D1613117

READING WAGNER

OTHER BOOKS BY L. J. RATHER

Mind and Body in Eighteenth-Century Medicine: A Study Based on Jerome Gaub's "De regimine mentis," 1965

Addison and the White Corpuscles: An Aspect of Nineteenth-Century Biology, 1972

The Genesis of Cancer: A Study in the History of Ideas, 1978

The Dream of Self-Destruction: Wagner's "Ring" and the Modern World, 1979

Johannes Müller and the Nineteenth-Century Origins of Tumor Cell Theory (with Patricia Rather and John B. Frerichs), 1986

A Commentary on the Medical Writings of Rudolf Virchow. Based on Schwalbe's "Virchow-Bibliographie 1843–1901," 1989

TRANSLATIONS

Disease, Life and Man: Selected Essays by Rudolf Virchow, 1958

The Therapy of the Word in Classical Antiquity, by Pedro Laín Entralgo (with John M. Sharp), 1970

Rudolf Virchow: Collected Essays on Public Health and Epidemiology, 1985

Rudolf Virchow: Letters to His Parents, 1839 to 1864, 1989

READING WAGNER

A STUDY IN THE HISTORY OF IDEAS

L. J. RATHER

LOUISIANA STATE UNIVERSITY PRESS

BATON ROUGE AND LONDON

Copyright © 1990 by Louisiana State University Press
All rights reserved
Manufactured in the United States of America
First printing

99 98 97 96 95 94 93 92 91 90   5 4 3 2 1

Designer: Amanda McDonald Key
Typeface: Sabon
Typesetter: G & S Typesetters, Inc.
Printer and binder: Thomson-Shore, Inc.

Library of Congress Cataloging-in-Publication Data
Rather, L. J.
    Reading Wagner: a study in the history of ideas/L. J. Rather.
        p.   cm.
    Includes bibliographical references.
    ISBN 0-8071-1557-6 (alk. paper)
    1. Wagner, Richard, 1813–1883—Books and reading. I. Title.
ML410.W19R25   1990
782.1'092—dc20   89-37814
                                                                CIP
                                                                MN

The paper in this book meets the guidelines for permanence and durability of
the Committee on Production Guidelines for Book Longevity of the Council
on Library Resources. ∞

Richard Wagner, that is to say: the *greatest genius and greatest human being of our time,* simply incommensurable!

Friedrich Nietzsche, *Gesammelte Briefe*

For me Wagner remains the greatest man, not only of music, not only of dramatic art, but also of humanity. The more he is understood, the more overwhelming his greatness appears, out of all proportion to the rest of men, even to men of genius. A kind of demigod, Wagner: this creator of a world of appearances more alive than life itself, more real than reality. . . . The mind of Wagner has seen and made evident things inexpressible, the sight of which is well for the well, but crushing for the feeble. . . . He is dangerous.—But this does not prevent him from being divine, the true God of Art.

Romain Rolland, *Cahiers VI. Printemps Romains*

For the strong, the intelligent, the healthy, the successful, those on whom, just because they are so, falls the duty of understanding weakness, stupidity, disease, and failure in order that they may cure them, Wagner's operas are essential, a constant source of delight. They *must* listen to him. But who should never be allowed to listen to Wagner? The unhappy, the disappointed, the politically ambitious, the self-pitying, those who imagine themselves misunderstood, the Wagnerians.

W. H. Auden, *Notes to New Year Letter*

CONTENTS

PREFACE

My purpose in writing this book is not to present and defend a particular set of theses on Richard Wagner but rather to paint a multifaceted picture of some neglected aspects of the man, his work, and his times—which, as will become plain to the reader in the second half of the book, are in many ways our times as well. My picture is, admittedly, a montage or, to employ a term more applicable to a piece of writing, a cento. I have relied on a predominately nonlinear method, one that assembles, juxtaposes, and interrelates often very diverse materials. These bits and pieces were garnered from my reading of Wagner's own poetry and prose, from the writings of authors on whom he drew, consciously or unconsciously, and, finally, from authors of his own or later times with whose work he was unacquainted. As in the case of my earlier book, *The Dream of Self-Destruction: Wagner's "Ring" and the Modern World*, such unity as the present book may claim is secured by linkages among repetitions and transformations of motifs audible in Wagner's day and still to be heard in ours. I am aware that my procedure involves the danger that even a very attentive reader—especially if that reader is looking for a unifying argument—may be taken by surprise when I seem to jump from one subject to another without any apparent transition. I can only apologize for this in advance and hope for the necessary indulgence.

The subtitle, *A Study in the History of Ideas,* is acceptable, I believe, if it be understood that many ideas, rather than a single leading idea, are in question here, and that none of them is dealt with systematically. The main title, *Reading Wagner,* is the clue to the genesis of the book. In the course of reading Wagner's own voluminous writings I was drawn further and further into the reading of writers in whom he expressed interest and to whom he was, in one way or another, indebted. In this way I came across a large number of unexpected parallels. To give only two examples: As we know from his autobiography, Wagner became acquainted with Pierre Joseph Proudhon's book *What Is Property?* during his first stay in Paris (1839–1842). Wagner's own, much later writings on credit-money and property reflect a general agreement with Proudhon's ideas on these subjects. And we learn from Cosima Wagner's recently published diaries that a few days before his death in Venice in 1883 Wagner again expressed his approval of Proudhon's views on property. In rereading Proudhon's book I was surprised by an anticipation of Siegfried's slaying of the gold-hoarding dragon Fafner (in Wagner's *Ring*) in the form of Proudhon's "proletarian," who, armed with the magic answer to the question posed in *What Is Property?,* slays the "monster," the "old serpent," the "sphinx" of capitalism. The second example comes from the work of a writer and musician avidly read by Wagner and bearing more than a passing resemblance to Wagner himself, namely E. T. A. Hoffmann. The harmonies and parallels between the writings of Hoffmann and those of Wagner were pointed out long ago by Hans von Wolzogen, in a book that made its appearance before the publication of Wagner's autobiography. Von Wolzogen was therefore unable to comment on the striking resemblance between Wagner's description of his own, quite unusual somnambulistic experience at La Spezia, when the opening notes of *Das Rheingold* came to him in a kind of half-dream, and E. T. A. Hoffmann's description in his novel *Kater Murr* of the quite usual creative experience enjoyed by the gifted tomcat-hero of this magnum opus.

Chapter One gives an account of Wagner's Dresden collection of books, based on Curt von Westernhagen's untranslated work on the subject. This library of some four hundred books was thought to have been dispersed and sold to pay off one of Wagner's debts, but it turned up intact after World War II in the basement of a bombed-out building in Leipzig. Chapter One also contains the first account, in English at least, of the contents of Wagner's much larger collection of about two thousand books at Bayreuth. This account is based on a typed list that I obtained early in 1985 through the courtesy of the custodian at Bayreuth. In continued pursuit of Wagner's reading, I have systematically gone through Cosima Wagner's diaries to find out just what books she and her husband read together between 1869 and 1883, and what they thought about them. The harvest was rich.

Chapter Two is entitled "On the Quality of Wagner's Poetry and

Prose." My demonstration here that Wagner's considerable stature as a poet was recognized by certain of his contemporaries (*e.g.*, Schopenhauer, Ferdinand Lassalle, and Nietzsche) is of some importance, since it now has become the fashion to consider Wagner's libretti distinctly second-rate writings, more doggerel than poetry. Needless to say, Wagner's poetry, like all poetry, tends to be lost in translation, and it is not as a rule to be found in English and French versions of the libretti. As I point out also in this chapter, Nietzsche's admiring description of Wagner's plastic use of the German language corresponds very closely to what has been said in our own day of Heidegger's use of that tongue. Chapter Three, "Wagner in France," follows, more or less sequentially, my discussion of the prose writings of Wagner published during his impoverished years in Paris and commented on in Chapter Two. It will be seen that Wagner, if he had not existed, would have had to be invented—indeed that he *was* invented in France, in a short story by Balzac published two years before Wagner's arrival in Paris.

Chapter Four, "Wagner on the Human Use of Animal Beings," is intended, among other things, to lead into my showing that the ethical basis of Wagner's attitude toward the use and abuse of animals is also the basis of his attitude toward the use and abuse of human beings. It was partly for this reason that Wagner so enthusiastically welcomed the writings of Darwin on the kinship between animals and human beings. The material gathered together in Chapter Four is of much more interest at present than it would have been only a very few years ago. The strong anti-vivisection movement of the late nineteenth century has become the animal rights movement of today. Direct action, reminiscent of Wagner's description of similar direct action in Germany a little over one hundred years ago, has been taken here and there against facilities for animal experimentation in the United States. Extreme activists in the animal rights movement go so far as to compare the animal facilities of major university medical schools with so many Auschwitzes. Official spokesmen have been forced to take notice of this movement (*cf.* the editorial in *Science,* January 29, 1988). Chapter Four leads into Chapter Five, where Wagner's notion of "active compassion" toward human beings is shown to be the foundation stone of his ethics. It was borrowed, of course, from Schopenhauer, the philosopher whom he most admired during the second half of his life. In Chapter Five I point out also that the remarkable likeness between the ethical stance of Tolstoy and that of Wagner was recognized in the

1890s, and that Tolstoy's antiwar writings at this same time are pre-figured on a smaller scale in the writings of Wagner two decades earlier.

Chapters Five and Six may prove to be stumbling blocks for many readers, for they deal with religious issues and, among other things, with the problem of Wagner's antisemitism. My treatment of the latter subject is in some ways quite original. I believe that no one before me has introduced materials from Kierkegaard's newly available diaries into this context. I offer as well a close reading of Wagner's essay "Judaism in Music" in connection with both Marx's essay "On the Jewish Question" and the conflicting writings of Marx's quondam admirer Moses Hess on this subject (ranging from Hess's early attacks on what he saw as the spirit of Judaism to his final espousal of a race-based Zionism). Benjamin Disraeli comes into the picture at this point because he was an influential advocate, in his political writings as well as in his novels, of the crucial importance of race in the historical development of civilizations. Disraeli, who in some ways anticipated the racial theorizing of Joseph-Arthur Gobineau, is the coiner of the slogan, notorious in midcentury England, "All is race; there is no other truth." Acknowledging Disraeli as his master, Houston Stewart Chamberlain picked up the slogan and passed it on from England to Germany. The doctrine itself was consciously implemented, for the first time in the twentieth century, by Hitler and the Nazis, with predictably disastrous results. Chapter Six also presents various aspects of what the religious philosopher and Zionist Martin Buber called the "German-Jewish symbiosis," and what, before him, the philosopher and anti-Zionist Hermann Cohen (1842–1918) had referred to approvingly as the "kindred spirit linking Germanism and Judaism." In the third section of Chapter Six I discuss in detail Wagner's message to the people of the United States of America, published in the *North American Review* of 1879, in which he contrasts what he believes the "German spirit" ought to be accomplishing in the world—by virtue of the power of music—with what it actually seemed bent on accomplishing by reliance on the power of arms.

Chapter Seven, "The Insurrection of Woman," contains some remarks on the first of Wagner's operas to be produced, *Das Liebesverbot* (referred to by Wagner in 1879 as *The Love-Veto*, but better known, since its revival in 1976, as *The Ban on Love*), in connection with some relatively obscure nineteenth-century aspects of the perennial problem of the right relationship between the sexes, a problem with which Wagner was concerned throughout his life—he was, in fact, in the midst of an essay on the subject at the very moment of his death. Chapter Seven includes a survey of Proudhon's paradoxically gynecophobic writings (best exemplified by his *Pornocracy, or Women in Modern Times*) and his attack on the outspokenly feminist George Sand. I comment here also on the writings of George Sand herself, on Richard and Cosima Wagner's relatively positive assessment of Sand, and on the negative judgment of Proudhon to be found in the writings of Cosima Wagner's gifted mother, the Countess d'Agoult (who wrote under the pen name of Daniel Stern). The section of this chapter dealing with the Oedipus myths as structured by Claude Lévi-Strauss and the "Ring" myths as structured by Wagner presents material which is, I believe, wholly new.

Chapter Eight, the concluding chapter, introduces some old and some new mythic material in connection with Wagner's *Parsifal*, including Hitler's deliberate misinterpretation of that work. After World War II, this misinterpretation was picked up by Theodor Adorno and others and used in their attacks on Wagner. The last section of Chapter Eight, "Musico-Sociology: Wagner's Christian Harmony," presents a hitherto almost neglected aspect of Wagner's world view, specifically the intimate connections that he discerned between the development of chromaticism in music and the development of an all-embracing human community.

Further remarks in justification and explanation of my procedure in composing this book will be found in the opening section of the first chapter, "Wagner's Reading," to which the reader is now invited to turn.

ACKNOWLEDGMENTS

I dedicate this book to the memory of my late friend Dr. John B. Frerichs and to our fifty years of close personal and working association. In 1982 he furnished me with a painstakingly accurate line-by-line editorial review of the text and notes of a much longer first version of this work. Death prevented him from carrying out a similar review of the completely revised and retitled second version. For much-needed encouragement during its composition I am indebted also to my son Dr. Lee Rather, to Dr. William Byron Webster, and to Professor Gerald Gillespie of the Department of German Studies and Comparative Literature at Stanford University. I warmly thank Beverly Jarrett, former Associate Director and Executive Editor of the Louisiana State University Press, for her continued interest, patience, and forbearance. I am grateful to three anonymous readers, called on by the Press to evaluate the work, for pointing out a number of shortcomings and errors. I am also grateful to my copy editor, Shannon Sandifer, for her meticulous work. Finally, I thank the Ford Foundation Emeriti Faculty Development Program at Stanford for a grant covering the costs of typing the manuscript.

READING WAGNER

CHAPTER ONE

WAGNER'S READING

In a self-confirming aphorism, Goethe tells us that everything worth saying has already been said by others before us, and that our task is to think it over again and express it in our own way. Karl Mannheim, writing as a sociologist of knowledge, puts it that the individual thinker thinks not as an individual but rather participates with others in thinking further what has been thought before. Broadening the scope of our indebtedness to past generations, the philosopher Morris Cohen stated near the end of his life: "None of us are self-made men, and those who think they are, are generally no credit to their makers. The language in which our thinking moves, the ideas to which we are attuned in the formative years of our childhood . . . even our gestures, facial expressions and intonations, are . . . the social products of generations of teaching." And, giving vivid expression to the specific indebtedness of scholars to the books they have read, the Spinoza scholar Harry Austryn Wolfson wrote, "As for Spinoza, if we could cut up all the philosophical literature available to him into slips of paper, toss them up into the air, and let them fall to the ground then out of these scattered slips we could construct his *Ethics*." Contrariwise (Wolfson might have added) we can cut the *Ethics* into slips of paper and reconstruct from the bits and pieces the books, some of them at least, available to Spinoza. Wolfson of course presupposes that we have at hand an intact copy of the *Ethics* to guide and confirm our reconstruction of it from the *disjecta membra* of Spinoza's reading; and in the contrary case we assume that we have at hand the intact books themselves. There is a more than casual relationship between these two procedures and the claim of Carl Gustav Carus in 1846 that we can achieve an understanding of the unconscious (*des Unbewussten*) by examining the contents of the conscious mind, and that contrariwise it is possible "to reconstruct the content of the unconscious from the content of the conscious mind" ("zu rekonstruieren von dem bewussten Sein ins Unbewusste").[1] But here, obviously, there is no way in either case of confirming the results.

Within the limits of rhetorical exaggeration, then, we can recognize each new book as a kind of Frankenstein creation, dug from the graves of dead books and patched together into a semblance of independent new life by the daedal artifice of the author of its being. Morris Cohen's "self-made men" are simply ignorant of their origin. The plagiarist filches wholesale, conceals his borrowings, and contributes little or nothing of his own. Most of the better authors work unconsciously, aided by what a depth psychologist of the early nineteenth century called the "hidden poet" within us; and so the shorn fragments are welded into a more or less organic whole. There are exceptions: in T. S. Eliot's *The Wasteland*, which one critic implicitly compared to Robert Burton's *The Anatomy of Melancholy* and another called a "scrap-heap of quotations," the borrowings are meant to stand out—including the four lines from Wagner's *Tristan und Isolde* inserted in "The Burial of the Dead." Eliot missed the point of the comparison until it was explained to him, but in fact Burton's *Anatomy* is the closest approach we have to Walter Benjamin's ideal of a completely objective literary creation, one made up entirely of acknowledged citations and paraphrases. Burton modestly called his great book—in print almost uninterruptedly since its first publication in 1621—a mere cento, a macaronic assemblage of quotations drawn from the works of better men than himself, a *macaronicon*, the book of a pygmy standing (as Lucian said) on the shoulders of giants. Burton, here borrowing from a graceful tribute of Lucretius to Epicurus as expanded by Joest Lips of Leyden, says that he too is no spider to spin the thread of a text out of himself alone (to catch the flitting attention of the reader) but rather a scholarly bee who has sipped freely in the flowery groves of Oxford's libraries, his own (some two thousand volumes) and the Bodleian included. Improving on Terence, Burton concludes: "*Nihil dictum quod non dictum prius, methodus sola artificem*

1. Cited by Sidney Hook in "Morris Cohen—Fifty Years Later," *American Scholar*, XLV (1976), 426–35; Harry Austryn Wolfson, *The Philosophy of Spinoza* (1934; rpr. 1958), 3; L. J. Rather, *The Dream of Self-Destruction: Wagner's 'Ring' and the Modern World* (Baton Rouge, 1979), 114–15.

ostendit, we can say nothing but what hath been said, the composition and method is ours only, and shows the scholar." [2]

Using a less time-worn analogy, we may say that just as each new living being represents the realization of a new grouping of words and phrases based on an ancient genetic code, so each new book represents a rearrangement—hopefully in the light of a life-giving idea—of words and phrases that are our spiritual heritage from past generations. [3] To believe otherwise is on par with believing in the spontaneous generation of threadworms in rain barrels, or believing that a child reared in total isolation will come to speak the original tongue—Chinese, Sanskrit, Hebrew, or whatever—of humankind.

And so, in order to read Wagner more fully, we turn first to a brief account of the literature available to him, specifically to a survey of the books with which he surrounded himself in Dresden in the 1840s, of the more than two thousand books left behind in Bayreuth on his death in 1883, and of the copious comments on these books to be found in Cosima Wagner's diaries.

Wagner's paternal uncle Adolf, philologist, polymath, editor of the *Parnasso italiano* edition of the Italian classics, and devotee of the Greek and Latin classics, was one powerful influence on his early life; another was his beloved stepfather, the actor, painter, and playwright Ludwig Heinrich Christian Geyer. The latter introduced him to the world of the theater (Wagner's father, an amateur actor and lover of the theater, died in 1813, the year of Richard's birth), the former to the world of books. Wagner's siblings, a rather talented lot, were probably influenced by their stepfather as well: Albert, the eldest, and three of the sisters, Rosalie, Luise, and Klara, were to have moderately successful theatrical or singing careers. Julius, who became a goldsmith, and Ottilie, who married the orientalist Dr. Hermann Brockhaus (brother of the publisher Friedrich, who had married Luise a few years earlier), may have been the exceptions.

After the sudden success of *Rienzi* in 1842 brought Wagner and his

2. Jay Martin (ed.), *A Critical Collection of Essays on "The Waste Land"* (Englewood Cliffs, N.J., 1968), 34, 53; Robert Burton, *The Anatomy of Melancholy* (3 vols.; 1931; rpr. London, 1961), I, viii, 24–26. On Benjamin's ideal book, see Rather, *The Dream of Self-Destruction,* xx, 197.

3. *Cf.* L. J. Rather, "Alchemistry, the Kabbala, the Analogy of the 'Creative Word' and the Origins of Molecular Biology," *Episteme,* VI (1972), 83–103.

first wife Minna from the grinding poverty of Paris to the relative
affluence of Dresden, with all its promise for a settled existence, he
hastened to build up a personal library. Writing some quarter of a century later in his autobiography, Wagner says that

> above all, my house was made really a home for me by a library that I pro-
> cured without delay, all at once, in keeping with a thoroughly systematic
> plan of studies that I had drawn up. This library passed, after the collapse
> of my Dresden existence, oddly enough into the hands of Heinrich Brock-
> haus [the brother of Hermann and Friedrich], to whom I owed five hundred
> thalers at the time; he took it in pawn for a debt of which my wife was
> unaware, without her knowing this, and it was never possible for me to
> regain this distinctive collection of books.[4]

The collapse—one of many in his life—referred to here took place
in 1849, when Wagner fled empty-handed to Switzerland to escape the
arrest and long imprisonment meted out to his fellow revolutionaries
Mikhail Bakunin and August Röckel. Wagner never saw this library
again. The account of it in his autobiography is worth quoting at
length.

> The ancient literature of Germany and the closely related literature of medi-
> eval times were in general best represented. In this way I acquired many
> costly works, the *Romans des douze pairs,* for example. Arrayed with them
> were outstanding histories of medieval times and of the German peoples in
> general. I provided at the same time a place for poetic and classical litera-
> ture of all ages and languages; aside from French writers, whose language I
> could understand in a pinch, I included the Italian poets and Shakespeare in
> the original, hoping that I would still find time to acquire a firm grasp of
> these neglected languages also. As for Greek and Roman antiquity, I had to
> approach it by way of our [German] translations, themselves now classics,
> since I soon became aware from my Homer, which I had in the Greek, that
> if I expected to find time enough to reacquire my earlier understanding of
> Greek I would have to reckon on a bit too much leisure over and above my
> activities as Kapellmeister [at the Dresden court theater]; for in addition to
> all this I had made careful provision for the study of general history, not
> neglecting to provide myself with multi-volumed works.[5]

Wagner does not appear to have retained a list of the books in his
Dresden collection, but the above account is accurate as far as it goes.

4. Richard Wagner, *Mein Leben,* ed. Martin Gregor-Dellin (2 vols.; Munich,
1969), I, 274. Unless otherwise indicated all references to Wagner's *Mein Leben* are to
this edition.

5. *Ibid.,* 274–75.

Writing in the 1930s Ernest Newman—who supposed that the books had been lost or dispersed—regretted that individual titles were unavailable. Given, asked Newman, Wagner's revolutionary associations in Dresden with Mikhail Bakunin and August Röckel, did the library contain the *Communist Manifesto*? Given, we may add, Wagner's claim that the present age faced the task of bringing the unconscious to consciousness, did it contain the Dresden physician Carl Gustav Carus' *Psyche* (1846), a work opening with the statement that "the key to the understanding of the conscious psychic life lies in the realm of the unconscious"; given Wagner's conversations in Dresden with Berthold Auerbach (a Jew) on the Jewish question, did it contain Karl Marx's "On the Jewish Question" (1844), an outspoken attack on what Marx then perceived as the essence of Judaism?[6]

We now know that the answers to the above questions are in the negative. For Wagner's books are not lost, as Newman believed. Stored in a bunker at the Brockhaus publishing house in Leipzig, the collection even survived the American bombing raid of December 4, 1943, on that city of books. The Brockhaus firm moved to Wiesbaden, and in 1966, thanks to Dr. Curt von Westernhagen, a detailed account of Wagner's Dresden library became available in book form.[7]

No works on economics, social reform, psychology and the natural sciences, or religion are to be found in the Dresden collection, and there are only a few on philosophy. Works on ancient medieval and modern history (in the West; there is nothing on the history of Egypt, the Near East, Persia, India, or China) are present in fair number, but the bulk of the collection consists of poems, plays, sagas, and romances by Greek, Roman, German, Scandinavian, English, French, Italian, and Spanish writers, for the most part in German translation. French, which Wagner read and wrote after a fashion, is the only foreign language heavily represented. Although Wagner states in the first of his autobiographical writings that as a boy he translated parts of the *Odyssey* and read, or at least tried to read, Shakespeare in the original, his grasp of both languages was very weak. Shakespeare he read in the

6. Ernest Newman, *The Life of Richard Wagner* (4 vols.; New York, 1933–47), I, 377; II, 50–51; Curt von Westernhagen, *Wagner: A Biography*, trans. Mary Whittal (2 vols.; London, 1978), I, 94. On the works by Carus and Marx mentioned in the text, see Rather, *The Dream of Self-Destruction*, 23–24, 114–15. Wagner's talks with Auerbach in Dresden are to be found in Wagner, *Mein Leben*, I, 337–39.

7. Curt von Westernhagen, *Richard Wagners Dresdener Bibliothek* (Wiesbaden, 1966).

Schlegel and Tieck translation that we find in both the Dresden and the
Bayreuth collections. As we shall see later, he retained enough Greek
to be able to compare original texts with German translations that he
and Cosima were accustomed to read, as well as enough Latin to comment on the rhetoric of Saxo Grammaticus.

Curt von Westernhagen offers us two lists of Wagner's books. The
first consists of 169 items, some 400 volumes in all. A second list of
29 items (about 60 volumes) came from Minna Wagner, who had
long ago named them as part of the original collection. Minna's list includes Berthold Auerbach's tales of village life in the Black Forest (the
Schwarzwälder Dorfgeschichten, published in 1846), Heinrich Heine's
poems (*Gedichte* and *Buch der Lieder*), and 9 volumes of the *Romans
des douze paires* (*sic*), the latter of which Wagner singled out for comment in his autobiography.[8] Also in the second list is George Sand's
novel *La dernière Aldini* in the Paris edition of 1842. This cannot be
the edition that Wagner read on board the *Thetis* in 1839 (to improve
his French, Wagner says in his autobiography) in the course of his wild
flight over the Baltic Sea from Riga to Paris (by way of London) together with Minna and their gigantic Newfoundland dog.[9]

The works of Plato in Friedrich Schleiermacher's German translation, the works of Aristotle in a Stuttgart edition of 1836–1840
(Minna's list) and G. W. F. Hegel's *Lectures on the Philosophy of History* (in German) exhaust the category of philosophy. The Greek and
Roman historians in the collection include Herodotus, Thucydides,
Plutarch, Livy, Tacitus, and Caesar. After Saxo Grammaticus' *History
of the Danes* (in Latin) and a German translation of the *Gesta roman-
orum,* the well-known fourteenth-century collection of moral tales
of the days of chivalry, come modern historians: Edward Gibbon's
Decline and Fall of the Roman Empire (in Johann Sporschil's twelve-
volume German translation of 1840), F. A. Mignet's *History of the
French Revolution,* Simonde de Sismondi's *History of the Medieval
Italian Republics* (both in French), B. G. Niebuhr's *Roman History,*
J. G. Droysen's *History of Hellenism,* Friedrich Raumer's *History of the
Hohenstaufens,* and selected works of J. G. Herder (all in German).

Sismondi's *History* points to Wagner's interest in Cola di Rienzi, the
hero of his opera of that name. As early as 1836 Wagner had read a

8. Called the "rare old work *Romans des douze Paris*" in the authorized translation, *My Life* (2 vols.; New York, 1911), I, 316.
9. Wagner, *Mein Leben,* I, 171.

German translation of Edward Bulwer-Lytton's *Rienzi, the Last of the Roman Tribunes*. During Wagner's brief stay in London in 1839 he made an attempt to seek out Lord Lytton, who proved to be not at home. Wagner was then taken into the House of Lords by a kindly English gentleman. There he saw in action the great Duke of Wellington ("with both hands in his pockets"), the Bishop of London (who, Wagner writes, "made an uncomfortable impression on me, perhaps due to my prejudice against the spiritual estate"), and other notables. Likewise, Raumer's history of the Hohenstaufen emperors points up Wagner's interest in Frederick II—who held court in Sicily, wrote poetry in Italian, and was suspected of having unholy ties with Saracens and Jews—emperor of Germany and king of Jerusalem, and in his father, Barbarossa. Manfred, the son of Frederick II, is the protagonist of Wagner's prose draft *The Saracen Woman* and Barbarossa is the central character of another unproduced fragment. With reference to the triumphant reception said to have been accorded Manfred by the Saracens, Wagner writes in his autobiography: "Even then it delighted me to find in the German spirit a capacity for transcending the narrower boundaries of nationality and grasping the purely human (*rein Menschlichen*), however strange its garb; this, to me, seemed related to the Greek spirit." [10]

If we except mathematics and the natural sciences, Wagner's Dresden collection encompassed the cultural heritage of Western Europe. Homer, Pindar, Aeschylus, Sophocles, Euripides, Aristophanes, Xenophon, Horace, and Vergil have their places, at times in several different translations.[11] In company with the *Parnasso italiano* edition of Dante, there are two German translations of the *Divine Comedy*, one the excellent version by "Philalethes." Also in his uncle's edition, Wagner had the works of Boiardo, Boccaccio, Ariosto, Tasso, Petrarch, Buonarroti, and Tassoni. (Readers of Wagner's essay of 1870 on Beethoven will recall the night in Venice when the music of Tasso's verses chanted by gondoliers seemed to reach Wagner as a "night-dream of tones." [12]) In German translation he had Boiardo's *L'Orlando innamorato*, Ariosto's *L'Orlando furioso*, Tasso's *Gerusalemme*

---

10. *Ibid.*, 178–79, 221.
11. *Cf.* Pearl Cleveland Wilson, *Wagner's Dramas and Greek Tragedy* (New York, 1919); L. J. Rather, "The Needed Destruction of the State: Wagner's Interpretation of the Oedipus Myth," in *The Dream of Self-Destruction*, 47–62; and Michael Evans, *Wagner and Aeschylus: The 'Ring' and the 'Oresteia'* (London, 1982).
12. Rather, *The Dream of Self-Destruction*, 138.

liberata, and the complete works of Boccaccio. Minna's list includes a French version of Tasso, *La Jerusalem delivrée,* by a Prince Lebrun.

The works in French include a complete Molière, some of Victor Hugo, Alain-René Lesage's *Histoire de Gil Blas de Santillane,* and a French translation of Cervantes, *L'ingénieux hidalgo Don Quichotte de la Manche* (Sand's *La dernière Aldini,* as already noted, appears on Minna's list). There is also a study of Provençal poetry by Eugene van Bemmel, *De la langue et de la poésie provençales.* From Spain there are the novellas of Cervantes, the complete plays of Schopenhauer's great favorite (as Wagner would later learn) Pedro Calderón de la Barca (eight volumes, translated by J. D. Gries), the *Spanish Theatre* of August Wilhelm von Schlegel and the *Spanish Theatre* of Friedrich von Schack. From England, the *Canterbury Tales,* the complete works of Lord Byron, the complete plays of Shakespeare in the Schlegel and Tieck translation, together with a two-volume work on Shakespeare's sources by a group of scholars including Karl Simrock. The German classics are represented by the complete works of G. E. Lessing, Goethe (the J. G. Cotta edition of 1840, in forty volumes), and Schiller. Not in the collection unearthed after World War II but on Minna's list are two volumes of J. Scheible's *Dr. Faust,* possibly a precursor of Scheible's great twelve-volume compendium of Faust legends. Aside from Auerbach and Heine (on Minna's list), there are works by Wagner's countrymen Heinrich von Kleist and Ludwig Uhland (author of *Siegfried's Sword*), Uhland being represented by his poems and his essay on the twelfth-century poet Walther von der Vogelweide. The medieval German poets are heavily represented. There are three editions of von der Vogelweide, respectively by Karl Lachmann, Karl Simrock, and Friedrich Koch, two editions of Gottfried von Strassburg's poem on Tristan and Isolde (by Hermann Kurtz and H. F. Massman, respectively), Karl Simrock's edition of Wolfram von Eschenbach's *Parzival und Titurel,* and a *Lohengrin* edited from a manuscript in the Vatican by Johann Görres, that implacable foe of the first Napoleon. A collection of Hans Sachs's plays, fables, and sayings, and Friedrich Furchau's *Hans Sachs* are listed by Curt von Westernhagen.

Wagner's books on Norse, German, English, Irish, French, Dutch, and Wallachian legends, folktales, and sagas are too numerous and little known to be named in their entirety here. The central position of Wagner's own great poem *The Ring of the Nibelung* requires us to note that his Dresden library contained four different editions of the medieval German *Nibelungenlied* (including Karl Simrock's translation of the poem into modern German), three editions of the Eddas (translated from the Icelandic), three editions of *Kudrun* (in which a King Hagen is the grandfather of Kudrun rather than, as in Wagner's poem, the half-brother of Gutrune), and Ludwig Ettmüller's *Vaulu-Spa* (the Voluspa, the "Sayings of the Prophetess") in the Old Norse, with a German translation, a commentary, and a vocabulary. Jacob Grimm's *German Mythology,* his *On Old German Master-Songs* and his *German Grammar,* Wilhelm Grimm's *The German Heroic Saga,* and *German Sagas* by the brothers Grimm also deserve mention.

There are only three books on music in the Dresden collection. They are N. A. Janssen's *True Groundrules of Gregorian or Choral Song,* K. E. P. Wackernagel's *German Church Song From Martin Luther to Nicholaus Herman and Ambrosius Blaurer,* and Alexander von Ulibischeff's *Life of Mozart with a Survey of the General History of Music and an Analysis of the Chief Works of Mozart* (all in German). Ulibischeff, a Russian nobleman, was born at Dresden, where his father was Russian ambassador to Saxony. This work was first published in Moscow in 1844 as *Nouvelle Biographie de Mozart.* *Grove's Dictionary of Music and Musicians* (1918) credits it with reawakening interest in Germany in Mozart's music at a time when Meyerbeer and Spontini were all the rage. Mozart was one of Wagner's two great musical passions. The famous credo "I believe in God, Mozart and Beethoven" comes from a poverty-stricken musician's outburst in one of Wagner's short stories. This tale of a German musician's death in Paris earned the twenty-six-year-old Wagner the praises of Hector Berlioz and Heinrich Heine, the latter remarking (according to Wagner): "Even Hoffmann couldn't have written anything like this!"[13] (The credo was later borrowed by Wagner's great admirer George Bernard Shaw.)

To return to Harry Austryn Wolfson's rhetorical maneuver, by cutting up the books in the Dresden collection into slips of paper and tossing them into the air we might well be able to reconstruct the verbal content of Wagner's operas and music dramas from the scattered fragments. Alternatively, we could simply note down passages from these books on the margins of Wagner's pages at appropriate points—

13. *Grove's Dictionary of Music and Musicians* (1918), V, 195; Wagner, *Mein Leben,* I, 201.

much as Sir John Harrington did for Queen Elizabeth in his translation of *L'Orlando furioso,* where account is taken of each imitation by
Ariosto of Vergil, Ovid, Catullus, and others.[14] Thus when we read (or
hear sung) the words of the ghostly Alberich in Wagner's *Götterdämmerung,* "Do you sleep, Hagen my son? / Do you sleep, and hear me
not, / Whom rest and sleep betrayed?," we may remember Nestor in
the *Iliad* addressing Agamemnon in the form of a dream, "O warrior-
son of Atreus, sleepest thou?," or perhaps the ghost of Patroclus reproaching his friend, "Achilles, sleepest thou, forgetting me?" And
recalling how Hagen had refused to mix his Nibelung blood with
that of his half-brother Gunther and Siegfried in the drink to "blood-
brotherhood," we may even be reminded of the later exhortation of a
Zionist group in Constantinople: "Sleepest thou, O our nation? What
hast thou been doing until 1882? Sleeping and dreaming the false dream
of Assimilation."[15]

Whether or not Wagner intended it, there is a distinct parallel between the fate of Troy in Vergil's *Aeneid* and the fate of Valhalla in
Wagner's *Ring of the Nibelung.* The walls of Troy were built by Apollo
and Neptune for King Laomedon, in the expectation of a reward. The
reward was not forthcoming, and the defrauded gods vowed eternal
vengeance. After the fall of Troy, when Aeneas is about to kill Helen,
Venus appears to tear the veil of illusion from his eyes so that he can
understand that the gods themselves, not Paris and Helen, are the real
destroyers of Troy. Aeneas *sees* the daimonic numina of the great gods
at work in the flames. Wagner's Valhalla was built for Wotan as an
impregnable stronghold by the giants Fafner and Fasolt. Wotan first
attempts to cheat them out of their promised reward (the goddess Freya)
and then is compelled to yield up the ravished gold of the Rhine—which
he himself took from Alberich by force and fraud. Alberich too swears
eternal vengeance. At the close of the *Ring* we, the audience, see—

14. Lodovico Ariosto, *Orlando Furioso, Translated into English Heroical Verse by
Sir John Harington (1591),* ed. Robert McNulty (Oxford, 1972). As Harington points
out, the opening lines of Ariosto's poem imitate the *Arma virumque cano* of the *Aeneid,*
and its closing lines imitate Vergil's closing hexameter, *Vitaque cum gemitu fugit indig-
nata sub umbras.*

15. William Cullen Bryant, *The Iliad of Homer* (Boston, 1870), Bk. II, 30; Bk.
XXIII, 81; Walter Laqueur, *The Israel-Arab Reader: A Documentary History of the
Middle East Conflict* (New York, 1969), 3. *Cf.* Psalms 44:23: "Awake, why sleepest
thou, O Lord? arise, cast us not off for ever."

behind the foreground action—Valhalla and the gods themselves caught up in the final ecpyrosis.

Without insisting too much on parallels of this kind, it is at least evident that Wagner's future operas and music dramas can be related to books in the Dresden collection. The titles of *Lohengrin, Tristan und Isolde,* and *Parsifal* speak for themselves. As for *Tannhäuser,* both Wolfram von Eschenbach and Walther von der Vogelweide make a personal appearance in this story of the knightly minnesinger of Germany. Matched with Wagner's *Die Meistersinger von Nürnberg* we have the two volumes of Hans Sachs. Practically all Wagner's sources for the greatest of his dramatic poems, *Der Ring des Nibelungen,* are to be found in the collection. For *Rienzi* we have Sismondi's history, Bulwer-Lytton's novel and, perhaps, the long section on Rienzi in Gibbon's *Decline and Fall.* Wagner's earliest operas are *Die Feen* (1834) and *Das Liebesverbot* (1835). *Die Feen* is based on Carlo Gozzi's dramatic fairy tale *La donna serpente* (not in the Dresden collection), and *Das Liebesverbot* on Shakespeare's *Measure for Measure.* Wagner's strong early bent for the fantastic no doubt attracted him to Gozzi's tale of "the lady serpent." But in typical Wagnerian fashion he worked into it certain themes that recur in his later dramas: redemption, compassion for animals (*Parsifal*), and the "forbidden question" (*Lohengrin*).[16] *Achilleus* (1849) and *The Saracen Woman* (1841–1843), both mere sketches, have obvious ties with the collection. Wagner's earliest sketch for an opera was *Die Hochzeit* (*The Wedding*), a blood-and-thunder tragedy involving the children of two feuding princely families. Wagner says in his autobiography that he took it from J. G. Busching's study of chivalry, *Ritterzeit und Ritterwesen.*[17] Finally, the fragment *Jesus von Nazareth* (1849) can be related, if need be, to Martin Luther's translation of the New Testament from Greek into German, a copy of which was in Wagner's library at Dresden.

Wagner had read Heine's "The Memoirs of Mr. von Schnabelewopski" (*Memoiren des Herrn von Schnabelewopski*) while in Riga. The narrator of Heine's novella of 1834 tells of witnessing, in Amsterdam, a play on the subject of a damned sea captain who can be redeemed only by the love of a woman "faithful unto death." And Eve in the audience tempts the narrator away in the midst of the stage action. He

16. Westernhagen, *Wagner: A Biography,* I, 36–7.
17. Wagner, *Mein Leben,* I, 75.

returns just in time to watch the faithful woman throw herself into the
sea (in order to ensure her "faithfulness unto death"), whereupon the
ship itself sinks. The narrator satirically concludes that women should
not marry Flying Dutchmen; as for men, they should be careful to
avoid women who, to improve matters, involve them in general shipwreck.[18] Wagner's passionately felt drama is a far cry from Heine's satirical tale. The faithless Minna, after having suffered near shipwreck
off Sandwike on the Norwegian coast during her flight from Riga to
London with her husband in 1839, would probably have been entirely
in sympathy with the first part of Heine's moral.

The Dresden collection seemingly gone for good, Wagner went about
accumulating a new library for himself. At his death in 1883 he left
behind some twenty-three hundred volumes at Bayreuth. Edward
Dannreuther (1844–1905), a pianist and an "active pioneer in Wagner propaganda" (as the editor of the latest *Oxford Companion to
Music* chooses to call him) knew Wagner well, and in *Grove's Dictionary* (1918) he wrote:

> All his life long Wagner was a great reader. "Whatever is worth reading is
> worth re-reading," he said. . . . The classics he habitually read in transla-
> tions. With Shakespeare (in German of course) he was as familiar as with
> Beethoven. To hear him read an act or scene was a delight never to be for-
> gotten. . . . A list of the principal books in the extensive and very choice
> library at Bayreuth would give a fair idea of his literary tastes, for he kept
> nothing by him that was not in some way connected with his intellectual
> existence. The handiest shelves held Sanscrit, Greek and Roman classics;
> Italian writers from Dante to Leopardi; Spanish, English, French drama-
> tists; philosophers from Plato to Kant and Schopenhauer. A remarkably
> complete collection of French and German medieval poems and stories,
> Norse Sagas, etc., together with the labors of German and French philolo-
> gists in those departments, occupied a conspicuous position; history and
> fiction old and new were well represented; translations of Scott, Carlyle,
> etc.[19]

18. Henri Lichtenberger, *Richard Wagner poète et penseur* (5th ed., rev.; Paris,
1911), 69–72. Lichtenberger doubts that any such play was shown in Amsterdam at the
time, but he suggests that Heine may have seen Fitzball's melodrama, "*the flying
Dutchmann [sic] on the phantom ship*" in London on April 7, 1827 (*ibid.*, 70 n. 1). *Cf.*
also Westernhagen, *Wagner: A Biography*, I, 60.
19. *Grove's Dictionary of Music and Musicians*, V, 410.

Dannreuther's statement need no longer be taken on faith. The curator at Bayreuth has prepared an informal typewritten list of the 2,310 volumes (a few of which must have been acquired after Wagner's death) there. This list is far from having the bibliographical fullness or accuracy of Curt von Westernhagen's account of the Dresden collection, but it is valuable as an index of the new and greater scope of Wagner's interests. As a guide to Wagner's reading during the last twenty-five years of his life, it supplements the enormous wealth of information on this subject contained in Cosima Wagner's recently published diaries.[20]

Wagner's stepfather and uncle both appeared on the Bayreuth list, Geyer in the form of a manuscript copy of *Der bethlehemitische Kindermord,* a play in rhymed Alexandrines on the slaughter of the innocents by King Herod (Matthew 2). This work is said by Wagner in his autobiography to have won praise from Goethe himself. Adolf Wagner's contributions include one work on the relationships of the Indian, Greek, Slavic, Celtic, and Teutonic languages to each other, and another on the theater and the public (*Theatrum und Publikum*) that would probably repay study in the light of Richard Wagner's own numerous writings on this topic. Karl Marx and Carl Gustav Carus are again conspicuous by their absence from the procession of names. We shall have something to say later of a work on the shelves by a "depth psychologist" who was one year younger than Carus, namely Gotthilf Heinrich von Schubert. As for the history of Judaism and the Jewish problem itself, there are seven books of pertinence, including the great account of the Jews down to A.D. 66 (*De antiquitatis Judaicis*) by Flavius Josephus, a Palestinian Jew who fought against Vespasian but was subsequently honored with Roman citizenship under Titus.

Many old friends are back on the shelves, among them the German translation of Dante's *Divina commedia* by Philalethes (King John of Saxony), Boiardo's "Enamored Roland," Ariosto's "Mad Roland," Tasso's "Jerusalem Liberated" (in Italian and German editions) and the works of Calderón (in German). With the epic poems now is Milton's

---

20. Cosima Wagner, *Die Tagebücher,* ed. Martin Gregor-Dellin and Dietrich Mack (2 vols.; Munich, 1976–77); Cosima Wagner, *Cosima Wagner's Diaries,* ed. Martin Gregor-Dellin and Dietrich Mack, trans. Geoffrey Skelton (2 vols.; New York, 1978–80). I have the curator at Bayreuth to thank for his courtesy in sending me a copy of the typewritten list of Wagner's books.

Paradise Lost in German (on which an interesting comment by Wagner is recorded in Cosima's diary) and Camoens' *Lusiads,* also in German. On the shelves too are Homer's *Iliad* and *Odyssey,* together with Anacreon, Pindar, Aeschylus, Sophocles, Euripides, Aristophanes, Lucian, Thucydides, Xenophon, Plato, Aristotle, Polybius, Plutarch, Diogenes Laertius, and Pausanias. Of the Latin authors, we find the comic poets Plautus and Terence, the historians Sallust, Suetonius, and Tacitus, and the poets Lucretius, Catullus, Vergil, Horace, Ovid, Tibullus, Propertius, Persius, Martial, and Juvenal, together with Caesar, Cicero, Seneca, Epictetus, Pliny, and Marcus Aurelius (in Latin, German, or both).

A new note is struck by a string of books in the field of science, among them studies on life and death by the great French histophysiologist François Bichat (1771–1802) and Georges Cuvier's landmark work in the history of the natural sciences (the multivolumed *Histoire des progrès des sciences naturelles*). Charles Darwin is well-represented: Wagner possessed a French translation of *On the Origin of the Species,* a German translation (1863) of the same, and German translations of *The Descent of Man* and *The Variation of Animals and Plants under Domestication.* There are three studies of prehistoric humanity: Edward Tylor's *Primitive Culture* (1871) in German translation, Wilhelm Baer's *Der vorgeschichtliche Mensch* (1874), and A. Müller's *Die ältesten Spuren der Menschen in Europa.* A work on astronomy, *Die Wunder des Himmels,* by J. J. and K. Littrow (with an atlas of the stars) completes this aspect of the Bayreuth collection.

Wagner's Dresden collection contained no works on the natural sciences, and there is strong evidence that behind his new interest in this field lay a very negative attitude toward those achievements in technology regarded by many—from Francis Bacon (whose *Novum organum* in German translation is on the Bayreuth list) down to the present—as of the essence of science. Wagner, like other perspicacious observers in the second half of the nineteenth century, had come to see that the power of knowledge cuts both ways, that destruction could easily outpace production. As early as 1861 Thomas Love Peacock (1785–1866) wrote in his last political and social satire: "See the complications and refinements of modes of destruction. . . . I almost think it is the ultimate destiny of science to exterminate the human race." Twenty years later Wagner wrote (in "Religion and Art"): "The military authorities have been made aware that, through the so-called natural sciences, physics and chemistry in particular, many more destructive forces and substances are yet to be discovered. . . . These sciences are especially favored." In the same essay Wagner expresses misgivings that the "advancing art of war" is relying increasingly on "mechanical" rather than "moral" force as its practitioners bring more and more of the "rawest forces of the underlying powers of nature . . . into play." Schopenhauer had perhaps been right, Wagner added, in discerning behind Judeo-Christian dogma the pessimistic belief that "God created the world so that the Devil might take it." In 1899, sounding rather like Wagner, George Gissing has the Tolstoyan protagonist of *The Crown of Life* (who is the son of an antimilitarist once associated with Bakunin) say that, although we were told that "science would be religion enough," science had failed as a "civilizing force"; it had "come to mean money-making and weapon-making . . . it is judged by its value to the capitalist and the soldier." Two years earlier, this time sounding like Bernard Shaw, Gissing has a character in *The Whirlpool* say that the "supreme concern of mankind is to perfect their instruments of slaughter." But not until 1903 will Shaw, in the Mozartian intermezzo of *Man and Superman,* have the Devil assert that man's "heart is in his weapons," that he "measures his strength by his destructiveness," and that when man "goes out to slay, he carries a marvel of mechanism that lets loose at the touch of his finger all the hidden molecular energies." Man's boasted "force of Life . . . is a force of Death," the Devil adds, anticipating Sabina Spielrein in 1912 and Sigmund Freud in 1920. Finally, Leo Tolstoy warned us in 1904 that the continued proliferation of new weapons and counterweapons would almost inevitably bring the hostile world powers to "mutual destruction, like spiders in a jar"—a fear that Wagner had expressed a quarter of a century earlier.[21] (As Goethe and Terence observed, everything worth saying has already been said, and much good does it do us.)

Equally disturbing to Wagner was his perception that the science of life—at least the medical science and technology that he had long admired as the truest expression of "active compassion" (*tätiges*

21. Thomas Love Peacock, *Gryll Grange,* in *Works* (10 vols.; London, 1924–34), V, 187; George Gissing, *The Whirlpool* (London, 1915), 391; Gissing, *The Crown of Life* (New York, 1899), 317 (for the protagonist's reading of Tolstoy, see p. 342); George Bernard Shaw, *Man and Superman* (New York, 1939), 106–107; Rather, *The Dream of Self-Destruction,* 178–80; Rather, "Tolstoy and Wagner: The Shared Vision," *Opera Quarterly,* I (Autumn, 1983), 12–24.

Mitleid)—had itself become suspect. Wagner's shelves at Bayreuth held a dozen or more books in French, English, German, and Italian opposing animal experimentation, or vivisection, as it was commonly called. Always an animal lover, Wagner adamantly opposed this activity, regardless of what benefits might be derived from it. The one book in favor of vivisection on the Bayreuth list is *Leçons de physiologie opératoire,* a manual of experimental surgical technique attributed, probably wrongly, to the French experimental physiologist Claude Bernard (1813–1898). Claude Bernard himself admitted freely that the physiologist's laboratory had come to resemble a bloody abattoir, in which the physiologist had no choice but to be completely without compassion—readers of H. G. Wells's *Island of Dr. Moreau* (1896) will recall the chant of the transfigured animals to the "House of Pain." Wagner perceived a link between the willingness of human beings to sacrifice animals in the physiologist's laboratory and in the slaughterhouse (*Schlachthaus*) and themselves—or, preferably, others—on the battlefield, the field of slaughter (*Schlachtfeld*). Hence his attraction to ethical vegetarianism, although ill health forced him to give up his attempt in this direction in Zurich in the 1850s. On the Bayreuth list are T. Grieben, *Le végétarianisme;* T. Hahn, *Der Vegetarianismus;* a book on vegetarianism in relation to social problems (P. Kroll, *Vegetarianische und sociale Fragen*); and Jean Antoine Gleize's *Thalysie; ou la nouvelle existence* (in German translation), a three-volume study of vegetarianism published in Paris during Wagner and Minna's stay there from 1839 to 1842.

To the meat eater, perhaps, some of Wagner's references to vegetarianism in Cosima's diaries will wear the aspect of King Charles' head—a gory vision always intruding itself into the mind of that amiable lunatic Mr. Dick in *David Copperfield* (the work of an author who unaccountably escaped the attention of Cosima and Richard Wagner). Cosima's entry of April 28, 1880, reads in part: "In the evening Herr [Josef] Rubinstein plays to us the sonata [Beethoven's opus] 111 . . . and at the end he [Wagner] exclaims: 'There lies my whole doctrine—the first movement is Will in its suffering and heroic desire, the other one is the gentler Will which human beings will possess once they become reasonable. Vegetarians!'" On June 24, 1880, Cosima and Richard have just read Aeschylus' *Agamemnon.* Wagner mentions Clytemnestra's contempt for the chorus, which has condoned the sacrifice of Iphigenia to the offended goddess Artemis by Agamemnon, urged by the priest Calchas. Cosima notes down her husband's words. " 'Those are these individual, unfathomable features; and all so bloody, drenched in blood. If Thyestes had been a vegetarian,' he adds jokingly, 'none of it would have happened.' " It would be interesting to know what Wagner thought of the great opening diatribe against religion in the first book of Lucretius, where the pitiful death of Iphigenia at the hands of her father on the altar of the offended goddess Diana culminates in the verse *Tantum religio potuit suadere malorum:* such was the power of religion to persuade men to evil deeds.

The works of Norse, German, English, Irish, and French legends, folktales, and sagas in the Dresden collection were back on the shelves at Bayreuth together with a great many new books along this line, including the twelve volumes of Scheible's monumental assembly of Faust legends, *Das Kloster.* History is proportionately even more heavily represented than before. The Bayreuth collection has an English as well as a German edition of Gibbon's *Decline and Fall,* and an English edition of Henry Buckle's fascinating *History of Civilization—* a work that although never completed offers far more than the title promises. Theodor Mommsen's history of Rome (*Römische Geschichte*) and a German translation of George Grote's eight-volume *History of Greece* are on the list. Five works by the writer, traveler, and diplomat Joseph-Arthur, Count Gobineau, are also on the list: *Amadis* (a poem), *La renaissance* (in German translation), *Three Years in Asia,* and *The History of the Persians* (both in French). And of course there is the now much-condemned but seldom intelligently read *Essai sur l'inégalité des races humaines,* an essay on the inequality of the actual historical accomplishments of the so-called white, black, yellow, and red races. This work, which lauds the accomplishments of the ancient Hebrews in Palestine as the model of what can be accomplished by strictly maintained racial purity, was present on the shelves at Bayreuth in the French original and the four-volume German translation. (It has never been fully translated into English.)

Here a digression is in order on the peculiar relation of Wagner to the writer, musician, and music critic Ernst Theodor Wilhelm Hoffmann (1776–1822), a man whose love for Mozart's music led him to substitute "Amadeus" for "Wilhelm" in his list of Christian names. E. T. A.

Hoffmann was on friendly terms with the actuary Friedrich Wagner (Richard's father), and in December, 1813, he met Wagner's uncle; a hyperbolic entry in Hoffmann's notebooks reads _"Adolf Wagner— a cultured man—speaks 1700 languages." They too became close friends.[22] Whether or not Richard Wagner was first made aware of Hoffmann's bizarre and fantastic tales (with their Dostoevskian doubles and mad young monks) by his uncle, he read them with a passion from boyhood on. Hoffmann's complete works appear on the Bayreuth list, and almost every one of them receives some notice in Cosima Wagner's diaries (one not-too-puzzling exception is Hoffmann's tale of the mad musician Kreisler and the musician-poet-tomcat Kater Murr). Wagner's own powerful audiovisual imagination was responsible for some near-hallucinatory, Hoffmannesque episodes in his boyhood and youth, and they are described moreover with a truly Hoffmannesque flair in his autobiography: The spectral portraits that seemed to move out of their frames in the bleak old house at Eisleben (Luther's birthplace) where his uncle, his aunt, and an "eccentric old maid," Jeannette Thomé, had quarters; the enchanting but daimonic world that the boy Wagner sensed behind the scenes at the theater; the terrible shrieking childhood nightmares that made his brothers and sisters refuse to sleep anywhere near him; and his terrifying vision at Brünn in 1830 of the cholera (then epidemic in that part of Austria) taking on bodily form, entering his bed, and seizing him in an icy embrace. (We recall Heine's remark to Wagner in Paris that even Hoffmann could not have done better.)

The tales of E. T. A. Hoffmann are of special interest to us in relation to Wagner and the macaronic theory of literary reproduction. Anticipating Harry Austryn Wolfson by some three decades, the Wagner scholar Hans von Wolzogen put the theory into practice by assembling a large number of what he called "harmonic and parallel" passages from the writings of Wagner and Hoffmann. For example, Wagner stated in his autobiographical fragment of 1842 (published at the time of the success of _Rienzi_) that reading Hoffmann had once brought him to the point of having "visions in half-sleep, in which tonic, third and fifth appeared before me in bodily form and disclosed their mo-

---

22. Walther Harich, _E. T. A. Hoffmann; Das Leben eines Künstlers_ (2 vols.; Berlin, 1920), I, 204, 229.

mentous meaning" (in "Halbschlafe hatte ich Visionen, in denen mir Grundton, Terz and Quinte erschienen und mir ihre wichtige Bedeutung offenbarten"). In parallel, Wolzogen cited Hoffmann's *Ritter Gluck*, a spectral tale of the musician Christoph Gluck, in which the narrator dreams that "two colossi . . . tonic and fifth" ("zwei Kolosse . . . Grundton und Quinte") were joined by a "gentle, delicate youth, the third" ("der sanfte, weiche Jüngling, Terz"), and another tale of Hoffmann's fictitious musician Kreisler, who sees musical quavers and semiquavers "become alive and spring like little black many-tailed imps from the white pages." A half century later Charles E. Passage gave further support to Wolfson's notion by citing parallel passages from Hoffmann and Dostoevsky. It is worth noting here that Dostoevsky not only read Hoffmann assiduously, but spent some time in Dresden and took steps toward preparing a translation of Carus' *Psyche*.[23]

Another Hoffmannesque parallel or harmony—not mentioned in Wolzogen's book—calls for attention here. Wagner states in a well-known passage in his autobiography that the undulating, broken E-flat major chord whose figured repetitions open *Das Rheingold* came to him of itself as he lay on his bed in Spezia, after an exhausting trip by foot over the Alps, in "a kind of somnambulistic state" ("in eine Art von somnambulem Zustand"). He awoke from his "half-sleep," he says, terrified by the feeling that waves were breaking over his head (a reminiscence, perhaps, of his voyage on the *Thetis*) but with the idea for the overture complete in his mind. In words bearing the clear hallmark of German romanticism, Wagner adds that for him the lesson of Spezia is that "the life-stream was to flow to me not from without but only from within." Now if we turn to E. T. A. Hoffmann's masterpiece, the story of the feline musician, scholar, and poet Tomcat Murr (*Kater Murr*), the fragments of whose autobiography are scattered through another of Hoffmann's tales of the mad musician Kreisler, we find something quite similar. Tomcat Murr is said by his owner to spend

23. Hans von Wolzogen, *E. T. A. Hoffmann und Richard Wagner; Harmonien und Parallelen* (Berlin, 1906), 41; Charles E. Passage, *Dostoevski the Adapter: A Study in Dostoevski's Use of the Tales of Hoffmann* (Chapel Hill, N.C., 1954), 188, *passim; cf.* Konstantin Mochulsky, *Dostoevsky: His Life and Work*, trans. Michael A. Minihan (Princeton, 1967), 167. See also Marc A. Weiner, "Richard Wagner's Use of E. T. A. Hoffmann's 'The Mines of Falun,'" *19th Century Music*, V (Spring, 1982), 201–14.

much of his time "in dreamy meditation, in somnambulistic delirium, in short in that strange state between sleeping and waking which is, for the poetic spirit, the right time for receiving original ideas" ("in das träumerische Hinbrüten, in das somnambule Delirieren, kurz, in jenen seltsamen Zustand zwischen Schlafen und Wachen, der poetischen Gemütern für die Zeit des eigentlichen Empfanges genialer Gedanken gilt"). Heinrich Heine's satirical poem "Young Tomcat's Association for Poetry-Music" ("Jung-Katerverein für Poesie-Musik") is said by Ernest Newman to contain "caddish references" to Franz Liszt. But Wagner too was much offended by this poem, according to E. M. Butler, and seldom had much good to say of Heine thereafter. One wonders whether Wagner sensed in Heine's poem an implied comparison between himself and Tomcat Murr.[24]

We need not suppose that Wagner was embellishing his experience at Spezia in retrospect, or that he was drawing, consciously or unconsciously, on the autobiography of E. T. A. Hoffmann's amusingly feline scholar, poet, and musician. The shape Wagner gave his experience mirrored the spirit of the time. In another revealing sentence Tomcat Murr tells us that his habit of musing often precipitated him into "that delirium (*jenes Delirium*) which is not to be called sleep but a battle between sleeping and waking, as Moriz, Davidson, Nudow, Tiedemann, Wienholt, Reil, Schubert, Kluge and other writers on physiology who have written on sleep and dreaming, and whom I have not read, rightly insist."[25] Murr perhaps, but not E. T. A. Hoffmann. The opening sentence of Gotthilf Heinrich von Schubert's work of 1814 on the symbolic language of dreams is: "In the dream, and already in that state of delirium (*jenem Zustand des Deliriums*) which commonly pre-

24. Wagner, *Mein Leben*, II, 512; E. T. A. Hoffmann, *Lebensansichten des Kater Murr*, in *Poetische Werke* (12 vols.; Berlin, 1957–62), IX, 27; Newman, *The Life of Richard Wagner*, I, 277n; E[liza] M. Butler, *Heinrich Heine: A Biography* (London, 1956), 253. Butler says that Wagner had been one of only three Germans to defend Heine in the Ludwig Börne affair, the other two being the poet Franz Dingelstedt and the sixteen-year-old Ferdinand Lassalle (*ibid.*, 158, 167–68).

25. Hoffmann, *Kater Murr*, in *Poetische Werke* (1957–62), IX, 257. The acute suggestion has recently been made that Wagner, in his autobiographical account of the La Spezia episode, was "backdating a musical idea and combining it with an experience of some other kind," since no such episode is mentioned in his correspondence at the time it was supposed to have occurred. See John Deathridge and Carl Dahlhaus, *The New Grove Wagner* (New York, 1984), 39–40.

cedes sleep, our soul seems to speak in a tongue quite other than the usual one." Schubert has much to say of the irony and the tortuous reversals of meaning that mark the activity of the "hidden poet" (*versteckter Poet*) whose work is revealed in states of somnambulism, dreaming, and delirium. E. T. A. Hoffmann wrote to the publisher of Schubert's book on the symbolism of dreams (*Die Symbolik des Traumes*) that he "thirsted" after the book.[26] Wagner may not have read Schubert with the same avidity, but a copy of *Die Symbolik des Traumes* is among his books at Bayreuth.

G. H. von Schubert (1780–1860) was professor of natural sciences of Erlangen, and very much in the tradition of Kant, Schopenhauer, Jean Paul, and the many others interested in the unconscious workings of the mind (or soul). He was particularly drawn by the philosopher of nature Friedrich Schelling, his contemporary, who spoke of the "eternal unconscious" always at work in the depths impressing its identity on the apparently free, surface actions of the soul (or mind). These currents of thought made themselves felt in France and England at a later date. Wagner's already quoted remark on the "life-stream" of inspiration flowing from within is worth matching up with the English physiologist Henry Maudsley's claim that the "results of the mind's unconscious workings flow as it were from unknown depths into consciousness . . . [hence] great writers or great artists . . . have been astonished at their own productions and cannot conceive how they contrived to produce them." These lines were written in 1867. Wagner was writing at the same time. But one could almost suppose that he had intended to illustrate Maudsley's generalization with a specific instance. Wagner's river is indeed within: in the beginning, in the at first undisturbed depths of the Rhine, the mythic world of the *Ring* comes into being in the music of its prelude. In the third of the *Four Quartets*, T. S. Eliot writes: "The river is within us, the sea is all about us"—the strong brown Mississippi, no doubt, or the turbid Thames, rather than the peacefully flowing Rhine of Heinrich Heine and Richard Wagner. Although the extent of T. S. Eliot's borrowings from Wagner has only

26. Gotthilf Heinrich Schubert, *Die Symbolik des Traumes* (1814; rpr. Heidelberg, 1968), 1, 56, 79, 104, and xxiv of Gerhard Sauder's well-documented afterword. See Rather, *The Dream of Self-Destruction*, 119, for later interest in France in the "night-side" of human existence. An entire chapter is devoted to Schubert's study of dream symbolism in Albert Béguin's *L'Ame romantique et le rêve: essai sur le romantisme allemand et le poésie française* (Paris, 1946).

recently been revealed, in this particular instance there is probably as little reason to relate him to Wagner as to Maudsley.[27]

The age seems to have given a Hoffmannesque aspect to the experiences of Wagner's revered older friend Count Tyskiewicz, who was one of the leaders of the Polish uprising against Russia in 1830–1831. Of Tyskiewicz, Wagner wrote in his autobiography, "on him there lay a shadow which, to a sympathetic heart, made him especially attractive. He told my sister Luise [in 1831, when her husband Friedrich Brockhaus entertained the count and other Polish rebels] the story of the frightful fate that had been his. He had been married once before, and with his first wife had visited one of his outlying castles. During the night a spectral figure appeared at the window of his bedroom; after repeatedly challenging it the count, to protect himself, seized a weapon and shot his own wife, who had had the eccentric idea of teasing her husband in the form of a phantom of the night." This story inevitably recalls *Die Hochzeit,* which was sketched in 1832 by Wagner and scrapped at the request of his sister Rosalie. But before writing it Wagner says that reading Busching's book on medieval chivalry, at a time when he was fascinated by the treatment given to musical mysticism by E. T. A. Hoffmann, led him to envision a story in which a fatal trio of young people would become involved with a peculiar old organist. He deserted this theme for the projected opera *Die Hochzeit.* In the latter, an unknown figure appears at the bedroom window of a princess who is to be married on the next day. After a fierce struggle she hurls the intruder to the castle courtyard far below. On the next morning, the body proves to be that of a neighboring prince, who had been sent by his father to fill the breach between the two noble houses. Wagner says only that he took the story from J. G. Busching. Aside from its remote resemblance also to *Romeo and Juliet* (although the would-be lover receives a rather different reception), it has harmonies and parallels with the strange tale of the death of Count Tyskiewicz's first wife. And to these, if we are so inclined, we can add the parallels and har-

27. Rather, *The Dream of Self-Destruction,* 111, 113–14; Wagner, *Mein Leben,* I, 68, 75. On T. S. Eliot and Wagner, see G. L. K. Morris, "Marie, Marie, Hold on Tight," *Partisan Review,* XXI (March–April, 1954), 231–33; Herbert Knust, *Wagner, The King, and "The Waste Land"* (University Park, Pa., 1967); and Stoddard Martin, *Wagner to "The Waste Land": A Study of the Relationship of Wagner to English Literature* (London, 1982). Wagner receives rather scanty mention in Jay Martin's *A Critical Collection of Essays on "The Waste Land."*

monies between Wagner's account of his journey to Austria in the company of Count Tyskiewicz and Thomas Mann's novella *Death in Venice,* a masterpiece constructed almost entirely of bits and pieces dug out of Wagner's autobiography.[28]

We return to the Bayreuth collection. Aside from its much greater size and its inclusion of books on science and related topics, it differs most from its Dresden counterpart in the amount of space accorded to religious, philosophical, and Eastern literature. The five relatively recent philosophers on the Bayreuth list are Hobbes, Descartes, Spinoza, Schopenhauer, and Nietzsche. Ludwig Feuerbach, to whom Wagner dedicated his 1849 essay "The Art-Work of the Future" (a title borrowed from Feuerbach's *Fundamentals of the Philosophy of the Future* [1843]), is not on the Bayreuth list, although there are a great many references to his works in Cosima's diaries. So also Eduard von Hartmann, whose *Philosophy of the Unconscious* and *Self-Destruction of Christianity* elicited little praise from Wagner. Schopenhauer's complete works are on the list, including his translation of the aphorisms of the seventeenth-century Spanish moralist Baltasar Gracián y Morales. Also present are Wilhelm Gwinner's biography of Schopenhauer and the *Schopenhauer Lexikon* of Julius Frauenstadt, Schopenhauer's devoted Jewish disciple and literary executor.[29] Hobbes's *Opera omnia* are present in Latin, the *Oeuvres* of Descartes in French, and Spinoza's collected works in the German edition prepared by Berthold Auerbach, Wagner's acquaintance from Dresden days. There are eight works by Nietzsche, including his tribute to Schopenhauer (*Schopenhauer als Erzieher*) and his tribute of 1876 to Wagner (*Richard Wagner in Bayreuth*).

28. Wagner, *Mein Leben,* I, 69, 75–76. On the borrowings from Wagner in *Death in Venice,* see Werner Vordtriede, "Richard Wagners 'Tod in Venedig,'" *Euphorion,* LII (1958), 378–96. Vordtriede did not exhaust the list of Mann's borrowings: Gustav von Aschenbach's near-hallucinatory vision at the Nordfriedhof in Munich, his dream of a Dionysian procession during his stay in Venice, the beautiful Polish boy, the name *Tadzio* (*Tadziu, Thaddaeus*), and the cholera motif likewise come from Wagner.

29. On Wagner and Schopenhauer see the encyclopedic and indispensable work of Edouard Sans, *Richard Wagner et la pensée schopenhaurienne* (Paris, 1969); Rather, *The Dream of Self-Destruction, passim* (on both Feuerbach and Schopenhauer); and Bryan Magee, *The Philosophy of Schopenhauer* (London, 1983), the appendix of which, "Schopenhauer and Wagner," appears also in the 1983 autumn and winter issues of *Opera Quarterly.*

Some of the books relating to the Near and Far East are: M. Uhlemann's encyclopedia of Egyptology (*Handbuch der gesammten ägyptischen Alterthumskunde*), a book on Egyptian art by C. R. Lipsius, W. Ahlwardt's *Poesie und Poetik der Araber*, the *Rubaiyat* of Omar Khayyam, L. de Lacy's *Le mille et une nuits*, Karl Ullman's *Koran*, and the works of the Persian poet Hafis in Persian and German. Many of the books are devoted to the literature and philosophy of India: Kalidasa's *Sakuntala* (in German translation), the *Bhagavad-Gita* (in Sanskrit and German), the *Ramayana*, the *Rig-Veda*, the *Mahabharata*, the *Oupnek'hat, theologia et philosophia* (in French and German), M. E. Burnouf's *Introduction à l'histoire de Buddhisme indienne*, a collection of Indian legends edited by Hermann Brockhaus, Friedrich von Schlegel's *Sprache und Weisheit der Inder*, and, moving further east to the ancient Chinese wisdom literature, A. A. Schott's *Werke des chinesischen Weisen Kung-Fu-Dsü*.

It may be asked, given Wagner's enormous creative output in the fields of music, poetry, and polemic prose, given his intimate involvement with the stage production of his masterpieces, and his role as a public figure at a time when pilgrimages were made to Bayreuth as they were later made to Tolstoy in Yasnaya Polyana, when did he find time to read? Did these books merely decorate the shelves? The answer can be drawn from the two massive volumes, well over a thousand pages each, of Cosima Wagner's diaries, which were published in 1976. They cover the period from 1869—which is a bit further than the autobiography goes—until Wagner's death in 1883. The diaries, to a very large extent, are made up of comments (whether by Richard Wagner or Cosima herself) on the books listed above and on a great many that are not. Like many other nineteenth-century couples of their social and educational class, Richard and Cosima Wagner spent most of their leisure hours at home reading—reading alone, to each other, to their children, and, on occasion, to their guests. Thanks to Cosima's unfailing entries in her diary, we know more about the reading matter of this couple than of any other in history.

On Saturday, January 2, 1869, the children already in bed by 7:00 P.M., they decided to read together. What shall it be? Plato is not yet bound, Schiller's *Wallenstein* they have read a short time ago, Calderón is "too emotional," and they are left with a choice between one of Shakespeare's histories or the *Odyssey*. They fix on Homer. On

Sunday morning Homer is the first subject of their breakfast conversation, and on Monday evening Richard reads aloud four cantos from the *Odyssey*, Cosima "delighting in the sound of his voice." On January 9 they finish the *Odyssey*. Wagner, meanwhile, has been upset by Dr. Julius Fröbel's attack on him in the Munich press as the founder of a sexually, politically, and religiously subversive sect. Wagner tells Cosima that "he feels as if he had knocked with friendly attentions on the door of a house . . . and all he heard in reply was the grunt of a pig." On January 15 they read some of Schiller's letters while the children are out walking; on January 17 Wagner discusses verse meters (a book on Greek metrics by A. Apel was on his shelves) with Cosima, who is rereading *Wallenstein;* on January 19 Wagner reads *Henry VI* to Cosima, who has a severe headache at the time; on January 23 they discuss the *Agamemnon* of Aeschylus, on February 9 Calderón's *Great Zenobia*. On March 3 Wagner brings home "a splendid edition" of *Don Quixote* given him by Pauline Viardot (friend of George Sand and Turgenev and, with her sister Maria Malibran, a Maria Callas of her day), and Cosima remarks that "his passion for books grows daily." Wagner tells Cosima on October 16 that he would like to have a room honoring every genius such as Cervantes, whose "genius is absolutely unconscious, like an elemental force." (But he very much disliked the Doré illustrations in Viardot's gift, as he told Cosima on June 16.) As the year ends they are reading Heine (December 13), whose work Cosima finds "[a]s always of incomparable genius, but also [containing] very repulsive pieces." Wagner calls Heine "the bad conscience of our whole era . . . and yet one feels closer to him than to the whole clique he is so naively exposing." On December 14 Wagner reads aloud from *Tristram Shandy,* and on December 24, after the tree has been lighted and extinguished, they read Ludwig Geyer's *Der bethlehemitische Kindermord,* the slaughter of the innocents.

On January 9, 1870 Cosima is reading Grimms' fairy tales to her daughter Daniela, and Richard tells them how, at the age of twelve, he read Schiller's drama of Joan of Arc (*Die Jungfrau von Orleans*) aloud to his sister and mentor Rosalie. They finish Aristophanes' *The Frogs* on February 5, begin *The Acharnians* on the following day, and finish *The Wasps* on February 23. On March 27, apropos *The Merchant of Venice*, Wagner calls Shylock a "completely axiomatic" figure, devoid of harmony and the love of music. On May 28 Cosima remarks that they have "read three great poets one after another (Schiller, Sophocles and Shakespeare)" and are now reading *The Merry Wives of Windsor*. On the evening of August 31, Wagner "reads to us" Byron's account of the capture of the fortress at Izmail during the Russo-Turkish wars, and remarks, "He is the only true poet of this century who watched and described contemporary events; Goethe and Schiller turned their backs on them." Concerning a pamphlet by Wolfgang Menzel on Alsace-Lorraine that they read together on September 15 (after Sedan and the capture of the French emperor), Cosima notes: "The great question is what the Germans will do—restore Napoleon, more and more of whose dirty financial transactions (the real cause of the war) are coming to light? Negotiate with the republic, which is still behaving in a hostile manner?" On October 4 they read the *Persae* of Aeschylus. They read Aristophanes' *The Peace* on October 23, and Nietzsche turns up on October 24, to voice "fears that in the coming day militarism and above all pietism, will make their pressure felt everywhere."

At lunch on January 11, 1871, Wagner says that Hamlet's famous monologue reveals "how utterly Shakespeare's characters are living persons, and just as incomprehensible," but that when an author "sets out consciously to write a monologue about suicide something emerges like Cato's monologue in Addison." (Two years later, on April 16, 1873, Wagner reads from Saxo Grammaticus, and Cosima notes: "We really had to laugh over the Latin rhetoric in which Hamlet indulges . . . some remarkable features, but still more remarkable what Shakespeare preserved and what he cast aside.") On November 1 Wagner plays passages from an opera based on Scott's *Ivanhoe*, Heinrich Marschner's *Der Templer und die Jüdin* (which centers on the love of Bois-Guilbert for Rebecca). "That is the Germans all over," he says, "clumsy and stupid, but capable amid all their idiocy of catching fire and producing ideas." On December 30, in the course of a long conversation on Balzac, Wagner reads from *Père Goriot* and "admires Balzac's mastery."

Returning to Aristophanes in January, 1874, they read *Lysistrata* ("great fun," notes Cosima). In March and April of that year they discuss *Antony and Cleopatra*, *Julius Caesar*, *The Tempest*, *Twelfth Night*, and *Two Gentlemen of Verona*. On March 30 Wagner reads bits of Champfleury's sketch of Balzac to Cosima and says: "They are charming, these French people." On November 18 she finds Wagner reading *Oedipus* in the evening after his work, comparing the translation with the text: "'It is like a Persian carpet,' he says, 'a torrent of beauty—now vanished forever: we are barbarians.' We then come to the *Oresteia,* the scene of Cassandra with the chorus, and R. declares it to be the most perfect thing mortal art has ever produced." On October 18, 1875, Wagner reads Cosima "Geraint and Enid" from the *Mabinogion.* On December 22, 1875, apropos *The Merchant of Venice* and a pamphlet on the Jews by an O. Beta, Cosima's entry reads: "privately printed; it is badly written, without style, but contains remarkable insights into the present nature of things; the comparison between Antonio's melancholy toward Shylock and the present behavior of the Germans toward the Jews is very apposite." In 1877 they return to *The Peace* ("the Athenians went laughing to their downfall," notes Cosima on March 1) and read *Plutus* as well ("how sublimely the downfall of this most talented people is reflected in the humor of this deeply discerning dramatist"—again Cosima, writing on April 4).

The German translation of Darwin's *On the Origin of Species by Means of Natural Selection, or The Preservation of Favoured Races in the Struggle for Life* appeared four years after the publication of the English original in 1859. The first reference to it in Cosima's diaries is as follows: "R. has a cold and cannot work today; in Darwin (*The Origin of Species*) he reads the case of a dog which, while being dissected, licks the hand of its master, who is doing the operation; the fact that the latter does not then stop upsets R. greatly. . . . In the evening [we read] Gibbon." This entry is dated June 29, 1872. On July 2 she writes: "Darwin is giving him pleasure, and he agrees with him that, in comparison with the old world, there is moral progress in the fact that animals are now accepted as part of it. . . . In the evening Gibbon." On July 21: "In the evening R. reads me a chapter from Darwin (on social instinct)." There is an extended and rather farfetched comment by Wagner on February 10, 1873: "In the evening we begin Darwin's *Origin of Species,* and R. observes that between Schopenhauer and Darwin the same thing has happened as between Kant and Laplace: the *idea* came from Schopenhauer and Darwin developed it, perhaps even without having known Schopenhauer, just as Laplace did not know Kant." On September 28, 1877, she writes: "R. somewhat unwell. . . . In the evening he reads us some passages from Darwin's *The Descent of Man.*" And on October 23, "R. again had a wretched night; abdominal troubles—he reads Darwin (*The Descent of Man*), feels cold." Cosima's entry of April 25, 1881, notes that R. is indisposed and out of humor all day. "In the evening a slight vexation for him, caused by a letter from Darwin in favor of vivisection, or, rather, physiology." It seems to have been Wagner's fate always to read Darwin—a perennial invalid himself—in ill health.

The three English authors mentioned by Dannreuther in his account of Wagner's library at Bayreuth are Shakespeare, Walter Scott (1771–1832), and Thomas Carlyle (1795–1881). Several of Carlyle's works, translated into German by various hands, are on the Bayreuth list, and all make their appearance in Cosima Wagner's diaries: *The History of Friedrich II, Called Frederick the Great; Heroes and Hero-Worship; The History of the French Revolution;* and various essays. Voltaire's association with Frederick the Great was so much the subject of conversation that Cosima noted on December 15, 1870: "I dreamed [last night] that at table Voltaire and R. got into a quarrel about Albrecht Dürer." A very interesting note of May 29, 1879, reads: "R. is also very much struck by a coincidence: Carlyle pins his hopes on a proficient and goodhearted industrialist, and Turgenev shows us just such a person in Solomin in *Virgin Soil* . . . in the evening a game of whist with friend Rubinstein." If Wagner had been able to look into the future he would have seen Carlyle's industrialist hero "Plugson of St. Dolly Undershot" (in *Past and Present*) undergo a sea change into the industrialist hero and armaments king "Andrew Undershaft of Perivale St. Andrews" in Bernard Shaw's *Major Barbara* (1905). This play presents the revised ending of Wagner's *Ring* proposed by Shaw in *The Perfect Wagnerite* (1898), in the early editions of which the industrial saviors are actually named: "Lever of Port Sunlight" (England), "Carnegie of Homestead" (U.S.A.), "Krupp of Essen" (Germany), and others. Shaw, as it were, grafted Carlyle's Plugson onto Wagner's Wotan. Undershaft is a Wotan whose empire will *not* go up in flames—so Shaw hoped.[30]

We are told by Jerome Mitchell that Walter Scott "inspired more operas than did any other single writer," Shakespeare excepted.[31] Wagner is not among the inspired. But, as Dannreuther has indicated, the Wagners were enthusiastic readers of Scott. The Bayreuth list includes Scott's novels in English, French, and German. Comments on *Ivanhoe, Quentin Durward, The Fair Maid of Perth, Count Robert of Paris,* and *Woodstock* occur in the first volume of the diaries; further

30. Rather, *The Dream of Self-Destruction*, 149–67.
31. Jerome Mitchell, *The Walter Scott Operas* (University, Ala., 1977), 9; Sherwin and Irene Sloan, editors, *Opera Quarterly*, I (Winter, 1983), 1–2.

comments on some of these, and on *Old Mortality, Waverley, Kenilworth, The Heart of Midlothian,* and *The Pirate,* are to be found in the second volume. The Bayreuth list also has *Guy Mannering, Der Alterthümler (The Antiquary),* and *Die Presbyterianer (Old Mortality).*[32]

As usual, the comments often illuminate Wagner's own thinking. On February 15, 1878, for example, they are reading *Die Presbyterianer,* a tale of partisan warfare and terrorism on the part of the Scots and remorseless military butchery on the part of the English in 1679 during the conflict between the troops of Charles II and the unyielding Covenanters. Wagner tells Cosima that these "horrors . . . would be unbearable" were it not for the relief afforded by such incidents as the rescue of the moderate Presbyterian Henry Morton by the Royalist Lord Evandale (and the subsequent rescue of Evandale by Morton). Wagner then asserts that the "humane purpose of these [*i.e.,* Scott's] works is to show how, amid all the terrible happenings, the better side of the individual characters triumphs." This is a fair judgment. Often enough, Scott's protagonists are not heroic characters but "moderates," who try to mediate between fanatical extremists on both sides. Readers of *The Fair Maid of Perth* will recall also how Catharine, the fair maid, tried to woo her lover, the valiant armorer and citizen-swordsman Henry Gow, away from the use of violence, and how he, sickened at last by carnage if not convinced by her words, hangs up his broadsword forever and joins with Catharine in wedlock—a Siegfried who has learned the lesson taught Parsifal by Gurnemanz.

On November 30, 1878, after reading from Scott's *Life of Napoleon Buonaparte* (published twelve years after Waterloo), Cosima notes: "R. quotes Heine's criticism of it and talks about the discredit into which it subsequently fell. But he says that it interests him as a criminal case."[33] On December 2, 1878, they read Scott's account of the siege of

---

32. The reference to Scott's *The Presbyterians* in the index of the English translation of Cosima Wagner's diaries as well as to *Old Mortality* is an error caused by a back translation of the German title.

33. The translation "as interesting as a criminal case" in *Cosima Wagner's Diaries,* II, 216, is, perhaps, misleading. The German has: "Ihn aber interessiere es wie ein Kriminalfall" (Cosima Wagner, *Tagebücher,* II, 246), *i.e.,* the life of Napoleon *is* a criminal case. For Wagner's characterization of "Caesars" and "Napoleons" as brutal, hateful men who are "empty within" and forever "gobbling up what is without," see Rather, *The Dream of Self-Destruction,* 21. To George Gissing, who shared so many of Wagner's views, Napoleon I was a "wild beast with a genius for arithmetic" (Gissing, *The Crown of Life,* 197).

Toulon, the victory over the English occupiers in 1793 that made Napoleon famous. Cosima notes, "R. tells me that in Eisleben (at the age of seven) he dreamed, after reading about the siege in Bredow's history book, that he was standing somewhere in Toulon and seeing all the corpses and the other horrors." We have no reason to doubt Wagner's story that in 1820, while staying at the old house in Eisleben, he dreamed of the bloody field of slaughter at Toulon. But one wonders nevertheless whether this recollection had been retrospectively touched up after a reading of E. T. A. Hoffmann's nightmarish vision of the field of slaughter at Dresden. Hoffmann, who was in Dresden when the town was taken by Napoleon, saw the mass graves when he visited the battlefield a few days later, on August 29, 1813. He wrote in his notebook, "What I have so often seen in dreams has been realized for me—in a frightful manner—mutilated and torn human beings!!" Hoffmann's "Vision" (*Vision auf dem Schlachtfelde bei Dresden*) was written down in December, 1813, and the still victorious first Napoleon is depicted as a war criminal, a mass-murderer without parallel in modern times.[34] Scott's description of the fall of Toulon culminates in the following passage: "It was on this night of terror, conflagration, tears and blood, that the star of Napoleon first ascended the horizon; and though it gleamed over many a scene of horror ere it set, it may be doubtful whether its light was ever blended with those of one more dreadful."[35]

To sum up this cursory account of Richard Wagner's stance in relation to world literature, we recall the delight he took in the capacity of the old "German spirit"—exemplified in the polyglot court of Friedrich II, that thirteenth-century king of Jerusalem, king of Sicily, son of the Holy Roman Emperor, father of Manfred, troubadour, polymath, and *stupor mundi* of his day—to transcend the narrow grasp of nationality and grasp the universal "purely human." Wagner's feeling for this

34. Harich, *E. T. A. Hoffmann*, I, 218. Hoffmann's *Vision auf dem Schlachtfelde bei Dresden* was first published in 1814.

35. Sir Walter Scott, *The Life of Napoleon Buonaparte* (9 vols.; Edinburgh, 1835), II, 357. Gissing's characterization of Napoleon (note 33 above) recalls Wagner's "reckoning beast of prey" and may have been derived from a letter of recommendation by one of Napoleon's teachers at Corsica: according to the teacher the future conqueror of Europe had a considerable talent for mathematics but *none* for the humanities (Scott, *Life of Napoleon Buonaparte*, II, 330).

ideal is as evident in the make up of his personal libraries at Dresden and Bayreuth as it has always been, to discerning eyes, evident in his lifework as a whole. "For me," Arnold Schoenberg wrote in 1931, "Wagner's high ethos and the timeless value of his works stand fast." [36]

36. Arnold Schoenberg, cited on the title page of Anna Jacobson, *Nachklänge Richard Wagners im Roman* (Heidelberg, 1932). The original reads, "Das hohe Ethos Wagners und der Ewigkeitswert seiner Werke stehen für mich fest."

CHAPTER TWO

ON THE QUALITY OF WAGNER'S POETRY AND PROSE

Wagner's writings, including the nine volumes of collected works published during his lifetime, together with his voluminous correspondence and huge autobiography, constitute a formidable bulk of material, much of it still available only in German. William Ashton Ellis's *Richard Wagner's Prose Works,* an eight-volume edition of Wagner's essays, short stories, and posthumous writings, appeared in the 1890s; it has been reprinted as recently as 1972.[1] Wagner's ten-volume collected works in German (volume ten appeared in 1883, after his death), the *Gesammelte Schriften und Dichtungen,* have been reprinted often enough, most recently in 1976.[2] Neither of these two collections includes Wagner's "The Work and Mission of My Life," a long essay, published in two parts, in the *North American Review* in 1879.[3] Wagner's autobiography, *Mein Leben,* was privately printed and circulated among his friends in the 1870s. It was not made public until 1911, when it appeared simultaneously in German and in the very faulty, authorized English translation, *My Life.* The translation was reprinted in 1972, and in 1983 an entirely new and much improved English version of *Mein Leben* appeared, based on a new German text.[4] An older edi-

1. Richard Wagner, *Richard Wagner's Prose Works,* trans. William Ashton Ellis (8 vols.; 1895–99, 2nd ed.; rpr. St. Clair Shores, Mich., 1972).
2. Richard Wagner, *Gesammelte Schriften und Dichtungen* (10 vols.; 1887–88, 2nd ed.; rpr. Hildesheim, 1976).
3. Richard Wagner, "The Work and Mission of My Life," *North American Review,* CXXIV (August, 1879), 107–24 and (September, 1879), 238–58.
4. Richard Wagner, *Mein Leben* (Munich, 1911); Wagner, *My Life,* authorized translation (1911; rpr. New York, 1972); Wagner, *My Life,* trans. Andrew Gray, ed. Mary Whittall (Cambridge, 1983). *Cf.* my book reviews of the authorized translation

tion of Wagner's correspondence, edited by Erich Kloss, amounts to seventeen volumes, and a critical and complete edition of the correspondence is now under way in Germany.[5] As for Wagner's poetry, it takes up, in the form of the libretti of the music dramas, approximately two of the ten volumes of the *Gesammelte Schriften und Dichtungen.*

Wagner's letters to members of his family from 1833 through 1836 have a fresh, open, and often charming tone. A letter to his ten-year-older sister Rosalie on December 11, 1833, for example, tells her of the progress he is making on his second opera, *Die Feen (The Fairies,* based on Carlo Gozzi's *La donna serpente, [The Lady Serpent]*). He had already abandoned *Die Hochzeit,* we recall, because of Rosalie's distaste for the blood-drenched story. The letter to Rosalie is a spontaneous and ingenuous outburst of creative joy.[6] Wagner was then chorus master at Würzburg. His *Symphony in C Major* had already been performed. Confident of his future success, he would soon be directing the musical affairs of the Bethmann theater company and living the life of a carefree and popular young lady's man. This life ended in 1836, when he and a young actress in the Bethmann company, Minna Planer, were married. The marriage broke up almost at once, with Minna deserting him for another man. Wagner went on alone in 1837 to the Russian town of Riga, where he had been appointed musical director (the repentant and forgiven Minna subsequently joined him there).

During the three years that the couple spent in Paris (1839–1842), Wagner finished *Rienzi,* which he had begun in Riga, composed his *Faust Overture,* and wrote the words and music of *The Flying Dutchman.* Working for Maurice Schlesinger, editor of the *Gazette musicale,* Wagner arranged operatic numbers by Gaetano Donizetti and Jacques Halévy for the piano or cornet, and wrote short stories and critical articles. He scraped an existence for himself and Minna out of the purest Bohemian vein. The alternating episodes of abject despair alone

---

and the Gray-Whittall version in *Opera Quarterly,* I (Autumn, 1983), 179–81, and II (Winter, 1984), 164–65, respectively, for a discussion of the authorized translator's errors and Gray's corrections.

5. Richard Wagner, *Richard Wagners Briefe in Originalausgaben,* ed. Erich Kloss (17 vols. in 9; Leipzig, 1910–1913); Wagner, *Sämtliche Briefe,* ed. Gertrud Strobel and Werner Wolf (4 vols.; Leipzig, 1967–).

6. Wagner, *Sämtliche Briefe,* I, 136–42.

and wild gaiety in the company of friends (whom, as always, he quickly acquired) are amusingly and often brilliantly described in his auto-biography—although not the few days that he may have spent in a debtors' prison.[7] The Paris milieu in which Richard and Minna Wag-ner then lived is captured in Gustave Flaubert's *Éducation sentimen-tale,* the first version (discarded) of which was written between 1843 and 1845. The art dealer Jacques Arnoux and his wife in Flaubert's novel are said to have been drawn from Maurice Schlesinger and his Christian wife—for whom Schlesinger abjured Judaism, and with whom Flaubert himself had fallen in love at the age of sixteen. It may even be that the shade of Wagner haunts Flaubert's *Éducation senti-mentale* in the form of a poverty-stricken painter.[8]

We note only in passing that two essays by Wagner, "Pasticcio" and "On German Opera," were published in 1834 in journals edited, respectively, by Robert Schumann and Heinrich Laube, and that an essay entitled "Bellini" appeared in the Riga *Zuschauer,* a German-language paper, in 1837. Wagner's contributions, ten in all, to Schles-inger's *Gazette musicale* were published between 1840 and 1842. A long and rather favorable account of Halévy's opera *La reine de Chypre,* which made its appearance shortly after the Paris premiere in December, 1841, was subsequently published in German in a Dresden newspaper, thus helping to keep Wagner's name alive in Saxony. A few weeks before the Paris premiere of Carl Maria von Weber's first and most hauntingly mysterious opera, Wagner's essay "Der Freischütz" appeared in the *Gazette musicale* to inform the French that their logi-cal minds were, on the whole, little fitted for the understanding of such a work. He contrasted the civilized purlieus of the Bois de Boulogne with the mysterious depths of a remote German forest, and added that only a Berlioz, composer of the *Symphonie fantastique,* would fully understand Weber's score. Wagner tells us in his autobiography that the essay on Weber's opera came to the attention of George Sand, and that she had used some of its ideas to lead into a "legendary tale from French provincial life." He was much flattered, he says, to have thus

---

7. Wagner, *Mein Leben, passim.* A letter dated October 28, 1840, from Minna Wagner to Theodor Apel, a well-to-do friend, states that Richard has just been taken to debtors' prison. See Westernhagen, *Wagner: A Biography,* I, 61; Newman, *The Life of Richard Wagner,* I, 301.

8. Léon Guichard, *La musique et les lettres au temps du romantisme* (Paris, 1955), 177; Westernhagen, *Wagner: A Biography,* I, 60.

attracted the famous writer's attention. Wagner does not give the title of Sand's tale, but it proves to be *Mouny-Robin*. Wagner's name is not mentioned in Sand's lead-in to the story, but there are unmistakable references in it to his essay. *Mouny-Robin* begins at a performance of *Der Freischütz* in Paris, where the first-person narrator hears a Frenchman assert that Germans must be simpleminded to countenance such rubbish. To this a German retorts that the French are too skeptical to countenance the marvelous. A "cosmopolitan spectator" nearby then makes some of the points made in Wagner's essay, and the narrator sums up as follows: "The French, for love of truth, deny or fail to recognize any new truth; the German, for love of the marvelous, refuses to recognize any truth that denies his chimaeras." Sand, after commenting that no one has better depicted the German spirit than Heinrich Heine, then begins the story proper.[9]

Wagner's three short stories all have as their central character a young German musician, "R." The first of these, *A Pilgrimage to Beethoven* (1840), recalls E. T. A. Hoffmann's fantastic tale *Ritter Gluck* (1809), which was also the first of Hoffmann's stories to be published.[10] Hoffmann was eleven years old when Christoph Gluck died, Wagner fourteen when Beethoven died, and in both stories a first-person narrator encounters the shade of the eponymous musician in question. R. does so in the company of an unknown and erratic Englishman, a lover of music given to scattering gold pieces abroad and shouting "Goddam!" After presenting one of his own musical compositions to Beethoven for approval, the Englishman departs. Beethoven advises R. to stay in Vienna and compose galops, adding that this is what he himself should have done. So far the story is in a style somewhere between that of Hoffmann and Heine, but suddenly a serious, entirely Wagnerian note is struck: Beethoven tells R. that he intends to compose a choral symphony, making use of Schiller's sublime words in the *Ode to Joy*. Why, Beethoven asks R., should we not take vocal music as seriously as we do instrumental music, instead of completely subordinating the words so that light-minded virtuosi may use them to display their vocal wares? The human voice represents the human heart in its

9. Wagner, *Mein Leben*, I, 207; George Sand, *Mouny-Robin* (Paris, 1869), 251–77 (bound with *Simon*); Grange Woolley, *Richard Wagner et le symbolisme français: Les rapports principaux entre le wagnérisme et l'évolution de l'idée symboliste* (Paris, 1931), 28–29.

10. Hoffmann, *Poetische Werke* (1957–62), I, 11–27.

limited individuality, whereas the instruments of the orchestra represent the primary organs of creation; they express the inexpressible, the "chaos of first creation." Beethoven sighs for a musician capable of writing poetry fit to take its place beside music. Words are weak in comparison with tonal language. But when the elementary force of tone is limited by the word, Wagner says, speaking through the mouth of Beethoven, "the human heart itself will be . . . brought into [a state of] godlike consciousness." [11] In this passage, written when Wagner was at the very beginning of his career as composer, we have the core idea informing the Wagnerian music drama, together with an indication of how that idea was to be embodied in the orchestral prelude to the *Ring,* where a broken, repeated E-flat major chord culminates at last in the voice of the Rhine-maiden Woglinde. The "cosmological," or rather "cosmogonic," aspect of music had already been pointed to by Arthur Schopenhauer in the first volume of *The World as Will and Representation* (1819), but Wagner had not yet found his way to the writings of that philosopher. [12]

Whether or not Wagner knew it, he was putting into Beethoven's mouth words that had been used by Jean Paul twenty-seven years earlier with respect to E. T. A. Hoffmann. In introducing Hoffmann's first collection of tales, Jean Paul wrote: "The author is . . . music director at Dresden. Connoisseurs and friends of his, and the knowledge of and enthusiasm for music in the book itself, promise and assure the appearance in him of a great artist in tones. So much the better, so much the rarity! For up to now the sun-god has always thrown out the gift of words with the right hand and the gift of tones with the left to men who stand so far apart that to this day we are still waiting for the one who will simultaneously write the words and compose the music of a true opera." [13] Hans von Wolzogen was the first to call attention to this curious passage—which seems in retrospect to announce the coming of Wagner. It was written at Bayreuth on November 24, 1813, the day after the death of Wagner's father, when Wagner himself was only six months old. [14]

11. Wagner, "Eine Pilgerfahrt zu Beethoven," in *Gesammelte Schriften und Dichtungen,* I, 90–114, *passim.* According to Gustave Flaubert's dictionary of received views, the word *Goddam* is "the foundation of the English language" (Flaubert, *Bouvard et Pécuchet* [2 vols.; Paris, 1945], II, 272).

12. *Cf.* Rather, *The Dream of Self-Destruction,* 134–35.

13. Hoffmann, *Poetische Werke* (1957–62), I, 5–6.

14. Wolzogen, *E. T. A. Hoffmann und Richard Wagner,* 11–12.

"An End in Paris," Wagner's second contribution to Schlesinger's *Gazette musicale,* will call for further attention in a following chapter in connection with Wagner's attitude toward animals. It is the story of a young German musician who has come to Paris to give the world his art. The narrator of the story, a Heine-like figure, explains to the young German innocent that in Paris art is a business: commodities packaged with known names are sold to a public that would not otherwise know how to evaluate them. One must have a name to be heard, yet to have a name one must be heard. More important than talent is the influence of a powerful protector. The narrator assures R. that Beethoven is now a "name" in Paris, but let some piece of Beethoven's music be hawked about the city with an unknown name attached to it and there would be no buyer. R. refuses to accept this apparently cynical view, quarrels with the narrator, and drops out of sight. Fourteen months later he is found dying of starvation.

R.'s last words (which can be taken as the young Wagner's own confession of faith) are justly famous. They show us at a glance how unfitted this twenty-seven-year-old German idealist was to cope with the commercial world of Paris, where—after the bourgeois king, Louis Philippe, had been ushered into office by the predatory banker Jacques Lafitte in 1830—"the finance aristocracy made the laws . . . [and] dominated public opinion through the actual state of affairs and through the press, [and] the same prostitution, the same shameless cheating, the same mania to get rich was repeated in every sphere." The aim of the finance aristocracy was, adds Karl Marx, "to get rich not by production but by pocketing the already available wealth of others." [15] R.'s last words are as follows:

> I believe in God, Mozart and Beethoven, in the disciples and apostles likewise;—I believe in the Holy Spirit and the truth of art one and indivisible;—I believe that this art proceeds from God and lives in the hearts of all enlightened human beings;—I believe that whoever has even once luxuriated in the sublime delights of this high art must forever after be her subject,

15. Karl Marx, "The Class Struggles in France," in *Karl Marx and Frederick Engels: Selected Works* (3 vols.; Moscow, 1969), I, 206–208. Marx's characterization of the July monarchy as a "joint-stock company for the exploitation of France's national wealth . . . Louis Philippe was the director of this company—Robert Macaire on the throne" (*ibid.,* 208) is witty and probably accurate (Robert Macaire, rogue and cheat, was made famous by the celebrated actor Frederick Lemaitre in 1823 and caricatured later by Honoré Daumier; the latter's caricature of the bloated Louis Philippe swallowing enormous budgets cost him six months in prison.)

and can never deny her;—I believe that through this art everyone will be
blessed, and that it is therefore the privilege of everyone to die of hunger for
her;—I believe that death will give me great happiness;—I believe that I
was, on earth, a dissonant chord, which will at once be wholly and magnifi-
cently resolved by death. I believe in a last judgment with frightful damna-
tion for all those who dared to practice usury with high, chaste art in this
world, who shamed and dishonored her out of base desire and sensual lust,
and in the evil of their hearts; I believe that throughout eternity they will be
condemned to listen to their own music. In contrast, I believe that the true
disciples of high art will be transfigured in a heavenly fabric of fragrant and
radiant harmonies, and united for all eternity with the divine source of all
harmony.[16]

Occasional notes of self-irony are heard in this credo. Wagner's
characterization of R. as a dissonant chord on this earth is one such—
although Wagner could not have known how startlingly accurate it
would prove to be. The sentence passed on faithless musicians, who
will be forced to listen to their own music for all eternity, is an old one.
It is a joke; but the condemnation of those who "practice usury with
high, chaste art" coupled with it is meant seriously. The "privilege" of
dying of hunger for the sake of art, a traditional fate of artists, had
almost been granted to Wagner himself during his stay in Paris. As for
the "dissonant chord," it was not resolved at Wagner's death: the musician himself, if not his music, remains as controversial as ever.

The third in the trilogy of stories about the musician R. is entitled
"A Happy Evening." It was published in the *Gazette musicale* in late
1841 under the title "Une soirée heureuse; fantaisie sur la musique pittoresque." Wagner's *Rienzi* had been accepted in June, 1841, by the
Dresden court theater. Wagner's end in Paris had turned out to be a
happy one after all. The narrator of the story recalls a summer evening
in the public gardens of Paris when he and R. heard performances of
Mozart's *Symphony in E-flat* and Beethoven's *Symphony in A Major,*
and afterwards enjoyed a bowl of steaming punch together. They had
conversed on the contrasting features of the music of Beethoven and
Mozart, on program music and tone painting (*musique pittoresque*),
and other such topics. R. reveals himself as very much a musical pur-
ist. "Nothing is more insufferable," he tells the narrator, "than the
tasteless pictures and anecdotes that people attach to instrumental

16. Wagner, "Ein Ende in Paris," in *Gesammelte Schriften und Dichtungen,* I,
114–36.

works. What poverty of spirit and feeling is betrayed when someone
listening to a Beethoven symphony being performed is able to keep his
attention up only by imagining that the course of some romance or
other is being imitated by the torrential flow of the music!" R. says
also, "It is true once and for all that where human speech ends, music
begins." These last words stand in some conflict with what he had said
a year earlier on the subject in "A Pilgrimage to Beethoven." (They
present the more usual view. As George Sand wrote in *Consuelo*
(1842): "Music . . . is the manifestation of a higher order of ideas and
sentiments than any to which human speech can give expression."[17])
"A Happy Evening" ends with R.'s enthusiastic outburst: "Long live
happiness, long live joy! Long live courage that inspires us in the struggle
with our fate! Long live victory, gained by our higher consciousness
over worthless vulgarity! Long live love, that rewards our courage,
friendship, that keeps our faith upright, hope, that weds our foreboding!
Long live day and night! Hail to the sun! Hail to the stars! A triple
hail to music and her high priests! Let God be honored and praised,
the god of joy and happiness—the god who created music!"[18]

We are reminded here of Brünnhilde's cry when Siegfried awakens
her from her deathlike sleep:

> Hail, thou sun!
> Hail, thou light!
> Hail, thou shining day!
> Long was my sleep[19]

Wagner himself was rising up from the darkness that had almost covered
him in Paris: his *Rienzi* had been accepted in Dresden, and his
Flying Dutchman was almost ready to set sail for Berlin.

Back in Dresden now, Wagner was no longer the nameless youth
who had so nearly gone under in the giant metropolis of France. In
Saxony the name Wagner already had some renown. Richard's brother
Albert was a successful actor and teacher of singing in Leipzig. His
sister Luise, an actress in Dresden, was now the wife of Friedrich Brockhaus,
the publisher; Klara, another sister, was married to a well-known
singer; Ottilie, youngest of the sisters, was the wife of the In-

17. George Sand, *Consuelo: A Romance of Venice* (New York, [1856]), 331.
18. Wagner, "Ein glücklicher Abend," in *Gesammelte Schriften und Dichtungen*,
I, 136–49.
19. Wagner, "Siegfried," *ibid.*, VI, 166.

dologist Hermann Brockhaus. Rosalie, Richard's oldest sister and artistic conscience, had given up her acting career and married a doctor of philosophy, only to die in childbirth a year later. Richard's uncle, the polymath Gottlob Heinrich Adolph Wagner, had died in 1835, but he was still remembered as the editor of *Il parnasso italiano* and as the man to whom Goethe had presented a silver goblet in return for the dedication of that series to "al principe de' poeti." [20] A few may have remembered Richard Wagner's kindly stepfather, the actor and portrait painter Ludwig Heinrich Christian Geyer. [21] Wagner himself had contributed seventeen "letters from Paris" to the Dresden *Abendzeitung* between March, 1841, and January, 1842, and he became a celebrity overnight after the first performance of *Rienzi* on October 20, 1842. [22]

During the Dresden years, from 1842 to 1849, Wagner was busy conducting at the royal theater, and working on *Tannhäuser* and *Lohengrin*. The already finished *Flying Dutchman* was given its first performance in January, 1843, and *Tannhäuser* in October of 1845, but *Lohengrin* was not performed until 1850. Wagner, having escaped arrest by the police of Dresden during the Saxon uprising of 1849, had by then fled to Zurich, to begin his eleven-year period of exile from the Germanies. Under the auspices of Franz Liszt, the premiere of *Lohengrin* took place at Weimar, in the grand duchy of Saxe-Weimar, where Bach had been court organist and concertmaster a little over a hundred years earlier, and where Goethe—dead since 1832—had once been chief minister of state (a position that Wagner would later be accused of usurping, under Ludwig II, in Bavaria).

Wagner's account in his autobiography of the uprising in 1849 and of the part that he played in it is one of the most fascinating episodes in a work that has been called by its most recent editor, Martin Gregor-Dellin, "not the least" of Wagner's "dramas." [23] Wagner tells us, in an autobiographic sketch first published in 1843, that with the overthrow of the last Bourbon in France in July, 1830, "at one stroke I became a revolutionary and arrived at the conviction that every halfway-aspiring human being should be concerned with politics alone." [24] In *Mein Leben* he tells of the enthusiasm that gripped him after the Poles rose

20. Westernhagen, *Wagner: A Biography*, I, 20.
21. On Geyer's possibly closer relationship to Wagner, see Chapter 5 herein.
22. Newman, *The Life of Richard Wagner*, I, 288.
23. Wagner, *Mein Leben*, II, 795–96.
24. Wagner, *Gesammelte Schriften und Dichtungen*, I, 7.

up against their Russian overlords shortly thereafter. "It was the Polish freedom-fight (*Freiheitskampf*) against the superior strength of the Russians that soon filled me with growing enthusiasm. The successes that the Poles achieved for a short time in May 1831 moved me with astonishment and ecstasy: to me it seemed that a miracle had created the world anew." [25] A similar enthusiasm gripped him in 1849 during the Saxon uprising. But as the Polish uprising had been suppressed by the Russian troops so the Saxon uprising was quelled by Prussian troops.

During the uprising Wagner was closely associated with the Russian anarcho-communist Mikhail Bakunin (1814–1876), a young man of Wagner's own age. (Wagner thought Bakunin was older, but he was actually a few months younger.) On Palm Sunday, 1849, after Wagner had concluded a performance of Beethoven's *Ninth Symphony,* Bakunin stepped up to congratulate him and to announce "in a loud voice that if all music should be lost in the expected world-conflagration, we should bind ourselves at the risk of our lives to preserve this symphony." In one of the ironic asides frequent in his autobiography, Wagner adds that six weeks later Bakunin seems indeed to have taken on the office of chief incendiary. [26] Wagner says that Bakunin, a Russian officer of aristocratic background, had fled the army and Russia under the influence of the writings of Rousseau. In Berlin, he had eagerly taken to the Hegelian dialectic. Wagner was much impressed.

> Everything in him was colossal, with a weight suggestive of primeval freshness. I never had the impression from him that he made very much of my acquaintance, for he no longer seemed to be much concerned with intellectually gifted people, desiring instead only ruthless, active natures; but, as became plain to me later, here too theoretical demands were more active in him than purely personal feelings, for he had much to say and explain on these matters. He had in general accustomed himself to the Socratic mode of conversation, and he was obviously at ease when, stretched out on his host's hard sofa, he could hold forth at length before a motley group of people on the problems of the revolution. . . . In this connection he called attention to the childish-daimonic joy of the Russian people in fire, on which Rostopschin [the governor-general of Moscow] had reckoned in his stratagem against Napoleon at the burning of Moscow.

Bakunin was convinced that the "burning of the lord's castles" was the only goal worthy of a reasonable human being. "While Bakunin was preaching these frightful doctrines in his way," adds Wagner with an

25. Wagner, *Mein Leben*, I, 66–67.
26. *Ibid.*, 397–98.

unforgettable touch, "he never ceased, for a full hour, holding his broad hand before me, in spite of my protests, since he noticed that my eyes suffered from the harsh glare of the light." [27]

"As with his music," wrote an editor of Wagner's autobiography in 1923, "so also with *Mein Leben* he draws us into his magic circle." [28] The autobiography is at times quite frank, as when Wagner tells us of Minna's illegitimate daughter (who passed as her sister), whom he accepted along with Minna herself. The most brilliant set pieces are to be found in the first two of the four parts of the biography. Among them are Wagner's account of his relationship with Count Tyskiewicz, leader of the Polish uprising against Russia in 1830–1831, which culminates in Wagner's Hoffmannesque account of his semihallucinatory confrontation with the spirit of cholera while at Brunn; the perilous flight from Riga in 1838, accompanied by Minna and their gigantic Newfoundland, over a Russo-Prussian frontier guarded by Cossacks with orders to shoot to kill; the subsequent and even more perilous journey to London on the little *Thetis*, still with Minna and the dog, during which the sea-borne, unconquerable Wagner accumulated material for *The Flying Dutchman* and, as already noted, improved his French by reading Sand's *La dernière Aldini;* and, finally, the story of the uprising in Dresden and Wagner's flight to Switzerland.

Almost never does the authorized translation truly mirror Wagner's remarkable way with words. On occasion it is simply erroneous. Wagner says, for example, that the rocking, rolling E-flat major triad motif in the opening bars of the *Rheingold* overture came to him as he lay "in a kind of somnambulistic state," exhausted and still seasick, in a hotel room in Spezia; he suddenly had the feeling that he was being overwhelmed by rapidly flowing water, and he awoke with a start. The translation calls this "a kind of somnolent state," and thus fails to express the hypnagogic quality of the episode (all German editions read "eine Art von somnambulem Zustand"). Worse is the translation of a sentence that refers to the young Leo Tolstoy. Wagner says that in 1860 he met in passing a number of people, "among whom a Russian Count Tolstoy stood out especially favorably" ("unter denen ein russischer Graf Tolstoi sich besonders vorteilhaft auszeichnete," in the three German editions). The authorized translation has "amongst whom a Russian count Tolstoy was conspicuously kind." Adding to

27. *Ibid.*, 398–400.
28. Richard Wagner, *Mein Leben*, ed. Wilhelm Altmann (2 vols.; Leipzig, 1923), I, 10.

this puzzle is the absence of a Count Tolstoy from the indices of the German editions of 1923 and 1963. The limp translations of what Wagner wrote about the volcanic personality of his friend the singer and dramatic actress Wilhelmine Schröder-Devrient make it difficult to read *My Life* "musically" (as Gregor-Dellin advises us to do). Together with Beethoven and Shakespeare, Madame Schröder-Devrient was one of the three definitive factors in Wagner's artistic development. For Wagner she was a kind of embodied link between music and the drama, between tone and word. She was also, in his eyes, a thoroughly "daimonic" figure, careening through life and exhausting herself in a succession of love affairs and stage performances. The nine-year-older woman made Wagner an unwilling confidant of her love affairs in the 1840s. At times she gave him financial and artistic support. On one such occasion, however, Wagner says that she "laughed like a kobold" ("lachte wie ein Kobold") when he told her of his troubles with the proposed performance of Spontini's *La Vestale* in Dresden in 1845. The authorized translation reads "laughed as though she would never stop," and misses the Kundry-like element in the great diva's response. *Daimonic* is a word that recurs as frequently in the writings of Wagner as in those of Goethe. But Wagner's characterization of Schröder-Devrient's "almost daimonic warmth" ("fast dämonische Wärme," in all editions) comes to us in the authorized translation as "almost satanic ardour." Where he tells us that music was for him "a wholly daimonic realm, a mystic, sublime portent" ("durchaus nur Dämonium, eine mystische erhabene Ungeheuerlichkeit," in all editions), the authorized translation reads "a spirit, a noble and mystic monster." [29] Wagner wrote to Mathilde Wesendonck from Venice in 1859 that the Grail-messenger, Kundry, had risen up before his eyes in the form of "a wonderful world-daimonic woman" ("ein wunderbar weltdämonisches Weib"). [30] The word, like a recurring musical motif, reminds us that the features of Wilhelmine Schröder-Devrient are imprinted on the Kundry of Wagner's *Parsifal*. [31]

Wagner's self-irony in his autobiography seems to have largely escaped his biographer Ernest Newman. While living in Zurich in the early 1850s, Wagner took the water cure at Albisbrunn and gave up

29. I have used some of this material in a review of the authorized translation.

30. Richard Wagner, *Richard Wagner an Mathilde Wesendonck* (Berlin, 1904), 110.

31. *Cf.* Paul Bekker, *Richard Wagner: His Life in His Work*, trans. M. M. Bozman (1931; rpr. Westport, Conn., 1971), 487, 498–500.

alcoholic drinks. Newman says that Wagner then attempted to convince his friends Jakob Sulzer and Georg Herwegh that for "spiritual 'intoxication' regenerate man should look not to the juice of the grape but to love." According to Newman also, Wagner "argued with his friends about the evil effects of strong liquors, with such vehemence on both sides that they often came near quarrelling." After citing nine lines from Wagner's autobiography on the episode, Newman concludes: "For him the cosmos was always a matter of Wagner *contra* non-Wagner; and whenever he adopted a new faith it was the duty of humanity to change with him. In his last years, largely as the result of his horror of vivisection, he preached the virtues of vegetarianism."[32] Other than Wagner's autobiography, it should be noted, Newman cites no other source of information. Wagner's account of the episode in *Mein Leben* is as follows.

> I rejoiced to receive my Zurich friends again as visitors in our new quarters [at Albisbrunn], which were located more conveniently for them as well; but for a long time I spoiled all our friendly conversations with my passionate advocacy of the water cure and an associated polemic against wine and other narcotic drinks. From all this a new religion had taken shape for me: for example, if I were driven into a corner by Sulzer and Herwegh (the latter prided himself on his knowledge of chemistry and physiology) because of the untenability of Rauss's theory on the poisonous properties of wine, then I would hold fast to the moral-aesthetic factor, which allowed me to see in the enjoyment of wine merely a poor and barbaric surrogate for the ecstatic mood to be won only by love. . . . This led to a general critique of the modern relationship of the sexes to each other, to which I was led by observing the separation of men from women as it crudely presented itself here in accordance with Swiss custom. Sulzer stated that he had nothing at all against letting himself be intoxicated by association with women, but "where to get them without stealing?" Herwegh wanted to go somewhat deeper into my paradoxes, but he thought that wine had nothing to do with the matter and was in itself a strengthening nourishment, which, moreover, fitted in very well with the ecstasy of love, as Anacreon had shown. Looking more closely at my condition, however, my friends on their part found reason to be concerned about my strange and stubborn extravagance: I was exceedingly pale and haggard, slept little at all and betrayed in everything alarming overanimation. Although in the end sleep escaped me almost entirely, I insisted that I had never been so cheerful and well, and I continued to take my chilly baths very early in the morning in the greatest cold of

32. Newman, *The Life of Richard Wagner*, II, 274–75.

winter, to the torment of my wife, who had to light my way with a lantern on the necessary promenade.[33]

Wagner's account, dictated to Cosima ten or fifteen years after the event, is light and amusing in tone. As for his behavior at the time and that of his friends, for example, the vehement arguments on both sides, we know no more about it than Newman did.

Turning now to Wagner's poetry, that is, the libretti of his operas and music dramas, we find that opinions as to its quality have varied widely. In Wagner's day it was the alliterative verse of the *Ring* that came in for the most adverse criticism. In recent years, in English-speaking countries at least, blanket condemnations of all the libretti are often heard. In 1973, for example, the editor of a collection of Wagner's essays and stories mentioned previously devotes most of his short introduction to a total condemnation of Wagner's libretti. "Instead of collaborating with a dramatist of distinction," he tells us, Wagner "preferred to write his own libretti." He continues:

> The results are frequently as clumsily illiterate as the work of the worst of the Italian hack librettists whom he derides, and are additionally burdened by Wagner's teutonic inability to be precise. The drama . . . is provided entirely by the music, which is often seriously hampered by the portentous autodidactic doggerel churned out by the composer as poet. . . . The sad truth is that Wagner lacked any feeling for words as the raw material of art, though he possessed the artist's instinct as far as his own requirements were concerned. Wagner the composer needed Wagner the poet. He would not have been happy with, say, Goethe or Schiller.

So that we may approach Wagner in the right spirit, the editor tells us: "It is also unfortunately true that some of Wagner's theories, which he was venal enough to adopt and discard always at the expedient moment, are as conscienceless as his character: a character which allowed him to be callous in personal relationships, dishonest in business dealings, and unreliable in most other matters." [34] All this in the three paragraphs of his introduction.

To dispute these sweeping and unsupported conclusions (which come with an escape hatch in the form of the clause "though [Wagner]

33. Wagner, *Mein Leben*, II, 488–89. I have used some of this material in my review of Newman's *The Life of Richard Wagner*, in *Opera Quarterly*, I (Autumn, 1983), 184–86.

34. Richard Wagner, *Richard Wagner: Stories and Essays*, ed. Charles Osborn (London, 1973), 7–8.

possessed the artist's instincts as far as his own requirements were concerned") would be futile. After all, even greater writers have often been very hard on their predecessors: Leo Tolstoy found Shakespeare confused, repetitious, and morally repulsive, Dante's reputation unjustified, and *Paradise Lost* a bore, while T. S. Eliot's admirer Ezra Pound called Milton "donkey-eared," and was willing to throw out the whole of Vergil "without the slightest compunction."[35] On occasion all critics agree: Edward Young's long didactic poem *Night Thoughts* was widely admired in the eighteenth century, but today it is, as poetry, as unreadable as the poems of Henry Wadsworth Longfellow have since become. It is conceivable that we become "word-blind" with the passing of time, as George Steiner suggests with respect to the Pre-Raphaelite and decadent verse of one hundred years ago. "Our contemporary sense of the poetic, our often unexamined presumptions about valid or spurious uses of figurative speech have developed from a conscious negation of *fin-de-siècle* ideas," he writes.[36]

In a particular case, it may be that we ourselves lack the associations that give beauty and evocative force to lines, or even a few words, from a poet when they are apprehended by a suitably prepared hearer. In *Remembrance of Things Past* the narrator's boyhood friend Bloch is, or professes to be, enchanted by the beauty of a few words from Racine, *la fille de Minos et de Pasiphae*—words, Bloch says, that have the supreme merit of meaning nothing. Proust's narrator then speaks of the insoluble problem raised by the existence of "beauty denuded of reason."[37] But the magic of Racine's line, if it has any, depends entirely on its context and on the images it evokes, and not at all on the sound or look of the words. To one who grew up with the figures of Norse and Germanic mythology, the lines of Wagner's *Ring* may carry an added "Blochian" force.

For the *Ring*, Wagner forged an alliterative verse style entirely different from that employed in his earlier works. From the beginning the *Ring* has been both the most admired and the most denigrated of Wag-

35. *Cf.* Leo Tolstoy, *Journal intime,* trans. Natacha Rostova and Mgte. Jean-Debrit (Paris, 1917), 123; *Tolstoy's Letters,* ed. and trans. R. F. Christian, (2 vols.; London, 1978), I, 666; Ezra Pound, *Literary Essays of Ezra Pound,* ed. T. S. Eliot (New York, 1968), 28–72.

36. George Steiner, *After Babel: Aspects of Language and Translation* (New York, 1975), 14.

37. Marcel Proust, *A la recherche du temps perdu* (3 vols.; Paris, 1969), I, 90, 93.

ner's libretti. In 1909, in a doctoral dissertation on the language of the *Ring,* John Schuler commented:

> It is interesting to note that some important critics have unrestricted praise for the poetry of the "Ring" but speak disdainfully of the alliteration; while others extol its merits and condemn the poem. Julian Schmidt calls it "Old-Frankonian twaddle"; [Eduard] Hanslick "A frightfully short dog-trot"; and when "Parsifal" appeared he was glad "to be rid of this childish tittle-tattle" . . . Georg Witkowski thinks that the vast thought-content and the dramatic importance of the "Ring" place it in the domain of true elevated tragedy; but the freakish external form which applies alliteration with utter want of intelligence, the language which is intentionally antiquated and distorted by numberless word-plays, impair its dramatic value. Dr. Karl Koestlin, on the other hand, holds just the opposite view. He sees no value in it from the viewpoint of tragedy, but has almost unlimited praise for it as a poem.[38]

Wagner, who had been working on the text of the *Ring* since 1848, and who would continue to alter it until 1876, finished the first version of the work in 1852. In the following year he had a small private edition of the text published at his own expense (with borrowed funds) and sent out copies to a few friends. He himself gave a dramatic reading of the *Ring* to an invited audience at the Hotel Baur au Lac at Zurich in 1853.[39] During 1854 Wagner developed an enormous admiration for the writings of Arthur Schopenhauer, and on Christmas of that year he sent a copy of the *Ring* to the philosopher at Frankfurt.[40] Schopenhauer's assessment of it, coming as it does from a master of German prose in his own right, deserves notice. The philosopher remarked to one of his friends: "The man [Wagner] is a poet, not a musician!" And to one of his visitors Schopenhauer said: "Tell your friend Wagner . . . he should give music up, he has more genius as a poet! I, Schopenhauer, remain true to Rossini and Mozart." In a letter of 1855 Schopenhauer wrote that he had heard one of Wagner's operas in Frankfurt and intended to hear others; once again he praised the *Ring* as a work of poetry.[41]

---

38. John Schuler, *The Language of Richard Wagner's Ring des Nibelungen* (Lancaster, Pa., 1908), 45–46.

39. Westernhagen, *Wagner: A Biography,* II, 606.

40. Newman, *The Life of Richard Wagner,* II, 432.

41. Felix Gotthelf, "Schopenhauer und Richard Wagner," in *Viertes Jahrbuch der Schopenhauer-Gesellschaft* (Nendeln, Liechtenstein, 1968), 42. Schopenhauer's admiration was tempered by what he saw as Wagner's too-free use of the German language (*cf.*

The reaction of another reader of the *Ring*, Ferdinand Lassalle, is worth noting here. Lassalle was the son of a German Jewish merchant, the author of two scholarly works on philosophy and several political-economic pamphlets, and a founder (in 1863) of the German Workers Party. He was given a copy of the *Ring* by Hans von Bülow, at the time the husband of the future Cosima Wagner. In the spring of 1862 Lassalle wrote to von Bülow: "I began reading the *Ring* yesterday morning, was unhappy and angry when I had to go out for twenty minutes around two o'clock, returned as quickly as possible, gave orders not to be disturbed by anyone, was finished with the book at five o'clock, immediately began a second reading, finished this too on the same night, could hardly fall asleep, and even today my soul is so full that I can still think of nothing else, of nothing at all." Lassalle then says that a "*purely poetic* view of Wagner's work of art" as yet escapes him, for he is totally involved by the question, the answer to which is not yet clear, of the meaning intended by Wagner in thus restating the old Norse myths. He continues:

> Naturally this does not in the least, not in the slightest, diminish the quite inexpressible merit of the poet, the intoxicating beauties of the work, the incomparable power of expression, which often had me reading with bated breath, the ecstatic conception of the whole, accessible only to the expert connoisseur of the subject matter. Only Wagner, the poet of Elsa and Tann-häuser, was capable of this! To me Wagner is one of the *absolutely few* natures who offers and confirms the certainty that despite the terrible decay surrounding us, there is in the Germans something more than in any other people, provided the German spirit rises up in its true greatness.[42]

Aside from his lack of clarity as to the overall meaning of Wagner's *Ring*, Lassalle wondered whether the episode in which Wotan's spear (with its runically engraved law of contract) is shattered by Siegfried's sword could be found in the *Edda* or in *The Song of the Volsungs*. He himself, he told von Bülow, could recall it in neither of these old poems.[43] As Lassalle suspected, this episode (as well as numberless others in Wagner's *Ring*) were invented by Wagner himself and endowed with special meaning. I have argued elsewhere that the shatter-

Newman, *The Life of Richard Wagner*, II, 432–33, for Schopenhauer's marginal comments on his copy of the *Ring*).

42. Ferdinand Lassalle, *Ferdinand Lassalle; Der Mensch und Politiker in Selbstzeugnissen*, ed. Konrad Haenisch (Leipzig, 1925), 195–97.

43. *Ibid.*, 198.

ing of Wotan's lance—which bars the approach to Brünnhilde—by
Siegfried's sword and the appearance of the perfected, male-female human being of the future, represent the downfall of purely male egoism.
Wotan bears a relationship to Wagner's revised view of the swan-
knight Lohengrin. For in 1851 Wagner achieved a new understanding
of his Elsa, speaking of "my Lohengrin, whom I had to abandon in
order to arrive with certainty on the track of the *truly womanly* that
would bring salvation to me and all the world, after male egoism (even
in the noblest form) had shattered before this principle in self-destruction. Elsa . . . had made me a complete revolutionary."[44]

In writing the *Ring* Wagner made very free use of an alliterative
verse form (called in German *Stabreim*) found in the Norse poetic
Edda, the Old English poem *Beowulf,* and Old German poetry in general. After the celebrated musical prelude culminating in the lalling
song of the Rhine maiden Woglinde, the *Ring* opens at the bottom of
the Rhine, where three Rhine maidens are keeping watch over the
gold. The Nibelung Alberich, an ugly powerful dwarf, makes his way
up from the depths of the earth and accosts the Rhine maidens.

> He he! Ihr Nicker!
> Wie seid ihr niedlich, neidliches Volk!
> Aus Nibelheim's Nacht
> naht' ich euch gern, neigtet ihr euch zu mir.

An English and a French translation of this passage follow.

> Hey, hey, you nymphs!
> How inviting you look, enviable creatures!
> From Nibelheim's night
> I'd gladly draw near if you'd but come down to me

and

> He He! Les nixes!
> Que vous êtes mignonnes, et enviables!

44. Rather, *The Dream of Self-Destruction,* 58–59. Commentators on *Lohengrin,*
beginning with Joachim Raff in 1854, usually overlook Wagner's reinterpretation, in
1851, of Elsa, Lohengrin, and the "forbidden question." But Henri Lichtenberger, basing himself on the same passages in Wagner's writings that I made use of in 1979,
pointed to the Elsa = Brünnhilde and Lohengrin = Wotan equations eighty years ago in
his *Richard Wagner poète et penseur,* pp. 133–34. Charlotte Teller's feminist novel *The
Cage* (1907) appears to be structurally based on the reinterpreted *Lohengrin* (*cf. The
Dream of Self-Destruction,* 203).

Du ténébreux Nibelheim
j'aimerais venir vers vous si vous veniez vers mois.[45]

Although the alliterative *Nicker-niedlich-neidliches-Nibelheims-
Nacht-naht'-neigtet* sequence, and the alternating assonance of
niedlich-neidliches-Nibelheims-neigtet are reflected to some extent in
"nymphs-inviting-enviable-Nibelheim's-night-near" (less so in the
French translation), the effect is entirely different. The insistently repetitive "n" sounds that begin the seven words in the original German
express Alberich's forceful insistence, which he shows when he tries
and fails to seize each one of the Rhine maidens in turn. The word
Nicker, moreover, is not precisely the equivalent of "nymph" or "nixy"
(*nixe*). It suggests *Nickel* (a derogatory name for a female) and *Nick-
elmann* (a water sprite), but its current meaning is "nodder"—someone
whose head is nodding in an intermittent doze. This meaning points
back to a warning already given by Flosshilde, the most responsible of
the three Rhine maidens, that they are neglecting their assigned task.
When the gold comes into view one of the two sisters (Wellgunde) informs Alberich that from it can be forged a ring that will confer on the
owner power without limits, and the other (Woglinde) that only one
who will forswear love can "force" the gold into a ring. She and her
sister believe that no living being will do this. But Alberich sees things
differently: He curses love, seizes the gold, and hastily disappears into
the depths of the earth, laughing malignantly.

Woglinde's words are worth considering. She sings:

Nur wer der Minne Macht versagt,
nur wer der Liebe Lust verjagt,
nur der erzielt sich den Zauber,
zum Reif zu zwingen das Gold.

The translations, as before, are:

Only he who forswears love's power,
Only he who forfeits love's delight,
Only he can obtain the magic
To fashion the gold into a ring.

Celui seul qui renierait les lois de l'Amour,
en bannerait la joir,

45. The English and French translations here, as well as the original German, are
taken from the libretto accompanying the Philips recording of the Bayreuth *Ring*, conducted by Pierre Boulez.

> pourrait contraindre par un charme
> l'Anneau a sortir de l'or.

Both translations lack the poetic force of the original, and they fail to make the meaning, as Alberich understands it, plain. For, he reflects to himself, once the world is in his hands, can he not satisfy his sexual desires at will? Forget about love, then! Think about lust! Where Woglinde's words imply that love and its pleasures are inseparable, Alberich sees that he will be able to distill the pure alcohol of lust from the wine of love. He sings:

> Erzwäng ich nicht Liebe,
> doch listig erzwäng ich mir Lust?

This is given, without the force of the antithesis, in two translations.

> If I cannot extort love
> then by cunning can I obtain pleasure?

and

> Renoncant a l'Amour
> j'aurais cependant le plaisir?[46]

In his essay of 1848 on the Nibelung myth Wagner says that Siegfried was originally a god of light, a sun-god who kissed the earth and its treasures awake at dawn, only to be treacherously slain at the end of each day and drawn down into Nibelung darkness. The later Siegfried of the Norse sagas became a human hero, and the treasure of the earth became the Nibelung's hoard. The hoard represents earthly power; whoever possesses it becomes a Nibelung. Eventually, Wagner says, the treasure of the Holy Grail underwent mythical fusion with the hoard of the Nibelungs, and the West turned from Rome to Jerusalem in search of salvation; still later the Grail moved east to the homeland of the Aryan peoples.[47]

The image of Siegfried as sun-god is still evident in Wagner's *Ring*.

46. Libretto accompanying the Philips recording of the Bayreuth *Ring*, conducted by Pierre Boulez. For the most part, libretti supplied with recordings of *Das Rheingold* read, as in this instance, "versagt." An exception is the libretto accompanying Sir Georg Solti's recording, which has "entsagt." It is said on good authority that Wagner himself preferred "entsagt." Nevertheless, vol. V, p. 211, of Wagner's *Gesammelte Schriften und Dichtungen*, published during his lifetime, has "versagt." Julius Kapp in his translation has "entsagt" (Richard Wagner, *Richard Wagners gesammelte Schriften*, ed. Julius Kapp [14 vols. in 5; Leipzig, 1914], IV, 24).

47. Rather, *The Dream of Self-Destruction*, 42–43.

Alberich's attention is first drawn to the gold of the Rhine by Woglinde's outcry.

> Lugt, Schwestern!
> Die Weckerin lacht in den Grund.
>
> (Look, sisters! The waker smiles into the depths.)

Wellgunde adds:

> Durch den grünen Schwall
> den wonnigen Schläfer sie grüsst.
>
> (Through the green swell she greets the blissful sleeper.)

And Flosshilde:

> Jetzt küsst sie sein Auge,
> dass er es öff'ne;
> schaut, es lächelt
> in lichtem Schein:
>
> (Now she kisses his eye to open it;
> see! it smiles in the gleaming light:)

The "waker" (*die Weckerin*) here is female; the sleeping treasure, or "blissful sleeper" is male.[48]

In pursuit of this cluster of images we move on to the third act of *Siegfried*. After having penetrated the magic fire that surrounds Brünnhilde's mountain, the hero kisses her awake. Brünnhilde opens her eyes and hails Siegfried in the passage cited in connection with Wagner's short story "A Happy Evening."

> Heil dir, Sonne!
> Heil dir, Licht!
> Heil dir, leuchtender Tag!
> Lang' war mein Schlaf
>
> (Hail, O sun! Hail, O light! Hail, O
> shining day! Long was my sleep.)

This passage—and probably the similar passage in "A Happy Evening" as well—clearly reflects Brynnhild's "hailing" in the *Poetic Edda*, after she has been awakened from her long sleep by the hero Sigurd. Ludwig Ettmüller's translation of the *Edda*, published in 1837, could have been Wagner's source.[49]

48. Wagner, *Gesammelte Schriften und Dichtungen*, V, 209 (my translation).
49. *Ibid.*, VI, 166 (my translation). In Ludwig Ettmüller's "Songs of the Edda of

One of the images, like a recurring leitmotif, appears again in *Göt-terdämmerung,* after Siegfried has been stabbed in the back by Al-berich's half-human son, Hagen (who was engendered not by love, but by lust on one side and greed on the other). As light rapidly dims be-fore Siegfried's eyes he sings:

> Brünnhilde—
> heilige Braut—
> wach' auf! öffne dein Auge!—
>
> . . . .
>
> Der Wecker kam;
> er küsst dich wach.
> (Brünnhilde—holy bride—awake!
> Open your eyes! . . . The Waker came;
> he kissed you awake).[50]

Even without the pulsating musical phrase that so strangely points up the words "the Waker came" in *Siegfried,* as heard on the stage, this scene has unique evocative force. (The reader will note that throughout I ignore an all-important topic: the shifting relationship among the words, the melodies to which they are sung, and the intricate web of orchestral music in the background.) To feel that force, however, we must be aware that in the original myth, Siegfried was the "Waker," the sun-god who kissed the treasures of the earth awake each morning. The woman Brünnhilde—to one who has not forsworn love for power—is the greatest of these treasures (she is the daughter of the earth goddess Erda, by Wotan, in Wagner's free version of the myth). In *Das Rheingold* a gender transformation is evident: a "male" sleeper is kissed awake by a "female" (*die Weckerin, die Sonne*). In *Siegfried* the "Waker" is again male, and the sleeper female. The interchange of gender is perhaps meant to emphasize what Wagner wrote in explana-

---

the Nibelungs" Brynhild sings:
> Lang ich schlief
> lang schlummert' ich,
> lang ist der Leute Leid.

After telling Sigurd that she is called "Sigurdisa" and that she is a Valkyrie, she sings:
> Heil dir, Tag,
> Heil euch Tagessöhnen,
> Heil dir, Nacht und Nährling!

(In *Die Lieder der Edda von den Nibelungen. Stabreimende Verdeutschung* [Zurich, 1837], 21).

50. Wagner, *Gesammelte Schriften und Dichtungen,* VI, 246 (my translation).

tion to his friend August Röckel in January, 1854: "Siegfried alone (the man alone) is not the perfected 'human being' (*der vollkommene 'Mensch'*). He is merely the half; only with Brünnhilde does he become the savior." (The union of the two separated beings into a perfect whole is implied by Siegfried and Brünnhilde themselves when they sing their parting duet at the beginning of *Götterdämmerung*.)[51] Claude Lévi-Strauss has called Wagner "the undeniable originator of the structural analysis of myths." Although Lévi-Strauss made reference here to musical rather than verbal analysis, we can perhaps understand why he, borrowing from Stephen Mallarmé's poem, speaks of his lifetime reverence for "that God, Richard Wagner."[52]

Writing in 1904 on Wagner's verse, Wolfgang Golther says: "In the *Ring* a whole new language takes command, not simply because end-rhyme is dropped and *Stabreim* taken up, but above all because of the natural, free rhythms . . . Wagner . . . by no means adopts the old-German epic *Stabreim* verse line; rather he shapes his self-sufficient dramatic verse anew, basing it on the laws of German speech accent." There is, Golther continues, "free interchange of so-called iambic, trochaic, anapaestic, and dactylic feet—or, better, of combined feet of one, two, or three syllables."[53] As these words imply, the traditional classification of quantitative feet used in Greek and Roman poetry does not fit with the non-quantitative, accented feet of Norse, Germanic or Old English verse. In John Schuler's exhaustive analysis of alliterative and assonantal patterns in the verse of the *Ring*, the traditional classification of feet is ignored entirely. Schuler also illustrates the multiplicity of Wagner's verse forms as compared with the relatively unvaried patterns of traditional *Stabreim*.[54]

51. *Cf.* Rather, *The Dream of Self-Destruction,* 67.

52. Claude Lévi-Strauss, *The Raw and the Cooked: Introduction to a Science of Mythology: I,* trans. John and Doreen Weightman (New York, 1975), 15. Lévi-Strauss states that his own comparison of myth analysis to the analysis of a musical score was derived from "Wagner's discovery that the structure of myths can be revealed through a musical score." (Lévi-Strauss uses musical paradigms in his analysis of myths, *e.g.* "theme and variation," "sonata," etc.)

53. Wolfgang Golther, *Richard Wagner als Dichter* (Berlin, 1904), 7–9. This work forms part of a collection of monographs edited by the eminent Danish literary critic Georg Morris Cohen Brandes.

54. Schuler, *The Language of Richard Wagner's Ring des Nibelungen,* 50–63. The medieval German *Nibelungenlied (Song of the Nibelungs),* which Wagner had in his Dresden library in Simrock's modern German translation, is made up of stanzas of four

Unlike Schopenhauer, Lassalle, and Wagner's small circle of intimate friends and admirers, those of us who read the *Ring* today can hardly succeed in separating the verse rhythm from the accompanying musical rhythm. Since musical rhythms are by nature quantitative as well as accentual, it is possible to describe them in terms of the rhythms of Greek and Roman verse. (For the past one hundred years or so the reverse has been done, the quantitative feet being described by means of musical notation.) In her path-breaking book *Wagner's Dramas and Greek Tragedy*, Pearl Cleveland Wilson pointed out some resemblances between typical Greek lyric rhythms and Wagner's musical rhythms. The so-called Nature leitmotif in the *Ring* is a trochaic dipody $(-\cup\,/$ $-\cup\,/\,-\cup\,/\,-\cup)$, the final short syllable being omitted. She states that this leitmotif is used in the *Ring* to produce effects similar to those produced by references to Zeus in the choral odes of the *Oresteia*, adding, "It is interesting, therefore, to note that the rhythm of this motive is the same as the rhythm of the first lyric reference to Zeus in the *Agamemnon*, 160ff." Other Greek lyric rhythms used in the *Ring* are the iambic $(-\,/\,\cup-\,/\,\cup-)$, in Donner's leitmotif, the cretic $(-\cup-)$, in the "fate" motif, the logaoedic, in the "lalling" song of the first Rhine maiden, the dactylic, choriambic, ionic, and the dochmiac. The rhythms in Greek and Roman verse are determined by the length of the successive syllables. "But," says Wilson, "we may read Wagner's text without getting any idea of the variety of rhythm, even in the vocal parts, while the effects often produced by conflicting rhythms in the orchestra must, of course, be heard to be appreciated." She gives us as illustrative examples the sailor's song, "Frisch weht der Wind der Heimat zu," and Kurwenal's reply to Isolde, "Wer Kornwalls Kron' und Englands Erb'," both in the first act of *Tristan*, remarking that to the reader they seem rhythmically identical, but Wagner makes of the former a "graceful phrase in three-quarter metre," and of the latter a "heavy, emphatic phrase in four-four metre filling four measures." [55]

---

long lines rhymed *aabb;* each line is divided into two sections, one with a feminine ending, one with a masculine. Alliteration is not a feature.

55. Wilson, *Wagner's Dramas and Greek Tragedy*, 90–94, *passim.* The "victory" motif on which Beethoven's *Fifth Symphony* is based is a fourth paeonic foot $(\cup\cup\cup-)$. And the unifying rhythmic figure of the allegretto movement of Beethoven's *Seventh Symphony* is a continuous series of stately Vergilian dactyls and spondees $(-\cup\cup\,/\,--\,/$ $-\cup\cup\,/\,--)$ on which a rhythmic melody of the same character is superimposed.

Wagner's skill with words was perhaps most highly praised by Friedrich Nietzsche. Writing in 1876, in *Richard Wagner in Bayreuth,* Nietzsche has this to say:

> A zestful feeling for the German language runs through Wagner's poetry, a heartiness and ingenuousness in his dealings with it such as cannot be found in any German other than Goethe. Full-bodied expressiveness, audacious brevity, power and rhythmic variety, an extraordinary wealth of meaningful words, syntactical simplicity, an almost unique inventiveness in the language of surging feelings and longings, at times a quite pure, sparkling folkishness and proverbiality—such features might be added up yet others, the mightiest and most admirable of all, go unnoticed. Whoever reads two such poems as *Tristan* and the *Meistersinger* one after the other will feel the same astonishment and hesitation before the language as before the music: namely that it was possible to obtain creative command over two worlds as different in form, color and structure as they are in soul.[56]

Not only had Wagner shaped a new language for each new work, said Nietzsche, he had "forced language back into a primal state, where it hardly thinks in terms of concepts, where language is itself poetry, image, feeling. . . . Anyone else would have failed, for our language seems almost too old and worn out for such a demand." But Wagner's "blow on the rock set free an abounding source."[57]

This brilliant and apparently original insight into Wagner's creative use of language differs little from what Wagner himself had written sixteen years earlier in his "Open Letter to a French Friend (Frederic Villot)." The letter, some fifty pages in length, was prefaced to the prose translations into French of Wagner's *Flying Dutchman, Tannhäuser, Lohengrin,* and *Tristan* by Paul Challemel-Lacour, who translated the letter as well. (In 1861 the letter, ironically titled "*Zukunftsmusik*" ["*Music of the Future*"—the quotation marks are Wagner's] was published in the original German by J. J. Weber of Leipzig.[58]) Words, Wagner told his French audience, had lost touch with their

56. Friedrich Nietzsche, *Werke; Kritische Gesamtausgabe,* eds. Giorgio Colli and Mazzino Montinari, (8 pts; Berlin, 1967–77), pt. 4, vol. I, p. 59.

57. *Ibid.*, 58. Wagner used a similar metaphor in the Dresden *Volksblätter* in 1849, where he has the goddess of Revolution say, "I annihilate what exists, and whither I turn there wells forth fresh life from the dead rock" (Rather, *The Dream of Self-Destruction,* 47–48).

58. Newman, *The Life of Richard Wagner,* III, 54–55. Villot was Conservator of the Picture Museums at the Louvre (Wagner, *Prose Works,* III, 294).

metaphorical roots, and in consequence language was losing touch with concrete reality. Hence the importance of music in our time:

> The metaphysical necessity of the discovery of this entirely new means of communication precisely in our own time seems to me to lie in the ever more conventional forms taken on by modern verbal languages. When we look more closely at the developmental history of these languages we hit, in the so-called roots of words, even today on a primal origin that clearly reveals how the formation of the concept of an object corresponded in the first beginnings almost completely to the subjective feeling engendered by it; and the assumption that the first speech of human beings must have had a likeness to song may not appear entirely ludicrous. From what was in any case an entirely sensuous, subjectively felt meaning of words human language became ever more abstract, so that in the end only a conventional meaning of words remained, and thus all share in understanding was withdrawn from the feelings.[59]

The poet, Wagner continued, must now proceed in one of two directions, toward "an inner fusion with music," or further into "the field of the abstract." But the poet who made the second choice was abandoning the muse of poetry. True poetry is "that depiction of the living image of humanity in which all motives clarifiable solely by abstract thought vanish, to reappear instead as motives of purely human feeling (*rein menschlichen Gefühles*)."[60] Ten years later, in his essay on Beethoven, Wagner again touched on the lost paradise of primal poetizing, which he traced to the introduction of letters. "From that time on . . . language, which was until then taking shape, as if it were alive, in a steady process of natural development, deteriorates and stiffens in a process of crystallization; the poetic art becomes the art of decking out the old myths, now no longer to be invented anew, and ends as rhetoric and dialectic." The last downward steps in the degradation of verbal language was "the invention of newspapers, and the full bloom of journalism" in our time.[61] "Newspeak," Orwell would christen it in 1948.

The above statements by Wagner will perhaps recall to today's reader some of Martin Heidegger's utterances on the same topic, for example, his comment of 1935 on the need to counteract the decay of language that we see taking place all about us. "We . . . seek to win back again

---

59. Wagner, "Zukunftsmusik," in *Gesammelte Schriften und Dichtungen*, VII, 87–137; see also 110–11.

60. *Ibid.*, 94–95, 104.

61. Rather, *The Dream of Self-Destruction*, 147–48.

the undestroyed naming-force of speech and words; for words and speech are not mere hulls in which things are packed away for verbal and written interchange. Things first come into being and exist through the word, through speech. Hence the misuse of speech (*Sprache*) in mere chatter (*Gerede*), in catchwords and cliches, destroys our true relation to things."[62] Later, in 1950, Heidegger added: "Language is itself, in the essential sense, poetry . . . Language . . . guards and preserves the primordial essence of poetry."[63] Heidegger, a close student of Nietzsche, was no doubt aware of Nietzsche's assertion that Wagner had "forced language back into a primal state . . . where language is itself poetry, image, feeling," and that Wagner had released the living stream of language "with a blow on the rock."[64] The writings of Ezra Pound on the theory and practice of poetry, likewise, show a strong resemblance to those of Wagner.[65]

62. Martin Heidegger, *Einführung in die Metaphysik* (Tübingen, 1953), 11.

63. Martin Heidegger, *Holzwege* (Frankfurt am Main, 1950), 61.

64. "When dealing with German words," writes Thomas Langan, "Heidegger likes to re-invent something of the feeling of the 'ancient forests' first by splitting these words into their components . . . this at one blow cuts underneath the accumulations of habitual interpretation" (*The Meaning of Heidegger: A Critical Study of an Existentialist Phenomenology* [New York, 1959], 114).

65. In his essay "Vorticism" Pound distinguished two kinds of poetry: lyric poetry, "where music, sheer melody, seems as if it were just bursting into speech," and imagist poetry, "where painting or sculpture seems as if it were 'just coming over into speech.'" He castigated "contemporary poets who escape from . . . the indefinitely difficult art of good prose by pouring themselves into verses" (*Fortnightly Review*, CII [September 1, 1914], 461–71). The following statements are drawn from *Literary Essays of Ezra Pound*, ed. T. S. Eliot (New York, 1968): "Go in fear of abstractions" (p. 5); "compose in the sequence of the musical phrase" (p. 3); "poetry withers and 'dries out' when it leaves music, or at least an imagined music too far behind" (p. 437); "Poets who will not study music are defective" (p. 437). Pound refused to countenance the chopped-up prose put forward as poetry by some writers of *vers libre,* and he suggested that poets should "attempt to approximate classical quantitative metres" (p. 13). *Cf.* also the following statement by Ernest Fenollosa: "Our ancestors built the accumulation of metaphor into structures of language and into systems of thought. Languages of today are thin and cold because we think less and less into them. Nature would seem to have become less and less like a paradise and more and more like a factory. . . . A late stage of decay is arrested and embalmed in the dictionary. Only scholars and poets feel painfully back along the thread of our etymologies and piece together our diction, as best they may, from forgotten fragments" (Fenollosa, *The Chinese Written Character as a Medium for Poetry,* ed. Ezra Pound [New York, 1936] 28–29).

CHAPTER THREE

WAGNER IN FRANCE

Balzac's short story "Gambara" was published in 1837 in two successive issues of Schlesinger's *Gazette musicale*.[1] A reader of this story today might be forgiven for claiming that Balzac had invented a Wagner two full years before the unknown young musician himself reached Paris. The Gambara of Balzac's story, too, is a musician in quest of the absolute. Like the chemist Balthazar Claes in another of Balzac's philosophical short stories, Gambara aims to solve the world-riddle. The chemist Claes looked for a chemical solution of the riddle: "One Element common to all substances, modified by a unique Force."[2] The musician Gambara hopes for a solution mediated through the marriage of tone to word, of music to language. Like the Wagner of fifteen years later, Gambara hopes to compose a trilogy, a "great musical drama" in three parts. (It will be recalled that Wagner always looked on the *Ring* as a trilogy made up of *Die Walküre, Siegfried,* and *Götterdämmerung,* with *Das Rheingold* as a prologue.) Gambara tells his occasional patron, the rich, young Count Marcosini, that the trilogy will embrace "the life of Mahomet, a figure in whom the ancient Sabaean magi and the oriental poets of the Jewish faith are blended to produce one of the greatest of human epics—the domination of the Arab." Gambara has written the libretto himself, for, as he tells the count, "no mere poet could have wrought the subject adequately." The count, who can make little of Gambara's music, tells him—as Wagner

---

1. Honoré de Balzac, *The Works of Honoré de Balzac,* trans. J. Walker McSpadden (36 vols.; New York, n.d.), III, 329–91; Balzac, *Oeuvres complètes,* eds. Marcel Bouteron and Henri Longon (40 vols.; Paris, 1912–40), XXVIII, 37–107.

2. On the alchemical-chemical goal of Balthazar Claes, see Balzac, "The Quest of the Absolute," in *Works of Honoré de Balzac,* II, 72.

would be told later by Schopenhauer—that he is "more poet than musician."[3]

Gambara, however, does what Wagner would refuse to do twenty-four years later when *Tannhäuser* made its disastrous debut at the Paris Opera. Reluctantly, he allows a ballet scene to interrupt the continuity of his musical drama, with apologies to the count. "Here comes in one of those miserable ballets, which cut the thread of our finest musical tragedies." But to no avail. Gambara ends—as Wagner might well have ended—as an itinerant, half-mad street musician in Paris. His wife Marianna, who had fostered his genius and then deserted him, returns in the end to share his poverty. And so it was that to win his bread "one of the greatest musicians of his day, the unknown Orpheus of modern music, would play fragments of his compositions, selections so remarkable that they elicited a moderate number of sous from the Parisian idlers." But Gambara is content. "My music is beautiful. . . . My misfortune comes from having hearkened to the songs of angels, and having believed that mankind could understand them." Gambara's initial love for Meyerbeer's music and his subsequent distaste for it also recall Wagner.[4]

In Grange Woolley's study of Wagner and French symbolism, the Wagnerian features of Balzac's musician are recognized. "Gambara, the hero of the story, expresses some ideas on a projected musical drama very much like those that Wagner will express a few years later. . . . Although there is no reason to suppose that the story, which was very likely read by Wagner, appreciably influenced the development of his theoretical concepts, it is curious to find a literary figure of the French romantic period already interested in the problem."[5] And thirty years later George Piroué, in his book on Proust and the music of the future, speaks of "Balzac . . . whose character Gambara announces and prefigures Wagner."[6] The parallels between Wagner and the fictional musician Gambara are parallels in retrospect only; they could not have been evident to the author of Gambara or to Wagner himself at the time. To Balzac (who died in 1850, before Wagner's fame had spread) the prototype of the mad musician Gambara was none other than E. T. A. Hoffmann. We have the clue from Balzac him-

---

3. Balzac, "Gambara," in *Works of Honoré de Balzac*, III, 358, 363.
4. *Ibid.*, 385, 391–92.
5. Grange Woolley, *Richard Wagner et le symbolisme français*, 22.
6. Georges Piroué, *Proust et la musique de devenir* (Paris, 1960), 38.

self, who credits the invention of Gambara, "that personage worthy of Hoffmann, bearer of untold treasures, pilgrim seated at the gate of paradise," to the Marquis de Belloy, his friend, collaborator, and secretary. Addressing the marquis, Balzac states, "You have created Gambara; I merely clothe him."[7] Gambara's ideas do in fact resemble those of Hoffmann's mad musician, Kreisler.

Another fictional character who seems to bear the features of Richard Wagner is the musician Landara in Emile Augier's play *Ceinture Dorée* (*The Golden Band*), first produced in Paris in 1855. The play deals with an idealistic young man's suit for the hand of the daughter of an unscrupulous French financier (part of whose money comes from slum rentals). On discovering the "poisoned source" (*source empoisonnée*) of the father's funds the young man prepares to reject the daughter, but the situation is saved by a happy accident. Landara, a minor character in the play, is introduced merely as a musician of the "ideological school" who believes that music is destined to become the universal language of humanity; he is also the composer of a "philosophical symphony" entitled *The Golden Calf.*[8] Emile Augier is mentioned in the March 15, 1887 issue of Edouard Dujardin's *Revue wagnérienne* as one of those present (along with Emmanuel Chabrier, Léo Delibes, and Jules Massenet) at a presentation of *Die Walküre* in Brussels.[9] Although we may assume that Augier was something of a Wagnerian in his later years, it seems less likely that he could have been aware of Wagner's philosophy of music and of his plans for the *Ring*. Augier's Landara probably owes more to Balzac's Gambara than to Wagner himself. Nevertheless, as I have pointed out elsewhere, Augier's *Ceinture Dorée* was to furnish William Archer with the plot of a comedy tentatively entitled "Rhinegold," and when Archer enlisted Bernard Shaw as his collaborator in 1884, "Rhinegold" underwent a Tarnhelmian transformation into Shaw's first play, *Widowers' Houses* (1892). The subsequent reappearances of the essentially anti-Wagnerian idea that Shaw developed from Archer's "Rhinegold" took place in Shaw's *Major Barbara* (1905) and in the third and succeeding English editions of *The Perfect Wagnerite.*[10]

7. Balzac, *Works of Honoré de Balzac,* III, 329; Balzac, *Oeuvres complètes,* XXVIII, 450.

8. Emile Augier, *Théâtre complet* (6 vols.; Paris, 1885–86), III, 291–425; Rather, *The Dream of Self-Destruction,* 150–51.

9. *Revue wagnérienne,* March 15, 1887, pp. 33–34.

10. Rather, *The Dream of Self-Destruction,* 149–67.

One wonders whether or not Balzac or his collaborator the Marquis de Belloy, or at a later date Emile Augier, were acquainted with an essay of 1833 entitled "Filosofia della Musica" ("Philosophy of Music") by the Italian patriot, revolutionary, and exile Giuseppe Mazzini. That essay is a detailed exposition of ideas similar to those motivating Gambara and his counterpart Landara. Addressing younger musicians rather than the maestri and professors, Mazzini declares, "The Art you cultivate is holy, and you must render your lives holy, if you would become its priests." He asks, "Who has ever imagined that the fundamental idea of Music might be identical with the progressive conception of the terrestrial Universe itself, and that the secret of its development might have to be sought in the development of the general synthesis of the epoch?" Again, "Who ever looks for a *general* idea in a musical drama?" Mazzini adds in a footnote: "The poetry of the musical drama can only be regenerated simultaneously with the regeneration of Music itself. A libretto such as I should require would probably find neither a composer to set it, nor a theatre wherein it could be represented at the present day." Mazzini hears hints of the "music of the future" in the works of Meyerbeer and Rossini; indeed he finds that Rossini must certainly have foreseen the coming of "social music, the musical drama of the future" ("la musica sociale, il dramma musicale dell' avvenire"). We need only wait in patience for the fulfillment of the prophecy. "That genius will arise," says Mazzini, "[w]hen the times are ripe for his coming, when there is a public of believers ready to reverence his creations, he will surely come." But he will not come to take a place in a world "where Poetry is required to be the servant, not the sister of Music, which in its turn is the venal servant of managerial speculation." He will instead sweep aside these vestiges of a corrupt past and give music its rightful place as the "social art" par excellence of our day. Mazzini asks rhetorically: "What! shall an entire synthesis, a whole epoch, a whole religion, be sculptured in stone; shall architecture thus sum up the ruling thought of eighteen centuries in a cathedral and music be unequal to the task?"[11]

There is a passage in Mazzini's "Philosophy of Music" in which Wagner's leitmotif technique seems to be anticipated. Every character worth being represented in a drama is given by the dramatist a certain

11. Giuseppe Mazzini, "The Philosophy of Music," in *Life and Writings of Joseph Mazzini* (6 vols.; London, 1890–91), IV, 7, 10, 12–13, 34, 35, 40; Mazzini, *Filosofia della Musica*, ed. Adriano Lualdi (Milan, 1943), 140n.

style, bearing, and idea belonging to that character alone, Mazzini says:

> Why not endeavour to render that idea a form of musical expression, special and peculiar to him? . . . Why not study more carefully how to avail yourselves of the power of instrumentation to symbolise, through the medium of the accompaniment that surrounds each of the personages, that tumult of affections, habits, instincts . . . playing so large a part in the formation of their destiny? . . . Why not vary the nature and character of the melodies and accompaniments according to the nature and character of the personages on the stage? Why not, through the well-timed repetition of a special musical phrase, or of certain fundamental and striking chords, suggest the disposition of each, or the influence of the circumstances or natural tendencies that urge him along? [12]

Mazzini was of course not looking forward to the Wagnerian use of leitmotifs here, nor did he have in mind the musical *idée fixe* employed by Hector Berlioz in the *Symphonie Fantastique* (composed in 1830–1831, but little played at the time). Instead, as he tells us, Mazzini has in mind Mozart's musical depiction of the unrepentant Don Giovanni and Meyerbeer's depiction of the archfiend Bertram (in *Robert the Devil*). To the first he knew no equal, to the latter he could cite as a literary parallel only the Mephistopheles of Goethe. "In a period of transition like our own," writes Mazzini, "we may not expect the High Priest of the Music of the future to appear amongst us; but Meyerbeer is the precursor spirit sent to announce his coming." In the *Huguenots* Meyerbeer had revealed his hand in "the exquisite blending of the Italian and German elements of melody and harmony, which the Music of the future is destined to combine." Mazzini concludes his philosophy of the new music with the following: "Of German descent, though born in Italian Istria, one might almost fancy this combination of the two elements in his own person, significant, symbolic and prophetic. The figure of Giacomo Meyerbeer appears before us as the first link between the two worlds, the complete union of which will constitute the highest Music of the future." [13] One wonders what Wagner would have thought of this picture of the German Jew Giacomo Meyerbeer as the John the Baptist of the "Music of the future." [14]

12. Mazzini, "The Philosophy of Music," in *Life and Writings*, 42–43.
13. *Ibid.*, 43, 55.
14. Mazzini's name does not appear in the indices of Newman's *The Life of Richard Wagner*, Westernhagen's *Wagner: A Biography*, or Wagner's *Mein Leben*. In an

We return now to the real Wagner in France. In 1849, seven years after quitting Paris as a failure, Wagner returned as a political exile and musician of some reputation. His purpose was to find a place in the French journal *Le national* for his newly written essay "Art and Revolution." For whatever reason, the essay did not appear, and Wagner returned to Zurich and Minna. In February of the following year he made another sally into France, this time to see a promised performance by the orchestra of the Société Ste Cécile of the overture to *Tannhäuser*. The performance did not take place. After a "sentimental interlude with Jessie Laussot, a young Scotswoman whom Wagner had known slightly in Dresden, now married to a merchant of Bordeaux" (as Georges Servières wrote in 1923, in a special issue of *La revue musicale* devoted entirely to the subject of Wagner and France), Wagner again retreated to the mountains of Switzerland.[15]

The promised performance of the overture by Société Ste Cécile finally took place on November 24, 1850. In attendance as an invited guest was the poet Gérard de Nerval, who was then forty-two years old. Nerval was a former medical student, a translator of Goethe's *Faust*, a Swedenborgian visionary, and an amateur of the Kabbala—altogether a Hoffmannesque figure. Already apparently a Wagnerian, Nerval had journeyed to the grand duchy of Saxe-Weimar three months earlier expressly to hear the first performance (under the baton of Franz Liszt) of Wagner's *Lohengrin*. In 1852 Nerval wrote that Wagner had "submitted music completely to the rhythms of poetry," and he added, "Every poet, if he had some understanding of musical notation, could easily make music of his [own] verse." Nerval had a special interest in the theory of verse, and in 1854 (one year before committing

open letter of February, 1860, to Hector Berlioz, Wagner disclaimed the phrase "music of the future." Calling it a "silly and malicious misunderstanding" (of his essay "The Art-Work of the Future"), Wagner attributed the phrase to a Professor Bischoff of Cologne (*Gesammelte Schriften und Dichtungen*, VII, 83, 101, 136). "Wagner—smirk when his name is mentioned, and make a few humorous remarks about the music of the future," we read in Gustave Flaubert's dictionary of received views (*Bouvard et Pécuchet*, II, 281). Mazzini appears to have been forgotten.

15. Georges Servières, "Les visées de Wagner sur Paris," *La revue musicale*, October 1, 1923. This special issue has recently been reprinted as *Wagner et la France: numéro spéciale de la Revue musicale, 1ᵉʳ Octobre, 1923* (New York, 1977); see pp. 94–97. For Newman's account of the Laussot affair, see his *Life of Richard Wagner*, II, 138–58.

suicide) he wrote to his psychiatrist Antoine-Emile Blanche, "My theories, which I seldom discuss, are close enough to those of Richard Wagner."[16] The use of musical notation in connection with the study of verse rhythms, and of verse rhythms in the study of musical themes, was uncommon at the time.[17]

"Baudelaire," Arthur Symons stated in 1899, "discovered Wagner."[18] Did Baudelaire's Wagnerism anticipate that of Gérard de Nerval? On November 1, 1922, another French Wagnerian, André Suarès, published in *La revue musicale* a letter written by Baudelaire to Wagner a few weeks after the composer conducted selections from *The Flying Dutchman, Tannhäuser, Lohengrin,* and *Tristan* at the Théâtre Italien in the opening months of 1860.[19] In commenting on the letter, Suarès took it for granted that Baudelaire had no prior knowledge of Wagner's music, and indeed the letter suggests none. In 1925, however, Jacques Crepet made public for the first time a letter of recommendation, dated July 13, 1849, by Baudelaire of a certain "Schoman," and in this letter Wagner is praised in the highest terms. Baudelaire writes: "The matter concerns Mr. Schoman, a musician of great talent, who had to quit Dresden after the revolution. Mr. Schoman wishes to publish a study of *Tannhäuser* and a series of articles on the evolution of music." The conclusion that "Schoman" is merely a cover name for the composer

16. Servières, "Le visées de Wagner sur Paris," in *Wagner et la France,* 96–97; Woolley, *Richard Wagner et la symbolisme français,* 30–33; Gérard de Nerval, *Oeuvres,* ed. Henri Lemaître (2 vols.; Paris, 1966), I, 864; Robert Emmett Jones, *Gérard de Nerval* (New York, 1974), 157–58.

17. Joshua Steele in 1775 used musical notation in his study of Vergil, Shakespeare, and other poets, as did Sidney Lanier (who shows no awareness of Steele's work) one hundred years later. *Cf.* Joshua Steele, *An Essay Towards Establishing The Melody and Measure of Speech* (1775; rpr. as No. 172 of the series *English Linguistics 1500–1800,* ed. R. C. Alston [Menston, Eng., 1969]); Sidney Lanier, *The Science of English Verse and Essays on Music,* ed. Paull Franklin Baum (Baltimore, 1945). Lanier remarks in one of his essays that the musician is, in our time, the necessary complement of the scientist. "The latter will supervise our knowing, the former will supervise our loving." This essay closes with a Wagnerian statement: "And as music takes up the thread which language drops, so it is that where Shakespeare ends Beethoven begins." Another of the essays, "Mazzini on Music" (1878), expresses Lanier's agreement with Mazzini's belief in the regenerative power of music (*ibid.,* vii, 274, 285, 290, 307).

18. Arthur Symons, *The Symbolist Movement in Modern Literature* (rev. ed.; New York, 1919), 114.

19. André Suarès, "La première lettre de Baudelaire à Wagner," *La revue musicale,* November 1, 1922, pp. 1–10.

of *Tannhäuser* is contradicted by Baudelaire's next sentence. "Our common admiration for Wagner leads me to anticipate on your part a favorable reception of Mr. Schoman." The next sentence, if it is taken to refer to Wagner, seems too prophetic to be true: "In assisting him [*i.e.,* Schoman] you will save the cause of one whom the future will honor as the most illustrious of masters."[20] Commentators on this letter, including Crepet, tacitly read an *and* in the first sentence: "Mr. Schoman [and] a musician of great talent." Crepet suggests that Schoman was the father of the Gobinist Ludwig Schemann. The most recent editors of Baudelaire's correspondence, however, rule out Schemann *père* and Robert Schumann as a possible Schoman.[21] Who was this ghostly personage who wished to write on *Tannhäuser* and the evolution of music? Neither his identity nor that of the person to whom this letter was written has ever been ascertained.[22]

Baudelaire cannot have had any knowledge of Wagner's music in 1849. The supposition that he had is incompatible with the content of the letter he wrote to Wagner shortly after the concert at the Théâtre Italien in 1860, for Baudelaire states that his knowledge of German music had until then been limited to a few works by Beethoven and von Weber. At the concert, however, he had at once succumbed to the spell of Wagner's music. "At first," he tells Wagner, "it seemed to me that I knew this music; later, after considering the matter, I understood the source of that illusion: it seemed to me that this music was *mine,* and I recognized it just as every man recognizes what he is destined to love. . . . In your work I found everywhere the solemnity of the grand aspects, the great tumults of nature, and the solemnity of the great passions of humanity . . . I felt all the majesty of a life larger than our

20. Charles Baudelaire, *Oeuvres complètes de Charles Baudelaire,* ed. Jacques Crépet (19 vols.; Paris, 1923–53), XIV, 112–13.

21. *Ibid.;* Charles Baudelaire, *Baudelaire: Correspondence,* eds. Claude Pichois and Jean Ziegler (2 vols.; Paris, 1966–73), I, 157, 787.

22. No "Schoman" figures in Wagner's autobiography. Newman, in discussing this letter, casts doubt on its date and is unable to identify "Schoman" (*The Life of Richard Wagner,* III, 9 n. 12). Newman doubted that Baudelaire could have had any acquaintance with Wagner's music at the time Marcel Ruff supposes that he had been introduced to it by the painter Champfleury (Baudelaire, *Oeuvres complètes,* ed. Marcel Ruff [Paris, 1968.], 510). The validity of the letter and its reference to Wagner are taken for granted by T. J. Clark, *The Absolute Bourgeois: Artists and Politics in France* (1973; rpr. Princeton, 1982), 142.

own."[23] Baudelaire then makes reference to his own interest in synaesthesia, in this instance to the supposed correspondence between certain colors and certain emotions. "Finally, and I ask you not to laugh, I also experience certain sensations probably deriving from my turn of spirit and my frequent preoccupations . . . For example, to make use of a comparison borrowed from painting, I imagine before my eyes a vast extent of somber red. If this red represents passion, I see it arrive gradually, by all transitions of red and rose, to the incandescence of a furnace." Baudelaire himself blushes for his country, he tells Wagner, for almost daily he runs across "shameful ridiculous articles in which every effort is made to defame your genius."[24]

Thirteen months after Wagner conducted selections from his works at the Théâtre Italien, several performances of *Tannhäuser* were given at the Paris Opera under his direction. Apparently the anti-Wagnerian cabal had been busy in the meantime. Hector Berlioz, whose feelings about Wagner seem to have been mixed, wrote to his son shortly before. "There is much excitement in our musical world over the scandal this production of *Tannhäuser* is going to cause." This remark would suggest that Berlioz had wind of a planned disruption of the performances. Berlioz added: "Wagner is plainly mad. He will die . . . of a

23. Suarès, "La première lettre de Baudelaire à Wagner," *passim.* The initial response of writers to Wagner's music deserves an essay of its own. Commenting in 1855 on the "exclusion of melody" from Wagner's *Lohengrin*, George Eliot wrote: "Tannhäuser is still the music of men and women, as well as of Wagnerites, but *Lohengrin* to us ordinary mortals [the other, in this case, being George Lewes, her lover] seemed something like the whistling of the wind through the keyholes of a cathedral . . . whatever the music of the future may be, it will not be a music which is in contradiction with a permanent element in human nature—the need for a frequent alternation of sensations or emotions; and this need is *not* satisfied in *Lohengrin*" (George Eliot, "Liszt, Wagner, and Weimar," *Fraser's Magazine,* LII [1855], 48–62). But even *Tannhäuser* was too much for Amiel in May, 1857: he notes in his journal that the overture struck him as "enormous, savage, elementary, like the murmur of forests and the roar of animals . . . like nature before man appeared" (Henri Frédéric Amiel, *Amiel's Journal: Being the Journal Intime of Henri Frederic Amiel,* trans. Mrs. Humphrey Ward [New York, 1928], 81). As late as 1877 Amelia Ann Edwards, a now almost forgotten English novelist (and amateur Egyptologist), could speak of "the crash and clang, the involved harmonies, and the multitudinous combinations of Tannhäuser," and characterize the music further as "dominant, tyrannous, overpowering, unintelligible," and "*difficult*" (Amelia Ann Edwards, *A Thousand Miles up the Nile* [London, 1877], 175–76).

24. Suarès, "La première lettre de Baudelaire à Wagner," *passim.*

brain fever." After the second performance he wrote to his son: "The press is unanimous as to exterminating him. . . . As for myself, I am most cruelly avenged." All three performances were disrupted by disorderly behavior on the part of a vocal segment of the audience and by the blowing of dog whistles held in the white-gloved hands of the aristocrats of the Paris Jockey Club, angered because their mistresses in the *corps de ballet* had not been allowed by Wagner to cut the thread, a la Gambara, of *Tannhäuser*. Newman, who gives a detailed account of the affair, says that "the aristocratic ruffians and their Press hirelings . . . had made no secret of their intention of ruining Wagner and his work," and that Meyerbeer and his "journalistic myrmidons" were left in full possession of the field. Not until twelve years after Wagner's death was *Tannhäuser* to be heard again in Paris.[25]

Baudelaire was present at the rehearsals and at one or more of the performances. He had written an article on Wagner for the *Revue européenne* (published April 1, 1861), and to it, in a separately published brochure entitled *Richard Wagner and "Tannhäuser" at Paris,* he added a few remarks on the fiasco. The "whistlers and cabalists," Baudelaire wrote, were all crying out with joy that "the music of the future" was now dead and buried. But, he added: "The people who believe themselves rid of Wagner have rejoiced much too soon; we can assure them of that. . . . The immensity of the injustice has engendered a thousand sympathies, which now show themselves on all sides." He advises the members of the Jockey Club, "Watch over your harem and religiously conserve the traditions, but allow us to have a theater where those who think otherwise may find pleasures more to their taste." He thanks Berlioz for having the "negative courage" to have at least added nothing to the universal injury, he castigates the press (with the single exception of a M. Franck Marie, writing in *La patrie*), and again he says that he blushes for France: "What will Europe think of us, what will they say of Paris in Germany?"[26]

The main part of Baudelaire's essay is devoted to the concert at the Théâtre Italien and the course thereafter of Baudelaire's growing interest in Wagner's ideas. He comments briefly on some bizarre behavior on the part of an anti-Wagnerian music critic, Pierre Scudo, who stood in the lobby of the Théâtre Italien waving his arms and inveighing

25. Newman, *The Life of Richard Wagner*, III, 99–128, *passim*.

26. Baudelaire, "Richard Wagner et *Tannhäuser* à Paris," in *Oeuvres complètes,* ed. Ruff, 510–26, *passim*.

loudly against Wagner to all and sundry, and he mentions the attacks on Wagner in the *Gazette musicale* by the music critic and theorist François Joseph Fêtis, an inveterate anti-Wagnerian. He recalls the enchanted state of synaesthesia that overcame him on hearing the overture in *Lohengrin,* and he quotes the first two strophes of his own poem the *Correspondances.*

> La nature est un temple où de vivant piliers
> Laissent parfois sortir de confuses paroles;
> L'homme y passe a travers des forets de symboles
> Qui l'observent avec des regards familiers.
>
> Comme de long echos qui de loin se confondent
> Dans une ténébreuse et profonde unité
> Vaste comme la nuite et comme la clarté,
> Les parfums, les couleurs et les sons se répondent.

"But," he adds, "what would be truly surprising would be for sound *not* to suggest color, for colors *not* to give the idea of a melody, and for sound and color to be incapable of translating ideas; for, ever since the day that God uttered the world as a complex and indivisible totality, things have always been expressed in reciprocal analogy."[27] These words recall the fragmentary writings found in the pockets of Gérard de Nerval after his suicide: "Everything in nature assumed new aspects . . . out of colours, odours, and sounds, I saw unknown harmonies come forth."[28]

Baudelaire says that after the concert at the Théâtre Italien he immersed himself in Wagner's theories of poetry and music. Not being acquainted with German, he had read an English translation of Wagner's treatise *Opera and Drama,* an article by Franz Liszt on Wagner and Lohengrin, and Wagner's own *Lettre sur la musique* (the "Open Letter" to Frederic Villot). To the anti-Wagnerians in France who had leveled the charge of dilettantism against this presumptuous German musician who claimed to be poet, dramatist, mythologist, and theoretician of music all in one, Baudelaire replied: "How could Wagner not have admirably understood the sacred, divine character of myth,

---

27. *Ibid.,* 512, 513.
28. Symons, *The Symbolist Movement in Literature,* 88–89. A story that Wagner tells of his early youth in *Mein Leben* (I, 59) suggests a synaesthetic impulse on his own part at the time: in 1830, in writing out the score of his *Overture in B-flat Major,* he originally intended to use red for the strings, black for the brasses, and green for the winds.

he who is at once a poet and a critic? . . . Those who reproach the
musician Wagner for having written books on the philosophy of his
art and who derive from this the suspicion that his music is not a
natural and spontaneous product must equally deny that da Vinci,
Hogarth and Reynolds could have produced good paintings simply because they deduced and analyzed the principles of their art. Who
wrote better on painting than our own great Delacroix?" Nor, added
Baudelaire, had Gluck's interest in the theory of music and poetry
hobbled his practice.[29]

Wagner's use of recurring musical phrases to characterize the action
and personalities of his dramas had already attracted Baudelaire's attention in 1860. He points out now that this procedure gives the music
itself a poetic, not to say literary, character.

> I have already spoken of certain melodic phrases whose regular return in
> various passages of the same work vividly impressed my ear during the first
> concert Wagner gave at the Italien . . . the recurrence of the two principal
> themes in *Tannhäuser*, the religious motif and the song of voluptuousness,
> awake the attention of the audience and bring it into a state analogous to
> the situation depicted. . . . In effect, even without the poetry, Wagner's
> music would still be a poetic work, since the music is endowed with all
> the qualities of well-made poetry: self-explanatory, all things in it well-
> united, joined together, reciprocally adapted, and if a barbarism may be
> coined to express the superlative of this quality, far-seeingly *concatenated*
> (*concatenée*).

Without mentioning Nerval, Baudelaire remarks that Théophile Gautier had returned from Germany a few years earlier very moved by a
presentation of *Tannhäuser* and he had given his impressions in the
Moniteur with "that plastic certitude which gives irresistible character
to all his writings." Baudelaire finds it "not surprising that men of
letters in particular should have shown themselves sympathetic to a
musician who glories in being a poet and a dramaturge." And he adds,
"In the same way the works of Gluck were acclaimed by writers in the
eighteenth century, and I cannot but observe that those people who are
most repelled by Wagner also manifest a decided antipathy for his
precursor."[30]

29. Baudelaire, "Richard Wagner et *Tannhäuser* à Paris," in *Oeuvres complètes*,
ed. Ruff, 514, 517. According to Ellis (Wagner, *Prose Works*, II, xviii), an English translation of *Opera and Drama* was published in 1855–56 in *Musical World* (London).

30. Baudelaire, "Richard Wagner et Tannhäuser à Paris," in *Oeuvres complètes*,
ed. Ruff, 521, 523.

Wagner promptly acknowledged the article in the *Revue euro-péenne* with a letter to Baudelaire two weeks later. He wrote:

> You can well believe how much I want to tell you of the immense satis-faction that you gave me in your article which honors me and encourages me more than anything else that has ever been said of my modest talent. Would it not be possible to tell you soon, aloud, how intoxicated I felt in reading those pages that told me—as would a poem—of the impressions that I may boast of having made on a spirit so superior as yours?
>
> A thousand thanks for the pleasure you have given me, and believe me that I am proud to call you a friend.[31]

Subsequently the two met at Wagner's lodgings in Paris, and an amus-ing contretemps that shows how little Wagner shared Baudelaire's sense of synaesthesia took place.[32]

Baudelaire's knowledge of Wagner's place in musical history in rela-tion to Gluck probably came from Wagner's *Lettre sur la musique*. Wagner speaks there of his concern with the problem of the right rela-tion between poetry and music in musical drama. "In Italy, but still more in France and Germany, this problem busied the most significant minds in literature. The battle between the Gluckists and Piccinnists in Paris was nothing other than a controversy, by its nature undecidable, as to whether or not the ideal of the drama could be attained in opera."[33] A little less than one hundred years earlier Gluck himself had explained his intent in his preface to *Alceste* (1776).

> I endeavoured to reduce music to its proper functioning, that of seconding poetry by enforcing the expression of the sentiment. . . . My idea was that

31. Baudelaire, *Oeuvres complètes*, ed. Ruff, 34.

32. While playing on the piano, Wagner paused to change from a blue dressing gown to a yellow one, then to a green one. Baudelaire asked whether the change of col-ors symbolized anything in the music. Wagner, who at first thought he was being made fun of, explained that the colors meant nothing: it was merely that he became over-heated when he played (Unsigned review of Lawrence Gilman's *Aspects of Modern Opera*, in *Nation*, December 17, 1908).

33. Wagner, "Zukunftsmusik," in *Gesammelte Schriften und Dichtungen*, VII, 102. The disputes between the champions of Christoph Willibald Gluck (1714–1787) and those of Niccola Piccinni (1728–1827) are said to have become so furious that the subject was no longer safe to discuss; society was divided into irreconcilable "Gluckists" and "Piccinnists" who challenged one another in the streets of Paris (*s.v.* "Piccinni," in *Grove's Dictionary of Music and Musicians*). There were other similarities to the dis-putes of a hundred years later between Wagnerians and anti-Wagnerians. The Piccin-nists claimed that Gluck's music had no melody, that his singers shrieked, and that his orchestra was too large and noisy (*s.v.* "Gluck," in *Grove's Dictionary of Music and Musicians*).

the relation of music to poetry was much the same as that of harmonious colouring and well-disposed light and shade to an accurate drawing, which animates the figures without altering the outline. . . . My idea was that the overture ought to indicate the subject and prepare the spectators for the piece they are about to see . . . and that it was necessary above all to avoid creating too great a disparity between the recitative and the air of a dialogue, so as not to break the sense of a period or awkwardly interrupt the movement and animation of a scene.[34]

Gluck sent a copy of *Alceste* to Jean-Jacques Rousseau. In an open letter to Dr. Charles Burney, an English composer and historian of music, Rousseau subsequently wrote: "I have said, and I believe, that Greek tragedies were true operas. The Greek language, a truly harmonious and musical one, has a melodious accent in itself, and the addition of rhythm to make music of a declamation is not required . . . the poets rightly said *I sing*, an expression that we, most ridiculously, have preserved." With respect to *Alceste*, Rousseau observed: "Here there is a great and fine problem to be resolved, that of ascertaining the limits to which language can be made to sing and music to speak." [35]

In his "*Zukunftsmusik*" (the *Lettre sur la musique*) Wagner pointed out that the question of the right relation between music and poetry in opera had been first raised in Germany by G. E. Lessing (1729–1781),

34. *S.v.*, "Gluck," in *Grove's Dictionary of Music and Musicians*.

35. Jean-Jacques Rousseau, "Lettre à M. Burney sur la musique, avec fragmens d'observations sur l'Alceste Italien de M. le Chevalier Gluck," in *Collection complète des Oeuvres* (17 vols.; Geneva, 1782–89), VIII, 571–76; see also pp. 558–59. *Cf.* the words of Franz Hüffer in "Richard Wagner," *Fortnightly Review*, XVII (March 1, 1872), 265:

> Posterity, as a rule, may be relied on to amend the injustices of former generations, and Richard Wagner has not acted unwisely in appealing for a fair judgment of his aspirations to those hereafter. For it is not otherwise that we have to interpret his adopting the malicious joke of a hostile journalist, and calling his new movement in art the 'Music of the Future.' The keynote of the new principle . . . is the urgent demand of a poetical basis of music. . . . This principle . . . came to a distinct utterance in Gluck's celebrated preface to *Alceste*, and it vibrates with unsurpassable power and beauty in the works of Beethoven's later period. . . . Wagner must be called the protagonist and eminent representative of this vital idea of modern music, for which he has fought with the philosopher's and artist's weapons, and as the highest development of which we have to consider his own music-drama.

A slightly different version of this essay may be found in Franz Hueffer (*sic*), *Richard Wagner and the Music of the Future* (London, 1874). Note that Hüffer, like Wagner himself, was not aware that Mazzini had originated the phrase "music of the future."

and that it had been discussed at length in the correspondence between Goethe and Schiller.[36] To these names Edward Rod (1857–1910), in a concise and informative essay on Wagner and the history of aesthetics in Germany, added the names of J. G. Herder and G. W. F. Hegel. Rod's essay was published in 1885 in a French journal of literature, politics, and philosophy. "The idea of a synthesis of the arts," he asserted, "is completely Hegelian, especially that of the union of poetry and music, the two *subjective* arts, as opposed to the *objective* arts of architecture, sculpture, and painting, and with the philosopher as with the musician [*i.e.*, Wagner] . . . the result is the supremacy of the dramatic form."[37] Rod also has some pertinent remarks to make on Wagner's view of the relation between art and religion. Wagner, he says, conceived of art and religion as "two manifestations of a single need, or, to employ the expressions that he took freely from Schopenhauer, two *intellectual representations* of one and the same idea." The true function of art is to express the otherwise inexpressible truth of religion by means of an ideal representation of religious allegories. Rod then cites the following sentence from Wagner's essay "Religion and Art" (1880): "While the priest endeavors to regard religious allegories as matters of fact, the artist on the other hand openly and freely presents his work as the fruit of his fancy." So it is, Rod concludes, that in *Parsifal* Wagner presents the idea of redemption through compassion and simplicity of spirit by "substituting a pure symbol (the Grail) for the entire mythology of the Hebrews . . . here we have the triumph of symbolic art."[38]

36. Wagner, "Zukunftsmusik," *Gesammelte Schriften und Dichtungen*, VII, 102.

37. Edouard Rod, "Wagner et l'esthétique allemande," *La revue contemporaine, littéraire, politique, et philosophique*, July 25, 1885 (rpr. Geneva, 1971), 305–15. Amiel called *Tannhäuser* "Neo-Hegelian" in 1857: "Man is deposed from his superior position, and the center of gravity of the work passes into the baton of the conductor. It is music depersonalized, neo-Hegelian music—music multiple instead of individual. If this is so, it is indeed the music of the future, the music of the socialist democracy replacing the art which is aristocratic, heroic, or subjective" (Amiel, *Journal*, 81).

38. Rod, "Wagner et l'esthétique allemande," *passim*. Rod lived for a time in Paris, but from 1886 on he was a professor at Geneva. Like Wagner, Tolstoy, and many other writers, Rod was appalled by the increasing militarization of Europe toward the close of the nineteenth century. "The mind revolts at the inevitable catastrophe awaiting us," he wrote. "For twenty years all the powers of knowledge have been exhausted inventing engines of destruction. . . . It is no longer as formerly a few thousand mercenary wretches who are under arms, but whole nations are preparing to kill one another. . . . And in order to fit them for murder their hatred is excited by assurances that they are

The *Revue wagnérienne,* a French periodical devoted entirely to
Wagnerian studies, was founded by Edouard Dujardin in 1885. Writing
in 1923, Dujardin says that until 1882 he had known little of Wagner's
music other than the occasional morsels served up at the Concerts
Lamoureux. In 1882, however, a performance of the *Ring*—originally
intended for Paris but blocked by anti-Wagnerian forces—took place
in London, and Dujardin was among those who attended it. Although
he hardly understood a word of German at the time, Dujardin says
that something in the *Ring* "responded to the deepest needs of [his]
unconscious." After these "four evenings of ecstasy," Dujardin had
become a Wagnerian, and he remained one for the rest of his life.
Wagner's death on February 13, 1883, according to Dujardin, came as
a shock that released a new wave of interest in his work in France. In
that same year the prelude to *Parsifal* was first heard in Paris (the
world premiere of the music drama had taken place in Bayreuth the
previous year). Dujardin traveled to Germany in 1884 to hear the *Ring*
at Munich and *Parsifal* at Bayreuth. It was at this time that the idea of
founding the *Revue wagnérienne* came to him. Later in Paris he discussed the project at length in daily meetings with his English friend
Houston Stewart Chamberlain (1855–1927) and their circle of French
friends at the *café* Roth and the *brasserie* Maximilien. "The aim of the
Revue wagnérienne," Dujardin writes, "was not, as some believed, to
promulgate Wagner's works, but to penetrate and make known their
profound meaning . . . we wanted, Chamberlain and I, to spread
abroad our discovery. Wagner the great musician? This was too obvious. Wagner the great poet rather, Wagner the great thinker, above all
Wagner the creator of a new form of art." The first number of the *Revue wagnérienne* saw the light of day on a Sunday in February, 1885,
at one of the Concerts Lamoureux.[39] The *Revue wagnérienne* lasted
until 1888, and its long list of contributors included such names as

---

hated . . . they will be so deceived by false high-flown words that they will call on God to
bless their bloody deeds" (cited by Tolstoy, *Recollections and Essays,* trans. Aylmer
Maude [1937; rpr. London, 1961], 22). For Wagner's similar views and predictions, see
Rather, "Tolstoy and Wagner: The Shared Vision," 11–24.

    39. Edouard Dujardin, "La revue wagnérienne," in *Wagner et la France: numéro
spéciale de la Revue musicale, 1ᵉʳ Octobre, Paris, 1923* (rpr. New York, 1977) 139–60,
passim.

Paul Verlaine, Villiers de L'Isle-Adam, Stéphane Mallarmé, Joris Karl Huysmans, Odilon Redon, and Ignace Fantin-Latour. Gérard de Nerval's "Souvenirs sur Lohengrin" (1849) was reprinted in the issue of February, 1887.

A poet, novelist, and playwright, the long-lived (1861–1949) Edouard Dujardin was also a student of the Christian tradition, which he saw as directly opposed to the Jewish tradition.[40] He is best remembered today for the novel from which James Joyce (1882–1941) drew inspiration for the so-called stream of consciousness technique, *Les lauriers sont coupés* (1888). Dujardin called it the "interior monologue" (*monologue intérieur*) in his book on Joyce in 1922. There he distinguishes the "interior monologue" from the traditional dramatic or psychological monologues employed by writers before him. He likens the structure of his *monologue intérieur* to a succession of Wagnerian "musical motifs" (*motifs musicaux*) or "little phrases" (*petites phrases*—probably a direct allusion to Marcel Proust's great work), and he regrets that he did not dedicate *Les lauriers sont coupés* to the inspirer of its literary technique, Richard Wagner. According to Dujardin, Joyce read the novel in 1901, and wrote to him on the subject in 1917.[41] In a short history of the free verse movement in France, also published in 1922, Dujardin writes: "Very early, I told myself that to the free music (*musique libre*) of Wagner there should correspond a *poésie libre*."[42] It is of interest that the great German student of comparative literature Ernst Curtius states—without mentioning Dujardin's novel—that the technique employed by Joyce in *Ulysses* (1922) is "an exact transposition of the use of motifs in musical struc-

40. Edouard Dujardin, *La source du fleuve chrétien; histoire critique de la judaïsme ancienne et du christianisme primitif* (Paris, 1906); Dujardin, *The Source of the Christian Tradition: A Critical History of Ancient Judaism*, trans. Joseph McCabe (rev. ed.; Chicago, 1911). A demythologized, revisionist history of Christianity in relation to Judaism, it is more or less in line with Tolstoy's similar undertaking of a decade earlier. Dujardin argues that the "Jewish prophets preached not the conversion of the world, but its conquest . . . [they] were the protagonists, not of justice, but of the claims of their people and their political party. . . . Its unconquerable nationalism has made the Jewish people one of the greatest in the world" (Dujardin, *Source of the Christian Tradition*, 195).

41. Edouard Dujardin, *Les lauriers sont coupés* (Paris, 1888); Edouard Dujardin, *Le monologue intérieur, son apparition, ses origines, sa place dans l'oeuvre de James Joyce et dans le roman contemporain* (Paris, 1922), 19–20, 54–55, 104.

42. Edouard Dujardin, *Les premiers poètes du vers libre* (Paris, 1922), 63.

ture, or, to be more precise, of the Wagnerian technique of the leitmotif."[43] More recently, the contributions of both Wagner and Dujardin to the Joycean procedure have been minimized.[44]

Stéphane Mallarmé was a recalcitrant Wagnerian. Naming him as
one, Dujardin writes in 1922, "I think I hear the clash of swords."
Dujardin took Mallarmé to a rendition of the Good Friday music from
Parsifal in 1885, and the poet succumbed to Wagner's spell. But when
Mallarmé, at Dujardin's insistence, wrote his famous "Revery of a
French poet on Richard Wagner" for the *Revue wagnérienne* it caused
something of a scandal because of its hardly comprehensible language,
and, says Dujardin, would have caused a greater one if readers had
understood that in it "the great poet was separating his cause from
that of the great musician."[45] Mallarmé's still more cryptic poem of
homage to Richard Wagner also made its first appearance in the pages
of Dujardin's *Revue wagnérienne*.[46]

We bring this short chapter to a close with a reminiscence of Wagner's story "A Happy Evening" that occurs in Huysman's novel of
1884, *A rebours* (*Against the Grain*). The decadent French nobleman
of the story, des Esseintes (who, like Proust's Charlus, owes something

43. Ernst Curtius, "James Joyce and His Ulysses," in *Essays in European Literature,* trans. Michael Kowal (Princeton, 1973), 351. Stuart Gilbert says that in 1920
Joyce told him to read Dujardin's novel and to note that "the reader finds himself, from
the very first line, posted within the mind of the protagonist." Gilbert, who was well
aware of Dujardin's contribution, passed the advice on to his own readers who were
interested in the origins of Joyce's technique (Stuart Gilbert, *James Joyce's Ulysses: A
Study* [New York, 1934], 12).

44. Writing in 1944, Harry Levin called Dujardin—who was still publishing as
late as 1943—a "half-remembered French symbolist . . . [who] survived to promulgate
a rambling definition of the style which he had invented." Levin asserts that the style was
"less of an innovation than Joyce or Dujardin would have liked to believe." As for Wagner, Levin calls him the "arch-symbolist" who had "forged the uncreated conscience of
the Third Reich" (Harry Levin, *James Joyce: A Critical Essay* [New York, 1941], 89–
91, 211).

45. Dujardin, "La revue wagnérienne," 141–60; Stéphane Mallarmé, "Richard
Wagner, rêverie d'un poète français," *Revue wagnérienne,* August 8, 1885, pp. 195–
200. Arthur Symons writes: "Carry the theories of Mallarmé to a practical solution,
multiply his powers in a direct ratio, and you have Wagner. It is his failure not to be
Wagner. And, Wagner having existed, it was for him to be something more, to complete
Wagner" (Symons, *The Symbolist Movement,* 180).

46. Stéphane Mallarmé, "Hommage," *Revue wagnérienne,* January 8, 1886,
p. 335. For a detailed exegesis of these fourteen lines, see Robert Greer Cohn, *Towards
the Poems of Mallarmé* (expanded edition, Berkeley, 1980).

to the real Comte Robert de Montesquiou-Fezensac), knows that there is "not a scene, not even a phrase, of an opera by the fabulous Wagner that [can] be removed from its context with impunity." He finds it most distasteful that "morsels cut off and served up on plates" are offered at concerts. Why, he asks, cannot one enjoy the music of Wagner, as one does a book, alone at home, instead of being forced to mingle with the crowd, to breathe "the atmosphere of a scullery" while watching "a man with the look of a carpenter beat mayonnaise in the air and massacre disjointed fragments of Wagner to the great joy of an ignorant crowd?"[47] And in Wagner's story the behavior of R. and the narrator at a concert in Paris is described as follows.

> We arrived and took our usual place beneath a great oak, for we had been taught by a well-confirmed observation that this place was not only at the greatest remove from the idle crowd, but also that from it one had the advantage of being able to hear the music best and most distinctly. We had always pitied the unhappy creatures in the gardens as well as in the halls, who were compelled, or perhaps actually preferred, to linger in the immediate vicinity of the orchestra; we were quite unable to understand how they could find pleasure in *seeing* rather than hearing the music, for we could not interpret otherwise the strained attention with which they, immovable and rigid, watched the various movements of the musicians, but especially how they observed the kettledrum player with enthusiastic participation when he, after counting off the pauses with wary anxiety, at last permitted himself to join in concussively. We were agreed that there is nothing more prosaic and dispiriting than the sight of the frightfully swollen cheeks and distorted physiognomies of the wind players, of the unaesthetic clawings of the double-bass and cello players, yes, even of the tiresome sawing back and forth of the violin bows, when what is at issue is the listening to a performance of a beautiful piece of instrumental music. For this reason we placed ourselves so that we could hear the finest nuances in the performances of the orchestra, without having to be disturbed by the sight of it.[48]

47. Joris-Karl Huysmans, *A rebours* (Paris, 1965), 250–51.
48. Wagner, *Gesammelte Schriften und Dichtungen,* I, 137–38.

CHAPTER FOUR

WAGNER ON THE HUMAN USE OF ANIMAL BEINGS

Richard Wagner's concern for the well-being of animals is evident in his already mentioned short story "An End in Paris." This tale of an overpresumptuous young German composer, known only as R., is the one that Heinrich Heine praised for its more than Hoffmannesque manner. The fictional narrator of the tale may, in fact, be based on Heine himself: he is a sophisticated, cynical but sympathetic fellow countryman of the young musician, and already at home in Paris. The story opens on a cold, overcast day. The narrator and an unidentified English gentleman (who also appears in another of Wagner's Paris stories) have just presided over R.'s burial. The narrator then recalls how R., accompanied by a magnificent Newfoundland, had come to Paris a year earlier filled with high hopes. The narrator had warned him that without money or patronage he would be unable to feed his dog, much less himself. "Although I know that you are frugal, your fine beast will eat a great deal. You will feed both him and yourself with your talent?—That's fine, self-preservation is the first duty, but a second and the finest is humanity toward animals." After repeatedly being told by the narrator what really goes on behind the scenes in the musical and artistic world of Paris, and how vanishingly small are his chances for success, the idealistic young R. stalks angrily away, predicting that within a year his name will be known to every street boy in Paris—or he will be dead.

Somewhat less than a year later, we find the narrator strolling in the Champs–Elysées, turning over in his mind the inevitable fate of the braggart Punchinello. In the end, he says to himself, "the daimonic principle, so strikingly represented by a chained cat with superhuman claws, humbles the vain presumption of arrogant mortals." At this point he meets R., whom he has not seen since their quarrel. As the narrator predicted, R. has gone under: he is utterly destitute, all but starving and half-mad. To feed the Newfoundland he had sold his grandmother's rug and part of his own clothing, and lived on scraps. The well-fed dog had attracted the eye of an elegant Englishman (later to attend R.'s funeral), who offered to buy it. The offer was refused indignantly, but the dog ran away with (or was stolen by) the Englishman. R. now fancies that he sees music embodied before him in the form of a cat. Asked by the concerned narrator about his plans, R. raves incoherently:

> "You will find out about them just as soon as they are carried out," he replied. "Quadrilles, galops! O that is my forte!—You shall see and hear!—Do you see that cat?—She is to help me to goodly author's fees! Look how sleek she is, how nicely she licks her chops! Just imagine coming out of this mouth, through those rows of pearly teeth, the most inspired embellishments, accompanied by the most delicate moans and groans in the world! . . . Everything depends on her . . . Fortune, honor and fame lie between her soft paws. Heaven guide her heart and give me her favor!—She looks friendly;—yes, that is feline nature! She is indeed friendly, and courteous, courteous beyond measure! But she is a cat, a perjured, false cat!" [1]

We have here a real dog, the Newfoundland that Wagner brought from Riga to Paris by way of London (and lost, as he tells us in his autobiography, in Paris), and a metaphorical cat. Music is, as always for Wagner, a woman and a daimonic force: in his autobiography he speaks of the great singer Wilhelmine Schröder-Devrient's "almost daimonic warmth," and says that for him music is, or was, "a wholly daimonic realm." [2] The existence of a link between E. T. A. Hoffmann's musician-poet Tomcat Murr and Wagner's cat in "An End in Paris," as well as Heine's "Young Tomcats' Association for Poetry-Music," is undeniable, but it cannot detain us here. The point to be made is simply that Wagner's lifelong concern with the welfare of animals is prominent in this story of a musician who (as we learn in its second paragraph) "invariably wept when men tormented the poor horses in the streets of Paris"—anticipating perhaps the tears shed by Dostoevsky several decades later over the similar fate of horses in the streets of St. Petersburg.

1. Wagner, *Gesammelte Schriften und Dichtungen*, I, 114, 116, 125–26, 130.
2. Wagner, *Mein Leben*, I, 39, 44.

During the nineteenth century northern Europeans were often re-
volted by the treatment accorded animals in the Latin countries, and
Wagner was no exception. Writing to his friend Theodor Uhlig from
Lugano on July 22, 1853, Wagner tells of his hazardous trip on foot
over the icy wastes of the Gries glacier down into the idyllic and
luxuriant valleys of northern Italy on his way to Spezia (and the composition of the *Ring* overture). Wagner's blissful mood was dispelled
while crossing Lago Maggiore. He saw that

> on the steamer—loaded with Italian Philistines, who are, after all, not so
> bad—there were poor animals, hens and ducks (in transport) that were
> being subjected to a frightful slow death, and were so abominably tor-
> mented that I was once again filled anew with furious anger at the revolting
> insensitivity of the human beings who had this spectacle constantly before
> their eyes. And to know that if any attempt were made to step in here one
> would be laughed to scorn!!—In general, dear friend, my views on the hu-
> man race become ever gloomier; indeed for the most part I am constrained
> to believe that this breed must perish utterly.[3]

The salutation of this letter is remarkable: "O Thou Human Being!
Homo terribilis (Lin. II, 53)" ("O Du Mensch! *Homo terribilis* [Lin.
II, 53]"). The *homo terribilis* or *homo troglodytes* of the Swedish physician and naturalist Carl Linné (Linnaeus) was a dwarfish, cave-
dwelling creature thought to be a species of primitive *homo* but identified by nineteenth-century naturalists as the immature orangutan.[4]
Where Wagner picked this up is an open question. Linnaeus was never
on Wagner's shelves, as far as we know, nor is his name mentioned in
Cosima Wagner's diaries. Schopenhauer—incidentally one of those
who believed, before Darwin, that human beings had arisen from an
apelike ancestor by a kind of quantum jump—suggests himself, but
the words *homo terribilis* occur nowhere in his writings. More interesting is the fear of a *Götterdämmerung* expressed in the closing line of
Wagner's letter. A parallel passage from George Gissing's diary, made
in Rome on Christmas, 1888, is also of interest. "I have noticed much
lately the gross cruelty with which fowls for the market are treated
here. Every day I see them being carried about the streets by the legs,

---

3. Wagner, *Briefe in Originalausgaben*, IV, 205.
4. The *Encyclopaedia Britannica* (1771), II, 789, gives an account of Linné's
homo terribilis: it is white, about one-half human size, and supposedly a distinct species
of primitive man.

heads hanging down; and they are often packed so closely together in crates that they can scarcely flutter a feather."[5]

Wagner's essay of 1879 on the humane treatment of animals (couched in the form of an open letter to Ernst von Weber, another champion of animal rights) will be cited from at length in the present chapter. But before approaching the letter two developments in the second half of the nineteenth century require comment. One was in Wagner himself; the other was a shift in the focus of interest of the animal-rights movement. The change in Wagner resulted from his encounter with the writings of Arthur Schopenhauer, which first took place, if only casually, in 1852; by 1854 he had become a convinced disciple of Schopenhauer, and he remained one for the rest of his life.[6] Wagner found in Schopenhauer a rational basis for his own deeply felt sentiments on the proper human treatment of animal beings, specifically the claim that we ourselves are animals and owe them a large measure of the compassion that we—rightfully, according to the ethics of Schopenhauer—owe each other.

The shift in focus—heretofore centered on domestic animals—on the part of champions of animal rights resulted from the rapid rise of experimental physiology and experimental pathology in the second half of the nineteenth century. The experiments, of course, were performed in all but the rarest cases on animals. Moreover, animals came to be used with increasing frequency by teachers of medicine and biology to demonstrate, for the benefit of their pupils, already established findings. Demonstrations of this kind, together with operative procedures carried out on animals by beginners, were often found offensive by a public willing to admit that experiments carried out by competent professionals in search of new knowledge were morally justified. A smaller number of people, Wagner among them, refused to accept the utilitarian argument under any circumstances. A part of the public feared too that the moral callousness of animal experimentation might in the end lead to experimentation on unwilling human beings. Wagner shared this concern, but he saw it as another manifestation of the utilitarian point of view, and therefore blind to the moral point at issue.

5. George Gissing, *London and the Life of Literature in Late Victorian England: The Diary of George Gissing, Novelist,* ed. Pierre Coustillas (Hassocks, Sussex, 1978), 109.
6. Sans, *Richard Wagner et la pensée schopenhauerienne,* 17–21, calls attention to Wagner's encounter with Schopenhauer's philosophy in 1852.

In the history of Western medicine and biology, experimentation on living beings is nothing new. Celsus, a writer who flourished during the reign of Tiberius, claims that even Hippocratic physicians approved the procedure of "Herophilus and Erasistratus [in Alexandria in the third century B.C.E.] . . . when they cut open alive criminals sent from prison by the kings," whereas the rival school of empiricists regarded this as a cruel, unproductive, and atrocious misuse of the art. Galen, the greatest of Greek physicians after Hippocrates, left a written record of his many surgical experiments on live animals, five centuries after Herophilus. In the early seventeenth century it was "from the dissection of living animals" (*ex vivorum dissectione*) that William Harvey, as he himself wrote, came to understand the movements of the heart and blood. René Descartes, Harvey's contemporary, held that animals were soulless machines; his followers are said to have concluded, quite logically, that the cries of living animals called for no more compassion than the creaking of a windlass.[7] We might suppose that no such argument was needed in an age that condoned the burning, drawing and quartering, and worse, of human offenders. But this would be as mistaken as to suppose A's love of dogs will prevent her from enjoying the flesh of calves, or from approving the use of napalm and fragmentation bombs against enemies of her people. It is possible that many of the early practitioners of vivisection found it difficult to do what they did, and that the development of reliable chemical means of anesthesia at midcentury was one reason for the increased frequency of the practice. In the closing decades of the nineteenth century, "vivisection" came to include all forms of animal experimentation involving an encroaching on the body of the subject, for example, inoculation procedures.[8] But this took place with the rise of bacteriology and immunology, and at a time when the initial furor over vivisection had led to the enactment of laws regulating the practice in Germany, England, and elsewhere.[9]

7. Celsus, *De medicina*, trans. W. G. Spencer (3 vols.; London, 1948), I, 15, 23; see L. J. Rather, *The Genesis of Cancer: A Study in the History of Ideas* (Baltimore, 1978), 20–21, for an account of one of Galen's experiments; Rather, "Old and New Views of the Emotions and Bodily Changes: Wright and Harvey versus Descartes, James and Cannon," *Clio Medica,* I (1965), 1–25.

8. By 1990, according to Stephen Paget ("vivisection," in *Encyclopaedia Britannica* [11th ed.]), 95 percent of animal experiments involved inoculation.

9. For a well-documented account, see Richard D. French, *Antivivisection and Medical Science in Victorian Society* (Princeton, 1975).

Compassion (*Mitleid*) is the cornerstone of Schopenhauer's ethics. In the fourth book of his magnum opus, *The World as Will and Representation* (1819), ethics is presented as the culmination of the entire philosophical system. Ethics, he says, is concerned with *action* and its significance. To suppose that Schopenhauer's compassion or *Mitleid* ("suffering with") is simply a matter of having or expressing the right sentiments at the right time is to miss the point entirely. Wagner later clarified the matter by making use of the phrase "active compassion" (*tätiges Mitleid*) and held that such compassion was best exemplified in the work of the healer—who might even on occasion seem pitiless to the onlooker. Schopenhauer's *Mitleid* has much in common with the specifically Christian concept of "love" (called in the Greek New Testament *agape* and translated into Latin as *caritas*, whence the misleading term *charity* in the King James version). Schopenhauer writes: "All true, pure love is compassion, and all love that is not compassion is selfishness; selfishness [*i.e.*, selfish love] is *eros*, compassion is *agape*." The egoist feels himself surrounded by enemies; the good human being, on the contrary, lives in a friendly, cheerful world where all living beings are of essentially the same character, and the good of one is the good of all. All beings, according to Schopenhauer, are phenomenal manifestations of the one underlying metaphysical reality, the *will*. "Which truth," he adds, "in respect of practice I cannot better express than in the already mentioned formula of the Veda, *tat tvam asi!* (that art thou!) Whoever can say this to himself with clear understanding and firm conviction about every being with which he comes in contact is thereby certain of all virtue and bliss, and on the straight way to salvation."[10] Schopenhauer's reason for turning to India is twofold: he wants philosophical rather than religious underpinnings for his ethical system, and he wants to emphasize—as Christianity hardly does—the essential unity of *all* living things. (Wagner made a pun on the Sanskrit "formula" that would have amused Schopenhauer: he was reading a French version of the Bhagavad-Gita in 1878, when he laughed and said to Cosima "tat tvam asini."[11])

10. Arthur Schopenhauer, *Die Welt als Wille und Vorstellung,* in *Sämtliche Werke,* ed. Wolfgang Freiherr von Lohneysen (5 vols.; Stuttgart, 1960–65), I, 375–76, 509–511; Schopenhauer, *The World as Will and Representation,* trans. E. F. J. Payne (2 vols.; 1958; republished with minor corrections, New York, 1958), I, 271–72, 374–76.

11. Cosima Wagner, *Diaries,* II, 97. With a Latin noun in the place of a Sanskrit verb the phrase cannot be construed, but the intended meaning, clearly, is that human beings most resemble asses.

A more extended treatment of ethics is given in Schopenhauer's "On the Basis of Morality," a prize essay submitted to the Royal Danish Society of Sciences in 1840.[12] This work includes a critique of earlier systems of ethics, in particular those of Spinoza (whom Schopenhauer admired, while differing with him in important respects) and Kant (whose categorical imperative was, in Schopenhauer's opinion, completely ungrounded and drawn entirely from theological morality). Here Schopenhauer asserts that the moral foundation of his own system rests on the metaphysical identity of all living things, and therefore requires that the principle of *Mitleid*, or compassion, be extended to beings who are, like ourselves, capable of suffering. The Cartesians in particular draw his fire. "The supposed rightlessness of animals, the delusion that our actions with respect to them are without moral meaning . . . is in plain terms a shocking crudity and barbarity of the West, whose source lies in Judaism. In philosophy it rests on the assumed—in the face of all evidence—total difference between human beings and animals; this, as is well known, was most decisively and vividly expressed by Descartes, as a necessary consequence of his errors."[13] Schopenhauer calls Spinoza a "very great man" but nevertheless a man whose attitude toward animals never rose above the most primitive level of the Old Testament, that is, the view that animals exist solely for us to make use of them as we see fit.[14] It is true that Spinoza did say as much, although he was by no means a Cartesian. In Scholium I, proposition 36 of part 4 of his *Ethics,* Spinoza states that if we are led to spare animals it will be by virtue of "empty superstition and womanish compassion" rather than sound reason. "I do not deny," he adds, "that brutes feel, but I deny that for this reason we are not permitted to consult our interests and use animals at will . . . since their nature differs from our nature and their emotions from human emotions."[15] Schopenhauer was of course aware that Spinoza had been cut off from the Jewish community at Amsterdam by the tribal elders because he rejected, among other things, the belief that the Jews

12. Schopenhauer, *Über die Grundlage der Moral,* in *Sämtliche Werke,* III, 629–815.
13. Schopenhauer, *Sämtliche Werke,* III, 773.
14. *Ibid.,* II, 828.
15. Baruch Spinoza, *Benedicti de Spinoza opera omnia quotquot reperta sunt,* ed. by J. van Vloten and J. P. N. Land (4 vols. in 2; The Hague, 1914), II, 209.

were a race apart, chosen by God.[16] Nevertheless, it is Schopenhauer's belief that Spinoza's attitude toward animals stems from the great philosopher's inability to cut himself free from primitive Old Testament Judaism. "Entirely Jewish," Schopenhauer writes, "and, moreover, absurd in conjunction with [Spinoza's] pantheism, and at the same time revolting, is his contempt for animals."[17]

As will be shown later, Schopenhauer's claim that contempt for animals in our society has its roots in Old Testament Judaism has been used in our day to support the charge that he was anti-Semitic. Since Judeo-Christianity accepts the authority of the Old Testament as well as the New Testament, it could of course be said that Schopenhauer was anti-Christian. He believed, however, that Christian—not Judeo-Christian—morality was in theory on a higher plane than that of other religions, however little there was to be said for it in practice. A decision in favor of Christianity on the plane of practice will hardly be made (writes Schopenhauer) by anyone who "recalls the long list of inhuman cruelties that have accompanied Christianity in the numerous religious wars, in the extermination of a great part of the aboriginal inhabitants of America and the repopulation of that part of the world with negro slaves brought in from Africa torn without justice, without a shadow of justice, from their families, their homeland, their part of the world, and condemned to endless forced prison labor, in the unceasing persecution of heretics, in the courts of the Inquisition that cry to heaven, in St. Bartholomew's Night, in Alba's execution of eighteen thousand Netherlanders, and so on, and so on"—a diatribe that fittingly expands what Lucretius said of a single instance, the sacrifice of Iphigenia at Aulis by her father.[18] Wagner, we recall, was of the same mind as Lucretius about this crime.[19]

The Inquisition, the St. Bartholomew's Day massacre of the Huguenots, and the Duke of Alba's slaughter of dissidents in the Netherlands

16. Spinoza stated that the Jews could arrogate to themselves nothing with respect to virtue or intellect beyond that possessed by other human beings, and also that the continued existence of the Jews after the diaspora had nothing of the miraculous about it, "for they so separated themselves from every other nation as to draw down on themselves universal hatred" (Spinoza, *The Chief Works of Benedict de Spinoza*, trans. R. H. M. Elwes [London, 1891], I, 55–56.

17. Schopenhauer, *Sämtliche Werke*, II, 828.

18. *Ibid.*, III, 768.

19. See Wagner's comment on the *Agamemnon* of Aeschylus in Chapter 1 herein.

being the deeds of adherents of Rome, Schopenhauer could be called an anti-Catholic as well as an anti-Semite. The same may be said of his strictures against the maltreatment of animals, since the dominant tradition of the Catholic church is that of Thomas Aquinas rather than Francis of Assisi—quite like the tradition that Schopenhauer finds in Judaism. The works of Aquinas contain nothing more than a rationalization of the Old Testament doctrine of man's absolute superiority over brute beasts. Only man has an immortal soul, only man has free will (*electio*), whereas the lower souls of beasts perish with their bodies, and their actions while they are alive are those of clockwork automata, set in motion by God ("animalia bruta . . . diriguntur a Deo sicut horologia"). Although animals lack free will we are yet justified in punishing them for their sins, Aquinas tells us, since we thereby demonstrate our abhorrence of the sin (*detestationem peccati*); in other instances we may be indirectly punishing their owners, somewhat as God visits the sins of the fathers on the children. Thus Aquinas in the *Summa Theologica*. In the *Summa contra Gentiles* he cites Psalms 13:6–8 to prove that God made the beasts, fowl, and fish subject to the domination of man, and (possibly to drive another nail into the coffin of the Albigensians), God's decree that for man "[e]very living thing shall be meat" (Genesis 9:3). It is a theological error to believe that we cannot kill animals or use them in any other way we please ("unde absque injuria eis utitur homo vel occidendo, vel quolibet alio modo"); the closing "or in any way we please" ("vel quolibet alio modo") would obviously allow animal experimentation. Aquinas assents also that if any passage in the Scriptures prohibits a specific act of cruelty toward animals, such as killing a bird with young, its intent is to prevent the habit of cruelty from broadening its scope to include man, or to prevent pecuniary loss, or for some other reason, as when Paul expounds for us the true meaning of the Deuteronomic injunction "Thou shalt not muzzle the ox when he treadeth out the corn" (Deuteronomy 25:4).[20]

All this far from exhausts the official Catholic attitude toward animals, still less that of individual Catholics. The same may be said of Judaism and Jews. To call attention to the sources of this attitude in the

20. Thomas Aquinas, *Divi Thomae Aquinatis Summa Theologica* (editio altero; 6 vols.; Rome, 1894), VI, 89–90, gives access to all references to animals and their treatment. See especially the *Summa Contra Gentiles*, VI, 461. St. Paul explains (1 Corinthians 9:9–10) that the passage bears on the well-being of man, not on that of the ox.

WAGNER ON ANIMAL BEINGS

Old Testament does not, by itself, imply reprehensible anti-Catholicism or anti-Judaism, that is, anti-Semitism, on the part of a writer. But it may help explain why "[e]vangelicals, and those of similar faith and sympathy, occupied almost all of the chief positions in the anti-vivisection societies," as Lloyd Stevenson (an anti-antivivisectionist) pointed out in 1955.[21] Nevertheless, there were—and continue to be—Catholics, Protestants, and Jews on both sides of the controversy. In England Cardinal Manning (1808–1892) championed animal rights (as well as workingmen's rights) and was a strong supporter of the antivivisectionists. Louis (or Lewis) Gompertz, a nineteenth-century English philanthropist, was the first honorary secretary of the Royal Society for the Prevention of Cruelty to Animals. Gompertz, a devout Jew, is said to have solved the problem, for himself at least, of ritual Jewish slaughter by abstaining entirely from flesh foods.[22]

The ritual slaughter of animals for food according to the procedure implied by the Old Testament offended Gompertz, but it was as nothing to what had gone on in Christian circles until the end of the eighteenth century. Thus Percy Bysshe Shelley, in his "Essay on the Vegetable System of Diet" (written in 1813, but not published until 1929): "Sows big with young are indeed no longer stamped upon and sucking pigs roasted alive; but lobsters are slowly boiled to death and express by their inarticulate cries the dreadful agony they endure; chickens are mutilated and imprisoned until they fatten; calves are bled to death that their flesh may appear white; and a certain horrible process of torture furnishes brawn for the gluttonous repasts with which Christians celebrate the anniversary of their savior's birth."[23]

The procedure of a Jewish ritual slaughter involves bleeding an animal to death without preliminary stunning. Since most Jews were unwilling on religious grounds to relinquish it, or to abandon flesh foods entirely, as Gompertz had done, there was friction between Jews and non-Jews within the humane movement. According to a recent histo-

21. Lloyd G. Stevenson, "Science Down the Drain," *Bulletin of the History of Medicine*, XXIX (1955), 1–26. An unusual and interesting treatment of the subject will be found in Major C. W. Hume's *The Status of Animals in the Christian Religion* (London, 1957).

22. Charles D. Niven, *History of the Humane Movement* (New York, 1967), 67–71.

23. Percy Bysshe Shelley, *Shelley's Prose, or the Trumpet of Prophecy*, ed. David Lee Clark (Albuquerque, 1954), 94.

rian of the antivivisectionists in Victorian England, Richard D. French, the failure of the movement to retain the support of "the Humane Jews of England" (as they were then called) was followed by a certain hostility toward Judaism on the part of some of the antivivisectionists. Attacks bred counterattack. In 1894 Morris Rubens published a tract entitled *Anti-Vivisection Exposed, Including a Disclosure of the Recent Attempt to Introduce Anti-Semitism into England*. Rubens charged that the eminent surgeon Lawson Tait and the antivivisectionist leader Francis Power Cobbe were using "the envenomed weapon of Anti-Semitism" to threaten the progress of science, and he urged the Jews to follow the Chief Rabbi of England in refusing to support the antivivisectionist movement."[24]

Although the Jews in England had been among the pioneers of the humane movement in England, many of them seem to have abandoned it when it failed to win orthodox support. The controversy over ritual slaughter still continues in our day, especially in England, and the same charges are still being made. The Moslem religion calls for a similar procedure, but in recent years the Imam of the Shah Jehan Mosque in Woking gave way in response to pressure from the Humane Slaughter Association in England. But the Orthodox Jews of England did not. They claimed (and received) exemption from the law requiring animals to be stunned before killing. The result was that in England "gentile slaughtermen could be prosecuted for failing to stun while under the same roofs Kosher killings can quite legally take place," and this despite the subsequent sale of the ritually slaughtered animals to "gentile" consumers. A bill proposing to include the Kosher slaughtermen was said to show "racial prejudice" and to involve "racial discrimination." It was rejected, and a second reading of it did not take place. There are said to be commercial as well as religious forces arrayed against the disallowing of ritual slaughter: the shed blood is used as fertilizer and in the preparation of albumen.[25]

In the United States today, says another historian of the subject, "Jews—the pioneers of the Humane Movement—are now obstructing the completion of the humane slaughter project," and in Germany "a retrograde step was taken after the Second World War because Jewish

24. French, *Antivivisection and Medical Science in Victorian Society,* 347–48.
25. Monica Hutchings and Mavis Caver, *Man's Dominion: Our Violation of the Animal World* (London, 1970), 110–11.

ritual slaughter had been suppressed under the Hitler regime."[26] It is
true that in Germany on November 24, 1933—two years before the
Nuremberg Laws deprived Jews of certain civic rights and inadver-
tently supported Orthodox Jewry by forbidding marriages between
Jews and non-Jews—a far-reaching law for the protection of animals
had been passed. Among other things the law prohibited force-feeding
of geese and other fowl in the production of fatty liver paste, the tear-
ing off of the legs of live frogs, and Jewish ritual slaughter procedure.
In 1945 the occupying powers nullified the law for the benefit of Jews
still living in Germany (reduced from 500,000 to less than 30,000),
and as late as 1956 German animal protection societies were still try-
ing to reinstate the old law.[27] Many non-Jews will sympathize with the
desire of Jews in Europe to do away with all laws even remotely sug-
gestive of anti-Jewish bias, as well as with the readiness of their liberators to accommodate them, even at the expense of a guiltless third
party unable to protect itself. A like sympathy for the English Jews of
late Victorian times who could see nothing more in the antivivisection
movement than a disguised form of anti-Semitism will be harder to
come by.

Although the Germans, Swedes, and Danes were pioneers of the
modern animal-rights movement, the English were the first to initiate
formal legislation against cruelty to animals, whether domestic or scientific, that is, experimental. The Cruelty to Animals Act, the most
comprehensive of its time, became law in England in 1876. This was
three years before Wagner wrote his "Open Letter to Mr. Ernst von
Weber, Author of the Paper 'The Torture-Chambers of Science.'"[28]
Niven believes it unlikely that the act would have become law of the
land had it not been for what Thomas Henry Huxley called the "wantonly and mischievously brutal" character of the testimony against it
given by an Austrian experimentalist by the name of Emmanuel Klein.[29]
Klein's words were in fact more guarded than those long since current

26. Niven, *History of the Humane Movement*, 125.

27. *S.v.* "Tierschutz," in *Der Grosse Herder* (Freiburg, 1956).

28. Richard Wagner, "Offenes Schreiben an Herrn Ernst von Weber, Verfasser der
Schrift: 'Die Folterkammern der Wissenschaft,'" in *Gesammelte Schriften und Dichtungen*, X, 194–210. Translated as "Against Vivisection" in Wagner, *Prose Works*, VI,
193–210.

29. Niven, *History of the Humane Movement*, 97–98; French, *Antivivisection
and Medical Science in Victorian Society*, 103–105.

in France and Germany, where the power of the state-controlled universities and the influence of their professors was far greater than in England. Clause Bernard, the leading experimental medical physiologist of his day, spoke for most of his colleagues when, in 1865, he stated: "A physiologist is not a man of fashion, he is a man of science, absorbed by the scientific idea which he pursues: he no longer hears the cry of animals, he no longer sees the blood that flows, he sees only his idea and perceives only organisms concealing problems which he intends to solve."[30] The cries from the "House of Pain" perhaps fell on deafer ears in a country where both Descartes and Aquinas could be cited in support of the view that animals were mere mechanisms, like the famous astronomic clock in the Strasbourg cathedral. Huxley may have shared this view in theory, but in practice he was shocked.[31]

Animal lovers often referred to themselves—probably in order to escape the pejorative sense of a term used by their opponents somewhat as "nigger lovers" was used in the southern United States until a generation ago—as zoophilists. French, after calling attention to a slur cast on the (Jewish) race of the editor of the *British Medical Journal* in the 1890s by an antivivisectionist, remarks that in Germany there were close ties between anti-Semitism and antivivisectionism, and that in reviewing a German antivivisectionist tract in 1881 the editor of the *Zoophilist* (a British journal) "did not scruple to refer to 'the uncongenial influences of Judaism and Materialism.'"[32] Whether or not the antivivisectionist whom French mentions in connection with the editor of the *British Medical Journal* was an anti-Semite in the worst sense of the term, there is surely no reason for putting the editor of the *Zoophilist* in the same category. His remark has to do with a system of beliefs and practices. To those of us who are neither devout Catholics, orthodox Jews or, for that matter, orthodox materialists, there is no reason why opposition to the theory and practice of Catholicism, Ju-

30. Claude Bernard, *An Introduction to the Study of Experimental Medicine*, trans. Henry Copley Greene (New York, 1949), 103.

31. On Huxley's belief that we are conscious automata and on his admiration for Descartes, see "On Descartes' 'Discourse Touching the Method of Using One's Reason Rightly and of Seeking Scientific Truth,'" in Thomas Henry Huxley, *Lay Sermons, Addresses, and Reviews* (New York, 1870), 320–44.

32. French, *Antivivisection and Medical Science in Victorian England*, 347. For Cesare Lombroso's scientific diagnosis of Wagner as a zoophilomaniac (*Zoophilomane*), see his "Neue Studien über die Genialität," *Schmidt's Jahrbücher der in– und ausländischen gesammten Medicin*, CCXCIII (1907), 145.

daism, or materialism should be considered suspect. In the case of
anti-Judaism, however, any criticism of Jewish beliefs and practices
is today too often pejoratively labeled with the blanket term *anti-
Semitism*, and all dialogue ceases. Anti-Semitism, as Alfred M. Lilienthal suggests, has come to seem—to certain Christians and Jews—
original sin, the sin against the Holy Ghost, something utterly beyond
the pale. And yet as late as October, 1933, the English Zionist Sir
Lewis Bernstein Namier granted that some anti-Semites were "sane
and civilized," and moreover cautioned his fellow Jews that "not
everyone who feels uncomfortable with regard to us must be called an
anti-Semite, *nor is there anything necessarily and inherently wicked in
anti-Semitism"* (emphasis mine).[33] But today, if Spinoza—not to mention Christ—were to walk the earth again he would be anathematized
as an anti-Semitic Semite, in some quarters at least.

It is unwise to see every protest against certain doctrines found in
the Old Testament, the Torah in particular, as another manifestation
of all-pervasive anti-Semitism—misleading, too, since the attitudes
thought to have been inculcated by these doctrines are shared by most
Christians. Writing as a historian of technology in 1976 for readers of
Science, Lynn White, Jr., suggested that the historical roots of what
he sees as the present ecological crisis lay in the "Judeo-Christian
teleology" generally accepted in the Western world. Relying on the
Jahvistic rather than the Elohistic creation myth in Genesis, White
writes: "Finally, God had created Adam and, as an after thought, Eve
to keep man from being lonely. Man named all the animals; thus establishing his dominance over them. God planned all of this explicitly
for man's benefit and rule: no item in the physical creation had any
purposes save to serve man's purpose." White then asserted that if the
exploitative process now being carried out by Western science hand in
hand with Western technology is truly out of control then "Christianity bears a huge burden of guilt." He proposed that the objectionable
Old Testament "teleology" be shelved, and that Francis of Assisi be
recognized as "patron saint for ecologists."[34]

White, quite properly, puts the onus on Judeo-Christianity. A more

33. Arthur Ruppin, *The Jews in the Modern World* (London, 1934), xiii. *Cf.* "Exploiting Anti-Semitism," chap. 9 of Alfred M. Lilienthal, *The Zionist Connection: What
Price Peace?* (New York, 1978).
34. Lynn White, Jr., "The Historical Roots of Our Ecological Crisis," *Science*,
CLV (1967), 1203–207.

apocalyptic version of White's thesis appears in an address by Ian L. McHarg, an ecologist, given in 1971 at the North American Wildlife and Natural Resources Conference in Portland, Oregon. The message of the God of Abraham, Isaac, and Jacob, "explicit in Genesis, central to Judaism, [and] absorbed and changed into Christianity," that man is to have dominion over the earth and all living creatures is, says McHarg, "absolutely horrifying." It may have had survival value in the past, but today it represents the "best guarantee of [our] extinction." McHarg was careful to make plain that at issue was a certain interpretation of a particular passage in the Old Testament. Carefully guarding himself against the charge of antireligious bias, he writes: "This is not an anti-Jewish, anti-Christian, anti-Catholic, anti-Protestant view. My view has been espoused by every important theologian I know—Martin Buber, Schweitzer, Karl Barth, the lot." As part of this lot, he named Paul Tillich (Protestant), Gustave Weigel (Catholic), and Abram Heschel (Jew).[35]

Commenting on the generally more favorable treatment accorded to animals by northern Europeans, the Germans in particular, Charles D. Niven in his *History of the Humane Movement* writes, "The horrible truth is that people are usually cruel to animals unless somebody has told them not to be, and Germans have been told not to be cruel to animals for a longer period of time than the people of any other nation."[36] No inherent moral superiority is here involved, nor is there any guarantee that a prescribed aversion to cruelty to animals will include human beings within its scope. For good as well as for bad we are, as Morris Cohen stated, all of us "the social products of generations of teaching."[37]

But by the middle of the nineteenth century the physiological laboratories of Germany were no different from those in France. Schopenhauer, who studied medicine at Göttingen in 1809–1811, wrote at midcentury:

> When I studied in Göttingen, [Johann] Blumenbach spoke to us very seriously in his lectures on physiology on the frightful character of vivisection, and showed us what a cruel and revolting thing it was; hence one should

35. Ian L. McHarg, *Man: Planetary Disease*, the 1971 B. Y. Morrison Memorial Lecture, presented in cooperation with the North American Wildlife and Natural Resources Conference, Portland, Ore. (Washington, D.C., n.d.), 7–8.

36. Niven, *History of the Humane Movement*, 97–98.

37. See Chapter 2, note 1 and corresponding text herein.

resort to it very rarely, and only in investigations involving very important and immediate benefits, and then only with great openness in the main lecture room after all medical men had been invited, in order that the cruel sacrifice on the altar of science should bring the greatest possible benefits. But today, in contrast, every charlatan considers himself qualified to carry out the worst cruelties toward animals in his torture chamber—to solve problems whose solutions were long since present in the books in which he is too lazy and ignorant to put his nose. Our physicians no longer have the classical education they once had, which gave them a touch of nobility and a certain humanity. Now they go to the university as soon as possible to learn poultice-smearing and the art of prospering in the world.

The French physiologists had set the example, Schopenhauer claimed, and the Germans were doing their best to emulate them.[38]

Wagner was aware of what was going on behind closed doors in the university schools of medicine. His loyal supporter Malwida von Meysenbug (later a close friend of Romain Rolland) was ill-advised enough to defend (on the grounds of their scientific value) some experiments carried out in the 1870s on the brains of live dogs—involving the selective destruction of parts of the cerebrum—by professor Friedrich Goltz of Strassburg. Wagner grew pale with anger as he told her of his utter contempt for such procedures.[39] This was in the spring of 1878. In July of the following year Wagner received from Wiesbaden a pamphlet attacking vivisectionists and a written request that he join the fight "against the prevailing cruelty of the—largely Jewish— physicians." It is not clear from Glasenapp's account of this incident whether "largely Jewish" is his or the correspondent's interjection, nor do we learn anything of the correspondent other than her sex.[40]

The brief delay was occasioned by the illness of Wagner's son, the ten-year-old Helferich Siegfried Wagner.[41] Wagner then joined the animal protection society in Bayreuth and wrote to the Dresden protectionists for literature and statutes of organization. On August 14,

38. Schopenhauer, "Über Religion," in *Sämtliche Werke*, V, 441; Schopenhauer, "On Religion," in *Parerga and Paralipomena: Short Philosophical Essays*, trans. E. F. J. Payne (2 vols; Oxford, 1974), II, 373.

39. Carl Friedrich Glasenapp, *Das Leben Richard Wagners* (6 vols.; Leipzig, 1911), VI, 145. For the experiments see Friedrich L. Goltz, *Gesammelte Abhandlungen über die Vernichtungen des Grosshirns* (Bonn, 1886), *passim*.

40. Glasenapp, *Das Leben Richard Wagners*, VI, 240.

41. On their son's insistence that he be called "Helferich," see Cosima Wagner, *Diaries*, I, 652; on Wagner's plans for his future, see *ibid.*, II, 156.

1879, he explained to the founder and chairman of the Dresden society, Ernst von Weber, why he had hitherto taken no part in the antivivisectionist movement. This letter shows that Wagner by now fully shared Schopenhauer's ethical position. It reads, in part:

> So far I have honored the activities of associations such as yours, but I have nonetheless always regretted that in their instructive work with the public they base themselves on a showing of the usefulness of animals and the uselessness of torturing them. It may be useful to address a heartless people in this fashion, but it seemed to me that the time had come to move forward and invoke compassion as the sole basis for the ennoblement of Christianity. The great Brahmin proverb *tat tvam asi,* "that art thou," must now be addressed to human beings with reference to animals—even though it will be difficult to make the proverb understandable in our Old Testament-judaized world.[42]

On September 12 a gathering of Wagnerians, mostly from France, included Ernst von Weber: Joseph Rubinstein appropriately played a piano arrangement of the *Parsifal* prelude. On September 18 Cosima jotted down her husband's comment on recent progress of the sciences. "'God grant it may all be for nothing' R. observes, 'when one sees all this equipment made in the name of vivisection as well as militarism.'" Wagner had come a long way since writing (in 1849, in "The Art-Work of the Future") that the "sole achievements of the present age that offer us consolation and succor from madness and futility" were "modern natural science and modern landscape painting," both being achievements in which the human being no longer occupied the "egoistic center of the work."[43]

The phrase "Old Testament-judaized world" (*alttestamentarisch-verjudeten Welt*) in Wagner's letter refers to precisely the same world view rejected in our time by the Catholics, Protestants, and Jews who find themselves in more or less agreement with the views of Lynn White, Jr., Ian McHarg, and a host of other spokesmen. In a considerably expanded form this letter became Wagner's "Open Letter to Mr. von Weber," which was published in the October, 1879, issue of

42. Glasenapp, *Das Leben Richard Wagners,* VI, 241–42, 248–49; Cosima Wagner, *Diaries,* II, 354.

43. Cosima Wagner, *Diaries,* II, 363, 365; Wagner, *Gesammelte Schriften und Dichtungen,* III, 146–47.

Wagner's house organ, the *Bayreuther Blätter*, and gave him enduring fame (now somewhat muted) among proponents of animal rights.[44]

Wagner begins his "Open Letter" by locating the problem of vivisection in the context of the larger problem of the use of "science" by the state (the German universities were state institutions, and animal experimentation took place in them alone). "In the matter before us," he writes, "we are again confronted from the first by the same specter of science that has risen up from the cutting table and the arms factory as the daimon of the cult of utility, the sole cult looked on as friendly to the state." He then expands his earlier objections.

> What has so far kept me from joining one of the existing societies for the protection of animals was my recognition that all demands and doctrines emanating from them were based almost solely on the principle of utility. It may well have been necessary up until the present time for philanthropists concerned with the protection of animals to concern themselves above all else with a showing of the utility of this behavior, in order to persuade the folk to treat animals with consideration. For the outcome of our present-day civilization allows us to take into account no other mainspring for the actions of bourgeois humanity than the quest for utility. How far we have distanced ourselves from the sole ennobling motive for the friendly treatment of animals, and how little can really be reached on the path that has been followed, is very plain these days: the representatives of the so-far firmly held policy of animal protection societies against the extremely inhumane torture of animals practiced in our state-supported halls of vivisection have no valid argument to bring forward once the utility of these procedures is adduced to defend them. We find ourselves almost limited to questioning this utility, and if such utility were to be proved without the shadow of a doubt the animal protection society itself would have favored the most inhumane cruelty toward its own charges, given the policy that it has so far followed.[45]

The "sole ennobling motive" referred to by Wagner above is, of course, *compassion,* a moral sentiment not based on cost-benefit ratios. "The curse of our civilization, the proof of the profane charac-

44. Wagner, *Gesammelte Schriften und Dichtungen,* X, 194–210. Wagner's contributions to animal protection were honored in the United States in 1933 by M. R. L. Freshel in her *Selections from Three Essays by Richard Wagner with Comment on a Subject of Such Importance to the Moral Progress of Humanity That It Constitutes an Issue in Ethics and Religion* (Rochester, N.H.: 1933).

45. Wagner, *Gesammelte Schriften und Dichtungen,* X, 194–96.

ter of our established-church religions," says Wagner, is that we do not
make compassion the sole mainspring of our moral actions. Referring
here indirectly to Schopenhauer's essay "On the Basis of Morality"
and the unfavorable view taken of it by the Royal Danish Society
of Sciences in 1840, Wagner says that in our day a philosopher did indeed attempt to make "*compassion* the sole true basis of morality."
But this view

> was scorned, and even indignantly rejected by the senate of a learned so-
> ciety; for virtue, [they held] where it was not enjoined by revelation, must
> be founded only on considerations of reason. Compassion, regarded from
> the standpoint of reason, was in contrast even explained away as a potenti-
> ated form of egoism: the sight of another's suffering was said to cause us
> pain, and was thus the motive of our compassionate actions—not the
> other's suffering in itself, which we tried to remove only because this was
> the sole way of relieving the pain it caused us. How resourceful we had
> become, mired in the basest selfishness, in insisting against any disturbance
> due to feelings of common humanity! Moreover, compassion was also de-
> spised because it was supposed to be met with most commonly, among
> even the most ordinary human beings, as a very low grade expression of
> life; here diligence was exerted to substitute for [true] compassion the com-
> miseration that so readily manifests itself in all cases of public and domestic
> misfortune among the bystanders and, what with the great frequency of
> such cases, finds its expression in the head-shaking and shoulder-shrugging
> of someone who in the end turns away—until, perhaps, out of the crowd
> the one person moved by true compassion to give active help steps
> forward.[46]

Compassion (or whatever else we choose to call it) can of course be
written off as a mere form of self-gratification even if we include what
Wagner calls "active compassion" (*tätiges Mitleid*) under this heading.
In commenting on the above passage, Wagner's translator William
Ashton Ellis pointed out that it clearly alludes to Nietzsche's *Human,
All Too Human*. Ellis cited Nietzsche's aphorism 50, in which La
Rochefoucauld and Plato are said to have warned us against the en-
feebling effect of pity on the soul. Nietzsche adds that "one should
shew pity, but take heed not to *have* it: for the unfortunate are really
so *stupid* as to take a show of pity for the greatest good in the world"
(Ellis' translation).[47] This cynical advice to be Tartuffian in our show of

46. *Ibid.*, 196–97.
47. Wagner, *Prose Works*, VI, 197.

morality—if this is indeed Nietzsche's meaning—as well as in our show of religion does express a kind of low wisdom, since the show of compassion is often what is most called for, and it costs nothing. The true face of active compassion may deceive the beholder, for it can be as energetic, vulgar, and apparently pitiless as the face of Giotto's *Caritas* at Padua was to Marcel Proust.[48]

Many years earlier Wagner had found himself too unskilled to provide first aid at the scene of an accident. Only then, he told his biographer Carl Glasenapp, did he understand why Goethe has the peripatetic hero of *Wilhelm Meister* acquire some skill in treating wounds and travel about always equipped with a surgeon's kit. Wagner named his son Helferich ("helpful") Siegfried after Helferich the physician in his sketch *Wieland der Schmied*. An entry of September 26, 1878, in Cosima Wagner's diary reads: "[W]e resolve to have him [Helferich] trained as a surgeon so that he may become a useful and beneficent person, here in the place where his father brought a glorious ideal into being; he must of course provide aid without charging for it, thereby earning himself the right to live independently in the world and, if possible, to represent his father's ideas." How unwarlike and antimilitaristic his ideas then were is suggested by an entry of July 27, 1880, in Cosima's diary, two and a half years before Wagner's death: he tells her of his desire to go to America, perhaps to stay there, in order to put his son "out of reach of the 'horrible soldier business.'"[49] Wagner is here no battle-lusty Siegfried, but a Parsifal; he is not a warrior, but a healer who has learned from Hippocrates that the physician's first duty is to do no harm, the second to offer aid where possible.

Continuing with the "Open Letter," Wagner remarks that whereas we have little reason to hope that the Christian church will extend the scope of its compassion to embrace animal beings as long as it follows Genesis in considering them created solely for the sake of human beings, we might have expected something better from the physician.

> The physician should appear to us really as the secularized savior of life (*bürgerlicher Lebensheiland*), the immediately ascertainable benefit of

48. Proust, *A la recherche du temps perdu*, I, 81.
49. Glasenapp, *Das Leben Richard Wagners*, VI, 116–17; Cosima Wagner, *Diaries*, II, 156, 519. In Ellis' deliberately archaized translation "Wieland the Smith" (Wagner, *Prose Works*, I, 217–48), Helferich is called a "Leech," although the original has *Arzt*, the ordinary German word for a physician or doctor (Wagner, *Prose Works*, III, 178).

whose professional work is beyond all comparison. We must honor and trust what it is that gives him the means to effect our recovery from serious illnesses; medical science is therefore looked on by us as the most useful and precious of all the sciences, to whose practice and demands we are ready to make every sacrifice. For from this science issues the truly qualified practitioner of personally active compassion (*persönlich thätigen Mitleides*), elsewhere so seldom to be met with among us.[50]

Wagner thus saw that in the secularized middle-class society of nineteenth-century Lutheran Germany the physician was well on the way to occupying, as "savior" of the body, the position formerly held by the priest, the mediating "savior" of the soul. In the old aristocratic society of Europe the priest was honored (if only because of the power of the church), but the physician was often little more than a kind of superior servant. Wagner himself shared both the secularized estimate—which made the physician into the high priest of the body—of medical science and the corresponding depreciation of theological science. But he had his misgivings.

When Mephistopheles warns of the "hidden poison" [*Faust*, l. 1,986] of theology we may look on that warning as just as malicious as his doubtful praise of medicine, whose practical outcome he, to the comfort of physicians, wants to leave to the "pleasure of God" [*Faust*, l. 2,014; evidently cited, incorrectly, from memory]. But just this spiteful complacency toward medical science leads us to fear that precisely here not a "hidden" but a completely visible "poison" may be present, which the wicked rascal seeks only to conceal behind his provocative praise. In any case it is astounding that the more this "science," which is regarded as the most useful of all, seeks to withdraw itself from practical experience and base itself on ever more positive findings to attain infallibility on the path of speculative operation, the more it becomes apparent that medicine is not really a science at all. It is the practicing physician who shows us the way here. The teaching surgeons of speculative physiology may assert that these physicians are conceited, insofar as they presume to suppose that in the practice of medicine the experience available to practicing physicians alone, perhaps also the perceptive eye of the unusually gifted medical individual, and finally the deep-seated zeal of the physician to help in all possible ways the patient entrusted to his care, are more pertinent.[51]

50. Wagner, *Gesammelte Schriften und Dichtungen*, X, 198–99.
51. *Ibid.*, 199.

The "poison" in question, feared by Wagner to be working on the body of medicine, is one that kills compassion (*Mitleid, agape, caritas*). Once compassion is dead, the way is open to any kind of frightfulness, even in the benevolent realm of medicine.

> Mohammed, after he had run through all the wonders of creation, at last recognized as the most wonderful of all that human beings had compassion for each other; we presuppose this unconditionally in our physician as long as we trust ourselves to him, and we believe in him therefore, rather than in the speculative operative physiologist striving for fame and abstract knowledge in the dissecting room. But this trust too should desert us when we hear, as happened recently, that a congress of practicing physicians was so moved by fear of "science" and dread of seeming sanctimonious or superstitious that it denied the one trust-giving quality presupposed by the ill and made itself humbly subservient to speculative animal torture by declaring that practicing physicians would soon become unable to help the ill if their lordships the medical students were unable to continue operating on living animals.[52]

To Wagner's way of thinking, the last bastion of "*the religion of compassion*" (his emphasis) in our everyday life, namely the practice of medicine, had thus fallen. Compassion was being rooted out of our law books. Our medical institutes, under the pretext of humanitarian care, were "being transformed into institutes for teaching disregard for compassion." The logical next step, Wagner predicted, would be to "experiment also on human beings who chance to be unprotected—all for the sake of 'science.'"[53] This prophecy, interestingly enough, had been made four years earlier, in 1875, by the author of *Alice in Wonderland*. Calling it a fallacy to suppose that the practice of vivisection "would never be extended to include human subjects," Lewis Carroll wrote, speaking as a Samaritan:

> And surely the easy-going Levites would take an altogether new interest in this matter, could they only realise the possible advent of a day when anatomy shall claim, as legitimate subjects for experiment, first, our condemned criminals—next perhaps, the inmates of our refuges for incurables—then the hopeless lunatic, the pauper hospital-patient, and generally 'him that hath no helper'—a day when successive generations of students, trained

52. *Ibid.*, 199–200.
53. *Ibid.*, 200–201.

from their earliest years to the repression of all human sympathies, shall
have developed a new and more hideous Frankenstein—a soulless being to
whom science shall be all in all.

Engraved on the forehead of this monster, said Carroll, inverting
Terence's "Homo sum humani nil a me alienum puto," would be the
proclamation "Homo sum: quidvis humanum a me alienum puto." To
the cold eye of the new man everything human will appear utterly
alien. We see that Mary Shelley's monster was already familiar under
the name of his creator (and double) Dr. Frankenstein; unlike the
author of *The Strange Case of Dr. Jekyll and Mr. Hyde* (1886), she
had given him no name of his own. It is worth recalling that Dr.
Frankenstein, in the course of his studies at Ingolstadt, "tortured the
living animal to animate the lifeless clay [of his monstrous creation]."[54]

Wagner can therefore be, with some justice, accused of "antiscientism." But there are at least two categories here. One includes all those
who require that the findings of science conform to doctrines derived
from a literal reading of the Old Testament as the word of God. Cos-
mology, astronomy, geology, and biology are scrutinized in the light of
this demand by inquisitors who range in sophistication from Cardinal
Bellarmin (in the case of Galileo) to William Jennings Bryan (in the
Scopes case). The inquisitors in such cases enjoy the support of the
church, the state, or both—of the state alone, if the demand is that of
conformity to a certain reading of Marx, as in the Lysenko controversy in the USSR. "Antiscientists" in the second of the two categories
are less concerned with scientific knowledge as such than they are with
the uses to which it is put. More often than not they find the powers of
the state arrayed against them. Scientists unconditionally committed
to the advancement of science, whatever the means, are apt to write
off—and often in a rather bitter fashion—those who have moral
objections to the acquirement and use of scientific knowledge as no
different from antiscientists in the first category. Aside from moral objections based on humanitarian sentiments rather than on divine revelation, antiscientists in the second category often share a fear and
dislike of the many and at times quite unforeseen consequences of

54. Lewis Carroll, "Some Popular Fallacies About Vivisection," *Fortnightly Review*, XXIII (June, 1875), 845–54; Mary Shelley, *Frankenstein; or The Modern Prometheus*, in Leonard Wolf (ed.), *The Annotated Frankenstein* (New York: 1977), 68.

technological innovation—consequences of which they were aware long before Marx offered to explain how this came about.

The antivivisectionists of Victorian England, we are told by Richard D. French, "foresaw the cold, barren alienation of a future dominated by the imperatives of technique and expertise."[55] A case in point is Francis Power Cobbe. Writing in 1888, Cobbe—who was accused by his opponents of being anti-Catholic and anti-Jewish—stated that the scientific temperament was "hard and pitiless," and that this absence of compassion was reflected in the very language of science. "Men and beasts are . . . alike 'specimens' (wretched word!), and if men be ill or dying, they become 'clinical material' . . . Nor has she [science] more pity than Nature for the weak who fall in the struggle for existence."[56] (This was at the high tide of the social Darwinism that had manifested itself as the illegitimate son of Darwin's biology.) But the most eloquent expression of antiscientism of the second kind came from the pen of the humanist George Gissing in 1903.

> I hate and fear "science," because of my conviction that, for a long time to come if not for ever, it will be the remorseless enemy of mankind. I see it destroying all simplicity and gentleness of life, all the beauty of the world; I see it restoring barbarism under a mask of civilization; I see it darkening men's minds and hardening their hearts; I see it bringing about a time of vast conflicts, which will pale into significance "the thousand wars of old," and, as likely as not, will whelm all the laborious advances of mankind in blood-drenched chaos . . . Oh, the generous hopes and aspirations of forty years ago! Science was then seen as the deliverer; only a few could prophesy its tyranny, could foresee that it would revive old evils and trample on the promise of its beginning.[57]

The distinction between these two categories is evident in the dispute over Darwin's *The Origin of Species* (1859) and *The Descent of Man* (1871). While the Wilberforces of England anathematized these two books as heretical, the Cobbes supported them, insofar as they revealed the kinship between animals and human beings and made our

55. French, *Antivivisection and Medical Science in Victorian Society*, 411–12.

56. Francis Power Cobbe, "The Scientific Picture of the Age," *Contemporary Review*, LIV (July, 1888), 126–39. On Cobbe see French, *Antivivisection and Medical Science in Victorian Society*, especially p. 347.

57. George Gissing, *The Private Papers of Henry Ryecroft* (New York, 1903), 253–54.

mistreatment of them all the more inacceptable. Cobbe wrote in 1888, "Every biologist now has tenfold better reasons than had St. Francis for calling the birds and beasts 'little brothers and sisters.'" Wagner, as we have already seen, approved of Darwin, and in 1874 one of Wagner's most enthusiastic supporters (who was later to become Thomas Mann's father-in-law) told Cosima that he had discovered a link between "Darwinism" and "Wagnerianism."[58] (Curiously enough, the provivisectionist, anti-Catholic Rudolf Virchow, whose testimony blocked Ernst von Weber's antivivisection petition on the floor of the Reichstag, won reluctant praise at this time from Catholic quarters because of his strictures against those who saw Darwinism as the new revelation.[59]) The educated classes of France and Germany were at this time far less subservient to primitivistic Old Testament doctrine than was the case in England; there the so-called higher criticism of the Bible took root rather late and scantily—long after the working classes had been alienated by the Church of England's role as handmaid of the established order.[60]

With reference to a prominent German physiologist who continued to defend animal experimentation on an Old Testament basis, Schopenhauer wrote in 1839 that nothing should be more calculated to lead us to recognize the essential identity of animal beings and human beings than the study of comparative anatomy and physiology. He added: "What then are we to say to a canting animal-dissector [Rudolph Wagner] who now makes so bold as to claim that there is a radical difference between human beings and animals, and goes so far

58. Cobbe, "The Scientific Picture of the Age," 136; Cosima Wagner, *Diaries,* I, 802. Cosima notes: "Wrote to Dr. [Alfred] Pringsheim, who claims to have found the connection between Darwinism and Wagnerianism in primitive human beings who are singing." Pringsheim was a wealthy German Jewish academician. On the Pringsheims and Thomas Mann, see L. J. Rather, "The Masked Man[n]: Felix Krull is Siegfried," *Opera Quarterly,* II (Spring, 1984), 67–75.

59. *Cf.* Erwin Ackerknecht, *Rudolf Virchow: Doctor, Statesman, Anthropologist* (Madison, Wisc., 1953), 200–201. For Virchow's very provisional acceptance of Darwinian natural selection, see also L. J. Rather, *Disease, Life and Man: Selected Essays by Rudolf Virchow* (Stanford, Calif., 1958), 148.

60. Charlotte Brontë's *Shirley* (Leipzig, 1849) depicts anti–Church of England, antitechnological stance of workers in Yorkshire at the time of the Luddite riots toward the close of the Napoleonic Wars. As late as 1888 the disavowal of biblical miracles in Mrs. Humphrey Ward's novel *Robert Elsmere* drew a sharp attack by England's prime minister (temporarily out of office); see William E. Gladstone, "'Robert Elsmere' and the Battle of Belief," *Nineteenth Century,* XXIII (May, 1888), 766–88.

as to attack and calumniate the honest zoologists who go their way
with the help of nature and the truth, far from all priestly trickery, lip-
service and Tartuffianism?" In the course of a conversation with his
Jewish disciple and literary executor Julius Frauenstädt, Schopenhauer
expressed his belief that human beings had arisen from apes. "At the
right moment a chimpanzee became a human being . . . The human
being was originally black and an animal living cleanly, like the ape,
on vegetables." But, continued Schopenhauer: "Once he had forced
his way north he could no longer subsist without flesh food, and thus,
along with his clothing, took on an unclean and loathsome aspect."[61]
This account of the "descent" and subsequent perversion of man antedates Darwin's *Descent of Man* by several decades.

Wagner of course did not need Schopenhauer to inform him that
human beings were animal beings, closely related to anthropoid apes.
The *homo terribilis* or *homo troglodytes* of Linnaeus, mentioned in
Wagner's letter of 1853 to Theodor Uhlig, had been looked on by
some observers, as, if not a man, a near-relative of man. Writing in
1816, Georges Cuvier expressed his disapproval of "the grave surmises
of soi-disant philosophers, who have alarmed the rest of mankind with
the representations of their relationship to the anthropomorphous
tribes" (he himself nevertheless placed man in the class mammalia).
"The pongo seems as little like man as the most brutal of baboons,"
continued Cuvier.

> The Chimpansé, like the Orang Outang, with whose history it has been
> very generally confounded, has proved a copious source of the marvellous
> to those whose interest or whose pleasure led them to cater for the in-
> discriminating and importune appetite of credulity. It appears to have
> been . . . the *homo troglodytes* of Linnaeus. It is impossible to ascertain
> from his description whether he means to designate an animal or a man. He
> also calls him *homo nocturnus,* and attributes to him many of the pecu-
> liarities of the Albino variety of the human race.[62]

To the aborigines of Borneo who first named him, too, the orangutan
was the "man of the woods," "man's sylvan double." The notion of the

61. Schopenhauer, *Sämtliche Werke,* III, 775; Schopenhauer, *Schopenhauers Gespräche und Selbstgespräche nach der Handschrift εἰς ἑαυτον,* ed. Edward Griesbach
(Berlin, 1898), 46.
62. Georges Cuvier, *The Animal Kingdom arranged in conformity with its Organization. With Additional Descriptions of all the Species hitherto named, and of many
not before noticed,* trans. Edward Griffith *et al.* (16 vols.; London, 1827–36), I, 250.

"missing link," still alive in the popular mind as late as the 1920s, was already being exploited by P. T. Barnum in the 1840s. The point deserves emphasis, for even today we continue to be told that it was Darwin who first revealed our kinship with animals or, more narrowly, with apes.[63]

Before continuing with the "Open Letter," it is worth noting here that Walter Scott's *Count Robert of Paris* (1831), a novel that Wagner read in 1876 with "unalloyed enjoyment" (according to Cosima), features a giant orangutan appropriately called "Sylvan." Before seeing the creature, which he encounters in the dungeons of the Byzantine emperor, the crusading knight hears it speak in a "strange, chuckling voice, in a language totally unintelligible." Later, after Count Robert had succeeded in terrorizing the giant ape, its "melancholy cry . . . excited [his] compassion." Scott's rather sympathetic version of *homo terribilis* antedates by ten years the orangutan of Poe's "Murders in the Rue Morgue," and we recall that the harsh, shrill voice of this murderous creature seemed to its auditors always to be speaking in some language other than their own. Apropos of *Count Robert of Paris,* Wagner may have recognized the Frankish crusader and his equally valiant warrior-bride Brenhilda as forerunners of his own Brünnhilde and Siegfried.[64]

Continuing with his "Open Letter," Wagner manages to find some solace in that precisely at a time when experimental physiologists and pathologists assault our consciences every day in their bloody laboratories help has come from science itself—as if, Wagner adds, to con-

63. Arthur O. Lovejoy, *The Great Chain of Being* (Cambridge, Mass., 1936), 231–36. Norman O. Brown tells us that we are to "learn from Copernicus that the human world is not the purpose of the universe . . . from Darwin that man is a member of the animal kingdom; and . . . from Freud that the human ego is not even master in its own house" (Brown, *Life Against Death: The Psychoanalytical Meaning of History* [New York, 1959], 16). Freud was somewhat more knowledgeable and modest. In his discussion of these three "narcissistic illusions," as he called them, he mentioned Schopenhauer along with himself, Pythagoras and Aristarchus, and Copernicus, and noted that Darwin's belief was shared by children, *Urmenschen,* and surviving "primitives" (Sigmund Freud, "Eine Schwierigkeit in der Psychoanalyse," *Imago,* V [1917], 1–7).

64. Cosima Wagner, *Diaries,* I, 625, 907, II, 933, 936; Sir Walter Scott, *Count Robert of Paris* (2 vols.; New York, 1880), I, 365–73. Poe's Dupin in *The Murders in the Rue Morgue* refers to Cuvier for his account of the orangutan. For harmonies and parallels among Wagner's Nibelungs, Stevenson's Mr. Hyde, H. G. Wells's Morlocks, and the *homo terribilis* of Linnaeus, see Rather, "Thematic Bibliography," in *The Dream of Self-Destruction,* 203–205.

firm what Mephistopheles has to say in *Faust* of his own frustrated
activities. Not mentioning Darwin by name, Wagner tells us that an
"honest investigator, a careful breeder and a truly comparative student
and scientific friend of animals, has revealed to us once again the
teachings of forgotten primal wisdom. And has told us that the same
life breathes in us as in animals, that we are in fact undoubtedly descended from animals." Again quoting *Faust,* Wagner points out that
the scientific student of animals need not of necessity use reason only
to become "more bestial than any beast." Indeed, given the unbeliev-
ing spirit of our age, the new science of life may prove to be our surest
guide to the love of animals as our kindred, perhaps even to the only
true religion, the "love of humanity" (*Menschenliebe*). In this way we
may return to the insights of the Hindu and Buddhist sages and to
those of certain Christian saints. For, says Wagner, "Legends tell us
how the animals trustingly gathered around these saints—perhaps not
only for the protection of which they were assured but also impelled
by a deep impulse of possibly germinating compassion: here were the
wounds, perhaps also a friendly, protecting hand to be licked." [65]

At this point Wagner—like the Whites and McHargs of our day—
traces the source of the evil back to the teachings of Jewish law in its
primitive form.

> These sagas are now forgotten. In our day the Old Testament has tri-
> umphed, and out of the rending beast of prey has arisen the "reckoning"
> beast. Our credo reads: Animals are useful, particularly when, trusting in
> our protection, they submit themselves to us; let us, therefore, use them in
> any way that seems good for our purposes; we have the right to torture a
> thousand faithful dogs all day long, provided we thereby assist a human
> being to enjoy the "cannibal" well-being of "five hundred swine."
>
> Our horror at the results of this maxim could, however, not reach true
> expression until we were more precisely informed of the monstrosities
> of scientific animal torture, and we are now at last forced to answer the
> question of how—since we can find no real support in the dogmas of our
> churches—our relationship to animals can be defined in a moral and
> conscience-quieting manner. The wisdom of the Brahmans, indeed that of
> all cultured pagan peoples is lost to us. With the misunderstanding of our
> relationship to animals we see before us a world that is bestialized in the
> worst sense, indeed more than bestialized, a diabolized world. There is not
> one truth, even supposing that we are capable of understanding it, that we

65. Wagner, *Gesammelte Schriften und Dichtungen,* X, 203.

are not ready to hide from ourselves out of egoism and selfishness. For it is precisely in this that our civilization consists.[66]

Wagner's above denunciation of the Old Testament code is no more, or less, anti-Christian or anti-Jewish than are the later utterances of a White or a McHarg. It is a specific attitude toward the world, not a specific people, that is being condemned: the attitude is strikingly described by the phrase "reckoning beast of prey." This new predator, the new man, relies on calculation rather than brute force. Wagner found the phrase (*rechnendes Raubtier*) in H. Haug's eccentric interpretation of the Old Testament.[67] To Haug the biblical Joseph was the prototype of this new species, a predator who, in the service of the Pharaoh, despoiled the Egyptian peoples of their lands and reduced them to total servitude. Haug's revisionist assessment of Joseph the Provider was elaborated later by Leo Tolstoy (in 1886) and Mark Twain (in 1899), apparently quite independently of each other.[68] The phrase "reckoning beast of prey" parallels, rather strikingly, George Gissing's description in 1899 of Napoleon Bonaparte as a "wild beast with a genius for arithmetic."[69]

Wagner then moves on in the "Open Letter" to consider another aspect of our treatment of our fellow animals, namely that we—unlike our presumed anthropoid ancestors, and unlike most apes of the present day—have made animal flesh the staple article of our diet. The view taken by Wagner, namely that the eating of flesh is a crime equivalent to cannibalism in the worst case and impiety in the best, is an ancient one, the echoes of which are most familiar to us in the form transmitted in the Old Testament: flesh food is the proper diet for a *fallen* creature (animal or human). There are other similar traditions: Albrecht von Haller, the eighteenth century's most erudite anatomist and physiologist, cites the third-century Neoplatonist Porphyry as his authority for the statement that the first flesh used by man as food was

66. *Ibid.*, 202–203. Wagner's "'cannibal' well-being of 'five hundred swine'" comes from the scene in Auerbach's cellar in *Faust* (2293–94): "Uns ist ganz kannibalisch wohl, / Als wie fünfhundert Säuen!"

67. Wagner's comments on Haug's *Das alte Testament* will be found in Cosima Wagner, *Diaries*, II, 355–60.

68. Leo Tolstoy, *What Then Must We Do?*, trans. Aylmer Maude (1935; rpr. London, 1960), 139–45; Mark Twain, "Concerning the Jews," *Harper's New Monthly Magazine*, XCIX (September, 1899), 527–35.

69. Gissing, *The Crown of Life*, 197.

impiously stolen from the altars of the gods; men were thereafter unable to restrain themselves from indulging in this "barbarous delicacy." Hence, according to von Haller, the growth of anatomical knowledge, so as to fulfill the needs of a race of hunters and butchers.[70]

Wagner accepted an idea that we have already seen expressed by Schopenhauer: the migration of peoples to the less fruitful north had forced this initially abhorrent diet on them for sheer survival.

> Peoples driven into harsher climates saw themselves compelled to preserve their lives by resorting to animal foods, but until recent times they remained aware that the animal belonged not to them but to a godhead. They knew that they were guilty of an impiety when they killed or slaughtered an animal, and that to make atonement they had to approach the god. And so they sacrificed the animal and thanked the god with an offering of the choicest parts of the booty. What was here a religious feeling lived on after the corruption of religions in philosophers of later times as a humanly dignified conviction. Let one read Plutarch's fine essay "On Reason in Land and Sea Animals," and then, fairly taught, return with shame to the views of our scholars and such.
>
> Thus far, and unfortunately no farther, can we follow the traces of our ancestors' religiously-based compassion for animals, and it seems that just as the advance of civilization made the human being indifferent to "the god" so it transformed him into a rending beast of prey.[71]

The characterization of man as a beast of prey unique in that it preys also on its own kind is already implicit in the adage "man is a wolf to man" (*homo homini lupus*) of Plautus. The phrase "beast of prey"—whether of the rending or reckoning variety—was in use in Germany, as we shall see in a later chapter, to characterize the human animal long before Darwin wrote. Its best known expression in the English-speaking world is that of William James in 1904: "Man, biologically considered . . . is the most formidable of all beasts of prey, and, indeed, the only one that preys systematically on its own species."[72] Nietzsche's outpourings, misunderstood, on the subject of the "blond beast" seemed to affirm this aspect of human behavior. A fe-

70. Rather, *The Genesis of Cancer*, 46; *cf.* Daniel A. Dombrowski, "Vegetarianism and the Argument from Marginal Cases in Porphyry," *Journal of the History of Ideas*, XLV (January, 1984), 141–43.

71. Wagner, *Gesammelte Schriften und Dichtungen*, X, 202.

72. William James, "Remarks at the Peace Banquet," *Atlantic Monthly*, XCIV (December, 1904), 845–47.

male character in Gissing's *Our Friend the Charlatan* (1901) predicts that Nietzsche will "do a great deal of harm in the world. . . . The jingo impulse and all sorts of forces making for animalism will get strength from him, directly or indirectly." Such was indeed the case, and, if we are to believe a French observer writing in 1910, President Theodore Roosevelt was persuaded to exhort the male citizenry of the United States to "choose as its ideal the veritable *Uebermensch*—the Warrior—of Nietzsche, to become a conquering people, a predatory race (*race de proie*)." These were dangerous words at a time when, as William James himself wrote in 1910, whole nations were in arms, and "the science of destruction vies in intellectual refinement with the sciences of production." [73]

The transformation of prehistoric man, nourished at first largely on fruits and plants, into a flesh-eating beast of prey brought with it "diseases and woes of all kinds, to which human beings who nourished themselves on vegetable products alone do not appear to have been exposed," the "Open Letter" continues. And it is precisely for such as these that "our physiologists vivisect animals, inject them with poisons . . . and artificially prolong their torment to learn, perhaps, how long they may keep the wretch from his last agony!" Money is required to purchase these dubious medical benefits. But, says Wagner, we cannot suppose that so much science would be used for the benefit of our poor workers. Instead, the "poor laborer who suffers from hunger, want and the over-taxing of his powers . . . is often made the object of highly interesting experiments aimed at the understanding of certain physiological problems: the poor are thus made to serve the rich in dying as well as while living." Wagner wishes that the "apes scrambling up the tree of knowledge" would look for once into the eyes of their experimental animals, and from there into the eyes of their "suffering fellow human beings born in naked need, condemned from early childhood on to health-shattering overwork," and, if nothing else, at least recognize the presence of another human being. They might then take action to restore the laborer's shattered health by "giving him the excess of food that had made the rich man ill." [74]

73. Jean Bourdeau, *Les maîtres de la pensée contemporaine* (Paris, 1910), 146; Gissing, *Our Friend the Charlatan*, ed. Pierre Coustillas (Rutherford, N.J., 1976), 25; William James, "The Moral Equivalent of War," *McClure's Magazine*, XXXV (August, 1910) 463–68.
74. Wagner, *Gesammelte Schriften und Dichtungen*, X, 204–208, *passim*.

Worth noting here is Wagner's conditional approval of extralegal violence to free the animals held captive in the laboratories. After calling for us to bethink ourselves, to undergo a conversion (*Umkehr*), he continues.

> Should not the horror surely felt by everyone at the use of the most unthinkable torture of animals for the supposed benefit of our health—the worst thing we could have in such a heartless world!—of itself have brought about such a conversion, or did we first find it necessary to learn that this utility was mistaken . . . ? Were we to wait until the sacrifice to "utility" extended to human vivisection also? Are the needs of the state to be placed above the needs of the individual? A Visconti, Duke of Milan, once ordered that political offenders be punished in such a way that their death agonies would stretch out for forty days. This man would seem to have given in advance a norm for our physiologists; they too know how to prolong the tortures of a soundly qualified animal for exactly forty days in favorable cases, although less from cruelty than from calculating parsimony. Visconti's edict was approved by state and church, since no one protested against it; only those who considered that to endure the frightful torment threatened was not the worst of all possible evils were driven to seize the state, in the person of my lord Visconti, by the throat. May the newer state itself take the place of these "political criminals" and simply throw my lords vivisectors, those disgracers of humanity, out of their laboratories. Or should we again leave this to "enemies of the state," as the so-called "socialists" are indeed called in the latest legislation? And indeed we learn—while state and church break their heads as to whether they should look into our ideas, or whether the possible anger of offended "science" is more to be feared—of a violent invasion of just such a vivisection laboratory in Leipzig . . . that has been ascribed to a raw outbreak of subversive socialistic agitation against the rights of property. But who would not become a socialist when he finds that our measures against the continuation of vivisection, and our demand for its absolute abolition are rejected by both state and Reich?[75]

This passage, it should be remembered, was written after the refusal of the Reichstag (prompted by Rudolf Virchow as spokesman for science) to permit Ernst von Weber's petition to be debated on the floor of that assembly.

The "Open Letter" contains Wagner's credo, which was to be given expression three years later in the first performance of *Parsifal:* "knowing through compassion" (*durch Mitleid wissend,* as Gurnemanz says).

75. *Ibid.,* 208–209.

The passage is given emphasis in the original: "As for human dignity our conclusion may be stated as follows. Human dignity first manifests itself precisely at the point where human beings are able to distinguish themselves from animals through compassion for the [other] animals as well; contrariwise, once we treat animals in a manner both reasonable and worthy of human dignity we can learn from them compassion for human beings." Wagner closes the "Open Letter" with a citation, apparently from memory, from Goethe's *Faust:* If the German antivivisectionists continue to be scorned and rejected by the intelligentsia, they will at least have the satisfaction of having separated themselves from a world in which "no dog would care to live any longer." [76]

Wagner's rejection of the "cult of utility"—the idol worship of the modern national state—has a close parallel in the writings of Ludwig Feuerbach, the philosopher whom he forsook in the early 1850s for Schopenhauer. Feuerbach's *Das Wesen des Christentums* was published in 1841 and translated as *The Essence of Christianity* by George Eliot thirteen years later. The Jewish God, who is also God of the Christians, represents, according to Feuerbach, the outwardly projected reification of a more or less integrated set of human passions, impulses, and ideas. The Yahweh of Genesis 2 : 6–23, who created the world for the sake of man, and only later—after none of the animals proved to be a "help meet" for Adam—created woman (also for the sake of man), is egoism personified.

> The [Christian] doctrine of creation comes from Judaism; it is the characteristic doctrine, the fundamental doctrine of the Jewish religion. The principle on which it is based is not so much the principle of subjectivity as it is that of egoism. The doctrine of creation in its characteristic form arises only at the point where man subjects nature for all practical purposes only to his will and needs, and hence also demotes his power of ideation to a mere piece of botchwork, a product of the will. . . . Utility (*Utilismus*), profit, is the highest principle of Judaism. The belief in a special divine Providence is the characteristic belief of Judaism; belief in Providence is the belief in the miraculous; but it is in the belief in the miraculous that nature is seen as only an object of the caprice, of the egoism, that uses nature only for arbitrary purposes. The waters divide or come together . . . the sun

76. *Ibid.*, 209–210. Faust, in the opening monologue, says of his desiccated world: "Es möchte kein Hund so länger leben!" Wagner has "kein Hund länger mehr leben möchte."

stands still in its course. . . . And all these unnatural things happen for the benefit of Israel, merely at the command of Jehovah, who is concerned only with Israel, who is nothing other than the personified selfishness of the Israelite people, to the exclusion of all other peoples, intolerance absolute—the secret of monotheism.[77]

This and nothing more is what Wagner means when he speaks of our "Old Testament-judaized" world—a world in which no dog would care to live (or for that matter, any other animal). This world is the lowest common denominator of Judaism, Christianity, and Islam, three religions sharing in common a base in the Old Testament, for the believers in all three sects are only too ready, in any sort of pinch, to throw off the restraints imposed by the later Hebrew prophets, by teachers such as Hillel, by the founders of Christianity and Islam, and by sundry Jewish, Christian, and Islamic commentators on the ferocious volcano-god of Moses and Joshua. This "God of Hosts" commands and approves deeds that are no less bloody and cruel today than they were when Joshua led the Hebrews into the promised land and slaughtered its inhabitants wholesale. To Wagner the modern warfare state is the reified ego of its people; science, the "daimon" of the state cult of utility, now miraculously intervenes with its columns of fire and smoke to guide the chosen people on its way. But there are too many such states and too little room on the earth. The end will be, as Tolstoy wrote in 1904 at the height of the Russo-Japanese War, that they will destroy each other "like spiders in a jar."[78]

One of the many disastrous consequences of the German attempt to usurp the position of the "chosen race" accorded to the ancient Hebrews by the writers of the Old Testament has been to persuade many people today, not all of them Jews, that adverse criticism of any aspect of Old Testament Judaism (and even of the modern state of Israel) is anti-Semitism and nothing more. It is true, as we have seen, that the conflict between defenders of the rights of animals and upholders of orthodox Jewish slaughtering procedures in the late nineteenth century was marred by the charge that one of the defenders was motivated by

77. Ludwig Feuerbach, *Das Wesen des Christentums*, in *Sämtliche Werke*, ed. Wilhelm Bolin and Friedrich Jodl (13 vols. in 12; Stuttgart, 1959–64), VI, 135–36; *cf.* Feuerbach, *The Essence of Christianity*, trans. George Eliot (New York, 1957), 112–14.
78. Leo Tolstoy, "Bethink Yourselves!" in *Recollections and Essays*, 226.

"envenomed anti-Semitism." But in our day, especially where Wagner is concerned, the conflict between critics and defenders of Old Testament doctrine has become far more bitter, and all critics run the risk of being charged with anti-Semitism. The most elaborate and far-reaching case of this kind against Wagner was made in 1950 by Leon Stein in his book *The Racial Thinking of Richard Wagner*.[79]

Stein, a well-known musicologist, begins by citing an "interesting instance of Schopenhauer's virulent anti-Semitism" from the pages of *On the Basis of Morality*. In the translation cited by Stein the passage reads: "The assumption that animals have no rights, the idea that our conduct toward them is without moral significance, or that there is literally no such thing as duty to animals is an absolutely revolting barbarism whose source resides in Judaism." Stein next asserts that "such passages as Exodus XXIII, 12; Deuteronomy XXII, 4; Isaiah I, 3; the 23rd Psalm (The Lord is My Shepherd); Job I-II completely refute this calumny." Moving then from Schopenhauer to Wagner, Stein writes: "That Wagner was familiar with this essay [*On the Basis of Morality*] is evidenced by his Open Letter to Ernst von Weber. . . . The statement that 'pity is the only true foundation of morality' is taken directly from Schopenhauer's essay . . . a thesis limited to animals—certainly it would not apply to Catholics, Jews, or to other composers." Finally, after scrutinizing Wagner's essay "Judaism in Music" (1850) in the light of what took place a century later, Stein concludes that the Wagnerian attitude towards Jews in Germany pointed irrevocably in one direction: to "Hitler, the laws of Nuremberg . . . and the ovens of Auschwitz."[80]

The passage from Schopenhauer's essay on morality that so offended Stein was cited earlier in the present chapter, and the reader will recall that it continues with the claim that the philosophical, as opposed to the religious, basis of the denial of rights to animals was most vividly expressed by Descartes. The passages Stein cites from the Old Testament, or Hebrew Bible, overlap those cited by Aquinas in the same connection. We recall also that Aquinas looked on any injunction against cruelty to animals in the sacred Scriptures as designed solely for the benefit of man, and that he branded the claim that we are morally unjustified in using animals at our pleasure a theological error.

79. Leon Stein, *The Racial Thinking of Richard Wagner* (New York, 1950).
80. *Ibid.*, 34, 176. Cf. Rather, *The Dream of Self-Destruction*, 96–98, 102.

We have also seen that Saint Thomas anticipated the "clockwork" animal of Descartes. But there was also a Saint Francis, who looked on
animals as his brothers and sisters. It seems likely that we would find
Franciscans as well as Thomists among the Talmudic commentators
on the passages referred to by Stein.

CHAPTER FIVE

ASPECTS OF PRO- AND ANTI-JUDAISM IN THE NINETEENTH CENTURY

> Then Ezekiel said: ". . . we so loved our God, that we cursed in his name all the deities of the surrounding nations, and asserted that they had rebelled: from these opinions the vulgar came to think that all nations would at last be subject to the jews."
>
> "This," he said, "like all firm perswasions, is come to pass; for all nations believe the jews' code and worship the jews' god, and what greater subjection can be?"
>
> William Blake
> *The Marriage of Heaven and Hell*

WAGNER'S CHRISTIANITY

Wagner's parents were Lutheran Christians. He himself, so he tells us in his autobiography, was baptized at the Lutheran *Thomaskirche* (St. Thomas Church) in Leipzig on May 24, 1813, two days after his birth.[1] This was a faulty recollection, since, as Newman and others have pointed out, the baptism actually took place on August 16.[2] On August 26, 1813, in nearby Dresden, Napoleon won the last of his bloody victories. We recall the horrified response of E. T. A. Hoffmann, three days later, to the sights and sounds of the field of slaughter.[3] The battle of Leipzig, in which Napoleon was defeated by the combined armies of Russia, Prussia, and Austria, took place in mid-October. Wagner's father, who was police registrar of Leipzig, died during the epidemic of fever that raged through the devastated city. Wagner calls it "nerve-fever" (*Nervenfieber*) in his autobiography (it was either ty-

---

1. Wagner, *Mein Leben*, I, 9.
2. *Ibid.*, II, 811*n*; Newman, *The Life of Richard Wagner*, I, 13.
3. See Chapter 1 herein.

phoid or typhus, more likely the latter).[4] Wagner's widowed mother became the wife of Ludwig Christian Geyer nine months after her husband's death. With her six surviving children (one child died in January, 1814) she then moved to Dresden, where Geyer held a position as actor at the Dresden Court Theater.

Ludwig Geyer, who came of a family that had been Protestant for generations, was baptized at Eisleben (Luther's birthplace in Saxony) on January 23, 1779.[5] Wagner has nothing to say in his autobiography of his stepfather's piety or lack of it, but he tells us that his mother was in the habit of regaling her children with "longish, pathos-filled, sermon-like discourses on God and on the divine in human beings," interrupted from time to time by "humorous" asides on her part. Wagner was confirmed at the Church of the Cross (*Kreuzkirche*) in Dresden on Easter, 1827. He writes in his autobiography: "The boy who had gazed with painful longing at the altarpiece in the *Kreuzkirche,* and yearned ecstatically and enthusiastically to take the place of the savior on the cross, had by now so far lost respect for the pastor, whose preparatory classes he attended before confirmation, that he willingly joined in the mockery of the pastor and, together with some comrades united in this purpose, spent part of the fee due him on sweets." When the actual ceremony took place, however, Wagner says that he was deeply moved. "What my real feelings were, in spite of all this, I learned almost to my horror as the call for distribution of the Lord's Supper sounded forth from the organ and choir, and as I moved forward in the procession of candidates toward the altar. The shudder of emotion when the bread and wine were offered and taken remained so unforgettable in my memory that in order to rule out a lesser impression I never again partook of communion, which was possible for me because there is of course no such requirement for Protestants."[6] One wonders if Wagner, perhaps with the concluding scene of *Parsifal* in mind, touched up this recollection in retrospect. In any case, it is plain that he is recalling the experience as one of *aesthetic* rather than *religious* character.

In 1848 Wagner sketched out a five-act drama entitled *Jesus of Nazareth* and provided it with an elaborate commentary. For reasons

4. Wagner, *Mein Leben*, I, 9. Typhoid and typhus fevers had not been distinguished clearly.

5. Newman, *The Life of Richard Wagner*, I, 18 n. 2.

6. Wagner, *Mein Leben*, I, 18, 27.

that will be explained shortly, he put the project aside and went to work on *The Ring of the Nibelung*. The sketch and its commentary were not published until four years after his death.[7] Wagner says in his autobiography that in 1849 he described the proposed drama to Franz Liszt and the Princess Caroline von Wittgenstein. "I saw Liszt lapse into doubtful silence," Wagner writes, "while the Princess protested vigorously against any plan to bring such material on the stage." A little earlier he had received a similarly negative response, although quite differently motivated, from Mikhail Bakunin. Wagner writes: "Inspired by a recent reading of the gospels, I had at that time just produced a sketch for a tragedy to be performed in the ideal theater of the future and to be entitled *Jesus of Nazareth;* Bakunin asked me to spare him any details about it; yet as I seemingly won him over by saying a few words about my general plan, he wished me luck but requested me with great vehemence to make certain Jesus would be represented as a weak character."[8] If Bakunin had been gifted with foresight, he would have seen his own fate curiously forshadowed by the fate of Barabbas in Wagner's proposed drama.[9]

The sketch in *Jesus of Nazareth* opens with an interchange between the "fiery patriot" Barabbas and his compatriot Judas Iscariot. Both men are in favor of mounting an armed insurrection against the Roman forces occupying Judea. Barabbas asks Judas whether Jesus, now proclaimed the son of David, is the long-awaited Jewish Messiah. Judas cannot answer the question; he knows only that Jesus is a highly-skilled healer. When Barabbas confronts Jesus with this question he is told to render Caesar what is Caesar's due. Disappointed by the answer, Barabbas then decides to mount the revolt himself. He leads a handful of his followers against the troops of Pilate; the revolt is quickly suppressed and the captured Barabbas is condemned to death by crucifixion. Meanwhile the high priest Caiaphas and the elders of Zion have concluded that Jesus is a greater threat than Barabbas to their own position. They plot to betray Jesus to the Romans, on the one hand, and on the other to reveal his "foolishness" (*Torheit*) to the

7. Richard Wagner, *Jesus von Nazareth. Ein dichterischer Entwurf aus dem Jahre 1848* (Leipzig, 1887); "Jesus of Nazareth," in Richard Wagner, *Prose Works*, VIII, 284–340.

8. Wagner, *My Life*, trans. Gray, 387, 413.

9. Bakunin was captured, imprisoned, and condemned to death by the Saxon authorities in 1849. The sentence of death was commuted, however, and Bakunin was turned over to the Russian authorities, who eventually exiled him to Siberia.

Jews—most of whom still remain convinced that Jesus is their promised earthly Messiah. Jesus then makes his triumphal entry into Jerusalem. He drives the money changers from the temple and proclaims his
true mission: he has come to redeem *all* peoples, not the Jews alone, by
sacrificing himself, and his kingdom is *not* of this world. The horrified
Jews fall into the utmost confusion. Jesus disappears in the tumult, and
his disciples try in vain to explain the true nature of his mission on
earth. There follows the Last Supper, the betrayal of Jesus to the Romans by Judas, the death sentence, and the offer of Pilate to free one or
the other of the two condemned men. Caiaphas, the elders, and the
Jewish people as a whole call for the release of Barabbas. Jesus is cru-
cified, and Peter announces that the promise of redemption has been
fulfilled.[10]

Wagner's extensive commentary on *Jesus of Nazareth* is several
times the length of the sketch itself. One passage is of particular interest
in that it foreshadows Wagner's later commitment to nonviolence in
Parsifal and, more explicitly, in his essay "Religion and Art" (1880).[11]
Wagner writes:

> When Jesus was baptized by John he was accepted by the Jewish people as
> the heir of David. But Jesus withdrew to the wilderness and took counsel
> with himself. Should he assert his Davidic origin, in the sense understood
> by the people? Were he to be successful [as earthly Messiah], what would
> he be other than a fellow to the great ones of the world who draw their
> support from the rich and heartless? Yet could he not, as scion of the oldest
> race (*Geschlecht*), lay claim to supreme domination of the world; could he
> not threaten the base Roman rule of violence? Were he to succeed, would
> the exchange of violence for violence—under a different (perhaps juster)
> name—be of advantage to humanity?

The exchange of the violent rule of one faction (the Romans) for the
violent rule of another (the Jews) would leave humanity as a whole no
better off than before. This, at least, is the answer of Wagner's Jesus
to the question posed. An earthly Messiah of the Jews might well
lead them into a triumphant battle against their foes. But the Jesus of

10. Wagner, *Jesus von Nazareth*, 1–21, *passim*. Barabbas "made insurrection"
and "committed murder in the insurrection," according to Mark 15:7.

11. In *Parsifal* Wagner implicitly extends the rule of nonviolence to cover the world
of animal as well as of human beings (*cf.* Gurnemanz's reproaching of Parsifal for the
"murder" of the swan in act 1). For citations illustrative of Wagner's strongly antiwar
stance, see Rather, "Tolstoy and Wagner: The Shared Vision," and Rather, *The Dream
of Self-Destruction*, 173–79.

the gospels preaches a kingdom *not* of this world to *all* its peoples. Wagner adds: "And so Jesus cast off his Davidic origin; through Adam he was of God, and all human beings were now his brothers."[12]

Wagner repeatedly emphasizes the absolute incompatibility of Mosaic "law" and Christian "love" in his commentary on *Jesus of Nazareth*. Mosaic law, Wagner says, is "loveless." It is motivated by external compulsion, where love operates as a spontaneous impulse from within. Further, Moses was lawgiver to the Jews alone, to the chosen race, whereas Christ's love "extended . . . to the whole human race." Self-love, love of one's family, love of one's tribe, nation, or country— these are, according to Wagner, the successive steps toward universal love taken by the human race as a whole. Using a Hegelian technical term, Wagner then calls for the transcendental overthrow (*Aufhebung*) of Mosaic law. Only by doing so, Wagner writes, can "the reconciliation of the world" be brought about.[13]

In the sketch for *Jesus of Nazareth*, we recall, Judas tells Barabbas that Jesus is a skilled healer. In this role, however, Wagner's Jesus reminds us less of the first-century worker of miraculous cures depicted in the gospels than of a nineteenth-century German naturopath. Wagner's Jesus says (in the commentary):

> The physicians come and boast of their science, which understands nothing. They do not or cannot see where the root of the ailment is seated, and they take from the ill and hungry that which preserves the last remnants of health. My medicine is simple. Live in accordance with my commandment and you will need no physician. Therefore I say to you that if your bodies are disordered, see to it that your children are sound and do not inherit your infirmities. Live actively in the community. Do not say "This is mine," but say "all is ours." Thus you will grow healthy and none will starve. The ailments that will yet visit you from nature are readily cured. Does not each animal in the forest know the herb that will be of use to it? . . . But your eye is blind and you cannot see what is simplicity itself as long as you pursue the path of gluttony and want, of usury and starvation.[14]

The above passage anticipates by thirty years a passage in the third act of *Parsifal*. "Each finds herbs and roots for himself; we learn this from the animals of the forest," Gurnemanz tells Kundry in explaining to her why the "Arabian Balsam" she had brought on a previous occa-

12. Wagner, *Jesus von Nazareth*, 22–25, *passim* (see note 96 following.)
13. *Ibid.*, 63, 67–68.
14. *Ibid.*, 44–45.

sion to relieve the pain of the Grail-king's unhealing wound will no longer be needed.[15]

One final passage from the commentary must be cited. It has to do with the prohibition of oaths in the New Testament. Jesus said, "Again, ye have heard that it hath been said by them of old time, Thou shalt not forswear thyself, but shalt perform unto the Lord thine oaths: But I say unto you, swear not at all" (Matthew 5 : 33–34 [AV]). Wagner interprets these words in the light of what he sees as the Christian freedom to do as love commands us.

> In a world that did not know love the binding law was the oath. Let each human being be free to act at all times according to love and his capacity. When bound by an oath I am not free. If in fulfilling the oath I do good, the fulfillment loses value (as does every enforced good), the value of conviction; if the oath causes me to do evil, I sin with conviction. The oath engenders every vice. If I am bound by it to my disadvantage I will try to circumvent it (thus every law is circumvented). Because of the oath, that which I might rightly do in pursuit of my advantage becomes a crime; and if I find the oath advantageous to me (without disadvantaging my opponent) I rob myself of the moral satisfaction of acting at all times in keeping with my sense of what is right.[16]

We shall return to this subject in connection with Tolstoy's exegesis, forty years later, of the prohibition of oaths found in the Sermon on the Mount.

In what higher power, if any, did Wagner believe? "I believe in God, Mozart and Beethoven" was the credo uttered by the expiring German musician in Wagner's story "An End in Paris" (1841). It was no doubt Wagner's credo as well, and the linkage of three names in this fashion implicitly rules out belief in a transcendental deity. In this connection, an interchange of letters that took place in 1853 between Franz Liszt and Wagner is most revealing. Wagner was living in bitter exile at the time. Liszt wrote a consolatory letter from Weimar on April 8, 1853. A devout Catholic, Liszt admonished Wagner as follows: "Your greatness makes also for your misery—both are inseparably intertwined and cannot but torment and martyr you . . . until you sink down in *belief* and allow both to rise up!" (Liszt was asking Wagner to do what

15. William Ashton Ellis may have been the first to note this parallel; *cf.* Wagner, *Prose Works*, VIII, 310.

16. Wagner, *Jesus von Nazareth*, 26–27. Part of this passage is incorrectly translated by Ellis in Wagner, *Prose Works*, VIII, 299.

Nietzsche, nearly thirty years later, would claim that Wagner actually had done, in *Parsifal*). Obviously aware that Wagner was not a professing Christian, Liszt added, "However bitterly you may mock this feeling, I cannot but long for it and see in it the sole salvation."[17]

Wagner replied on April 13, 1853, that "mockery" was the last thing that any of Liszt's heartfelt utterances would ever elicit from him. He felt at one with Liszt in substance, if not in form. "The forms," Wagner wrote, "through which we seek to win consolation for our unhappy states of being take shape entirely in accord with our nature, our need, and the character of our culture, of our more or less artistic feelings; who could wish to be so loveless as to believe that in him alone the solely valid form has taken shape?" Wagner continues:

> Behold, my friend, I too harbor a strong belief, but one because of which I am bitterly mocked by our politicians and jurists: I believe in the future of the human race, and I derive this belief simply from my need. I have succeeded in grasping the manifestations of nature and history with such impartiality and love for their true character that I am unable to recognize anything evil in them other than—*lovelessness*. And this lovelessness I can explain to myself only as *going-astray* (*Verirrung*), a going-astray that has to lead us from the natural state of unconsciousness to knowledge of the uniquely sublime necessity of love. To attain this knowledge is the goal of world history.[18]

Whether or not Wagner had the *Divine Comedy* in mind at the time, the above passage sounds the chords that begin and end Dante's account of his long journey.[19]

In 1853 then, Wagner pinned such faith as he had on the human race and its ability—operating under the sign of love—to better its condition. He was what is today called a humanist. Given his commitment to compassionate love, Wagner can justifiably be called a Christian humanist. Although he himself had no faith in the transcendental

17. Wagner, *Briefe in Originalausgaben*, IX, 226–27.
18. *Ibid.*, 230–31. *Cf.* Henri Lichtenberger's comments on this letter, in his *Richard Wagner poète et penseur*, 199–201.
19. Wagner's use of the word *Verirrung* ("going-astray") recalls the word used in the third verse of the opening stanza of Dante's poem in the German translation at his disposal in Dresden. The line reads "Weil ich vom rechten weg verirrt mich hätte" (*i.e.*, "Because I had gone astray from the right path"). Further, the closing line of the *Divine Comedy* ("the love that moves the sun and other stars") gives the goal of world-history described in Wagner's letter to Liszt.

God of the Old and New Testaments, Wagner retained throughout his life the high estimate of Christian universalism that is present by implication in *Jesus of Nazareth*. In 1865, in an essay entitled "What Is German?," Wagner stated, "The Christian religion pertains to no one national tribe of people (*nationalen Volksstamme*): Christian teaching addresses itself to purely human nature" (*die reinmenschliche Natur*).[20] And in 1881, after some words of praise for the religion of the ancient Aryans of India, Wagner adds, "Its sole defect was that it was a race-religion" ("Sie hatte den einzigen Fehler, dass sie eine Racen-Religion war").[21] "The purely-human" (*Das Reinmenschliche*) was and remained Wagner's ideal, rather than any fancied purity of race. On this phraseology see the notes.[22]

The Christian religious trappings of Wagner's *Parsifal* (1882) were so utterly unlike the pagan trappings of the *Ring*—produced in its entirety at Bayreuth for the first time only six years before *Parsifal*—that he was thought by some of his admirers to have returned to the bosom of the Christian church. One of these admirers was Nietzsche, who now broke completely with Wagner. Nietzsche's poem "To Richard Wagner" (written probably as early as 1882) expresses his distaste for the religious atmosphere of Wagner's *Parsifal* and celebrates his own narrow escape from Klingsor's spell. The poem reads, in part:

> Woe! That even you sank down before the Cross!
> Even you! Even you—vanquished!
>
> For long I stood before this play,
> Breathing confinement, sorrow and anger, and the tomb,
> Between clouds of incense and church perfumes
> To me strange, to me gruesome and frightening.
> Dancing, I throw my fool's cap in the air,
> For I escaped!

20. Wagner, "Was ist deutsch?," in *Gesammelte Schriften und Dichtungen*, X, 40.

21. Wagner, "Heldenthum und Christenthum," *ibid.*, X, 281. *Cf.* "Hero-Dom and Christendom," in Wagner, *Prose Works*, VI, 281.

22. In German *Mensch* means a "human being," without regard to sex; *Menschlichkeit*, the abstract substantive derived from it, means "humaneness" (or "humanity," in its special sense). Goethe used the phrase *reine Menschlichkeit* and similar phrases, so also did Schelling. Wagner and his contemporaries took up these phrases (for another instance see note 88, this chapter). *S.v. Mensch* and *Menschlichkeit* in Keith Spalding, *An Historical Dictionary of German Figurative Usage* (Oxford, 1959–   ). Carried by speakers of Yiddish-German, *Mensch* has made its way into the English language. In *A*

And in a second poem entitled "Parsifal-Music" and written at about the same time, Nietzsche calls the music of *Parsifal* "sugar-sweet," "nun-eyed," and "sultry-screeching." He asks, rhetorically, whether such music could have come from a truly German heart. The closing lines indicate that the cross before which Wagner supposedly prostrated himself was a Catholic one (Nietzsche, like Wagner, was a Lutheran by religious upbringing). "For what you hear is Rome / *Rome's belief without words*" (Nietzsche's emphasis).[23]

Nietzsche, implacably anti-Christian in his later years, seems to have thought that Wagner had heretofore been worshipping at the foot of a pagan German oak. Perhaps he had seen Wagner's Siegfried as a preliminary version of his own soon to be forthcoming superman, blond beast, and anti-Christ. To Wagner, however, Christ, Siegfried, and Parsifal were three aspects of the same mythic figure. In 1848, in an essay on the historical-mythic background of the story of Siegfried and the Nibelung's hoard, Wagner asserted that medieval German and Frankish poets had re-embodied Siegfried's quest for the hoard in Parsifal's quest for the Holy Grail. "The Grail," he writes, "must be seen as the ideal representative and successor of the Nibelung's hoard."[24] And in 1851, in his essay "A Communication to my Friends," Wagner wrote that he had put aside unfinished a drama of redemption based on the life of Jesus of Nazareth, because of possible misunderstanding

---

Supplement to the Oxford English Dictionary (1976), vol. II, it is defined as a "person of integrity or rectitude." The earliest citation given is from Saul Bellow's *Adventures of Augie March* (1953), the latest from the *New Yorker* of June 24, 1972: "What is a *mensch?* . . . It means you're a substantial human being."

23. Friedrich Nietzsche, *Gedichte und Sprüche* (Leipzig, 1916), 115–16 (my translation). In Nietzsche's *Parsifal-Musik* we have the lines:

> Dies zuckersüsse Bimbambaumeln?
> Dies Nonnen-Augen, Ave-Glocken bimmeln?
> Dies ganze falsch verzuckte Himmeln-Ueberhimmeln?

Cf. Mephistopheles' reply to Faust's irritation at the continual ringing of the Angelus:

> Wer leugnet's! Jedem edlen Ohr
> Kommt das Geklingel widrig vor.
> Und das verfluchte Bim-Bam-Bimmel,
> Umnebelnd heitern Abendhimmel
> (*Faust*, 11261–64)

24. Wagner, "Die Wibelungen," in *Gesammelte Schriften und Dichtungen*, II, 151–52.

on the part of the public; he had decided to embody the myth of human redemption in the story of Siegfried.[25] *Parsifal* was aptly called "a
re-interpretation, from the natural [realm] to the moral, of the meaning of the *Ring*" by Otto Weininger in 1903.[26] And the Freudian ana-
lyst Sabina Spielrein, in 1912, pointed to what she saw as a striking
resemblance between the "Oriental Christ" of the New Testament and
the "Nordic Siegfried" of Wagner's *Ring*.[27] Having long since been
made plain by Wagner, this insight hardly called for the refined procedure of the psychoanalyst. One had only to read what Wagner had
written more than a half-century earlier.

THE DIALECTIC OF KIERKEGAARD'S ANTI-JUDAISM

Of the four men whose attitude toward Judaism will be examined in
this and the following section, two—Søren Kierkegaard and Karl Marx
—were born in 1813 (the year of Wagner's birth). The other two—
Moses Hess and Benjamin Disraeli—were born, respectively, one year
earlier and nine years earlier. Kierkegaard (1813–1855) was Danish
by birth and Lutheran by religious upbringing. The father of Karl Marx
was a German Jew who converted to Lutheran Christianity in 1824;
Marx himself (1813–1883) became a professed atheist in his early
years and remained one until his death. Moses Hess (1812–1875),
who was successively to become a forerunner of Marxian thought and
a pioneer of Zionism, was born into a long-established family of Orthodox Jews who lived in the German Rhineland. Benjamin Disraeli
(1804–1881), by birth an English Jew, was baptized an Anglican
Christian in 1817, at the behest of his father, Isaac D'Israeli. The views
of Kierkegaard, Marx, and Wagner on the nature of Judaism variously
overlap, as we shall see in this chapter. Disraeli exalted the Jewish race,
as he called it, in his fictional and nonfictional writings of the 1840s
and 1850s, and he was perhaps the first to claim that race is the motivating force of human history. Marx, of course, held that class was

25. Wagner, "Eine Mittheilung an meine Freunde," *ibid.*, IV, 331–32, 343.
26. Otto Weininger, "Zum Parsifal," in *Über die letzten Dinge* (6th ed.; Vienna,
1920), 92. Siegfried's role as Grail-seeker was recognized by Jessie L. Weston in *The
Legends of the Wagner Drama* (1903) but lost sight of in her *From Ritual to Romance*
(1920).
27. Sabina Spielrein, "Die Destruktion als Ursache des Werdens," *Jahrbuch für
psychoanalytische und psychopathologische Forschungen*, IV (1912), 464–503. *Cf.*
Rather, *The Dream of Self-Destruction*, 203.

that motivating force. Hess championed class during his Marxian phase, and race during his subsequent Zionist phase.

It is to Søren Kierkegaard's diaries (or journals) rather than to any of the works published during his short lifetime that we must turn to find explicitly stated his analysis of the dialectical opposition between Christianity—"true" Christianity, as he sees it—and Judaism. These journals have become available in their entirety only within recent years, although selections from them appeared (in Danish) as early as 1869. A complete edition, including the journals and posthumous papers, began to appear in 1909, but it was 1948 before all twenty volumes had been published. A German translation of this edition by Hayo Gerdes is now available; it includes five volumes of diaries proper and was published between 1962 and 1974. Ronald G. Smith's English translation of the later journals (1853–1855) appeared in 1965. The most complete selection of Kierkegaard's journals and posthumous papers in English (conveniently arranged according to topics) is the four-volume translation by Howard V. and Edna H. Hong, assisted by Gregor Malantschuk.[28] According to Walter Lowrie, writing in 1938, "Kierkegaard was first made known to the European world outside Scandinavia by the publication of Brandes' Literary Character-Sketch in German in 1879."[29] General interest in Kierkegaard among the American public largely postdates the appearance of Lowrie's book.

Rejection of the Old Testament Yahweh and a strongly held belief on the part of a significant minority of Christians that Judaism and

28. Sören Kierkegaard, *Die Tagebücher,* trans. Hayo Gerdes (5 vols.; Düsseldorf, 1962–74); Kierkegaard, *Søren Kierkegaard's Journals and Papers,* ed. and trans. Howard V. Hong and Edna H. Hong, assisted by Gregor Malantschuk (4 vols.; Bloomington, Ind., 1967–75); Kierkegaard, *Søren Kierkegaard, The Last Years: Journals 1853–1855,* ed. and trans. Ronald Gregor Smith (New York, 1965).

29. Walter Lowrie, *Kierkegaard* (London, 1938), 3. Lowrie points out on the following page that German theologians were already interested in Kierkegaard and that German translations of his writings began to appear as early as 1873. Georg Morris Cohen Brandes was a well-known Danish literary critic. Lowrie calls him a "freethinking Jew" and says that Brandes hazarded the guess that if Kierkegaard had lived till Darwin's time he would have ridiculed Darwin's "doctrine." Lowrie adds: "Very likely—but this suspicion does not seem so dreadful now, when everybody has abandoned that doctrine" (p. 3). Lowrie's statement will strike very oddly on the ears of anyone who was intellectually aware during the 1930s—Lowrie's "now"—unless that person happens to be a "parson" rather than a "professor" (Lowrie claims the former status, [p. xiii]).

Christianity are irreconcilably opposed doctrines can be traced back to Marcion, founder of the Marcionite Christian church in the second century of our era.[30] In post-Reformation times the reaction began anew; it is evident in the writings of such men as Thomas Hobbes and Benedict Spinoza in the seventeenth century, Immanuel Kant in the eighteenth, and Friedrich Schleiermacher (1768–1834) in the early nineteenth century.[31] Adolf von Harnack (1851–1930), our authority on Marcion, believed himself that "what Marcion wanted was basically right: the Old Testament should be deposed from canonical rank."[32] Aside from his purely doctrinal and historical reasons, Harnack argued that since the Reformation the Old Testament had been especially unwholesome in its effects under the Protestant dispensation; there it was read *literally*, as the word of God. The result was that "in some circles it [the Old Testament] aroused an Islamic fanaticism, in others it called forth a new kind of Judaism, and throughout it favored a legalistic attitude. . . . Had Marcion appeared again in the era of the Huguenots and Cromwells he would have encountered again, in the midst of Christendom, the warlike God of Israel whom he abominated."[33] Precisely the same characterization of the warlike God of these Christian zealots will be found in Scott's *Life of Napoleon Buonaparte*, a work that Wagner read and admired.[34]

Leaving aside the existential character of his thoughts on the human condition, which later proved so attractive to Martin Heidegger, Karl Jaspers, and other philosophers of this school, Kierkegaard belongs in

30. Adolf von Harnack, *Marcion; Das Evangelium vom fremden Gott* (1929, 2nd ed.; rpr. Darmstadt, 1960).

31. Emil G. Kraeling, *The Old Testament Since the Reformation* (1955; rpr. New York, 1969); *cf.* chap. 4, "The Reaction Against the Orthodox View of the Old Testament," 43–58.

32. *Ibid.*, 148. Von Harnack wrote: "To have rejected the Old Testament in the second century would have been a mistake . . . [and] to have retained it in the sixteenth century was a fatality . . . but to retain it even today, after the nineteenth century, as a canonical document in Protestantism is the result of religious and ecclesiastical paralysis" (Harnack, *Marcion; Das Evangelium vom fremden Gott*, 217).

33. Harnack, *Marcion; Das Evangelium vom fremden Gott*, 220.

34. See Chapter 1 herein. Scott compares the "fanatics of yore," the men who "studied the Old Testament for the purpose of finding bad actions to vindicate those which [they] themselves were tempted to commit," with the "desperate and outrageous bigots of the [French] Revolution, [who] read history to justify, by classical instances, their public and private crimes" (Scott, *Life of Napoleon Buonaparte*, II, 23).

126   READING WAGNER

the long tradition of Christians who reject the authority of the Old
Testament in their search for true Christianity. Kierkegaard's older
brother Peter was the Lutheran bishop of Aalborg, and Kierkegaard
himself had intended to follow in his brother's footsteps. But in 1843
he underwent a religious crisis, and according to Emil C. Kraeling,
thereafter "had no use for the Old Testament."[35] (No positive use, we
must add, for Kierkegaard did find a negative use for the Old Testament in defining the character of the New Testament.) "Christendom
is a conspiracy against the Christianity of the New Testament," wrote
Kierkegaard in one of his posthumously published papers.[36]

Lowrie's book contains little information on Kierkegaard's attitude toward Judaism. The word does not appear in the index, and the
only indexed reference to the Jews themselves is the following from
Kierkegaard's journal: "The present age is the age of despair, the age
of the Wandering Jew (many reforming Jews)."[37] But the fact is that
Kierkegaard was concerned with the troubling relationship of Judaism
and Christianity throughout his adult life. An entry dated July 8,
1834, reads as follows.

> I am surprised that none of the theologians who otherwise have observed
> often enough that Christianity in the New Testament still has a strong fla-
> vor of Judaism have also treated the doctrine of unrestricted grace in the
> same manner. If, for example, we observe that particularism appeared in its
> strongest possible form in the Jews, in such a way that it even bordered on
> fetishism (see Schleiermacher), then it would certainly be reasonable that
> the tendency toward universalism in Christianity would not please the
> Jews. Examples of such dissatisfaction are numerous in Acts. At the same
> time this very essential element in Christianity (its universalism) had to as-
> sert itself.[38]

Here we see Kierkegaard concerned with the same antithetical relationship (Jewish particularism versus Christian universalism) that

35. Kraeling, *The Old Testament Since the Reformation*, 248.
36. Lowrie, *Kierkegaard*, 536.
37. *Ibid.*, 91. See also Hayo Gerdes' translation in Kierkegaard, *Die Tagebücher*, I,
75. Gerdes dates the note between 1834 and 1837. Lowrie adds that in Kierkegaard's
"day the Jews (men without political attachments) were prominent as instigators of liberal reform in Denmark, as they were also in other lands, and as they are today"
(Lowrie, *Kierkegaard*, 91).
38. Kierkegaard, *Journals and Papers*, 167; Kierkegaard, *Die Tagebücher*, I, 33. In
his notes to this entry Gerdes cites the following statement from the writing of Friedrich
Schleiermacher: "In limiting Jehovah's love to the tribe of Abraham, Judaism still shows
a trace of fetishism" (*ibid.*, I, 358).

Wagner, fourteen years later, would deal with in his notes on *Jesus of Nazareth:* "And so Jesus cast off his Davidic origin; through Adam he was of God, and all human beings were now his brothers." [39]

At this point it will be convenient to move ahead to 1854 and to quote at length from two entries in Kierkegaard's journals.

> Judaism is really of all religions outspoken optimism . . . divinely sanctioned optimism, sheer promise for this life.
>
> And just because Christianity is renunciation, Judaism is its presupposition. *Opposita juxta se posita. . . .*
>
> But instead of seeing this, in the whole history of Christianity there is a constant tendency to resuscitate Judaism as being on a level with Christianity, instead of making use of it as a repelling force, or as something to be forsaken, since Christianity preaches renunciation, absolute renunciation. [40]

In the second entry, made later in the same year, Kierkegaard writes, "It cannot be made clear enough or be repeated often enough that Christianity certainly is related to Judaism, but in such a way, please note, that Judaism serves Christianity by helping it become negatively recognizable, is the repulsion of offense, yet they belong together for the very reason that this repulsion is an essential part, for otherwise Christianity would lose its dialectical elevation." Kierkegaard goes on to say that "Christianity means renunciation," whereas Judaism makes "promises of all kinds for this life"; Christianity "means virginity," whereas "Judaism is marriage and again marriage"; Christianity tells us "[m]y kingdom is not of this world," whereas "[i]n Judaism everything is promise for this life . . . and from this a conception of a theocracy here on earth." Having thus listed the antitheses, Kierkegaard concludes, "But men would rather be Jews—sensately holding fast to this life and with divine sanction to boot—than be Christians, that is, be spirit." [41]

Not only would human beings rather be Jews (in the Kierkegaardian sense) than Christians (again in the Kierkegaardian sense), the established churches of Christendom are, Kierkegaard insists, themselves

39. Wagner, *Jesus von Nazareth*, 22–25; see text corresponding to note 12 above.

40. Kierkegaard, *The Last Years: Journals and Papers 1853–1855*, 130. It should be understood that Kierkegaard did not, at any time, place Judaism on the same level as Christianity. A note, written in 1839, reads, "Christianity is the actual proprietor who sits in the carriage; Judaism is the coachman; Mohammedanism is a groom who does not sit with the coachman but behind" (Kierkegaard, *Journals and Papers*, I, 176).

41. Kierkegaard, *Journals and Papers*, II, 509–10. This passage does not appear in Kierkegaard, *The Last Years: Journals and Papers.*

strongholds of Judaism. An entry of 1848 in his diary states, "The only
Christianity there is in Christendom is really Judaism."[42] And again in
1848, "Established Christianity, insofar as it has any fear of God, is
actually Judaism."[43] Kierkegaard, in a Kafka-like parable, then describes the transformation of Christianity into its dialectical opposite,
Judaism.

> Imagine a fortress, absolutely impregnable, furnished with provisions
> for an eternity.
> Then a new commandant arrives. He has the idea that it would be best
> to build bridges across the trenches—in order to attack the besiegers.
> Splendid! He has transformed the fortress into a village—and naturally
> the enemy took it.
> So with Christianity. The method was changed, and of course the world
> triumphed.[44]

Sixty years earlier, we recall, William Blake had said (in the person of
Ezekiel) that in our day "all [Christian] nations believe the jews' code
and worship the jews' god."[45]

When did this capitulation take place? Walter Lowrie (who cites the
above parable in connection with Kierkegaard's claim that Christendom, *i.e.*, the Christianity of the established churches, is a conspiracy
against New Testament Christianity) argues that Kierkegaard "does
not mean to say that it is a new conspiracy in our day, for it dates at
least from the Peace of the Church in the fourth century."[46] Christianity became the state religion of Rome in the fourth century, under the
emperor Constantine. In issuing forth from its impregnable stronghold
Christianity did not *conquer* Rome—it was *conquered by* Rome. As
Kierkegaard tells us, "the world triumphed." The warlike spirit of ancient Israel expressed in the Old Testament was easily grafted on the
warlike spirit of Rome. Meanwhile, the message of Christ was completely forgotten. Christianity was stood on its head. Christianity became, as Wagner wrote in 1880 (in his essay "Religion And Art"),
a "state-religion for Roman emperors and hangmen of heretics."[47]
Like Wagner, Kierkegaard was critical of all established churches,

42. Kierkegaard, *Journals and Papers*, I, 154.
43. Kierkegaard, *Die Tagebücher*, III, 60.
44. Kierkegaard, *The Last Years: Journals and Papers 1853–1855*, 131.
45. William Blake, *The Marriage of Heaven and Hell*, in *Blake: Complete Writings with Variant Readings*, ed. Geoffrey Keynes (London, 1966), 153–54.
46. Lowrie, *Kierkegaard*, 536.
47. Wagner, *Gesammelte Schriften und Dichtungen*, X, 214.

Protestant as well as Catholic. In 1850, Kierkegaard took note that the Danish state, in its dispute with Prussia over the sovereignty of Schleswig-Holstein, was firmly supported by the Danish Lutheran church. "The Jewish [strain in Christianity] leads to an increased national zeal," Kierkegaard writes in his diary, "and now (since Christendom has been inverted in all respects), just now, it has become true orthodoxy for one to be a national zealot, just like any other politician."[48]

An early (February 6, 1839) entry in Kierkegaard's journals calls it "very characteristic of Judaism that it is only able to see the back of Jehovah."[49] Christianity, it is implied, sees the face of Jehovah. Judaism and Christianity, accordingly, would appear to be two aspects of the same whole, rather than two incompatible doctrines. Perhaps Kierkegaard still felt this to be the case before he underwent his religious crisis of 1848. Thereafter, Judaism and Christianity were for him thesis and antithesis, dialectical opposites, *opposita juxta se posita.* Thus, *Judeo-Christianity*—a term not often in use in the nineteenth century, and never used by Kierkegaard—is an oxymoron, an absurd coupling of opposites. A more vivid picture of the attempted union is to be found in Schopenhauer, a philosopher with whose work Kierkegaard was intimately acquainted. Writing in 1844, Schopenhauer calls the attempt to graft New Testament Christianity on a Jewish stem the equivalent of grafting a human head on the neck of a horse.[50] The problem, obviously, is one that Judaism does not have to face, for Judaism is under no compulsion to reconcile its doctrines with the teachings of the New Testament.[51]

48. Kierkegaard, *Die Tagebücher*, IV, 84. The Hongs do not include this passage in their collection.

49. Kierkegaard, *Journals and Papers*, II, 503. The reference is to Exodus 33:23, where the Lord says to Moses: "And I will take away mine hands, and thou shalt see my back parts: but my face shall not be seen."

50. Schopenhauer, *Sämtliche Werke*, II, 623; Schopenhauer, *The World as Will and Representation*, II, 488. Schopenhauer cites Horace's lines here: "Humano capiti cervicem pictor equinam / Jungere si velit" (*De arte poetica,* 1–2).

51. In *The Myth of the Judeo-Christian Tradition* (New York, 1957), Arthur Cohen speaks of the "fundamental and irreconcilable disagreement" between Judaism and Christianity. He suggests that it may some day find resolution in "Judeo-Christian humanism" (pp. 51–52, 219–23). Worth noting in this connection is Kierkegaard's journal entry of 1850: "Of all religions, the Jewish religion is closest to humanism. Its formula is: stay close to God and things will go well with you in this world" (Kierkegaard, *Journals and Papers*, II, 505).

MARX, HESS, AND DISRAELI

In 1844 a two-part essay by Karl Marx entitled "On the Jewish Question" was published in a short-lived periodical edited by Marx and Arnold Ruge.[52] This essay was a reply to an essay, "The Jewish Question," written by Bruno Bauer and published a year earlier. Bauer, a young Hegelian, saw the Jewish question as one hinging on religious belief, and he held that the emancipation of Jews from religious Judaism was really at issue. Marx, of course, having inverted Hegel's doctrine, directed his attention to the economic substructure of Judaism on which, as he saw it, the religious superstructure rested. "Jews," Marx writes in reply to Bauer, "have [already] emancipated themselves insofar as Christians have become Jews." In other words, says Marx, "the practical-Jewish spirit, Judaism, has . . . attained its highest development in Christian society." To Marx religion is a shadow without a Peter Schlemihl, an illusion without a future; his Judaism is a socioeconomic category. It embraces a kind of socioeconomic behavior generated by a bourgeois capitalist society. "The Jew," he writes in "On the Jewish Question," "is perpetually created by civil society from its own economic entrails." It follows that Bauer's statement on the emancipation of the Jews must be broadened. Marx does so, stating that "the *emancipation of the Jews* is the emancipation of mankind from *Judaism*" (Marx's emphasis).[53]

To illustrate his assertion that Christians have become Jews (in the economic sense) Marx offers in evidence the following passage from Thomas Hamilton's *Men and Manners in North America* (1833): "The devout and politically free inhabitant of New England is a kind of *Laocoön* who makes not the least effort to escape from the serpents which are crushing him. *Mammon* is his idol which he adores not only with his lips but with the whole force of his body and mind. In his view the world is no more than a Stock Exchange, and he is convinced that he has no other destiny here below than to become richer than his neighbour. Trade has seized upon all his thoughts, and he has no other recreation than to exchange objects." Marx adds, "In North America the practical domination of Judaism over the Christian world has

52. Karl Marx, "Zur Judenfrage," *Deutsch-Französische Jahrbücher* (1844; rpr. Darmstadt, 1967); Marx, "On the Jewish Question," in Karl Marx and Frederick Engels, *Collected Works* (New York, 1975–   ), III, 146–74.

53. Marx, "On the Jewish Question," in Marx and Engels, *Collected Works*, III, 170–71.

achieved as its unambiguous and normal expression that the *preaching of the Gospel* itself and the Christian ministry have become articles of trade, and the bankrupt trader deals in the Gospel just as the Gospel preacher who has become rich goes in for business deals."[54]

"Christians have become Jews" (Marx) and "Christianity . . . in Christendom is really Judaism" (Kierkegaard) are similar in phraseology; although different in meaning, they have in common the metaphorical use of the terms *Jew* and *Judaism*. Kierkegaard's Jews are nominal Christians, and for Marx the Jew in pure culture exists in Yankeeland as a professing Christian who worships Mammon.[55] Kierkegaard and Marx were apparently unacquainted with each other's writings.[56] But both men had read Ludwig Feuerbach (1804–1872), a German stylist whose work bristles with antitheses.[57] In 1844, in *The Essence of Christianity* (George Eliot's translation of Feuerbach's *Das Wesen des Christentums*), he had written, "Judaism is *worldly Christendom*, Christendom *spiritual Judaism* [Feuerbach's emphasis]; the Christian religion is the Jewish religion purified of national egoism."[58] We know that Kierkegaard purchased a copy of Feuerbach's *Das Wesen des Christentums* from his bookseller on March 24, 1844. Commenting on this book in elaborately ironic fashion, Kierkegaard suggests that Feuerbach, rather than having launched

54. *Ibid.*, 171. *Cf.* Bruce Barton's discovery that Christ is "the true founder of modern business," which was announced in his highly successful book *The Man Nobody Knows* (Indianapolis, 1924) 162–63.

55. On the metaphorical meaning of *Jude* (Jew) and *Judenthum* (Judaism) in Germany, and of *juive* (Jew) in French at this time, see Elisabeth de Fontenay, *Les figures juives de Marx* (Paris, 1973), 38–41; Robert C. Tucker, *Philosophy and Myth in Karl Marx* (Cambridge, 1967), 110–12; and the editor's remarks in Marx and Engels, *Collected Works*, III, 170.

56. Marx's name does not occur in the indices of Gerdes' translation of Kierkegaard's diaries (*Die Tagebücher*) or in the index of Lowrie's *Kierkegaard*, nor does Kierkegaard's name appear in the index of S. S. Prawer's comprehensive *Karl Marx and World Literature* (Oxford, 1978).

57. Feuerbach, *Sämtliche Werke*.

58. *Ibid.*, VI, 143. In the original, the passage cited from *Das Wesen des Christenthums* reads: "Das Judenthum ist das weltliche Christenthum, das Christenthum das geistliche Judenthum. Die christliche Religion ist die von Nationalegoismus gereinigte jüdische Religion" (emphasis in original). In my translation I have tried, with doubtful success, to distinguish "Christendom" (a realm) from "Christianity" (a religion). In George Eliot's translation (1854) the passage reads: "Judaism is worldly Christianity; Christianity, spiritual Judaism. The Christian religion is the Jewish religion purified from national egoism" (Feuerbach, *The Essence of Christianity*, 120).

a frontal attack on orthodox Christianity as a professed unbeliever, should have bored from within, "like a mole"—in effect, we may say, "like a Kierkegaard."[59]

Marx, by contrast, welcomed Feuerbach's writings (at first) with open arms. In a letter of August 11, 1844, to Feuerbach he expressed his "great respect" and "love" for the older man; *The Essence of Christianity* and *The Philosophy of the Future* (*Philosophie der Zukunft*) "provided . . . a philosophical basis for socialism and the Communists have immediately understood them in this way."[60] Feuerbach's writings were also welcomed later in the 1840s by Richard Wagner, who had in the meantime been much impressed by Hegel's *Philosophy of History*.[61] Probably no later than 1848, while still in Dresden, Wagner had been introduced to the writings of Feuerbach by a young German Catholic priest and political agitator named Metzdorf.[62] Wagner's essay "The Art Work of the Future" (1849), written in exile in Zurich, was originally dedicated to Feuerbach and owed its title to the latter's *Philosophy of the Future*. Newman remarks acutely that the "clockwork antitheses" abounding in Wagner's essay were also borrowed—in style, not in content—from Feuerbach.[63] The same may be said of Marx's "On the Jewish Question," as well as of Bruno Bauer's essay on the Jewish question of which it was a critique.

Marx's essay on the Jewish question is still an authoritative source drawn on by left-wing radical thinkers in their opposition to Zionism, their espousal of assimilation, and their reinterpretations of the mean-

59. Kierkegaard, *Das Buch über Adler*, trans. Hayo Gerdes (Düsseldorf, 1962), 58, 223 n. 79a). This constitutes vol. 36 of the works of Kierkegaard translated into German under the supervision of and largely by Emmanuel Hirsch.

60. Marx and Engels, *Collected Works*, III, 354–57. Marx adds in his letter that an English translation of *Das Wesen des Christenthums*, under the supervision of Engels, and a French translation, under the supervision of "the German Communist Ewerbeck," are almost ready for printing (p. 354). The English translation seems not to have found a printer, but the French translation by A. H. Ewerbeck was published in 1850 (*ibid.*, 606 n. 115).

61. Wagner, *My Life*, trans. Gray, 429–30.

62. *Ibid.*, 407, 430. In Cosima Wagner's diaries an entry dated August 19, 1870, reads: "When R. goes to town [Lucerne], he is addressed by a man he does not recognize; he turns out to be one of the Dresden revolutionaries, *Metzdorf*, who spent the last 20 years in Paris, earning his living by giving lessons, and has recently been banished! All in the name of civilization!" (Cosima Wagner, *Diaries*, I, 259).

63. Wagner, *My Life*, trans. Gray, 430; Newman, *The Life of Richard Wagner*, II, 431 n. 8.

ing of Jewish history.[64] Moses Hess, four years before he became acquainted with Marx in 1841, wrote down his own interpretation of
Jewish history. It was, as we shall see, of quite "un-Marxian" character. Later, after having met Marx, his writings on the Jewish question
took on a new character, compatible with those of Marx. Still later,
Hess broke with Marx and became the founding father of modern
Zionism, and in doing so he inverted Marx's view of the relative importance of race and class. The subject has recently been given exhaustive treatment by Julius Carlebach in a book written from the
standpoint of a religious Jew and a political Zionist.[65] It should be
understood that Carlebach's book deals solely with left-wing radical
critiques of Judaism (as its title indicates); right-wing radical critiques
of Judaism, Zionism, or both, whether carried out by Jews or Christians, are left untreated.

As mentioned earlier, Hess came from a family of Rhineland Orthodox Jews. Moreover, he was indebted to his grandfather, a learned Tal-
mudist, for part of his early education. In 1837 (four years before
meeting Marx) Hess published a book entitled *The Sacred History of
Humanity. By a Disciple of Spinoza* (*Die heilige Geschichte der
Menschheit. Von einem Jünger Spinozas*).[66] It was a highly unorthodox work, from a Jewish standpoint at least; the reader will see
later that it had features in common with the so-called Young Germany movement in Germany and the Saint-Simonian movement in
France. Following a paradigm that goes back to Joachim of Floris in

64. *Cf.* Abram Leon, *The Jewish Question: A Marxist Interpretation* (New York,
1970). Leon, a Jew, directed party work among the "proletarian [German] soldiers of
the Wehrmacht" in occupied Belgium, and even after his capture by the Gestapo he was
able to establish contact with the Trotskyists; he died at Auschwitz (see biographical
sketch by Ernest Germain, in Leon, *The Jewish Question*, 23–26). Nathan Weinstock's
introductory essay, written in 1969, takes issue with an essay by Maxime Rodinson introducing a new French edition of Leon's book. The New York edition of *The Jewish
Question: A Marxist Interpretation* reprints the English text of a limited edition published in Mexico City in 1950 (*ibid.*, 7), ten years after Trotsky's assassination in that
city. *Cf.* also Vladimir Il'ich Lenin, *Lenin on the Jewish Question*, ed. Hyman Lumer
(New York, 1974). Lumer cites in his introduction the works of Abba Eban (then foreign minister of Israel): "Anti-Zionism is merely the new Anti-Semitism" (*ibid.*, 19).

65. Julius Carlebach, *Karl Marx and the Radical Critique of Judaism* (London,
1978).

66. Moses Hess, *Philosophische und Sozialistische Schriften, 1837–1850*, ed.
Auguste Cornu and Wolfgang Mönke (Berlin, 1961). For *Die heilige Geschichte der
Menschheit*, see pp. 1–74.

the twelfth century, Hess sees three revelations marking the successive steps forward taken by humanity as a whole on the way to perfection. Respectively, they are the revelations of God the Father, of God the Son, and of God the Holy Spirit. In the closing section (entitled "The New Jerusalem and the Last Days") of his history Hess paints an idyllic picture of the alternative society. "Woman as well as man will rejoice in a *humane* (*humanen*) education, man and woman will be united by the bond of *free love* (*freien Liebe*) . . . [and] youth will no longer be subjected to the arbitrary rule of parents and guardians, nor woman to man, nor the poor and weak to the rich and powerful." The "New Jerusalem," however, will not be Jewish, for both Judaism and Christianity will be transcended by the third kingdom, the "kingdom of truth" (*Reich der Wahrheit*). Hess warns the Jews that they should not "bewail the seed-corn when it decays, if it bear fruit." For the impetus toward the "kingdom of truth" came from the Jews, who were a "people (*Volk*) called upon from the beginning to conquer the world—not, as did heathen Rome, by the force of its *arm* but through the inner virtue of its spirit."[67] And in the closing sentence of Hess's first book we are told that a time will come when "the human being, grown old, will no longer have any other wishes than those which his or her artistic activity (*Kunstthätigkeit*) can at once provide."[68]

Hess met Marx for the first time in Bonn, toward the end of August, 1841. On September 2 he wrote a glowing letter to Berthold Auerbach in Dresden. "You will rejoice to know of a man here who now belongs to our circle of friends. . . . As far as his stance and philosophic spirit is concerned he surpasses not only Strauss but Feuerbach as well, and the latter means a lot! . . . Dr. Marx, so my idol is called, is still a very young man (at most 24 years old); he will deal the final stroke to medieval religion and politics; he combines the deepest philosophical seriousness with the most cutting wit; imagine Rousseau, Voltaire, Holbach, Lessing, Heine and Hegel united in one person, I say *united*, not thrown together—then you have Dr. Marx."[69]

Four years later Hess published an extraordinary essay entitled "On the Nature of Money."[70] Carlebach notes that scholars such as Edmund Silberner (Hess's biographer), David McLellan, and Robert C. Tucker

---

67. *Ibid.*, 67–72, *passim.*
68. *Ibid.*, 74.
69. *Ibid.*, xxiv.
70. Hess, *Über das Geldwesen, ibid.*, 329–48.

claim that Marx drew heavily on this essay in writing "On the Jewish Question." Carlebach himself rejects this claim, but he does give three pages of parallel passages from Hess's "On the Nature of Money" and Marx's posthumously published *Economic and Philosophic Manuscripts of 1844* and seems to give Hess priority here.[71]

Startlingly different from his earlier version of the world-historical task of the Jews is the one set forth in Hess's "On the Nature of Money." The images employed here are highly colored, not to say fantastic; some of them will reappear, twelve years later, in the first volume of Marx's *Capital*. Hess calls money the "clotted, sweated blood of wretches who bring their life-activity itself to the market to exchange it for its *caput mortuum*, so-called 'capital.'" Human beings have, in the course of history, become transformed into

> *social beasts of prey,* finished, *conscious egoists* who in *free competition* sanction the war of all against all, who in so-called *human-rights* sanction the rights of isolated individuals, of private persons, of the "absolute personality," who in *freedom of trade* sanction mutual exploitation and the thirst for money—the *thirst for money,* which is nothing other than the *thirst of the social beast of prey for blood.* We are not *herbivorous,* like our good-natured ancestors who were, it is true, social animals also, but not as yet social beasts of prey . . . we are *bloodsuckers who exploit and consume each other.* As the animal enjoys its own life only in blood, so the human being enjoys his own life, but in a *brutal, bestial, cannibalistic* way, in money. *Money* is the *blood of society,* but it is alienated blood, shed blood [Hess's emphasis].[72]

How did we reach this sorry state? Who watched over our development, or rather degeneration, into "social beasts of prey" quite unlike our "herbivorous . . . good-natured ancestors"? The Jews—so Hess would have us believe.

> The *Jews,* whose *world-historic* calling it was, in the natural history of the social world of animals, to develop beasts of prey from human beings, have now at last completed this their assigned task. The mystery of Judaism and Christianity is now revealed in the modern *Jewish-Christian shopkeepers'*

---

71. Carlebach, *Karl Marx and the Radical Critique of Judaism,* 110, 120–122.

72. Hess, *Über das Geldwesen,* in *Philosophische und Sozialistische Schriften,* 335, 345. The *caput mortuum* (dead head) is the residue left behind in the alchemist's alembic after the spirits have been boiled away. Combining Hess's images, Marx calls capital "dead labour, that, vampire-like, only lives by sucking living labour" (Karl Marx, *Capital,* ed. Frederick Engels [3 vols.; New York, 1967], I, 233).

world. The mystery of *Christ's blood*, like the mystery of the *ancient Jewish veneration of blood*, appears here at last quite nakedly as the *mystery of the beast of prey*. In ancient Judaism the cult of blood was merely *prototypical;* in *medieval Christianity* it became actualized in a *theoretical, idealistic, logical fashion,* i.e. one actually consumed the *shed blood of humanity,* the *blood of the God-man,* but only in the imagination. In the modern, Jewish-Christian shopkeepers' world this inclination and craving of the social animal world came forward no longer in *symbolic* or *mystical,* but in quite *prosaic* form.[73]

Carlebach does his best with this essay. He asserts that the main thrust of Hess's "attack on religion" is directed against Christianity; he rejects David McLellan's claim, cited from the latter's book *The Young Hegelians and Karl Marx* (1969), that for Hess "Judaism represents in their grossest form the evils of bourgeois society."[74] In attempting to defend Hess against the charge of anti-Judaism, Carlebach perhaps overstates his case. It is true, however, that Hess uses the phrases "Jewish-Christian shopkeeper's world" and "Christian shopkeeper's world" interchangeably. Further, Hess asserts that "our shopkeeper's world is Christendom *realized*" (Hess's emphasis), and that this world was created by "*enlightened* and *practical* Christians who could not rest satisfied with legislating the *beyond* but wished instead to have the Christian world, their heaven, on earth."[75] (We recall that a few years later, in 1848, Kierkegaard would note in the privacy of his diaries, "The only Christianity there is in Christendom is really Judaism."[76])

A stubbornly literal reading of Hess, Marx, or Kierkegaard in the passages cited above will never yield their intended meaning. Carlebach, however, argues for a literal reading of Marx's "On the Jewish Question." He says, "In spite of the frequent assertions that in writing about Jews, Marx was really writing about capitalism or commercialism or the bourgeoisie, I have rejected this view, that this same Marx, master of the written word . . . was not capable of finding the right terminology for his arguments . . . and [I] have assumed that Jews and Judaism mean what they are generally understood to mean."[77] The

73. Hess, *Über das Geldwesen,* in *Philosophische und Sozialistische Schriften,* 345.
74. Carlebach, *Karl Marx and the Radical Critique of Judaism,* 123.
75. Hess, *Über das Geldwesen,* in *Philosophische und Sozialistische Schriften,* 334, 338.
76. Kierkegaard, *Journals and Papers,* I, 154.
77. Carlebach, *Karl Marx and the Radical Critique of Judaism,* 5–6.

statement begs the question, of course, since what is at issue is precisely what they are "generally understood to mean." And when Marx, in his essay on the Jewish question, tells us that Yankee Christendom shelters the most devout worshippers of Mammon, and that the "*chimerical* nationality of the Jews is the nationality of the merchant, of the man of money in general" (Marx's emphasis), we can hardly miss his meaning.[78] (Kierkegaard too was a master of language, but few would insist that he be read literally when he writes, for example, that Christians would rather be Jews.) For Marx, religion, race, and nationality were alike chimeras, mere fictions. Class (*Klasse*), not race, nationality, or religion, was the reality. Religious wars, race wars, civil wars, and wars between nations mask the reality of class warfare. "The history of all hitherto existing society is the history of class struggles," is the opening sentence of the *Communist Manifesto* (1848).[79]

Returning to Hess, we find that he has still another volte-face in store for us. Fourteen years after the *Communist Manifesto* began to haunt Europe, Hess, who had broken with Marx, conjured up the specter of race struggle in *Rome and Jerusalem: The Last National Question* (1862).[80] Race struggle (*Rassenkampf*) took precedence, in Hess's new view, over class struggle (*Klassenkampf*). More or less parodying the opening sentence of the *Communist Manifesto,* Hess wrote: "All history hitherto has been motivated by race struggles and class struggles; race struggle is primary, class struggle is secondary."[81] Hess uses the words *race* (*Rasse*), *folk* (*Volk*), and *nationality* (*Nationalität*) more or less interchangeably in this book. He states that "folk-types" (*Volkstypen*) are forms stamped out by Nature, and that it is an error to "base the equality of rights of human beings on an [supposed] original equality of all races and types." Humanity as a whole is, he says, a "living organism" and its "organs" are the original

78. Marx, "On The Jewish Question," in Marx and Engels, *Collected Works,* III, 172.

79. Karl Marx, "Manifest der kommunistischen Partei," in Karl Marx and Friedrich Engels, *Werke* (38 vols.; Berlin, 1959–71), IV, 462: "Die Geschichte aller bisherigen Gesellschaft ist die Geschichte von Klassenkämpfen."

80. Hess, *Rom und Jerusalem; Die letzte Nationalitätsfrage; Briefe von Moses Hess,* ed. Theodore Zlocisti (Tel Aviv, 1935).

81. *Ibid.,* 199: "Die ganze bisherige Geschichte bewegte sich in Rassen—und Klassenkämpfen. Der Rassenkampf ist das Ursprünglichste, der Klassenkampf das Sekundäre."

races and tribes, each of which has its peculiar world-historical task to
perform. Among the "truly creative organs" of the superorganism (humanity as a whole) is that represented by the Jewish race. Hess states
that the "Jewish race (*Rasse*) is a primary race," and that the Jews are
"a folk, one folk (*ein Volk, Ein Volk*)." Jews cannot emancipate themselves from the Jewish race by abjuring the Jewish religion. Hess insists
that a "Jew remains a Jew by virtue of his racial origin, even though his
ancestors may have become apostates." Assimilation is undesirable. It
is also impossible, for the Jewish race cannot be destroyed by "mixed
marriages with Indo-Germanic stocks." [82]

Carlebach says that *Rome and Jerusalem* has never been given a full
and systematic analysis and that to do so is beyond the scope of his
own book. He sums up Hess's achievement as follows: "Hess was thus
the first Jewish socialist to attempt a synthesis between socialism and
Judaism. His essay, like Marx's [on the Jewish question], sank into
oblivion, and, again like Marx's, did not re-emerge until early in this
century when the socialist revolutionary of the nineteenth century became the prophet of political Zionism. Inevitably, in purely Marxist
terms, Hess's thesis was totally unacceptable, mainly because it denied
the predominance of economic factors as determinants of history, but
also because it accorded religion an independent function." [83] It would
perhaps be more accurate to say that Hess was the first Jewish socialist to attempt a synthesis between socialism and Jewish nationalism,
and that in this sense he was the prophet of modern *political* Zionism. Race, not religion, was the determining force of history that Hess
gave priority before Marx's class. [84] Hess's book eventually found a
publisher, but it seems to have been little read: in advocating a similar
view of the driving force of human history twenty years later Ludwig
Gumplowicz, another German Jew, made no mention of *Rome and
Jerusalem*. [85]

82. *Ibid.*, 27, 29–30, 86–88.
83. Carlebach, *Karl Marx and the Radical Critique of Judaism*, 193–97, *passim*.
84. It may perhaps be said that Hess was the unwitting prophet of another later
attempt in Germany to effect a synthesis of socialism and racial nationalism—that of the
German National Socialist Workers Party, under the leadership of Adolf Hitler, who
shared Hess's views on the primacy of race.
85. Ludwig Gumplowicz, *Ausgewählte Werke* (4 vols.; Aalen, 1973). Gumplowicz
writes: "*Race struggle for rule*, in its open and violent as well as in its hidden and peace-
ful forms, is . . . the actual *driving principle, the moving force of history*" (his emphasis). "The Race Struggle" was first published in 1883, then reprinted in 1909 and 1926

Hess sent the manuscript to his old friend Berthold Auerbach. "Do you want to intervene in this truly incendiary (I can find no other word) fashion," Auerbach wrote to Hess in reply, "in a field where others have for years, indeed for their whole lives, devoted all their forces to constructive order?" Auerbach continued: "And that you should turn precisely to me for intercession! I am indeed, I confess it gladly (although you may find it laughable or disgraceful), a Teutonic Jew, a German (*ein germanischer Jude, ein Deutscher*), and I believe, as good as any to be found. . . . It is not for nothing that we speak of a father-land and a mother-language. There is a home of the spirit, the innermost within us, born through language and the whole historical inner life."[86] And Otto Wigand, a leading publisher in the field of Jewish history and literature, responded harshly: "I read only half of your manuscript, and then it was no longer possible for me to read more. . . . I shall not advocate your claims or views with my firm. Your entire paper is an offense to my purely human nature (*rein menschlichen Natur*)."[87]

The third man whose writings are to be commented on in this section is Benjamin Disraeli, Lord Beaconsfield. Created first Earl of Beaconsfield in 1876 by Queen Victoria, under whom he served twice as prime minister, Disraeli was an adroit and far from scrupulous politician. He had an even longer career as a writer of fictions. His string of novels extends from *Vivian Gray* in 1826 to *Endymion* in 1880 (one year before his death). Disraeli's novels are never mere entertainment pieces; they carry a message, and are often openly didactic in form. One of these messages was the importance of race in world his-

---

(with approval), and again in 1973 (with apologies for its doctrine of "hate as a social force") (*ibid.*, III, xxiv, 219). Gumplowicz, however, was *not* a Jewish nationalist; indeed he argued that there were already enough racial antagonisms to fuel world history and no need to add one based on "mummified religious traditions" and "long since outlived cultural forms" (*ibid.*, 324). On leaders of Reformed Judaism in Germany, such as Abraham Geiger (1810–1879), who asserted that the Jews should discard the "Chosen People" doctine, see Joseph L. Blau, *Modern Varieties of Judaism* (New York, 1966), 38–39, 125.

86. Moses Hess, *Moses Hess Briefwechsel*, ed. Edmund Silberner, with assistance of Werner Blumenberg (S-Gravenhage, 1959), 375–76, letter dated April 8, 1861.

87. *Ibid.*, 376–77, letter dated May 2, 1861. The phraseology of Wigand's rejection of Hess's Jewish particularism in favor of universal humanism is characteristic of the time (see note 22, this chapter).

tory. In *Coningsby; or, The New Generation* (1844) we are told that the "Hebrew race" constitutes an "aristocracy of nature," boasting as it does "the most ancient, if not the only unmixed blood that dwells in cities."[88] We recall that Disraeli was a baptized Christian; in *Sybil; or, The Two Nations* (1845), however, we learn that "Christianity is completed Judaism or it is nothing."[89] In *Tancred; or, The New Crusade* (1847) Disraeli's racial theorizing peaks: its Sephardic Jewish hero Sidonia informs his young English protégé Tancred that "all is race; there is no other truth." Sidonia adds that the downfall of all past empires can be traced to racial intermixture and the consequent "decay of race," and he warns Tancred that the times now call for a "man."[90]

In 1852, in his biography of Lord George Bentinck (1802–1848), Disraeli put aside his Sidonian mask and spoke with his own voice in favor of the racial theories set forth in *Coningsby* and *Tancred*. The biography contains an interpolated chapter entitled "The Jewish Question" (the chapter is not entirely irrelevant, for Lord George Bentinck had been a parliamentary champion of Catholic and Jewish political emancipation). In this chapter Disraeli makes the following six statements: (1) "The Jews [are] a superior race [and] shall never be destroyed or absorbed by an inferior." (2) "The Jews . . . are a living and the most striking evidence of the falsity of that pernicious doctrine of modern times, the natural equality of man . . . a principle which, if it were possible to act on it, would deteriorate the great races and destroy all the genius of the world." (3) "The native tendency of the Jewish race, who are justly proud of their blood, is against the doctrine of the equality of man." (4) "Persecution, . . . although unjust, may have reduced the modern Jews to a state almost justifying malignant vengeance. They may have become so odious and so hostile to mankind, as to merit for their present conduct, no matter how occasioned, the obloquy and ill-treatment of the communities in which they dwell." (5) "Destruction of the Semitic principle, extirpation of the Jewish religion, whether in the Mosaic or Christian form, the natural equality of man and the abrogation of property, are proclaimed by the secret so-

88. Benjamin Disraeli, *Coningsby; or The New Generation* (Leipzig, 1844), 204.
89. Benjamin Disraeli, *Sybil; or, The Two Nations* (Leipzig, 1845), 117.
90. Benjamin Disraeli, *Tancred; or, The New Crusade* (2 vols.; Leipzig, 1847), I, 169, *passim*. This may fairly be called Disraeli's "Zionist" novel.

cieties, and men of the Jewish race are found at the head of every one of them. The people of God cooperate with atheists; the most skillful accumulators of property ally themselves with communists; the peculiar and chosen race touch the hands of all the scum and low castes of Europe!" (6) "Thus . . . the persecution of the Jewish race has deprived European society of an important conservative element and added to the destructive party an influential ally."[91]

Sidonia's thesis that a superior race must keep its blood "pure" lest there occur "decay of race" is now advanced by Disraeli himself. Sidonia had advised his English protégés Coningsby and Tancred that they too belonged to one of the superior races—admittedly one of far less antiquity than that of the Jews, and one in dire need of Jewish tutelage. And in the chapter on the Jewish question in his biography of Lord George Bentinck, Disraeli warns the founders of "the great Anglo-Saxon republic" in North America that they too must keep their blood pure and unmixed.

> What would be the consequences on the great Anglo-Saxon republic for example, were its citizens to secede from their sound principle of reserve, and mingle with their negro and coloured populations? In the course of time they would become so deteriorated that their states would probably be reconquered and regained by the aborigines whom they have expelled and who would then be their superiors. But though nature will never ultimately permit this theory of natural equality to be practised, the preaching of this dogma has already caused much mischief and may cause more. The native tendency of the Jewish race, who are justly proud of their blood, is against the doctrine of the equality of man.[92]

Widely disseminated in Europe as well as in England in his fictional and nonfictional writings, Disraeli's racial theorizing gained added prestige in the second half of the nineteenth century by virtue of his role in 1868, and again in 1874–1880, as prime minister of Queen Victoria's empire. The reader should bear in mind that Disraeli's ad-

91. Benjamin Disraeli, *Lord George Bentinck: A Political Biography* (4th ed., rev.; London, 1852), 452–507, *passim*.

92. *Ibid.*, 496. Cf. the claim, made seventy years later by a German political leader, that the "racially pure and unmixed Teuton of the American continent has risen to become its master; he will remain master as long as he does not fall victim to blood-pollution" (Adolf Hitler, *Mein Kampf* [2 vols. in 1; Munich, 1939], 313–14).

vocacy of the rights of "superior" races and their role in world history antedates by as much as ten years the writings of Gobineau (1816–1882) on the subject: Gobineau's much-maligned but seldom read *Essay on the Inequality of the Human Races* was published (in French) between 1853 and 1855. The Count de Gobineau was a diplomat, littérateur, novelist, world traveler, and something of a scholar. In spite of the bad reputation he enjoys today, nothing in his writings, fictional or nonfictional, comes even close to the crude racism, to use today's pejorative term, of Disraeli, although there are several paragraphs in the *Essay* in praise of the ancient "Hebrew race" that sound rather like the effusions of Disraeli's Sidonia.[93]

Disraeli's treatment of the Jewish question in *Lord George Bentinck: A Political Biography* was given a rather rough reception on its appearance by the editors of *Punch:* "Well! The Jews, it seems, are conscious of their ill-treatment. *They* . . . join secret societies. *They* . . . topple over thrones with delight." *Punch* added, with a glance sidewise at Disraeli's *Tancred:* "'*All is race.*' What a picture of cool malignity is this! Shadrach luxuriates in locking up the Frank in a sponging house [*i.e.*, a debtors' prison]; he charges him for the 'Semitic Element'

---

93. Joseph Arthur, Compte de Gobineau, *Essai sur l'inégalité des races humaines* (4 vols.; Paris, 1853–55); Gobineau, *Essay on the Inequality of the Human Races,* trans. Adrian Collins (New York, 1915). Collins' translation consists only of book (*livre*) one of the first volume of Gobineau's essay. See Rather, *The Dream of Self-Destruction,* 24–28, for a brief account of Gobineau's theory of the rise and fall of civilizations in the course of world history (a forerunner of the differently based theories of Oswald Spengler and Arnold J. Toynbee). For a biologist's dispassionate critique of Gobineau's work, see John R. Baker, *Race* (London, 1974), 33–38; for a historian's critique, see Arnold Toynbee, *A Study of History* (12 vols.; London, 1939–64), I, 216–18. Georg Lukács' account, in his *The Destruction of Reason,* trans. Peter Palmer (Atlantic Highlands, N.J., 1981), 669–81, hardly rises above the level of political pamphleteering: Lukács' line is straight Gobineau-Chamberlain-Hitler. That Disraeli was as much a racial theorist as Hitler is passed over. Lukács refers to Moses Hess on one occasion, but not in connection with Hess's theory of the primacy of race-struggle in world history; however, he does give considerable space to the related theory of Ludwig Gumplowicz (*ibid.,* 687–94). See also Michael Biddis, *Father of Racist Ideology: The Social and Political Thought of Count Gobineau* (New York, 1970): here too the names of Benjamin Disraeli and Moses Hess do not appear. An assessment of Gobineau's fictional writings is given by Biddis (see also Baker, *Race,* 35, for a different assessment). Gobineau's complete works are now being edited by Jean Gaulmeier (Paris, 1983–   ). Gobineau's entertaining novel *Les Pléiades* (1874) has been translated by Douglas Parmée as *Sons of Kings* (London, 1966)

and sticks it on the chops and sherry."[94] Another protest, more cutting in tone, against Disraeli's Jewish chauvinism came in 1848 from the young George Eliot (1819–1880), after looking through *Coningsby* and *Tancred*. She wrote to a friend: "The fellowship of race, to which D'Israeli [*sic*] exultingly refers the munificence of Sidonia, is so evidently an inferior impulse which must ultimately be superseded that I wonder even he, Jew as he is, dares to boast of it. My Gentile nature kicks most resolutely against any assumption of superiority in the Jews, and is almost ready to echo Voltaire's vituperation. . . . Everything *specifically* Jewish is of a low grade" (Eliot's emphasis).[95] Later in life, however, Eliot was to execute a remarkable about-face with respect to things specifically Jewish, most notably perhaps in her novel *Daniel Deronda* (1876): the eponymous hero, raised as an English aristocrat, learns after reaching manhood that his mother is a Jewish diva who had broken with her father's religion and disposed of Daniel as a hindrance to her career. Daniel subsequently leaves for Palestine in order to regain his lost heritage.[96] One is inevitably reminded of the eponymous hero of Disraeli's *Tancred*, who, under the auspices of Sidonia, also undertakes a pilgrimage to Palestine, where he will seek to

94. Charles L. Graves, *Mr. Punch's History of Modern England* (4 vols.; London, 1921–22), I, 109.

95. George Eliot, *The George Eliot Letters,* ed. Gordon S. Haight (6 vols.; New Haven, Conn., 1954–55), I, 246. The following passage shows that while Eliot took for granted the existence of superior and inferior races, she favored—with the doubtful exception of the Negroes—racial assimilation: "As to his [Disraeli's] theory of 'races' it has not a leg to stand on. . . . Extermination up to a certain point seems to be the law for the inferior races—for the rest fusion for both physical and moral ends. It appears to me that the law by which privileged classes degenerate from continual intermarriage must act on a large scale in deteriorating whole races. . . . The negroes certainly puzzle me—all the other races seem plainly destined to extermination or fusion not excepting even the 'Hebrew-Caucasian.' But the negroes are too important physiologically and geographically for one to think of their extermination, while the repulsion between them and the others seems too strong for fusion to take place to any great extent."

96. By inversion, as it were, Eliot's *Daniel Deronda* was anticipated in 1837 in a fictionalized account of the life of Benedict Spinoza written by Berthold Auerbach. At the age of fifteen Auerbach's Spinoza learns that his mother was not by birth a Jewess; she was a Moorish woman of the Moslem faith who had been forced to masquerade as a Christian in Catholic Spain; she had converted to Judaism only in order to marry Spinoza's father. Spinoza then discovers that he is at heart not a "son of Israel" but a "son of humanity" (Auerbach, *Spinoza; Ein Denkerleben,* in *Werke* [15 vols. in 4; Leipzig, 1913], XIII, 76). This is, of course, precisely the discovery made by Jesus in Wagner's *Jesus of Nazareth* (which was written ten years after Auerbach's *Spinoza*).

achieve union with a daughter of his "Redeemer's race," the beautiful Jewess Eva.[97]

Among Disraeli's readers in Germany were Cosima and Richard Wagner. On March 24, 1874, Cosima noted in her diary: "I read some quotations today from a novel [*Coningsby*] by Disraeli—how he claims for Israel all the great men in art, science, even religion (the first Jesuits, he says, were Jews). A very curious phenomenon."[98] Four years later she and her husband were amused by Disraeli's *Tancred*. The entry of November 27, 1878, reads: "We have to laugh over Disraeli's glorification of the Jews: 'I have an idea what he is getting at,' says R., 'racial purity and great men; that ruling genius I dreamed about—only the Jews could produce him.' Yesterday R. called himself a 'tattooed savage.'"[99] On the following day the Wagners continued with their perusal of *Tancred,* and a note in Cosima's diary tells us why Wagner thought it important to find out just what Disraeli was "getting at": "During our reading we skip all the fictional parts in order to confine ourselves to the message. ('For that can't be taken lightly, he is the Prime Minister of England and has the whole Eastern world in his pocket.' During our walk R. said, 'I find it embarrassing to keep coming back to the subject of the Jews, but one can't avoid it when one is thinking about the future.'"[100] Only a year earlier, as the Wagners

97. On the thematic relationships between Disraeli's *Tancred* and Wagner's *The Saracen Woman* (written in 1843 but not published until 1889) and those between *The Saracen Woman* and Wagner's *The Ring of the Nibelung,* see Rather, *The Dream of Self-Destruction,* 22–23. Disraeli's Tancred and Eva have their counterparts in Wagner's Manfred and Fatima (who is Manfred's half-sister and a Palestinian). Eva ("Eve") and Fatima are purely fictional. The historical Manfred was the illegitimate son of Frederick II and the last Hohenstaufen king of Sicily. Disraeli's Tancred is a fictional nineteenth-century Englishman; the historical Tancred was a Norman hero of the First Crusade.

98. Cosima Wagner, *Diaries,* I, 744.

99. *Ibid.,* II, 212. Wagner's description of himself as a "tattooed savage" comes from a passage in *Tancred* where Sidonia so describes (in order to emphasize the superiority in culture of the "Hebrew race") the condition of the English bishops a few centuries ago. In an essay, "The Druidical Institutions," by Disraeli's father, the Britons of Caesar's day are said to have differed from red-tattooed Polynesian savages only in color: "The British savage chose blue, and made deep incisions in his flesh to insert his indelible woad" (Isaac D'Israeli, *Amenities of Literature, Consisting of Sketches and Characters of English Literature* [London, 1884], 3). Disraeli probably borrowed from the essay in his typical hyperbolic fashion.

100. Cosima Wagner, *Diaries,* II, 213.

were surely well aware, Disraeli had presided over Queen Victoria's assumption of the title of empress of India. The Near East, however, was still in the grip of the Turkish Porte.

The central message of *Tancred*—Sidonia's "all is race; there is no other truth"—seems not to have attracted Wagner's attention. To judge from the passage in Cosima's diary cited above, Wagner was somewhat unclear as to Disraeli's "idea . . . of racial purity and great men"; it required some "getting at." Wagner had first met Gobineau in 1876, but his acquaintance with Gobineau's *Essay on the Inequality of the Human Races* (or at least his first reading of it) dates from February 14, 1881.[101] It was an English-born Wagnerian and admirer of things German, Houston Stewart Chamberlain, who would, sixteen years after Wagner's death, advise the Germans to take heed of Disraeli's insistence on the virtues of racial purity (the same advice that Disraeli himself had given the North American "Anglo-Saxon republic" a half-century earlier). Chamberlain's *The Foundations of the Nineteenth Century* was written in the German language, and first published in Germany.[102] "Let Disraeli teach us," Chamberlain tells the Germans, "that the whole significance of Judaism lies in its purity of race, that this alone gives it power and duration." In a footnote, Chamberlain adds: "See the novels *Tancred* and *Coningsby*. In the

101. "Still in Rome . . . Made the pleasant acquaintance of Count Gobineau, the French ambassador in Sweden," notes Cosima in her diaries on November 30, 1876 (*ibid.*, I, 935). (Gobineau had previously served in similar capacities in Persia, Greece, and Brazil.) The next reference to him in Cosima's diaries is dated January 21, 1881: "[Wagner] praises Count Gobineau highly and takes great delight in the story *Les Amants de Kandahar*" (*ibid.*, II, 604). (This is a reference to a story in Gobineau's *Nouvelles asiatiques* [1876].) Gobineau's essay on the inequality of races is first mentioned by Cosima on February 14, 1881 (*ibid.*, II, 621). Wagner evidently decided to read it through. On April 18, 1881, Cosima notes: "Count Gobineau's book tires him, and he once again declares that one must beware of thick books" (*ibid.*, II, 657). On May 28, 1881, she notes: "His pleasure lies today in finishing the Count's book" (*ibid.*, II, 670). The final reference to the essay in Cosima's diaries is of interest for what in today's political jargon would probably be called its "pro-Arabism." She writes, on January 22, 1882: "we discuss yesterday's reading, the significance of the Arab people, and Gobineau's over-estimation of the Normans, who in fact simply took over the beautiful things they found [in the Near East] in order to enjoy them—they created nothing themselves" (*ibid.*, II, 794). (Gobineau prided himself on his Norman, purely "Nordic" descent, much as Disraeli, before him, preened himself on his Jewish descent.)

102. Houston Stewart Chamberlain, *Die Grundlagen des neunzehnten Jahrhunderts*, (5th ed.; 2 vols.; Munich, 1899).

latter [*sic*] Sidonia says: 'Race is everything: there is no other truth.'
And every race must fall which carelessly allows its blood to be
mixed."[103] As we have seen, the same doctrine is preached in Disraeli's
biography of Lord George Bentinck. Disraeli rather than Gobineau—
still less Chamberlain—is entitled to be called the father of nineteenth-
century racist ideology, if we are foolish enough to bestow such titles
on people who are merely repeating what they take to be the wisdom
of their own fathers. Sidonia was in fact repeating the postexilic doctrines of Ezra and Ezekiel when he warned against racial intermarriage, and these same doctrines gave biblical authority to Old Testament Christians in North America and South Africa to pursue their
policies of segregation and apartheid, respectively.

In a later chapter we shall return to Chamberlain in connection
with another Wagnerian, the Austrian-born Adolf Hitler, who was in
early youth inspired by Wagner's *Rienzi*—an opera based on the rise
and fall of the real-life Rienzi, a man of humble origins who became
supreme leader of medieval Rome—to envision himself as the future
leader of the German peoples. Still another Austrian-born Wagnerian
will call for our attention there as well: Theodor Herzl, Zionist leader
in the footsteps of Moses Hess and author of *The Jewish State. An Attempt at a Modern Solution of the Jewish Question* (1896). This book,
so we are told by Herzl himself, was directly inspired by the music of
Wagner's *Tannhäuser*.[104]

TOLSTOY'S CHRISTIANITY

In 1860, we recall, "a Count Tolstoy" stood out among Wagner's visitors.[105] It seems quite certain that the Count Tolstoy in question was

103. Cited in Houston Stewart Chamberlain, *The Foundations of the Nineteenth
Century*, trans. John Lees, with an introduction by Lord Redesdale (2 vols.; London,
1911), I, 271. In the introduction, Lord Redesdale recalls a conversation with a "distinguished Jewish gentleman" who had just come from a meeting with Disraeli (Redesdale
spells it *D'Israeli*). What had they talked about? "'Oh,' said my host, 'the usual thing—
the Race.'" (I, xxxiv). This Lord Redesdale was *not* the "future father-in-law of the British fascist leader Sir Oswald Mosley," as I erroneously stated in *The Dream of Self-
Destruction*, p. 28; he was the father of that father-in-law (the error was kindly called to
my attention by Jessica Mitford).

104. Theodor Herzl, *Der Judenstaat. Versuch einer modernen Lösung der Judenfrage* (Leipzig: 1896). See Herzl, *Theodor Herzls zionistische Schriften*, ed. Dr. Leon
Kellner (2 vols. in 1; Berlin, 1905), 18, for Herzl's account of his inspiration.

105. For the single reference to Tolstoy in Wagner's autobiography, see Chapter 2
herein.

Leo (Lev) Nikolayevich Tolstoy, since he was at the time engaged in a prolonged European tour. Then thirty-two years old, Tolstoy had written none of the novels and short stories that would later make him world famous. He was two decades away from his religious conversion and his subsequent near-total rejection of all forms of art—his own works and those of Shakespeare and Wagner included.[106] In the one reference to Leo Tolstoy in Cosima's diaries the visit of 1860 is not mentioned: the entry, dated December 3, 1882, tells us only that Wagner, at her instigation, is reading parts of Tolstoy's *War and Peace* (presumably in the French translation) with evident enjoyment.[107] Wagner's death in Venice came three months later, on February 13, 1883. He was never to know how close his thoughts on the nature of true Christianity were to those of Tolstoy, and Tolstoy himself, although he survived until 1910, seems to have been aware of Wagner only as a musician and poet.

In 1860 Tolstoy also paid a visit to Berthold Auerbach in Dresden. Tolstoy had been inspired to found a school for peasants on his estate at Yasnaya Polyana by one of Auerbach's novels, and, according to a biographer of Tolstoy, "took pleasure in telling him so."[108] In the same year Tolstoy made the acquaintance, in Brussels, of the French anarchist theoretician Pierre-Joseph Proudhon, author of *What Is Property?* (1840). On returning to Russia in the spring of 1861, Tolstoy paid a second visit to Auerbach. They discussed, among other topics, music, morals, and Christianity. In the diary that Tolstoy was keeping at the time (in German) Auerbach's definition of Christianity as "the spirit of humanity than which nothing could be higher" is cited with much approval. Tolstoy's biographer adds that "Auerbach's characterization of music as *pflichtloser Genuss,* as unethical pleasure leading directly to depravity, may have been the seed from which grew [Tolstoy's] tragedy of the Kreutzer Sonata' [1890]."[109]

106. Tolstoy ridiculed *The Ring of the Nibelung* in *What Is Art?* (1906) and *King Lear* in *Shakespeare and the Drama* (1906).

107. Cosima Wagner, *Diaries,* II, 965, 1152. See note 111 following for a comment on the French translation.

108. Nathan Haskell Dole, *The Life of Count Tolstoi* (New York, 1929), 138, 142. The novel in question was *Neues Leben;* in it a school for the common people is founded by Count Falkenberg. *Cf.* Anton Bettelheim's intoductory essay in Auerbach, *Werke,* I, 45.

109. Dole, *Life of Count Tolstoi,* 156–58. On Auerbach's religious sentiments, see note 96, this chapter.

Tolstoy's writings on the subject of religion begin with the story of his conversion, in *My Confession* (1879). *My Religion* (1884) sets forth in detail his reasons for rejecting the Old Testament Pentateuch together with dogmas of the Russian Orthodox church based on the book. A French translation of the Russian text of *My Religion* was published in 1885, and an English translation (from the French) in 1885; an English translation from the Russian original first appeared in 1904.[110] The similarity of Tolstoy's Christianity to that of Wagner at once attracted attention, and a long article entitled "The Religion of Richard Wagner and the Religion of Count Leo Tolstoy" on the subject by Teodor de Wyzewa was published (in French) in the *Revue wagnérienne* in the issue of October 8, 1885.[111] We shall return to this article later.

Tolstoy's religious studies were far more thorough than those of Wagner. Before writing *My Religion*, Tolstoy had mastered New Testament Greek and translated the Gospels. He had studied Hebrew and read parts of the Old Testament in the original, and had some acquaintance with the Talmud. Tolstoy was aware of the many points on which the Hebrew prophets and certain of the Talmudists were in full agreement with the teachings of Christ. Tolstoy writes in *My Religion:* "Some time ago I was reading, in Hebrew, the fifth chapter of Matthew with a Jewish rabbi. At nearly every verse the rabbi said, 'This is in the Bible,' or 'This is in the Talmud,' and he showed me in the Bible and in the Talmud sentences very like the declarations of the Sermon on the Mount. When we reached the words, 'Resist not evil,' the rabbi did not say, 'This is in the Talmud,' but he asked me with a smile, 'Do the Christians obey this command? Do they turn the other cheek?'"[112] Tolstoy was taken aback, because, as he says, he knew quite well that the "Christians, far from turning the other cheek, were smiting the Jews on both cheeks." Unwilling to let the *ignoratio elen-*

110. Leo Tolstoy, *My Religion, by Count L. N. Tolstoi,* trans. (from the French) Huntington Smith (New York, 1885); Tolstoy, *The Complete Works of Count Tolstoy,* trans. Leo Wiener (Vol. XVI of 24 vols.; Boston, 1904).

111. Teodor de Wyzewa, "La religion de Richard Wagner et la religion du comte Léon de Tolstoï," *Revue wagnérienne,* October 18, 1885, pp. 237–56 (Wyzewa says that the French translation of Tolstoy's *War and Peace* then available was "shamefully truncated" [*ibid.,* 237 n. 2]).

112. Tolstoy, *My Religion,* 17. The words "in Hebrew" do not appear in Leo Wiener's translation (Tolstoy, *Complete Works,* XVI, 19). Tolstoy studied Hebrew under a Rabbi Minor in Moscow (Dole, *Life of Count Tolstoi,* 296).

chi pass, however, he asked whether the Bible or the Talmud contained anything similar, to which the rabbi replied, "No . . . there is nothing like it; but tell me, do the Christians obey this law?"[113]

For Tolstoy, the central point of Christ's teachings, the "key to the whole mystery," is the total rejection of violence in human affairs that he finds expressed in the words of the Sermon on the Mount: "Resist not evil." Like Wagner and Kierkegaard, Tolstoy sees a fundamental contradiction between Judaism and Christianity, between the law of Moses and the law of Jesus. Because he himself had been inculcated in infancy with the notion that there was no such contradiction, he had theretofore managed to suppress his awareness of it: "I was taught to resist evil, that it was humiliating to submit to evil. . . . Then I was taught the soldier's trade, that is, to resist evil by homicide; the army to which I belonged was called 'the Christophile Army,' and it was sent forth with a Christian benediction. From infancy to manhood I learned to venerate things that were in direct contradiction to the law of Jesus,—to meet an aggressor with his own weapons, to avenge myself for all offences against my person, my family, or my race." And when he read Christ's words in the New Testament, "Ye have heard that it hath been said, An eye for an eye, and a tooth for a tooth: But I say unto you, That ye resist not evil," he tells us that he was for a long time simply unable to see that the words *But I say unto you, That ye resist not evil* "expressed the new law, which was a negation of the first."[114]

The contradiction, Tolstoy emphasized, does not exist for anyone who accepts the words of Jesus as the truth. Such a one simply ignored the law of Moses. Nor did it exist for the Jews, who "looked on the words of Jesus as foolishness, and believed in the law of Moses." It existed only for "those who would follow the law of Moses under the cover of the law of Jesus—for those whom Jesus denounced as hypocrites, as a generation of vipers." We ourselves, in other words—those of us who regard both laws as divine, but, when it comes to the test,

---

113. Tolstoy, *My Religion*, 17. See, however, Lamentations 3:30: "He giveth his cheek to him that smiteth him." Auerbach's fictional Spinoza objects: "When Christ says, 'If someone strikes you on the right cheek, offer him the left one as well,' this can be valid only in a time of oppression and lawlessness; otherwise it is more right and reasonable to give him who strikes you two blows in return . . . so that the wicked will not triumph in their wickedness" (Auerbach, *Werke*, XIII, 231). See Morton Smith, *Tannaitic Parallels to the Gospels* (Philadelphia, 1951) for a scholarly study.

114. Tolstoy, *My Religion*, 15–17.

always "reject the law of Jesus and follow that of Moses."[115] Only three years earlier, in "Know Thyself," Wagner had written: "Down to the present day, in spite of all dispersion, the Jewish tribes have remained one with the law of Moses, whereas our culture and civilization stand in the most crying contradiction to the teachings of Christ."[116] Tolstoy puts it in almost identical words. "Our entire social fabric," he writes, "is founded upon principles that Jesus reproved; we do not wish to understand his doctrine in its simple and direct acceptation, and yet we assure ourselves and others that we follow his doctrine, or else that his doctrine is not expedient for us." He continues: "Believers profess that Christ is God, the second person of the Trinity, descended upon earth to teach men by his example how to live; they go through the most elaborate ceremonies for the consummation of the sacraments, the building of temples, the sending out of missionaries, the establishment of priesthoods, for parochial administration, for the performance of rituals; but they forget one little detail,—the practice of the commandments of Jesus."[117]

Christ's command "*Resist not evil*" means precisely what it says, insists Tolstoy. It means "never resist, never oppose violence; or, in other words, never do anything contrary to the law of love."[118] To illustrate how the contradiction between law and practice had been glossed over in the New Testament, Tolstoy cites Matthew 5:21–22; in the King James version this reads (and must have read similarly in the version seen by Tolstoy): "Ye have heard that it was said by them of old time, Thou shalt not kill; . . . But I say unto you, That whosoever is angry with his brother without a cause shall be in danger of the judgment." Tolstoy saw clearly that the phrase "without a cause" destroyed the meaning of the verse. For there is always a cause, and who is to decide whether the anger is justifiable or not? In Tolstoy's Greek version (supposedly the original) of the New Testament the word εἰκῆ, meaning "heedlessly," "inconsiderately," hence "without a cause," was nevertheless present. The commentators whom he read had no help to offer; they simply attempted to define the conditions under

115. *Ibid.,* 67.
116. Wagner, *Gesammelte Schriften und Dichtungen,* X, 266. See Rather, *The Dream of Self-Destruction,* 178–79, for Wagner's equation of the "law of Moses" with "the law of Mohammed" (*das Gesetz Muhameds*).
117. Tolstoy, *My Religion,* 40.
118. *Ibid.,* 13.

which anger was justifiable. Eventually Tolstoy found that the word εἰκῆ "had not crept into the best copies of the Gospel as late as the fifth century." A "premeditated alteration of the text" had destroyed its moral, religious, and logical meaning.[119] Christ's command had been abrogated by an Orwellian copyist.

Tolstoy gives an equally close reading of other key passages in the New Testament. Matthew 5:43–44 ("Ye have heard that it hath been said, Thou shalt love thy neighbor, and hate thine enemy. But I say unto you, Love your enemies, bless them that curse you, do good to them that hate you and pray for them which despitefully use you, and persecute you") attracts his attention. Here, says Tolstoy, Jesus seems to calumniate Judaism, for all commentators agree that the words "hate thine enemy" are not to be found in the Mosaic law, but can offer no explanation as to why Jesus used them. Tolstoy himself finds it in the meaning of the key words, *neighbor* and *enemy*. The word *neighbor* in the Hebrew language means "invariably and exclusively, a Hebrew," and the word *enemy*, when used in the singular, means a "hostile people." Tolstoy writes: "The various passages scattered through the different books of the Old Testament, prescribing the oppression, slaughter, and extermination of other peoples, Jesus summed up in one word 'hate,'—make war upon the enemy. He said, in substance: 'You have heard that you must love those of your own race, and hate foreigners; but I say unto you, love everyone without distinction of nationality. . . .' His meaning was that the law of Moses established a difference between the Hebrew and the foreigner—the hostile peoples; but he forbade any such difference."[120] Tolstoy's interpretation of this passage was in all likelihood not the first of its kind, certainly not the last.[121]

Like many other readers, Jewish and non-Jewish, of the Old Testament, Tolstoy drew a sharp line of distinction between the universal

119. *Ibid.*, 70–75, 85. The phrase "without a cause" or its equivalent is absent from most other editions of the Bible, *e.g.*, the Jerusalem Bible (London, 1966), *La sainte Bible* (7th ed.; Paris, 1950), Luther's *Die Heilige Schrift,* and the Clementine *Biblia Sacra;* the word εἰκῆ does not appear in the *Novum Testamentum Graece et Latine* (Stuttgart, 1954).

120. Tolstoy, *My Religion,* 94–99.

121. In a review of Morton Smith's *Hope and History, An Exploration* (New York, 1980), J. R. Cameron took issue with Smith's similar interpretation of the ancient Hebrew attitude toward non-Israelites and called his book "savage and bilious" (*New York Review of Books,* XXVII, [April 17, 1980], 36).

Judaism of the prophets and the tribal Judaism of the Pentateuch. His strictures are always directed against the "law of Moses," and very rarely against the utterances of the Hebrew prophets. Tolstoy's conversations in Moscow with Rabbi Minor and his own perceptiveness in the matter had brought him to see how much Christianity could be found in these utterances. Hence Tolstoy's claim that Jesus himself drew the same line between two entirely different kinds of law. "And so Jesus sometimes speaks of law as the divine law (of Isaiah and the other prophets), in which case he confirms it; and sometimes in the sense of the written law of the Pentateuch, in which case he rejects it. To distinguish the difference, he always, in speaking of the written law, adds 'and the prophets,' or prefixes the word 'your,'—'your law.'" [122] This "written law of the Pentateuch" consists, Tolstoy asserts, of "minute doctrines, often absurd and even cruel in their purport." [123] Aside from the Ten Commandments, and not all of them, Tolstoy rejects the Pentateuch, that is, the Hebrew Torah, in its entirety. The violence of his invective against the tribal code of the ancient Hebrews far exceeds anything of the kind to be found in Wagner. One section of Tolstoy's *The Four Gospels Harmonized and Translated* is entitled "The Rejection of the Jewish God." We read there:

> In the Gospel we are prohibited not only from killing anyone but even from bearing anyone ill-will; in the Pentateuch: Kill, kill, kill women, children, and cattle.
> In the Gospel wealth is an evil; in the Pentateuch it is the highest good and a reward.
> In the Gospel bodily purity consists in having one wife; in the Pentateuch, Take as many wives as you please.
> In the Gospel all men are brothers; in the Pentateuch, all are enemies, except the Jews.
> In the Gospel there is no external divine worship; in the Pentateuch, the greater half of the books defines the details of the external ministration of God. [124]

In no reasonable sense of the word was Tolstoy what is today called an anti-Semite. On the contrary, the Jews of Russia often called on him for moral support during their late nineteenth- and early twentieth-century time of troubles, which began with the assassination of Tsar Alexander II in 1881 by a group of political terrorists (which included

122. Tolstoy, *My Religion*, 56–58.
123. *Ibid.*, 51, 63.
124. Tolstoy, *Complete Works*, XIV, 108–109.

some Jews). Tolstoy did so, but he made his moral position clear. His daughter Alexandra tells us that in 1903, on the occasion of the Jewish pogroms in Kishinev, Tolstoy spoke out "not because they are Jews but because we and they, and all human beings are sons of the one God and Father."[125] In 1890, on the occasion of another pogrom, Tolstoy expressed his sorrow to a Jewish journalist, and he suggested that much of the hatred was due to envy on the part of the "quasi-Christians" because Jews were better equipped to achieve the "aspirations of the majority." Tolstoy added, however, that "archaic outmoded Jewish principles of morality . . . [are] the very ones in whose names the persecutions are carried out."[126] He means, of course, the "archaic . . . principles of morality" to be found in the Pentateuch; these are the very principles to which "quasi-Christians" assent whenever they take to the warpath. Elsewhere, Tolstoy says that the kingdom of Christ on earth will have come when all men learn to live in peace with one another, and he adds, "It was thus that the Hebrew prophets conceived of the rule of God."[127]

We recall that Wagner, in his sketch of a drama based on the life of Jesus of Nazareth, made a case for the total prohibition of the taking of oaths laid down in the Gospels: "But I say unto you, Swear not at all" (Matthew 5 : 33 – 34). Forty years later, Tolstoy too insists that the taking of oaths constitutes a "terrible evil." It is the oath of obedience that Tolstoy has in mind, for such oaths bind us to obey the will of another person, or group of persons, or a document of less than divine origins, such as the military regulations. An ordinary man, put in the uniform of a soldier and pledged to obedience, can be made to burn, murder, and destroy at the will of his superiors. Tolstoy tells how he once reproached a soldier for committing such atrocities, asking the man whether he had ever read the New Testament; the soldier in turn asked Tolstoy whether he had ever read the military regulations. Sworn on the New Testament itself, an oath of absolute obedience to his military superiors required the Russian soldier to follow orders.[128]

---

125. Alexandra Tolstoy, *Tolstoy: A Life of My Father*, trans. Elizabeth Reynolds Hapgood (New York, 1953), 428.

126. Tolstoy, *Tolstoy's Letters*, II, 458–59.

127. Tolstoy, *My Religion*, 43.

128. *Ibid.*, 19–20, 44–45, 86–89. Morton Smith cites in connection with the prohibition against oaths in the New Testament a Tannaitic commentary on Deuteronomy 23 : 23: "It were good . . . that you vow not at all" (Smith, *Tannaitic Parallels to the Gospels*, 136).

Teodor de Wyzewa's paper of 1885 in the *Revue wagnérienne* makes all but one of these points of agreement between Wagner's and Tolstoy's Christianity. The one exception is the prohibition of oaths; Wagner's sketch *Jesus of Nazareth* had not yet been published. Wyzewa used the French translation of Tolstoy's *My Religion* and the German original of Wagner's essay "Religion and Art" (1880).[129] He cites parallel passages to buttress all claims. Tolstoy's rejection of the Pentateuch, for example, is paralleled by Wagner's rejection of the Judaic element in Christianity. Wyzewa writes: "Thus the religion of Wagner and the religion of Tolstoy are likewise Christian, but they are opposed to all teachings of the Christian Church. Are these religions therefore atheistic, forbidding all religious belief? *They are uninterested in such beliefs, because they are purely moral and positive religions*" (my emphasis). He goes on to say that Tolstoy's Jesus cares not at all whether you are a "materialist, an evolutionist, a Moslem, a Mormon, a Buddhist," or whatever; believe what you will in the way of metaphysical doctrine, says Tolstoy's Jesus, but follow my way of life while you live on earth. And, adds Wyzewa, "Wagner's religion admits, equally, all beliefs and all cults," for what is at issue for him too is how human beings behave themselves on this earth, not the beliefs, rites, and rituals of their particular religion.[130]

Rather inexplicably, Wyzewa held that there was a significant difference between the Wagnerian and the Tolstoyan concept of compassion (*Mitleid, compassion*). He asserts: "for Wagner compassion is pitying love, the inmost charity of the heart, itself suffering all suffering. Parsifal is the blessed savior because he has pity on the sufferings of Amfortas. And always the Maestro says to you: 'Love, show sympathy, enlarge your souls to embrace all souls!' Tolstoy, on the contrary, ceaselessly recommends to us active compassion (*compassion agissante*), the practical charity of the hands, labor, which alone is good, for the benefit of all."[131] Practical charity of the hands, however,

129. Wyzewa says that the Russian original of *My Religion* was published in Moscow in 1884, but he had been unable to obtain a copy. He calls the French translation (Paris, 1885) "magnificent in its clarity." He read "Religion and Art" in the October, 1880, issue of the *Bayreuther Blätter*, and he mentions that an excellent though anonymous translation of it appeared in the *Revue littéraire et artistique*, issue of November 15, 1881. *Cf.* Wyzewa, "La religion de Richard Wagner et la religion du comte Léon de Tolstoï," 237 n. 1, 238 n. 2.
130. *Ibid.*, 244–45.
131. *Ibid.*, 253.

does not consist solely of labor in the fields or factory, as Wyzewa's argument seems to presuppose. The work of the surgeon is handwork *par excellence*, a "chirurgeon" is, both literally and etymologically, a handworker. The healing hand of the physician may carry out its work unaided, as when fractures are set or dislocations reduced, or it may call in all the technical aids made available by the sciences. The practicing physician, Wagner wrote in 1879 in his polemic against vivisection, is (or should be) the foremost representative "of the personal active compassion (*tätigen Mitleides*) otherwise so rarely to be found in our midst." [132] The name Helferich ("rich in help") that he gave to his firstborn son was accompanied by the wish that the boy would become a surgeon or at least learn enough surgery "so that he can give first aid to human beings or animals." [133] As for Wyzewa's reference to *Parsifal*, it should have been obvious to him that the aim of Parsifal in returning to Monsalvat after he had learned compassion was to *heal* Amfortas rather than to shed tears of pity over his sad state.

132. Wagner, *Gesammelte Schriften und Dichtungen*, X, 199. One can only conclude that Wyzewa overlooked this passage.
133. Cosima Wagner, *Diaries*, II, 156; Glasenapp, *Das Leben Richard Wagners*, VI, 116–17.

CHAPTER SIX

GERMAN AND JEWISH QUESTIONS

WAGNER'S ESSAY "JUDAISM IN MUSIC" (1850)

Undoubtedly Wagner's most controversial and anathematized piece of writing, "Judaism in Music" was first published in September, 1850, in two successive issues of the *Neue Zeitschrift für Musik*, a musical journal founded in Leipzig in 1834 by Robert Schumann.[1] Since 1845 this journal had been owned and edited by Karl Franz Brendel, professor of music history and aesthetics at the Leipzig Conservatory. The essay appeared under the signature of "K. Freigedenk" (K. Freethought). Why did Wagner use a pseudonym, and why this pseudonym? It is true that Schumann himself—who, we recall, was one of the rejected candidates for the mysterious "Schoman" who visited Baudelaire in Paris in 1849—signed his own essays between 1834 and 1844 variously as "Florestan," "Eusebius," "Raro," and "Jeanquit."[2] It is true

1. Wagner, "Das Judenthum in der Musik," in *Gesammelte Schriften und Dichtungen*, V, 66–85; Wagner, "Das Judentum in der Musik," and "Aufklärungen über das Judentum in der Musik," in *Richard Wagners gesammelte Schriften*, 7–29, and 29–51, respectively. I have not seen the original version, as published in the *Neue Zeitschrift für Musik* in September, 1850. When Wagner reissued the essay in 1869 he made numerous changes and added the supplementary "Clarifications" (*Aufklärungen*). For translations see "Some Explanations Concerning Judaism in Music," "Judaism in Music," and "Appendix to 'Judaism in Music,'" in Wagner, *Prose Works*, III, 77–78, 79–100, and 1010–1122, respectively, and Wagner, "Judaism in Music," in Wagner, *Stories and Essays*, 23–39. The *Gesammelte Schriften und Dichtungen* contains only the 1869 version of the essay proper. Kapp and Ellis print the 1869 version and give the original wording (where changes were made) in footnotes. Ellis divided the "Clarifications" into two parts, printed before and after the essay proper, as noted above. Osborne prints his own translation of the 1869 version. For my comments on the translations of Osborne and Ellis, see notes 5, 16, 42, 43, and 45 following.

2. *S.v.* "Brendel" and "Schumann," in *Grove's Dictionary of Music and Musicians*. Schumann left Dresden during the rebellion of 1849. On the possibility that he

also that Wagner was at the time living in exile in Switzerland, and that a warrant for his arrest was in the hands of the royal police of Saxony. Whatever his reasons, Wagner's choice of pseudonym is evidence of recognition on his part that he was touching (none too delicately) on a taboo topic. No doubt he foresaw the reaction to the essay, although he may have been surprised by its violence; he would have been astounded could he have known that the reaction would still be in progress toward the end of the twentieth century, more violent than ever.

Wagner claimed in 1869—when "Judaism in Music" was published separately, with some changes in the original wording and some "clarifications" (*Aufklärungen*) by Wagner—that he had used the pseudonym in the hope of confining discussion of the essay to its contents and of avoiding *ad hominem* attacks on its author as "a composer doubtlessly envious of others." As for the purpose of the essay, Wagner wrote in his autobiography at about the same time that his intent had been to develop the "theme of the intervention of the Jews today in music, their influence on this art, and to ascertain the features characteristic of this problem."[3] Since the autobiography was, until long after Wagner's death, circulated only among friends or admirers we can assume that this statement is true as far as it goes, although perhaps hardly the whole truth.

Before turning to the matter in hand another passage from Wagner's autobiography will be cited here because of the interesting light it throws on relationships between Jews and Gentiles in France and Germany at the time. Wagner says that in Paris in 1841 he was conversing with Jacques Halévy (whose opera *La Juive* he much admired), the music publisher Maurice (or Moritz) Schlesinger, and several other (unidentified) Frenchmen. Suddenly Halévy addressed a few words to Wagner in German. There was a moment of surprise, says Wagner, until Schlesinger explained that "all Jews spoke German." Schlesinger was then asked by one of the company whether he himself was a Jew, to which Schlesinger replied that he had been, but that his wife was a Christian and at her request he had converted (the reader will recall what was said in Chapter 2 of Flaubert's *Éducation sentimentale*).

---

was the mysterious "Schoman" who visited Baudelaire in that year, see Chapter 3 herein.

    3. Wagner, *Mein Leben*, II, 479; Wagner, *Prose Works*, III, 102.

Wagner adds, "This relaxed conversation on a subject that among
Germans under similar circumstances would anxiously be avoided as a
thing painful to the person concerned gave me a pleasant surprise."[4]

The whole passage, to today's reader, bristles with unanswered implied questions. Why, assuming the truth of Wagner's remark, was the
subject taboo in Germany but not in France? Were the Gentiles in Germany restrained by a more formidable Jewish presence? Why painful
to the person concerned? Were French Jews more comfortable with
their "Jewishness" than were German Jews? (We know that Wagner
did find one German Jew, Berthold Auerbach, with whom he could
converse freely on the forbidden question.) What are the ramifica-
tions, and indeed the precise meaning, of Schlesinger's claim that *all*
Jews speak German? Some of these topics will be touched on briefly
here; others will receive consideration in the following section on the
German-Jewish symbiosis (a phrase coined, after the fact, by Martin
Buber). Finally, the attention of the reader is called to the apparent
lack of racial consciousness on the part of Wagner in his description
(written in the late 1860s) of the above episode in his life in Paris a
quarter of a century earlier.

The touchy character of the subject of "Judaism in Music" was
clearly obvious to Brendel, for he introduced Wagner's essay with the
following footnote: "However faulty her outward conformation, we
have always considered it a pre-eminence of Germany's, a result of her
great learning, that at least in the scientific sphere she possesses intellectual freedom. This freedom we now lay claim to and rely on in
printing the above essay, desirous that our readers may accept it in this
sense. Whether one shares the views expressed therein, or not, the author's breadth of grasp (*Genialität der Anschauung*) will be disputed
by no one."[5] But the outburst of rage and indignation that came at
once must have exceeded by far his worst expectations, for he could
hardly have thought that his own position at the Leipzig Conservatory

4. Wagner, *Mein Leben*, I, 219.
5. Wagner, *Prose Works*, III, 79. Osborne repeats Ellis' footnote verbatim, aside
from the omission of the German words in parentheses and the substitution of "foully"
for "faulty." He adds that Brendel wrote this apologia "with careful disingenuity." On
the same page Osborne calls "Judaism in Music" a "piece of obscene unreason . . . the
product of a mind so contorted with hate and envy that it merits little consideration"
(Wagner, *Stories and Essays*, 23). His translation of Brendel's words, as given, makes no
sense. Presumably "foully" is a typographical error: one wonders how it could have
been overlooked. See Chapter 2 herein for Osborne's assessment of Wagner's poetry.

would be endangered. Wagner, who was soon unmasked as K. Free-thought, was safe in exile from other than verbal reprisal. Not so Brendel: his fellow professors at the conservatory, including Joseph Joachim, Ignaz Moscheles, Ferdinand David, Moritz Hauptmann, and Julius Rietz, immediately sent off a letter calling for the dismissal of Brendel from the chair of music history and aesthetics.[6]

The Leipzig Conservatory, under the patronage of the king of Saxony, had first opened its doors on January 16, 1843. The conservatory was largely the creation of Felix Mendelssohn (1809–1847). When the essay was republished in 1869, Wagner wrote in the "Clarifications": "In consequence of the many years of rightly and deservedly honoured work which Mendelssohn had spent in Leipzig—at whose Musical Conservatorium Brendel filled the post of a Professor—that city had received a virtual Jewish baptism of music . . . it was exclusively becoming the metropolis of German music."[7] The signers of the letter calling for Brendel's dismissal had all been connected, in one way or another, with Mendelssohn: the great violinist Joachim had been taught by Mendelssohn as well as by David; Mendelssohn and David had been close associates; Rietz and Hauptmann were two former protégés of Mendelssohn; and the great pianist Ignaz Moscheles (1794–1870) had taught the young Mendelssohn in Berlin in 1824 and later became his intimate friend.[8]

Six years before the publication of "Judaism in Music" another acute observer had called attention to the prominence of Jews on the European musical scene. This was Disraeli's tireless spokesman Sidonia, celebrating in *Coningsby; or, The New Generation* one more triumph of the Hebrew race. According to Sidonia, "Rossini, Meyerbeer and Mendelsohn [*sic*] are of Hebrew race." In fact, so he instructs his young English protégé Coningsby: "Almost every great composer, skilled musician, almost every voice that ravishes you . . . spring from our tribes." Adding a note of prophecy that has been at least partially fulfilled, Sidonia continues: "There is not a company of singers, not an orchestra in a single capital that are not crowded with our children under the feigned names they adopt to conciliate the dark aversion

6. Newman, *The Life of Richard Wagner*, II, 218 n. 1.
7. Wagner, *Prose Works*, III, 101–102. Wagner says here that Brendel, with some difficulty, managed to ride out the storm.
8. *S.v.* "Mendelssohn," "David," "Hauptmann," "Rietz," and "Moscheles," in *Grove's Dictionary of Music and Musicians*.

which your posterity will some day disclaim with shame and disgust."
Sidonia seems almost to caper in triumph as he exults, "Musical Europe is ours."[9] Disraeli himself lets out all stops, including the note of
pathos, in his biography of Lord George Bentinck. "We dwell not,"
Disraeli writes, "on the fact that the most admirable artists of the
drama have been and still are of the Hebrew race, or that the most
entrancing singers, graceful dancers, and exquisite musicians are sons
and daughters of Israel . . . and when the Russian, the Frenchman, and
the Anglo-Saxon . . . yield themselves to the full spell of a Mozart or a
Mendelsohn [sic], it seems difficult to comprehend how these races can
reconcile it to their hearts to persecute a Jew."[10] (As far as Disraeli is
concerned Mozart, as well as Rossini, seems to be "of Hebrew race.")
This gasconading on the part of Disraeli, which had so annoyed the
young George Eliot, moved her slightly older contemporary W. M.
Thackeray to ridicule. In Codlingsby, his short parody of Coningsby,
Thackeray rechristens Sidonia "Mendoza," endows him with lethal
pugilistic skills, and traces his pedigree back to the union of Ivanhoe
and Rebecca, Ivanhoe having married Rebecca after the death of
Rowena and become "a rabbi of some note in the synagogue of Cordova." Thackeray adds to the list of Jewish notables hiding under
feigned names Carl Maria von Weber, Jenny Lind, the recently deposed Louis Philippe, and the Roman pope.[11]

There is no reason to suppose that Wagner was aware of the English
edition of Coningsby published in Leipzig by Tauchnitz in 1844. But
it may be that his attention to the Jewish influence on German music
was drawn in that year by Gasparo Spontini (1774–1851), who had
come to Dresden to oversee a production of his opera La Vestale at the
court theater. Spontini, an Italian by birth and Frenchman by naturalization, had dominated the musical scene in Berlin for two decades
under the patronage of Frederick William III. After the king's death in
1840 the irascible old musical dictator became involved in a quarrel
that culminated in his being convicted of lèse majesté with respect to
the new king of Prussia, Frederick William IV. Spontini was forced out
of Berlin. Wagner paints an amusing picture of the opinionated old

    9. Disraeli, Coningsby, 232, 235.
    10. Disraeli, Lord George Bentinck, 492, 494.
    11. William Makepeace Thackeray, "Codlingsby," in Works (22 vols.; Boston,
1899), VI, 15–28, passim.

composer in his autobiography. Spontini, says Wagner, was sincerely convinced that with him, the great Spontini, European music had reached the end of the road. Italian musicians, according to Spontini, were all "pigs," the French imitated the Italian *cochons;* as for the Germans, they were mere children whose musical promise had been "destroyed by the Jews"—in particular by the two "Wandering Jews" (*juifs errants*) who had usurped his place in Berlin.[12] These two were, of course, Giacomo Meyerbeer and Felix Mendelssohn. Meyerbeer was born Jakob Liebmann Beer, the son of a wealthy Berlin banker. *Meyer* was prefixed to *Beer* after he received a legacy from a rich relation of that name. Felix Mendelssohn became Mendelssohn-Bartholdy when, on the advice of his maternal uncle Salomon Bartholdy, he was baptized into the Christian faith. And Salomon Bartholdy had taken his last name from the "former proprietor of the garden belonging to the family."[13]

The reader fresh from a perusal of Marx's "On the Jewish Question" will find much that is familiar in Wagner's "Judaism in Music," for a central thesis of Wagner's essay is that the European world of art has been utterly commercialized, that is, judaized (in the Marxian sense). Quite recently "Judaism in Music" has been described as a piece of "obscene unreason," because of what it has to say—more accurately, what it is supposed to have said—about the Jews.[14] This description might with some semblance of justice be applicable to Moses Hess's "On the Nature of Money," when Hess asserts that it was the "world-historical task" of the Jews "to develop the *predatory animal* out of humanity . . . as blood-suckers, as Jews, as money-wolves."[15] But nothing of the like is to be found in Wagner's essay. It is really true that "Judaism in Music" is "far less intemperate than might be supposed," as a prominent Wagnerian, Edward Dannreuther (1844–1905), pointed out in his day. Happily unaware of such catchalls as "Jewish self-haters" and "anti-Semitic Semites," Dannreuther took note that among Wagner's "staunchest and most intelligent friends there were then, and there are still, many of Jewish descent who may

12. Wagner, *Mein Leben,* I, 301.
13. *S.v.* "Meyerbeer," in *Grove's Dictionary of Music and Musicians.*
14. See note 5, this chapter.
15. Hess, *Philosophische und Sozialistische Schriften,* 345–46. Cf. Chapter 5 herein.

have wished that he had left the subject alone, but who see no reason to disagree with him in the main."[16]

Marx and Hess were concerned with the total role played by the Jews in European political, economic, and religious thought. Wagner is concerned, he says, with the role played by the Jews in the development of German music. He asserts that the Jews have "long since ceased to be a foe deserving of [religious] hatred—thanks to all those [foes] found within the Christian religion itself, who have brought down upon themselves the hatred of the people." Nor has there been political conflict between Germans and Jews. "We even granted to them the establishment of an empire in Jerusalem," Wagner writes in "Judaism in Music," "and here we have had to regret that Herr von Rothschild was too clever to become king of the Jews, obviously preferring to remain 'the Jew of kings'"[17] The play on words probably comes from a bit of doggerel by W. M. Thackeray published in 1833 and dedicated to Nathan Rothschild: "The first Baron Juif; by the grace of his pelf / Not 'the king of the Jews,'; but 'the Jew of the kings.'"[18] (This sounds like something that Wagner might have picked

16. *S.v.* "Wagner," in *Grove's Dictionary of Music and Musicians.* Nevertheless, for today's sensitized reader, whether Jew or Gentile, it is not easy to read Wagner's "Judaism in Music" with understanding. The translation by Ellis is an additional hindrance. For example, Ellis has Wagner say of Felix Mendelssohn: "A like sympathy, however, can no other Jew composer rouse in us." The original German has "Jewish composer" (*jüdischer Komponist*). In the very next sentence Ellis has Wagner speak of another musician (commonly understood to be Meyerbeer) as a "Jewish tone-setter" (*jüdischer Tonsetzer*). To our ears, "Jew composer" sounds insulting, whereas "Jewish composer" is simply descriptive. "Jewish tone-setter" is merely confusing: the German word *Tonsetzer* means "composer" and is not pejorative. Ellis' reason, if he had one, for translating *jüdischer* on the first occasion as "Jew" and on the second as "Jewish" remains unclear. Osborne corrected Ellis here, giving "Jewish musician" for Wagner's *jüdischer Komponist* and "Jewish composer" for *jüdischer Tonsetzer* (Wagner, *Stories and Essays*, 36). But he translates Wagner's assertion that "Jewish musical works often make on us an impression as if, for example, a poem by Goethe were recited to us in the Jewish jargon" ("jüdische Musikwerke auf uns oft den Eindruck machen, als ob, z.B. ein Goethesches Gedicht im jüdischen Jargon uns vorgetragen wurde") as "works of Jewish music often produce in us the kind of effect we would derive from hearing a poem by Goethe translated into that Jewish jargon *we know as Yiddish*" (my emphasis on Osborne's gratuitous addition to the German text; Wagner, *Stories and Essays*, 33).

17. Wagner, "Das Judenthum in der Musik," in *Richard Wagners gesammelte Schriften*, XIII, 8. Hess had yet to write *Rome and Jerusalem*, but the idea of a Jewish return, with German help, to the Holy Land was already in the air. (Disraeli, of course, wanted the job done under the auspices of the British Empire.)

18. Thackeray, *Works*, XXII, 358.

GERMAN AND JEWISH QUESTIONS

up from Heine in Paris in the late thirties.) Wagner adds, in a passage shortly to be cited at length, his own play on words: the "creditor of kings" (*Gläubiger der Könige*) has become the "king of [Christian] believers" (*zum Könige der Gläubigen geworden*).[19] The pun works only in German. Something quite like it, which manages to survive translation, turned up not too many years later in Marx's *Capital:* "Public credit becomes the *credo* of capital. . . . Want of faith in the national debt takes the place of blasphemy against the Holy Ghost."[20]

The following passage from "Judaism in Music" puts one in mind of Marx's "On the Jewish Question." Marx, we recall, argues that the "Jew has [already] emancipated himself in a Jewish way . . . not only because he has acquired financial power, but also because through him and also apart from him *money* has become a world power and the practical Jewish spirit has become the practical spirit of the Christian nations."[21] (There are of course Kierkegaardian overtones to be heard here.) Wagner, in "Judaism in Music," writes:

When we fought for the emancipation of the Jews we were in fact fighters for an abstract principle rather than a concrete case, just as all our liberalism was a not very clairvoyant intellectual game, since we involved ourselves with the freedom of the folk without any knowledge of this folk, indeed with an aversion against any real contact with them. . . . Quite unperceived the 'creditor of kings' has become the king of creditors, and we can now find the plea of this king for emancipation nothing more than uncommonly naive, since we see ourselves rather in the position of fighting for emancipation from the Jews. The Jew is in fact, in the current state of things of this world, already more than emancipated. *He rules,* and he will continue to rule as long as money remains the power in the face of which all our acts and strivings lose force. That the historical misery of the Jews and the rapacious brutality of the Christian-German despots have placed just this power in the hands of the sons of Israel does not need to be set forth here.[22]

The reader's attention is called to the last sentence of the passage just cited, in particular to the two phrases "the historical misery of the Jews" and "the rapacious brutality of the Christian-German despots."

19. Wagner, *Richard Wagners gesammelte Schriften*, XIII, 9. Wagner used this same pun again in 1881: *cf.* Rather, *The Dream of Self-Destruction*, 173–76.
20. Marx, *Capital* (3 vols.; New York, 1967), I, 754.
21. Marx, "On the Jewish Question," in *Karl Marx Frederick Engels: Collected Works*, III, 170.
22. Wagner, *Richard Wagners gesammelte Schriften*, XIII, 9–10.

The Jews, it is implied, could only free themselves from their "historical misery" by winning power over money. And the "Christian-German despots" were, for their own purposes, willing to share this power with the Jews. Thirty years later, in 1880, Wagner wrote, "Jew and Junker are now reaching agreement over possession of the world." He may well have had in mind Otto von Bismarck and his Jewish banker Gerson Bleichröder.[23]

According to Arthur Ruppin, author of *The Jews in the Modern World* (1936) and a recognized authority on this subject, the Jews in their wanderings always borrowed the speech of the peoples among whom they pitched their tents. In the tenth century Arabic was the spoken and written language of the Jews of Africa and Spain. Jews who moved to the German-speaking countries took up German; those who migrated into Eastern Europe took up the Slavic tongues. A wide variety of what Ruppin calls jargons thus came into being, for the Jews did not speak the vernaculars precisely as did the original inhabitants: Ruppin mentions "Jew-French," "Jew-Italian," "Jew-Arabic" (written in Hebrew characters). Yiddish, he says, took form in German-speaking countries between the thirteenth and fifteenth centuries. When Jews began to migrate eastward to Poland in the thirteenth century they carried Yiddish with them. Not long afterwards Yiddish was adopted by the Russian Jews as well. Ruppin says too that until the beginning of the nineteenth century Yiddish, that is, Jewish-German, was the common language of all European Jews, aside from small communities of Ladino-speaking Sephardic Jews in Holland, France, and Italy, and that only in "exceptional cases had the Ashkenazic [*i.e.*, predominantly Yiddish-speaking] Jews in Holland, Southern and Central Germany, Bohemia, and Hungary adopted the vernacular."[24]

Wagner says much the same thing in "Judaism in Music." "The Jew," he writes, "speaks the tongue of the nation in which, from gen-

23. Wagner, *Gesammelte Schriften und Dichtungen*, X, 234. Wagner writes "über den Besitz der Welt verständigt jetzt der Jude mit dem Junker." Ellis, almost incredibly, translates the passage as follows: "the Jew now bargains with the Junior for possession of the world" (Wagner, *Prose Works*, VII, 234). "Junker" meant in Ellis' day and Wagner's precisely what it means in ours, namely an overbearing member of the Prussian land-owning nobility. On Wagner's description of Bismarck as an "ambitious Junker," see Rather, *The Dream of Self-Destruction*, 173; on Bleichröder, *ibid.*, 15–16, 174, 203.

24. Ruppin, *The Jews in the Modern World*, 284–87.

eration to generation, he lives, but he speaks it always as a stranger." In German, the language with which Wagner is primarily concerned, the "Semitic speech pattern" offends his ear. It is, he says, characterized by a "hissing, shrilling, humming and bungling pronunciation" and a "misuse and arbitrary twisting of words and phrase entirely uncharacteristic of our national language." As listeners, Wagner asserts, "our attention is instinctively held more by the repulsive *how* than by the *what* of Jewish speech."[25] At this point the present-day reader familiar with *The Ring of the Nibelung* may be put in mind of the shrill, pinched, nagging tones of Mime in the first act of *Siegfried* as he singsongs, for Siegfried's benefit, his repetitive praise of himself as the unselfishly protective parent—he claims to be both father *and* mother—and tutor of the young hero, who is as yet entirely ignorant of his true heritage.[26]

We are dealing here with several important features that should not be overlooked. Yiddish (*jüdisch*) is actually a German dialect in its own right, as much so as the Saxon dialect spoken by Wagner.[27] More so than any other of the German dialects, including the Bavarian, it developed a literature of its own. (That it was often printed in the Hebrew alphabet no more changed its character than would the printing of English today in, say, the Devanagari alphabet.) Unlike the other German dialects, however, Yiddish was ethnically, not regionally, bound. Moreover, as Ruppin pointed out, it had spread over all Europe and even penetrated into Russia. Accents offend us, please us, or amuse us in accordance with mysterious laws of their own, but in order to do so they must first be recognized as such. A Yiddish-speaking German Jew (or a German Jew speaking some other variant

25. Wagner, *Gesammelte Schriften und Dichtungen*, V, 70–71.

26. Mime is tutoring his protégé Siegfried only in order to win back Alberich's power-conferring ring from the dragon Fafner. After Siegfried has killed the dragon, Mime will try to poison his former protégé. Seen in a distorting glass, Disraeli's Sidonia, who packs off his English protégé Tancred to regain the Holy Land of the Jews, bears an odd likeness to Mime.

27. Wagner's Saxon pronunciation was not in general favor in Germany, and he himself disliked the barking tones of the Junker. In his autobiography he tells of a Latvian nobleman of German descent whom he encountered in 1863. This nobleman, says Wagner, "expressed his displeasure at the emancipation of the peasants by the Russian Tsar in the harshest German Junker-tones, and it became clear to me from this that any strivings for freedom on part of the Russians would receive no great aid from our German nobility living among them" (*Mein Leben*, II, 727–28).

of German with a Yiddish accent) might offend a German-speaking
Gentile, but a Yiddish-speaking Hungarian Jew would simply not be
understood by a Hungarian-speaking Magyar. What effect a Jewish
accent in the Hungarian language would have on that Magyar is an
open question. In the United States of only two generations ago the
speech style of black-face comedians such as Amos and Andy was in
great favor, if only among the white majority. Few people enjoyed Milt
Gross's Jewish-dialect parody of Longfellow's *Hiawatha* more than
American Jews themselves, and only a generation ago sophisticated
New Yorkers delighted in the verbal distortions of a H*y*m*a*n*
K*a*p*l*a*n.* In the United States these genres are moribund, dead,
or taboo. A French accent *à la* Maurice Chevalier is still fashionable in
some circles, but an English accent must be kept within decent bounds
lest the American be made to feel inferior. A German accent tends to
be detestable, sinister, or merely comic. The point to be borne in mind
here is that a Jewish accent in Germany, like an English accent in the
United States, held a peculiar place because Yiddish itself was a German dialect spoken only by Jews, just as "American" is an English
dialect.

If the German Jews—some of them, at least—could not speak German properly, according to Wagner's standards, what kind of music
could they produce? "The spoken word raised to the highest pitch of
passion is song: Music is the language of passion," Wagner asserts in
"Judaism in Music." And the source of the spoken word and the musical utterance characteristic of the German, the Frenchman, the Italian,
or the Russian lies among the folk: folk music is the living source of
the themes, rhythms, repetitions, and all else that appears, more or less
transfigured, in what we may call higher cultural music. But the Jew
has, that is, had, in Wagner's days, no folk—at least no folk rooted in
their own soil, for we recall Hess's cry, "We are a folk, *one* folk."
Where then lies the source from which Jewish music is to be drawn?
Wagner's answer, in "Judaism in Music," follows.

> To the Jewish composer (*Tonsetzer*) the musical celebration of Jehovah serv-
> ice is now the sole musical expression of his folk that offers itself: the syna-
> gogue is the sole source from which the Jew can draw popular (*volksthüm-
> liche*) motives, *intelligible to him,* for his art. However noble and sublime
> we may be inclined to picture for ourselves this musical divine service in
> its original purity, so much the more plainly must we recognize that this pu-
> rity has come down to us only in the most revoltingly sullied state: here, for

thousands of years, nothing has developed out of an inward fullness of life; instead, as in Judaism in general, everything has remained fixed in form and content. But a form that is not quickened by renewal of its content inevitably decays; an expression whose content is no longer alive with feeling becomes senseless and distorted. Who has not had occasion to convince himself of the caricature of the song of divine service in a real folk-synagogue (*Volks-Synagoge*)?[28]

Wagner, evidently, had at one time or another, heard this song, and to him it was a "gargling, yodelling, babbling confusion of sense and spirit." No doubt he witnessed an Orthodox Jewish service. For he adds, "In recent times the spirit of reform has actively attempted to restore the older purity of these songs, but what took place here among the higher, more reflective Jewish intelligentsia was, in accordance with its nature, merely a fruitless effort from above that could never take root below to the degree that the cultured Jew, who was looking for his artistic materials in the real source of life among the folk, could find his intelligent strivings reflected in this source."[29]

But the problem remained: How had the Jews risen to eminence in the musical arts? Disraeli's bombast aside, they really had done so and would continue to do so in Germany throughout the nineteenth century and well into the twentieth.[30] As Wagner himself said, it was unnecessary to "substantiate the Judaization of modern art; it springs to the eye and substantiates itself through the senses."[31] He puts it thusly in "Judaism in Music": "The Jew, who is *per se* incapable of presenting himself to us artistically, whether in his external appearance, his language, and least of all in his song, has nonetheless been able to arrive at mastery over the public taste in the most widespread of modern art forms, that of music."[32]

28. Wagner, *Gesammelte Schriften und Dichtungen*, V, 72, 76.

29. *Ibid.*, 76.

30. A German-Jewish Wagnerian raised the question again, on a broader scale, some seventy years later: "Moses Mendelsohn's [*sic*] translation of the Bible, from which the Jews of Prussia first learned German, appeared in 1790. By 1890 a good half of the thousand German poets, writers, scholars, critics, theatre-directors, actors, and academicians influential in Berlin were Jews. What does this mean?" (Theodor Lessing, *Europa und Asien, oder, Der Mensch und das Wandellose; Sechs Bücher wider Geschichte und Zeit* [Hannover, 1923], 331).

31. Wagner, *Gesammelte Schriften und Dichtungen*, V, 68. Ellis translates "Verjudung der modernen Kunst" grotesquely as the "be-Jewing of Modern Art" (Wagner, *Prose Works*, III, 82).

32. Wagner, *Gesammelte Schriften und Dichtungen*, V, 73.

Wagner's answer, part and parcel of the sociology of art first adumbrated in his "Art and Revolution" (1849) and "The Art-Work of the Future" (1849), is that ours is a bourgeois world in which "money confers nobility"—we recall Thackeray's lines on the newly created Baron Rothschild—and in which culture has become a "luxury article for sale." Stripped of its originally close ties to the folk, this abstracted culture can be more or less mastered by an intelligent person, including the cultured Jew. But the art forms thus produced, and in particular the music, leave the "deeper, core-feelings of the human heart" untouched. Of Mendelssohn, the only musician named in "Judaism in Music," Wagner writes:

> What other phenomenon will make all this [the position of the Jewish musician in Germany] more clear, indeed what else can make us inwardly aware of it, than the works of a musician of Jewish origin who was endowed by nature with a specific musical gift such as very few musicians had possessed before him? All that presents itself for consideration in examining our antipathy toward the Jewish character, all the contradictions of this character, in itself and with respect to us, all its inability, standing outside our soil, to have intercourse with us nevertheless on this soil, indeed to develop further the products of our soil, rise to a genuinely tragic conflict in the life and work of the recently departed Felix Mendelssohn-Bartholdy. He has shown us that a Jew may possess the richest measure of specific talent, the finest and most varied cultural education, the highest and most sensitive feelings of honor, and yet be unable, despite all these advantages, even once to elicit from us that deep heart and soul response that we expect from art because, having experienced this response any number of times as soon as a hero of our art merely opens his mouth to address us, we know that we are capable of feeling it.[33]

Nineteen years later Wagner would tell Cosima that Mendelssohn's *Hebrides Overture* was the work of a "landscape painter, incapable of depicting a human being . . . so clear, so smooth, so melodious, as definite as a crystal, but also just as cold; such an enormous talent as Mendelssohn's is frightening; it has no place in the development of our music."[34] Mendelssohn, Wagner tells us in "Judaism in Music," had found himself unable to go forward from the musical language newly forged by Beethoven. He had instead retreated to the language of Bach.

33. *Ibid.*, 73–75, 79.
34. Cosima Wagner, *Diaries*, I, 170, entry dated December 7, 1869.

Bach's musical language took form at a time in the history of our music when the common language of music was yet still striving for a secure, more individual mode of expression: the purely formal and pedantic still clung so tightly to music that her purely human expression first came to a breakthrough (*zum Durchbruche kam*) with Bach, due to the enormous force of his genius. The speech of Bach is to the speech of Mozart, and finally that of Beethoven, as the Egyptian sphinx is to a Greek statue of a human being: Just as the sphinx constantly strives to bring forth a human face from the body of an animal, so the noble human head of Bach strives to issue from the periwig. . . . The speech of Beethoven can be uttered only by a complete, whole, warm human being. . . . On the other hand, the speech of Bach can readily be spoken (although not in the sense of Bach) after him by a highly finished musician, because in it the formal is still preponderant, and the purely human expression is not yet so completely dominant that in it only the *what* can or must be stated, for it is still engaged in shaping the *how*.[35]

A "breakthrough" (*Durchbruch*) in music is, for Wagner, a breakthrough in the structure of society as well. To Wagner, so a recent writer on the sociology of knowledge tells us, "the problems of creative art are in the last analysis identical with the problems of public life." Wagner, this same writer asserts, "was almost as great a theoretician in his chosen field as he was a practitioner."[36]

The following passage from "Judaism in Music" reveals Wagner's recognition of the plight of the partly assimilated German Jew, who has cut all ties to his own people yet still finds himself a stranger amid the alien corn, a plight that will later be insisted on by Moses Hess and a host of other German Zionists. Wagner writes:

The cultured Jew has taken unthinkable pains to discard all obvious characteristics of his lower co-religionists: in many cases he has even thought it

35. Wagner, *Gesammelte Schriften und Dichtungen*, V, 80–81.
36. Werner Stark, *The Sociology of Knowledge: An Essay in Aid of a Deeper Understanding of the History of Ideas* (London, 1958), 10. Wagner's idea of the "breakthrough," also developed in his essay on Beethoven (1870), plays a crucial role in Thomas Mann's *Doctor Faustus* (1947). Mann's musician-hero in that novel speaks of the "psychology of the breakthrough" (*Psychologie des Durchbruchs*), in Mann, *Doktor Faustus. Das Leben des deutschen Tonsetzers Adrian Leverkühn erzählt von einem Freunde* (Frankfurt am Main, 1951), 459–63. The "breakthrough" here leads the musician Leverkühn (and the Germany that he represents) to musical and political self-destruction). Mann borrowed from Theodor Adorno the concept of the "breakthrough," and Adorno borrowed from Wagner. On Adorno's unacknowledged intellectual debt to Wagner, see Rather, *The Dream of Self-Destruction*, 147 n. 58.

useful by means of Christian baptism to obliterate all traces of his origin. But this zeal has never brought the Jew the desired fruits; it has brought about only his utter isolation and made him to such a degree the most heartless of human beings that we ourselves must lose our earlier sympathy for the tragic fate of his tribe. The Jew was unable to find a new connection with the society to which he had elevated himself to replace the connection with his former companions in suffering that he had wantonly broken. He stands in connection only with those who need his money, but money has never been able to knit an enduring bond between one human being and another. Alien and apart, the cultured Jew stands in the midst of a society that he does not understand, whose history and development have remained indifferent to him. We have seen the Jews, in this position, give birth to thinkers: the thinker is a poet turned backward; the true poet is a prophet who announces the future.[37]

From what source did Wagner draw his understanding, such as it is, of the Jewish plight? Berthold Auerbach seems a likely possibility. Wagner states in his autobiography that it was Alwine Fromman who brought Auerbach's highly successful short stories on village life in the Black Forest (the *Schwarzwälder Geschichten*, 1843–1853) to his attention. She was enthusiastic about them; Wagner too found the depictions attractive, vivid, and realistic. Auerbach was something of a celebrity in Dresden and, like Wagner, moved in its literary and artistic world. Wagner writes in his autobiography: "Soon I had just as little to do with all the painters, musicians and other art-enthusiasts of our group [as with Gutzkow, director of dramaturgy at the Dresden Theatre]. But at the same time I came into somewhat closer contact with Berthold Auerbach." Auerbach, says Wagner, was in appearance a "short, sturdy peasant youth" in the habit of wearing a green jacket and a green hunting cap. On Wagner he made a "thoroughly winning impression." Despite this dress, Auerbach moved in the highest circles: "Blunt, sensitive, original he mingled in his jacket with the high society that flattered him, and loved to show his letters from the hereditary duke of Weimar and his replies to them."[38]

The following paragraph from Wagner's autobiography describes the course of his relationship with Auerbach.

37. Wagner, *Gesammelte Schriften und Dichtungen*, V, 73–74. Wagner's concluding aphorism is perhaps an elaboration of Friedrich von Schlegel's "the historian is a prophet turned backward" ("der Historiker ist ein rückwärts gekehrter Prophet"; *cf.* Büchmann's *Geflügelte Worte* [22nd ed.], 264).
38. Wagner, *Mein Leben*, I, 337, 338.

What especially attracted me was that in him I met the first Jew with whom I could speak with cordial openness precisely about Judaism. It even seemed incumbent on him to break down all prejudice, in an agreeable fashion, against this attribute, and it was touching to hear him tell of his childhood in which he counted perhaps as the only German who had read Klopstock's *Messiah* in its entirety. He carried on this reading secretly in his village hut and missed school one day; when he came in late he was rebuked by the teacher: "You cursed Jew-boy (*verdammter Judenbube*), have you been lending money somewhere again?" Such experiences had only made him melancholy and thoughtful, but not embittered, and he had managed to summon up real pity (*Mitleiden*) for the rawness of his tormenters. These were features that drew me to him in a very heartfelt way. But in the course of time it became a matter of concern to me that he no longer moved outside of this circle of ideas and relationships at all, so that it seemed to me as if the whole world and its history contained for him nothing more than the clarification of the problem of Judaism. One day, therefore, I rose up against all this with good-hearted confidence and advised him to simply let the whole Jewish question drop; there were, after all, still other points of view to be won from which to judge the world. Curiously, he lost all his ingenuousness at this point; he assured me, taking on what seemed to me a not quite believable, tearfully ecstatic tone, that he could not, since there was still too much in Judaism that called for his full participation.[39]

It is perhaps not difficult to understand why Auerbach's response to the behavior of his coarse tormenters—there were presumably others in addition to the bigoted schoolteacher—so strongly attracted Wagner's sympathy. For in a way Auerbach had been, as Wagner's Parsifal would be much later, "enlightened by compassion" or "made knowing by suffering" (*durch Mitleid wissend*). As for Wagner's advice to Auerbach to let the whole Jewish question go hang, it is advice more easily given than taken, since there are people in the world who insist on regarding the Jews as a race apart, regardless of the stance of the individual Jew. Wagner himself was perhaps not the right man to be giving this advice, since he himself was apt to judge everything on the basis of whether it was good for the Wagnerian artistic project.[40]

39. *Ibid.*, I, 338.
40. The habit of judging the world solely from the standpoint of whether what takes place in it is good for the Jews has given rise to a familiar Jewish joke. It was recently retold by a professor of organic chemistry at the Hebrew University in Israel: "Someone goes into a synagogue and exclaims: 'There has been a flood in China and a million Chinese have been drowned!,' and is asked in return, 'Is this good or bad for Jews?'" (Israel Shahak, "The Divide Between Israel's Two Nations," *Middle East International* [August 10, 1984], 13).

Wagner concludes the above paragraph from his autobiography as follows:

> At a later date I could not help recalling the surprising anguish that I then noticed on the part of Auerbach when I learned that over the course of time he had repeatedly contracted Jewish marriages, of whose happy outcome I heard nothing special other than that he had hereby come into a fortune. When I saw him again in Zurich after many years, I found regrettably that even his physiognomy had changed in a doubtful manner: he looked really extraordinarily common and dirty, his former fresh liveliness had turned into the usual Jewish restlessness, and everything that he said came out in such a way that one could see he regretted not being able to have used what he said, rather, for the newspapers.

"Nevertheless," Wagner adds, "during that time in Dresden Auerbach's warm involvement with my artistic intentions was really good for me, even if it came from a Jewish-Swabian standpoint."[41]

We return again to "Judaism in Music." Other than Mendelssohn, only two German Jews, both writers, are named in this essay. Wagner writes of one:

> I said above that the Jews had produced no true poet (*Dichter*). We must now mention here Heinrich Heine. At a time when Goethe and Schiller poetized among us we know of no poetizing Jew, but at a time when poetry became a lie among us . . . it was the task of a very gifted Jewish poet to expose with delightful mockery this lie, this bottomless dullness, this jesuitical hypocrisy of our poetasters who still wanted to consider themselves poets. His famous musical compatriots too he lashed without pity for their pretending to pass as artists; no disguise deceived him. Driven by the pitiless daimon of denial he was ceaselessly urged on through all illusions of modern self-deception to the point where he deceived even himself into thinking himself a poet, and in return had his poetic lies set to music by our composers. He was the conscience of Judaism, just as Judaism is the bad conscience of our modern civilization.[42]

---

41. Wagner, *Mein Leben*, I, 338–39.

42. Wagner, *Gesammelte Schriften und Dichtungen*, V, 84–85. Osborne translates the last words cited here as "just as Judaism is the defaming conscience of our modern civilization" (Wagner, *Stories and Essays*, 39). This makes no sense and is incorrect. The German original reads, "wie das Judentum das üble Gewissen unsrer modernen Zivilisation ist" (Wagner, *Richard Wagners gesammelte Schriften*, XIII, 29). Ellis has "just as Judaism is the evil conscience of our modern Civilisation" (Wagner, *Prose Works*, III, 100).

And of the other, Ludwig Börne (Lob Baruch), Wagner writes, in the often deliberately misunderstood closing paragraph of "Judaism in Music":

> Still another Jew, who appeared among us as a writer, must be named. He came to us, out of his isolated position as a Jew, in search of redemption. He did not find it, and he had to become aware that he would be able to find it *only together with our redemption as well into genuine human beings.* To become, in common with us, a human being means, however, first of all for the Jew to cease to be a Jew. Börne did this. But it is precisely Börne who teaches us too that this redemption cannot be attained easily and with indifference, cold complacency, but that it costs, as it does for us, sweat, want, anguish, and a fullness of suffering and pain. Take part, without looking back, in this regenerative work of redemption through self-destruction, and we are one and indivisible! But be aware that only one thing can be your redemption from the curse resting on you: the redemption of Ahasuerus,—*going under!* ("die Erlösung Ahasver's—der *Untergang!*").[43] (The emphasis throughout is Wagner's.)

In view of the disagreement provoked in recent times by these closing words, a brief discussion is in order. Ahasuerus was supposed to have struck Jesus and hurried him on his way to the cross; he then became the "Wandering Jew," compelled to tarry on earth until Christ's second coming. According to another story, dating from the thirteenth century, the deed was done by Pontius Pilate's porter, Cartaphilus by name: he wandered the earth and, in the course of time, repented his deed and became a very holy man. The word *Untergang,* literally "a going-under," can refer to the decline and fall of a civilization or culture, the disappearance of a people, the sinking of a ship, the setting of the sun, and so on. The verb from which *Untergang* comes is *untergehen,* "to go under." We recall here that the German Jewish writer Ludwig Gumplowicz, author of *The Race Struggle* (1883), had no patience with the racial or the religious strivings of the German Jews. The twelve tribes of Israel, he says, first "conquered Palestine, whose inhabitants they partly exterminated, partly enslaved," and then "fantasized a common family tree" for themselves. In his opinion they should have long since rejected their separate status as a chosen people. But, says Gumplowicz, "the Jews did not understand, and even today

---

43. Wagner, *Gesammelte Schriften und Dichtungen,* V, 85. Osborne translates "der *Untergang!*" as "decline and fall!" (Wagner, *Stories and Essays,* 39).

by and large do not understand—how to go under (*unterzugehen*)."[44]
One wonders whether he had read the closing words of "Judaism
in Music."

"All is race; there is no other truth," Disraeli had written in 1847,
and he had insisted on the superiority and blood purity of the Hebrew
race above all others. To Marx, writing in 1844, the whole idea of race
was chimerical. To Moses Hess, after his break with Marx, race was
more important than class as a dynamic factor in the history of human
society. To Gumplowicz race was equally important, but he refused to
apply this category to the Jews. But to Wagner, at the time of the writing of "Judaism in Music," in 1850, there is no evident awareness of
race. The word does not occur in this essay. And yet we are asked to
believe, by one of Wagner's more recent critics, that in "Judaism in
Music" Wagner "for the first time sets forth his race theory as an answer to his critics," and that Wagner "supports his race theory with a
mythical account" (presumably the reference to Ahasuerus at the close
of the essay). We see here, this critic assures us, "the beginning of the
path to the 'final solution.'"[45] This was written in 1961. The claim
that the final lines of Wagner's "Judaism in Music" "pointed irrevocably in one direction: to Hitler, the laws of Nuremberg . . . [and] the
ovens of Auschwitz" had been made eleven years earlier by Leon Stein,
an American music critic.[46]

Stein mentions certain "anti-Wagnerian journalists who found the
reasons for Wagner's corrupt music in his Jewish descent." Stein, who
was not anti-Wagnerian as far as Wagner's music was concerned, believed that Wagner was of partly Jewish descent on his father's side
(Wagner's actual father being in Stein's opinion, Ludwig Geyer, whom

44. Gumplowicz, *Der Rassenkampf*, in *Ausgewählte Werke*, III, 323.
45. Otto Dov Kulka, "Richard Wagner und die Anfänge des modernen Anti-
semitismus," *Bulletin des Leo Baeck Instituts*, IV (April, 1961), 281–300, especially
281, 292, 294. The word *race* (*Rasse*) or *racial* (*rassisch*) appear nowhere in Wagner's
essay or in Ellis' translation of it. But they appear frequently in Osborne's version. Two
examples will suffice. Both have already been translated in the preceding text. I translated Wagner's "indem wir für die Freiheit des Volkes uns ergingen, ohne Kenntnis
dieses Volkes" as "since we involved ourselves with the freedom of the folk without any
knowledge of this folk." Osborne translates it "insofar as we proposed freedom for the
Jews with no knowledge of the race." I translated Wagner's "das tragische Geschick
seines Stammes" as "the tragic fate of his tribe." Osborne translates it "the tragic history
of his race."
46. Stein, *The Racial Thinking of Richard Wagner*, 176.

Nietzsche had hinted was really a Jew). Wagner, according to Stein, was aware of this, hence his anti-Judaism was traceable to "Jewish self-hatred." The same could be said of the anti-Judaism of Cosima Wagner, who, again according to Stein, was "one quarter Jewish" on her mother's side. Elsewhere in his book Stein asserts with equal conviction that "a Jewish 'race' does not exist," and that in general "no such genetic-cultural unit as a race [exists]." The reader is left puzzled: in what sense then was Cosima "one quarter Jewish"? Whatever Stein may have meant, his initial premise does not hold up. Genealogical studies have shown that the Geyers had been associated with the Lutheran church at Eisleben for two hundred years or more. (We grant, of course, that this brief span of time would have left Disraeli or Hess, or any believer in the eternal character of the Hebrew race, quite unimpressed.) As for the "Jewish grandmother" of Cosima Wagner, searched for and found by Leon Stein, she appears to be pure myth, although Stein was not alone in believing in her reality.[47]

The closing paragraph of "Judaism in Music" states plainly enough

47. Stein's statement in full is: "Cosima herself was one-quarter Jewish, her mother being the Countess Marie d'Agoult, her grandmother, the daughter of the Frankfort banker, Simon Moritz Bethmann" (*The Racial Thinking of Richard Wagner*, 90, n. 21). Ernest Newman refers to the "Franco-Hungarian-Jewish Cosima" in *Wagner as Man and Artist* (Garden City, N.Y., 1937), 133, but in his *Life of Richard Wagner*, a later work, there is no reference to the "Jewish" component; we must presume that Newman no longer believed in it. Sacheverell Sitwell, on the contrary, wrote in 1934 that the mother of the Countess d'Agoult was "the widowed daughter of a member of the Bethmann family, who were old-established bankers at Frankfurt" (*Liszt* [London, 1934], 35–36); in the revised edition in 1955, however, the passage reads "old-established Jewish bankers at Frankfurt" (*Liszt* [rev. ed.; London, 1955], 32). The Countess d'Agoult, mother of Cosima by Franz Liszt, and famous as a writer under the pen name of Daniel Stern, states in her autobiographical recollections that the Bethmann family traced its Protestantism back to Holland at the time of the Reformation, and she adds that the Bethmann banking house in Frankfurt was marked by a "pure savor of Protestantism, which distinguished it in the prejudiced eyes of the Lutheran, Catholic, and, above all, the Jewish groups that encumbered Frankfurt at the time." Her mother was the daughter of Johann Philip Bethmann (not of his brother, as Stein claims) and of Catherine Schaaf (Daniel Stern, *Mes souvenirs 1806–1833* [3rd ed.; Paris, 1880], 15–16). Marie Octave Monod, in her biography of the Countess d'Agoult, identifies Catherine Schaaf as an "intransigent Huguenot," a citizen of Basel, and the real head of the Frankfurt banking house. Monod asserts that the "austerity" of the Bethmann bank's "Protestantism distinguished it from the Catholic and Jewish banking houses then so numerous in Frankfurt" (Monod, *Daniel Stern, comtesse d'Agoult, de la restauration à la IIIe république* [Paris, 1937], 1–2).

that redemption, although difficult, is possible for Jew and Gentile alike. Judaism will have to go (Wagner was one with Marx on this point). But so will established Christianity, if we are to judge from Wagner's letter of 1853 to Liszt in which he states, "I believe in human beings and—need nothing further!"[48] To make the last sentence of "Judaism in Music" the first step on the way to the mass murder of Jews is as absurd as it would be to charge that Marx's "On the Jewish Question" is a concealed call for the bloody extermination of the Jews—a charge actually made in 1959 by Dagobert D. Runes.[49] On Wagner's essay as a whole, a recent comment by Bryan Magee is worth recalling here: "The degree of Wagner's originality in ["Judaism in Music"], as in so many things, is almost bewildering. As usual, he offered explanations for what other people had hardly noticed. . . . The trouble, as always, is that what is marvellous about this contribution was commingled with what is repellent to such a degree that it got overlooked and rejected along with the rest."[50] There is certainly a good deal of truth in these words. But when "Judaism in Music" is read (preferably, in the original German) and compared with the contemporary writings of Marx, Disraeli, and Hess on the Jewish question, it will probably be found by almost any unprejudiced observer to lose a considerable measure of its originality as well as of its repellency.

A few remarks, by way of an appendix to this section, on perceptions of Jewish control of the press in Wagner's day will be made here. The facts are harder to come by. Ernest Newman, writing in the 1930s, states: "A large proportion of the German Press is said to have been in the hands of the Jews, who naturally were not well-disposed toward Wagner after the publication of *Judaism in Music;* and certainly the papers, both musical and general, that had the largest circulation were then and for a long time after hostile to him." Newman—probably in the light of the rise of Nazism in Germany—described "Judaism in Music" as a "savage article."[51] Wagner himself wrote in his autobiography, "The unheard-of hostility that I have met with in the newspapers of Europe since [the publication of "Judaism in Music"] can

48. See Chapter 5 herein.
49. Karl Marx, *A World Without Jews,* trans. Dagobert D. Runes (4th ed.; New York, 1959). This is a translation of Marx's *Zur Judenfrage.* Runes claims that Marx cherished the "sanguinary dream . . . of a world without Jews" (*ibid.,* xi).
50. Bryan Magee, *Aspects of Wagner* (London, 1968), 43.
51. Newman, *The Life of Richard Wagner,* II, 218–19, 231.

be understood only by taking into account, bearing in mind that all European newspapers are almost exclusively controlled by Jews, the terrible effect of that essay."[52]

No doubt Disraeli's Sidonia would have agreed. The "Jewish mind," he tells us in *Coningsby*, exercises a "vast influence over Europe. . . . The first Jesuits were Jews . . . that mysterious Russian diplomacy which alarms Western Europe is organized and principally carried out by Jews: that mighty revolution which is at this moment preparing in Germany . . . is entirely developing under the auspices of Jews, who almost monopolize the professorial chairs of Germany."[53] And so on. But Sidonia—or for that matter Disraeli himself—is hardly a reliable witness in such matters.

Leaving the realm of fiction for that of fact, we find Wagner's old friend Mikhail Bakunin saying much the same thing about the European press, and oddly enough at almost exactly the same time. Bakunin had been captured by the Saxon police in Dresden in 1849 and handed over to the Russian authorities; he escaped from Siberia in 1861 and eventually reached Europe via the United States. In Switzerland he became a leader of the anarchist wing of the revolutionary socialists. In 1869, however, Bakunin was accused by a German-Jewish journalist, Maurice Hess, of being a secret agent of the Russian government. Bakunin sent a long letter of explanation to the editors of the journal in which the charges had been made. In this letter (sometimes mistakenly referred to as Bakunin's polemic against the Jews) he tries to make his position with respect to the Jews clear.

> First, gentlemen, let me explain the very special position in which I find myself vis-a-vis the Jews, German journalism in general, and Maurice Hess in particular. . . . I begin by asking you to believe that I am in no way an enemy or a detractor of the Jews. . . . I assure you that in my eyes all nations are equal. Each one, moreover, is an ethnographic, historical product, and in consequence responsible for neither its defects nor merits. It is in this

52. Wagner, *Mein Leben*, II, 479. For Wagner's treatment in the press see Wilhelm Tappert, *Richard Wagner im Spiegel der Kritik* (Leipzig, 1903). Tappert's book is ironically subtitled "A dictionary of discourtesy, containing the coarse, scornful, hateful and slanderous expressions used by the enemies and calumniators of the maestro Richard Wagner, his works and his followers, assembled by Wilhelm Tappert to delight the mind in leisure hours." By no means all of Wagner's enemies in the press were Jews; some were obviously anti-Jewish (see note 137, this chapter, for examples).

53. Disraeli, *Coningsby*, 202, 232.

spirit that one may observe, with respect to the modern Jews, that their nature hardly lends itself to free socialism. Their history, since well before the
Christian era, has imprinted on them a trait essentially mercantile and
bourgeois, which means, taken as a nation, they are par excellence the ex-
ploiters of the work of others, and they have a horror and a natural fear of
the masses of the people, whom, moreover, they hate, openly or secretly.
The habit of exploitation . . . gives them an aim . . . quite contrary to the
interests as well as the instincts of the proletariat.

But, Bakunin continues, an exploiting class often gives birth to individuals who strongly oppose the interests of that class (Bakunin himself was by birth a member of the Russian ruling class) and "two of the
most eminent socialists of our time [are] Marx and Lasalle." These
two men are "Jewish and giants"; Maurice Hess has his place among
the "Jewish pigmies." Bakunin then strikes a mingled Disraelian-
Wagnerian chord. "I am well aware that in uttering with such freedom
my intimate thoughts on the Jews I expose myself to enormous dan-
gers. Many people share them but few dare express them publicly, for
the Jewish sect (*secte juive*), far more formidable than that of the
Catholic Jesuits or the Protestants, constitutes a veritable power in Europe today. It weighs despotically in commerce and banking, and it has
enveloped three-fourths of German journalism and a very considerable
part of journalism in other countries. Woe to the person who has the
maladresse to displease it!"[54]

Wagner, too, was well aware that he had many supporters among
the Jews, and that these supporters were exposed to pressure from the
dominant Jewish group. He wrote in 1869, in connection with the re-
publication of "Judaism in Music":

> I cannot express myself on this subject [the hostility of much of the press]
> without constraint: this is the result, however, not of fear of my enemies (I
> have nothing to hope for from that quarter, hence nothing to fear), but
> rather of a careful regard for the self-sacrificing and truly sympathetic
> friends brought to me by the fates from the same national-religious element
> of modern European society whose implacable hatred I have brought on
> myself by discussing its peculiarities, which are so hard to eradicate, and so
> detrimental to our culture. Yet I can be encouraged by the recognition that
> these rare friends stand with me on precisely the same ground, indeed that
> they have to suffer more grievously, even shamefully, under the pressure

54. Bakunin, Mikhail, "Lettre adressée aux citoyens rédacteurs du Réveil (October, 1869)," in *Oeuvres* (6 vols.; Paris, 1907–1913), V, 242–44, 266–67.

that has fallen on *all* who are like me: for I cannot hope to make my position entirely plain without at the same time highlighting with the necessary clarity the pressure, crippling all free movement, of the dominant Jewish social group on the truly human (*wahrhaft humane*) development of their own kindred.[55]

THE GERMAN-JEWISH SYMBIOSIS

Martin Buber (1878–1965) seems to have coined the expression "German-Jewish symbiosis," although the idea itself was familiar a generation before him. A Jew, born in Vienna, Buber taught religion and philosophy at Frankfurt until the Nazi takeover in Germany in 1933. Looking back, a few months before the outbreak of World War II, in an essay entitled "The End of the German-Jewish Symbiosis" published in France in the German language, Buber wrote: "the symbiosis of German and Jewish character as I have experienced it during the four decades I spent in Germany has been, since the Spanish epoch, the first and only one which has found the highest confirmation that History can bestow: The configuration by *creativeness*. . . . This has not been a parasitic existence; the full weight of the human personality came into play and bore fruit. But even more profoundly than that through individual achievement the symbiosis found confirmation through a unique collaboration between the German and the Jewish spirit." Less than twenty years after penning this obituary, however, the ironies of history led Buber to assert that a new and horribly distorted version of the old collaborative spirit had come into being after World War II in Israel itself.[56]

Among biologists the term *symbiosis* refers to a way of life in which two organisms live together amicably as commensals, not only sharing the same table (*mensa*) but affording each other mutual benefits with-

55. Wagner, *Richard Wagners gesammelte Schriften*, XIII, 30–31.
56. Buber's essay was published in France in the *Jüdische Rundschau*, March 11, 1939. I have cited from the translated passage of the essay given in Alex Bein's "The Jewish Parasite: Notes on the Semantics of the Jewish Problem, With Special Reference to Germany," *Leo Baeck Institute Yearbook*, IX (1964), 38 n. 1. Nineteen years later, in an essay entitled "Old Zionism and Modern Israel" (*Jewish Newsletter*, XIV [June, 1958]), Buber wrote: "It was Hitler who brought the Jewish masses to Palestine. . . . *But the majority of the Jewish people preferred to learn from Hitler rather than from us* [Buber's emphasis]. Hitler showed them that history does not go the way of the spirit but the way of power, it can kill with impunity as many millions of another people as it wants to kill."

out which life for both organisms would be difficult or impossible. *Parasitism,* on the other hand, refers to a way of life in which one organism lives on (or within) another organism to which it contributes nothing and may be actively harmful; it is, of course, to the interest of the parasite that the host organism survive.

Alex Bein has pointed to a danger inherent in transferring biological concepts to the domain of sociology, namely that the distinctive factor of "human consciousness" may drop out of sight. The danger is greatest, he says, when Gentiles use such concepts in reference to the "relationship of Jews in the diaspora to their non-Jewish environment." While Jews may be allowed to speak of the Greek-Jewish symbiosis in ancient Alexandria or of the Spanish-Jewish symbiosis in medieval Spain with little harm done, there is grave danger when Gentiles speak in this way. For, says Bein, Jews think in a "more abstract manner" and are less aware of these "metaphorical associations" than are "other people," for whom, lamentably, the "graphic, naturalistic image often retains its original force." By way of making his point, Bein cites the following passage from a novel written by a Gentile: "If you call a man a bug, it means you propose to treat him as a bug"—the novel in question being Aldous Huxley's *Eyeless in Gaza* (1936).[57] Does Bein really believe that, say, Cochin Jews, Falasha Jews, and Yemeni Jews share, by virtue of their Jewishness alone, with Russian Jews, Polish Jews, French Jews, and German Jews this ability to "think in a more abstract manner"? The warning he issues is, however, not without validity.[58] The rhetoric of extermination has a long history,

57. Alex Bein claims that *parasite* is a word taken from classical Greek and used as a biological term at a comparatively late date, whereas "the word and concept 'symbiosis' was deliberately created to define a biological phenomenon" (Bein, "The Jewish Parasite," 38–39). While it is true that *parasite* was used as a biological term as early as the eighteenth century, and *symbiosis* not until the nineteenth, classical Greek has both *symbios* (a companion, partner, husband, or wife) and *symbioō* (to live together harmoniously), as well as *parasitos* (one who lives at another's expense) and *parasiteō* (to play the parasite).

58. The transfer of Darwin's metaphorical struggle for existence into sociological discourse and its literal use to justify unrestricted competitiveness between human beings, individually and in groups, is the best-known case in point. Some years ago J. B. Frerichs and I pointed out (in connection with the metaphorical wars waged in our day against cancer, the bacteria of infectious diseases, and so on) that in medicine the war metaphor is *only* a metaphor (hardly more than four centuries old), and that its use might conceivably have prevented the development of "symbiotic" drugs that would convert pathogenic organisms into harmless commensals—instead of "antibiotic" drugs

but it is important to bear in mind that neither the rhetoric nor the act has been or is now limited to Gentiles in their interactions with other peoples.[59]

The German-Jewish philosopher Hermann Cohen (1842–1918) too was a proponent of that symbiosis between Germans and Jews celebrated by Martin Buber in the decade of its demise. Cohen was an outspoken anti-Zionist, whereas Buber was a religious Zionist. In an open letter to Buber, Cohen stated in 1916 that "the Zionist believes that Judaism can be preserved only by an all-encompassing Jewish nationalism, [whereas] we are of the opposite view, believing that only a universal, mankind-oriented Judaism can preserve the Jewish religion." Zionism, Cohen continued, holds that "the Jew is a Jew only insofar as he is conscious of his Jewish nationality. We [the non-Zionists] . . . are read out of the Jewish people. . . . Ghetto mentality is not seen [by the Zionists] as a specter of Judaism but as its true spirit, or as the spirit of true Judaism." Cohen then speaks—as Buber will in 1939—of the bond of affinity between the German spirit and the Jewish spirit. "We

---

aiming to exterminate them (L. J. Rather, "On the Use of Military Metaphor in Western Medicine: The *bellum contra morbum* of Thomas Campanella," *Clio Medica*, VII [1972], 201–208). See also Rather, "On the Source and Development of Metaphorical Language in the History of Western Medicine," in *A Celebration of Medical History: The Fiftieth Anniversary of the Johns Hopkins Institute of Medicine and the Welch Medical Library*, ed. Lloyd G. Stevenson (Baltimore, 1982), 135–53.

59. The rhetoric of extermination at times followed by the deed has been employed against capitalists, proletarians, aristocrats, American Indians, Negroes, Jews, Gentiles, Persians, Arabs, and Germans. Marx wrote in 1844 that Marxist criticism has as its object an "enemy, which it wants not to refute but to *exterminate*" (emphasis in the original); Proudhon, in a letter to Marx dated May 17, 1846, argued that the proletariat thirsted for knowledge, not blood, and that "it would be bad politics for us to speak as *exterminateurs*" (Marx, *Karl Marx Frederick Engels: Collected Works*, III, 177; Pierre-Joseph Proudhon, *Lettres de Pièrre Joseph Proudhon*, ed. Daniel Halévy [Paris, 1929], 74). Eugen Dühring wrote of the need "to exterminate the parasitic [Jewish] race" (cited by Alex Bein, "The Jewish Parasite," 32). In the realm of fiction, Dickens' Marquis in *A Tale of Two Cities* calls Madame Defarge and her husband "dogs," whom he would willingly "exterminate . . . from the earth"; subsequently Defarge calls for the "extermination" of the "chateau and all the race" of the Marquis himself. Kurtz, in Joseph Conrad's *Heart of Darkness* (1902) cries out: "Exterminate all the brutes!" F. Scott Fitzgerald's Amory Blaine describes middle-class American rhetoric at the time of the Great War: "One minute it's 'the brutality and inhumanity of these Prussians'—the next it's 'we ought to exterminate the whole German people'" (*This Side of Paradise* [New York, 1920], 297–98).

love Germany and all it stands for not merely because we love our homeland as the bird loves its nest; nor do we love it merely because we draw our spiritual sustenance largely from the treasure-troves of the German mind. Weighty though these motivations for our love may be, they lose some of their significance when compared to our awareness of that innermost accord existing between the German spirit and our Messianic religiosity. The German spirit is the spirit of classical humanism and true universalism."[60]

During the Great War of 1914–1918 Hermann Cohen was as fervent a patriot as the most German of the Germans. He was convinced that the future belonged to the German spirit hand in hand with the Jewish spirit. He strikes a note of Messianic religiosity in the following passage.

> In these epoch-making times, so fateful for all nations, we Jews are proud to be Germans. And we are aware of our task to convince our coreligionists the world over of the religious import of the German ethos and of its influence as well as its claim on the Jews of all nations. . . . We know that we as German Jews share a central cultural force destined to unite all nations in the spirit of a Messianic mankind. . . . The German ethos must become the central force of such a federation which will establish world peace and with it the foundation for a world of true culture. A just war is the preparation for perpetual peace. . . . The kindred spirit linking Germanism and Judaism is thus focused on the most distant point of the world's historical horizon; and the lodestar guiding man's progress to perpetual peace is the Messianic idea of Israel's prophetism, that quintessence of the Jewish religion.[61]

The above passage is taken from Cohen's book *Deutschtum und Judentum* (*Germanism and Judaism*) as translated by Eva Jospe in 1971. She chose to omit the following passage: "We are also happily assured that the God of justice and love will ready, through the heroic victory of our fatherland, the end of the barbarian yoke that weighs on our fellow-Jews in the Russian empire, whose whole political existence speaks scorn to all justice, all state-reason, all religion, all morality, all human compassion, and all respect for the nobility of human value."

60. Hermann Cohen, *Reason and Hope: Selections from the Jewish Writings of Hermann Cohen*, trans. Eva Jospe (New York, 1971), 166–69. Cohen's words echo the response of Berthold Auerbach to the racial Zionism of Moses Hess, sixty years earlier, when Auerbach spoke of Germany as his spiritual home, and of himself as "a Teutonic Jew, a German, and, I believe, as good as anyone to be found" (Hess, *Moses Hess Briefwechsel*, 375–76).

61. *Ibid.*, 183–84.

Cohen goes on to say, in the passage omitted by Jospe, that the millions of Russian (and Polish) Jews who have in recent years left Europe to find a safe haven in America are Yiddish-speaking Jews, and that on this account alone they should "look back with piety to Germany as their emotional-spiritual home." Indeed, says Cohen, every Jew, whether English, French, Russian, or American, should look on Germany as the *"motherland of his soul"* (emphasis in the original).[62]

The symbiotic relationship between Germans and Jews remembered with nostalgia by Martin Buber in 1939 and championed by Hermann Cohen in 1915 was seen by both men as a spiritual relationship, hopefully one representative of a kingdom not (at least not entirely) of this world. In retrospect, the Messianic note in Cohen's utterance and his confidence that God was fighting on the side of the German "fatherland" may make us uneasy. But this note was characteristic of the times: *all* the combatants were convinced, or said they were convinced, that God was with them. And not only the ferocious God of the Old Testament. In the United States of America during the war to end all wars, "Jesus was dressed in khaki and portrayed sighting down a gun barrel," as Roland Bainton has pointed out.[63]

Far less palatable was the German-Jewish symbiosis, the earthly rather than spiritual, to which Wagner had called attention in 1880 with the words "Jew and Junker are now reaching agreement over possession of the world." The Second German Reich was then firmly in the grasp of Junker *par excellence* Bismarck, and among the most fervent admirers or supporters of the Bismarckian new order were the wealthy Jews of Berlin. In an essay entitled "Jew and Junker in Imperial Berlin," published in 1975, Lamar Cecil points out that the social ambitions of such wealthy Jewish families as the Bleichröders, the Schwabachs, and the coal-rich Friedländer-Fulds led them to cultivate Prussian Junkerdom and, where possible, marry into it. According to Cecil, Kaiser William I—the first emperor of the Second German Reich, which came into being in 1871 after the fall of Napoleon III—cared little for Jews, making an exception only in the case of his banker Bleichröder. The old Kaiser died in 1888 and was succeeded by Frederick III, whose wife Victoria had been princess royal of England

62. Hermann Cohen, *Deutschtum und Judentum. Mit grundlegenden Betrachtungen über Staat und Internationalismus* (Giessen, 1915), 35, 37–38.

63. Roland Bainton, *Christian Attitudes Toward War and Peace: A Historical Survey and Re-Evaluation* (New York, 1960), 209.

until their marriage in 1858. The new imperial couple, again according to Cecil, was "well-disposed toward Jews," and the emperor's unexpected death in 1888 (from laryngeal cancer) was "much lamented by Jewish society in Berlin." Next came their son, Kaiser William II. He threw over Bismarck (advisor to the throne of Prussia since 1862, and advisor to the imperial throne since its creation) but, says Cecil, continued to cultivate and ennoble wealthy German Jews.[64] We may note here that Kaiser William I was the second son of the Prussian king (Frederick William III) under whose patronage Meyerbeer and Mendelssohn had flourished in Berlin after the fall of Spontini.

This debased form of the German-Jewish symbiosis dreamed of by Cohen and Buber appears as a lower social level in Heinrich Mann's novel of 1914 *Der Untertan*. This is a story of *fin-de-siècle* chauvinism in Wilhelminian Germany (Mann's book has appeared in English translation, variously, as *The Patrioteer, Little Superman,* and *Man of Straw*). Diederich Hessling is the "underling" of the title, a chauvinist whose zeal is exceeded only by that of his symbolically symbiotic partner, a rabidly patriotic "Jewish gentleman from the Public Prosecutor's Office." These two puny men are at the beck and call of a local Junker, the brutal Governor von Wulckow; and they are of course utterly subservient to the "All-Highest" William II, he of the flashing eye and upturned moustaches. The voice of sanity in an era of crazy jingoism—in England, France, and the United States, as well as in Germany—is represented by Wolfgang Buck, son of a Jewish mother, and Buck's father, who was one of the "citizens of forty-eight." The father, condemned to death and then reprieved at the time of the uprising in Berlin, warns Hessling that "the curse of servility is spreading everywhere . . . that is what Herwegh, a survivor like myself, cried to those who were drunk with victory in the spring of 1870." (The senior Buck is referring here to the revolutionary poet Georg Herwegh, an associate of Karl Marx and a member of Wagner's circle in Switzerland in the 1850s; if Wagner had been taken by the police of Saxony, he would no doubt have shared the fate of the fictional Buck.) But the intoxicated Hessling is deaf to such warnings. "We are the *élite* among the nations," he

64. Lamar Cecil, "Jew and Junker in Imperial Berlin," *Leo Baeck Institute Yearbook,* XX (1975), 47–58. The Royal Automobile Club, whose headquarters was the former residence of the Bleichröders, admitted Jews to membership, as did the Union Club, which was modeled on the Jockey clubs of London and Paris. According to Cecil, "the Bleichröders and Friedlanders eventually embraced Protestantism, while the Schwabachs worshiped alternately at Catholic and Calvinist altars" (p. 51).

boasts in the deliberately ludicrous penultimate scene, while presiding over the dedication of a monument to "William the Great." But the offended heavens explode at this point and the "All-Highest," his fine feathers wilted by the downpour, is forced to beat a hasty retreat.[65]

Thomas Mann, Heinrich Mann's younger brother, touched on the character of the German-Jewish connection on at least two occasions in his fictions. His short story "Wälsungenblut" ("Blood of the Volsungs"), an elaborate parody of Wagner's *Die Walküre*, was written in 1906, translated into French in 1931 and into English in 1936 (it was not included in his collected works in German until 1958, three years after his death). "Wälsungenblut" not only plays on a number of Wagner's most important themes—including the Oedipal incest theme in relation to the "purely human" union of male and female principles—but also foreshadows Mann's half century of continued involvement with these themes, culminating in the *Confessions of Felix Krull, Confidence Man* (1954).[66] The one non-Wagnerian theme played on is the Jewish and (by that time) German obsession with the idea of race. Siegmund and Sieglind Aarenhold in Mann's parody are the twin son and daughter of a wealthy German Jew—an "Alberich" rather than a "Wotan," since his wealth comes from coal mines. The twins are mutually in love, but Sieglind is betrothed to a non-Jew, a certain von Beckerath. Mann's parody reaches its climax with the first act of incest committed by the twins; the act takes place after they have spent the earlier part of the evening alone together—leaving their "Hunding" behind—at a performance of *Die Walküre*. Siegmund describes the incestuous act as one of racial revenge against his twin sister's non-Jewish fiancé. "We've tricked him—the Goy!" was the closing sentence of Mann's first version. This sentence survives only in the authorized French translation of "Wälsungenblut" published in Paris in 1931, entitled "Sang Réservé."[67]

65. Heinrich Mann, *Der Untertan* (Leipzig, 1918), 106, *passim*. Mann finished this novel in 1914, but it was not then publishable. It appeared in English translation as *The Patrioteer* (New York, 1921), was republished in the same translation as *Little Superman* and republished again, in a new translation, as *Man of Straw* (London, 1972). For the citations, see *Little Superman* (New York, 1945), 86–87, 90–93, 309–13.

66. Rather, "The Masked Man[n]."

67. *Ibid.*, 69. Dr. Alfred Pringsheim (1850–1941), Thomas Mann's father-in-law, was an ardent Wagnerian, personally acquainted with Richard and Cosima Wagner. The scion of a wealthy German-Jewish family of industrialists, Pringsheim had taken a non-Jewish wife, the daughter of the then-prominent German feminist author Hedwig Dohm.

In Thomas Mann's *Doktor Faustus* (1947) the theme of German-Jewish relationships is developed at length, with obvious borrowings from Goethe, of course, and, if I am not mistaken, from both Hermann Cohen and Wagner himself. (Added, in the light of hindsight, is a predicted note of disaster should the relationship reach an impasse.) Mann's Faust, the German musician Adrian Leverkühn, is visited one day by a garrulous French Jew, Saul Fitelberg, a kind of pocket Mephistopheles who spreads out his mantle and tries to lure Adrian from his study into the great world of art. Unlike Goethe's Mephistopheles, he fails to do so. Before leaving, however, Fitelberg speaks a word for the German-Jewish relationship: "We are international—but we are pro-German and we are this like no one else in the world, simply because we cannot escape recognition of the role of Germanism (*Deutschtum*) and Judaism (*Judentum*) on the earth. *Une analogie frappante!* In like manner they are hated, despised, feared, envied, and in like manner they alienate and are alienated. People speak of the age of nationalism. But in reality there are only two nationalisms, the German and the Jewish, and every other kind is child's play by contrast." We catch an echo here of a debased version of Hermann Cohen's vision of the spiritual relationship between *Deutschtum* and *Judentum*. After a few more words, Saul Fitelberg continues:

> I say only one thing more. The Germans should leave it to the Jews to be pro-German. They will, with their nationalism, their pride, their plumage of superiority, their hate of being lined up and made equal, their hesitation in letting themselves be introduced into the world and joined to it socially— they will bring misfortune on themselves, a truly Jewish misfortune, *je vous le jure.* The Germans should let the Jew act as mediator between them and society, the manager, the impresario, the entrepreneur of Germanism—he is just the right man for it, one should not turn him out, he is international, and he is pro-German. . . . *Mais c'est en vain. Et c'est très dommage!*[68]

The senior Buck's warning to Diederich Hessling in Heinrich Mann's *Der Untertan* contains no note of irony. But this cannot be said of the above passage from *Doktor Faustus:* neither the warped arrogance

68. *Cf.* Thomas Mann, *Doctor Faustus. The Life of the German Composer Adrian Leverkühn as Told by a Friend,* trans. H. T. Lowe-Porter (New York, 1948), 407–408. Lowe-Porter omits four words (given as "the entrepreneur of Germanism" in my translation), and she incorrectly translates *Deutschtum* as "Germany" on two occasions in the passage cited. I have translated here from Mann, *Doktor Faustus,* 609–610.

of the German spirit represented by Adrian Leverkühn nor the hy-
perdeveloped commercialism of a Jewish spirit represented by Saul
Fitelberg is shown to us in an attractive light. From their symbiotic
union nothing of real value could have come. In real life, however, the
personal impresario (and sincere admirer) of Richard Wagner was
Angelo Neumann, a Jew.[69]

We have seen that Wagner recognized the symbiotic relationship
between Junker and Jew almost a hundred years before the publication of Cecil's essay "Jew and Junker in Imperial Berlin." Still earlier,
Wagner had recognized in Ferdinand Lassalle the prototype of the
German-Jewish "human being of the future." The year was 1864, and
Lassalle was involved in a love affair with Helene von Dönniges,
daughter of the Bavarian chargé d'affaires in Geneva. But there were
objections on the part of Helene's father. Lassalle asked his friend
Hans von Bülow to introduce him to Wagner, who was at the time
very close to the young king of Bavaria, that most passionate of Wagnerians. Ernest Newman puts it that since "both Lassalle and Helene
were ardent admirers of Wagner it was natural that the former should
suggest to Bülow that his now 'powerful friend' might lay his case personally before the King and ask for protection against Dönniges." Von
Bülow (who was still the husband of Cosima) complied with the request, and Lassalle paid a visit to Wagner at Starnberg, a town a few
miles from Munich, on August 17, 1864. According to Newman, the
"utmost that Wagner would do was hold out a half-hope that he
would bring the matter before the King." A few days later Lassalle,
who had in the meantime decided that Helene was unworthy of his
love, sent a telegram to Wagner withdrawing the request for help. On
August 28, says Newman, Lassalle was "wounded by his rival, Prince
Janko Rackowitza, in a duel, and on the 31st he was dead."[70] Shortly
thereafter, Wagner wrote to Eliza Wille:

> Just fourteen days before his death the unhappy man was with me (through
> Bülow) to urge me to intervene with the King of Bavaria against his minis-
> ter (Dönniges) in Switzerland. (I am now simply considered to be the all-
> powerful favorite . . .) What do you say to this? I still hardly knew Lassalle;
> on this occasion he displeased me deeply: it was a love story of pure vanity

69. Cf. Rather, *The Dream of Self-Destruction*, 176 n. 50.

70. Newman, *The Life of Richard Wagner*, III, 323–26. See Chapter 2 herein for
Lassalle's estimate of the *Ring*.

and false pathos. I saw in him the type of the significant human beings of our future, whom I must designate the Germanic-Jewish (*den Typus der bedeutenden Menschen unsererer Zukunft, welche ich die german-isch—jüdische nennen muss*).[71]

THE GERMAN QUESTION: WAGNER ON THE MISSION OF GERMANY

In a pamphlet entitled *De l'esprit de conquête et de l'usurpation* published in 1813 (the year of Wagner's birth) the political philosopher Benjamin Constant launched an attack against the martial French spirit that had been raging across Europe for the past two decades. Constant observes that the leader of even a warlike people cannot simply say, "Let us march on to the conquest of the world." For the people will then reply with one voice, "We do not want to conquer the world." Instead, says Constant, the leader must remind his people of the need to "round off frontiers," of "national honor" and "commercial interests." The leader must then accuse the targeted country of "plotting" and take military action against it. If the country defends itself this is to be taken as proof of its originally aggressive intent. The final note of hypocrisy was sounded, according to Constant, by the leaders of the French people. "During the French revolution," he writes, "a hitherto unknown pretext for war was invented, that of delivering peoples from the yokes of their governments, which are called illegitimate and tyrannical. . . . As if he had foreseen our history, Machiavelli says that the worst of conquests is that of hypocrisy."[72]

For more than a hundred years before Constant there had been, for the rest of the world, a "French question." Under a succession of Bourbon kings France had become the most populous, the most powerful, the most militarized, and the most centralized nation-state in Europe. Led by Napoleon, under the guise of introducing a new order based on liberty, equality, and fraternity, they seemed to be out to conquer Europe, perhaps even the world. Their military power reached from

71. Wagner, *Briefe in Originalausgaben,* XIII, 104. Newman translates the passage as "the type of the significant man of the future, which I would call the Germanic-Jewish" (*The Life of Richard Wagner,* III, 325). A more incorrect version, reported by Robert Weltsch, who was unaware of the original source, is "the type of the great man of our future, which I should like to call the German-Judaic" (Robert Weltsch, "Introduction," *Leo Baeck Institute Yearbook,* IX [1964], xv).

72. Benjamin Constant, *Oeuvres* (Paris, 1957), 985–1096, *passim.*

Spain to Russia, and from Sweden to Egypt and the Near East. Many of the French almost worshipped their leader. But to Walter Scott, Napoleon was at best a ruthless and bloody-handed adventurer; and to E. T. A. Hoffmann, as we have seen, Napoleon was the Hitler of his day—even the devils of hell turned away from Napoleon in horror.[73] To Richard Wagner, Napoleon was simply a political criminal.[74] To the Tolstoy of *War and Peace* he was more figurehead than leader of a murderous mass movement of peoples from west to east. To the Dostoevsky of *Crime and Punishment* (1866) Napoleon, as seen through the eyes of Raskolnikov, is the "real *Master* to whom all is permitted [who] storms Toulon, makes a massacre in Paris, *forgets* an army in Egypt, *wastes* half a million men in the Moscow expedition *and* gets off with a jest at Vilna." To George Gissing, in 1899, Napoleon is a "wild beast with a genius for arithmetic." To Joseph Conrad, in 1904, Napoleon is a "personality without law or faith, whom it has been the fashion to recognize as an eagle, but who was, in truth, more like a vulture preying on the body of a Europe which did, indeed, for some dozens of years, very much resemble a corpse."[75]

But the French question, however much it continued to haunt the European mind, was no longer a living reality after the defeat of Napoleon I and the breakup of the First Empire. The defeat of the Second French Empire under Napoleon III by the tiny state of Prussia underscored a witticism made two decades earlier by Karl Marx on the occasion of Louis Bonaparte's *coup d'état*. Reflecting on Hegel's claim that all facts and personages of great importance in world history occur, as it were, twice, Marx commented, "He forgot to add: the first time as tragedy, the second as farce."[76]

Early in the second half of the nineteenth century a new question, the "German question," was beginning to present itself. The old Germany, leaving aside militarized Prussia, was a loose collection of states whose people took pride in their renown as a nation of poets and

73. See Chapter 1 herein.
74. See Chapter 1 herein and Rather, *The Dream of Self-Destruction*, 50, 71, 98, 157, for Wagner's abhorrence of Napoleon I.
75. Fyodor Dostoevsky, *Crime and Punishment,* translated by Constance Garnett (New York, 1917), 278; Joseph Conrad, "Autocracy and War," in *Notes on Life and Letters* (Garden City, N.Y., 1900–1925), 86.
76. Marx, "The Eighteenth Brumaire of Louis Bonaparte," in *Karl Marx and Frederick Engels: Selected Works,* I, 398.

thinkers, *Dichter und Denker*. Thomas Henry Huxley wrote in 1868, "Ask the man who is investigating any question thoroughly—be it historical, philosophical, philological, physical, literary, or theological . . . whether he is not compelled to read half a dozen times as many German, as English books."[77] But another spirit was now abroad in Germany—the spirit of power. The German should leave his narrow Gothic chamber, and go into the great world, said the seductive voice of this spirit, in search of worldly power. "The German nation," Julius Fröbel wrote in 1859, "is fed up with principles, doctrines, literary greatness and the life of theory. What it demands is power—power—power. And whoever gives it power will be given honor, more honor than can be imagined." National "greatness" was what Fröbel and others like him (in all countries) were calling for, and to them greatness meant only one thing—power. On the opposing side were those who condemned the worship of the national state as the manifestation of a coming time of barbarism: such men were Lord Acton in England, Jacob Burckhardt in Switzerland, and Konstantin Frantz in Germany.[78] It was Frantz who wrote in 1866, "The German question is the most sombre, the most complicated, the most comprehensive problem of all recent history."[79]

Richard Wagner, too, posed the German question in 1865 and answered it to his own satisfaction in an essay entitled "What Is German?" ("Was ist deutsch?"). This essay went unpublished until 1878, when it appeared in Wagner's *Bayreuther Blätter*, together with a brief preface and a three-page postscript discussing events in Germany since the Franco-Prussian War and the founding of the Second Reich.[80] This would, he wrote, be his final word in respect of this "sadly serious theme (*traurig ernsten Themas*)."[81] He had thought to publish the essay in 1865 in a political journal edited by Julius Fröbel. "Unfortunately," Wagner writes in 1878, "I had to learn that Dr. Fröbel saw the

77. Thomas Henry Huxley, "A Liberal Education: And Where to Find It," in *Lay Sermons, Addresses and Reviews*, 48–49.

78. Golo Mann, *Deutsche Geschichte des neunzehnten und zwanzigsten Jahrhunderts* (Frankfurt a.M., 1958), 297–98.

79. Cited (as an epigraph) in Wilhelm Röpke, *The German Question*, trans. E. W. Dickes (London, 1946), 2 (first published in Switzerland in 1945 as *Die deutsche Frage*).

80. Wagner, "What Is German?," in *Prose Works*, IV, 149–69; Wagner, "Was ist deutsch?," in *Gesammelte Schriften und Dichtungen*, X, 36–53.

81. Wagner, *Gesammelte Schriften und Dichtungen*, X, 36.

problem in question from quite another standpoint than my own, and we parted one day when my idea that art should serve no useful purpose, but only its own values so strongly went against his grain that he burst into sobs and tears."[82]

In the original essay Wagner notes that it is usual for patriots to speak of their countries with unconditional admiration. But, he adds, the "more powerful a people (*Volk*) is, the less weight it seems to place on speaking of itself with this reverence." The English or the French are rarely heard praising their respective French or English virtues. It is the Germans, who are forever praising "German deepness," "German seriousness," "German loyalty," and so forth. Unfortunately, Wagner continues, it has in many cases become obvious that much of this praise is without a basis, that we have to do in fact with wholly imaginary qualities. Who are these peoples who call themselves "the Germans (*die Deutschen*)?"[83] Wagner then proposes to examine the question from the standpoint of history.

There is, he finds, no people (*Volk*) in the annals of history to whom the word *German* (*Deutsch*) specifically applies. Jakob Grimm had shown that *diutisk* or *deutsch* meant nothing more than the speech of those who spoke in an intelligible fashion. This speech was opposed by the "Teutonic tribes (*die germanischen Stämme*)" to the "Wälsch" spoken by the Gaelic-Celtic tribes. Wagner calls it a striking fact that only after the Goths, Vandals, Franks, and Langobards had crossed the Rhine and the Alps and adopted the languages of the peoples they overcame, did the Saxons, Bavarians, Swabians, and East Franks receive the collective name "the Germans (*die Deutschen*)." This was at the time of Charlemagne, who was crowned Holy Roman Emperor. As time passed, Wagner continues, the scepter was carried eastward and put into the hands of those peoples who still spoke German. Thus there came into being the curiously named "Roman Empire of the German Nation (*römisches Reich deutscher Nation*)." Wagner adds: "From the glorious memory that remained grew at last the pride with which we found it necessary, in order to console ourselves for the degeneracy of conditions in the present, to look back on the past. No great cultural folk (*Kulturvolk*) has come to the pass, as have the Germans, of constructing for itself a fantasy of fame. What advantage the

82. *Ibid.*, 51.
83. *Ibid.*, 37.

need for such a fantasied superstructure from the past might bring us will perhaps become clear if we first try to make its disadvantages understandable in an unprejudiced way."[84]

The disadvantages found by Wagner lie in the realm of politics. "Peculiarly enough," he writes, "the historical remembrance of the glory of the German name comes to us from precisely that period which was harmful to the German nature, namely the period of the power of the Germans over people who lived outside of Germany (*ausserdeutsche Völker*)." The Germans who had remained behind in Germany after the migrations of the Goths, Franks, and other tribes had no real wish to rule over other peoples. This was the reason for the invariable failure of "so-called German glory (*Herrlichkeit*)." Wagner asserts that the "concept of this [form of] glory was un-German." Only after the collapse of this false empire, indeed only after the indescribable devastation wrought on Germany by outside powers in the Thirty Years' War, could the true German spirit begin to assert itself. But now, once again in 1865, there are those in Germany who seem bent on following the dream of empire through the ivory gate into the upper world. Wagner writes: "German poetry, German music, German philosophy are today highly esteemed by all peoples of the world. But in his yearning for 'German glory' the German can as a rule still dream of nothing other than a restoration of something like the Roman empire (*Kaiserreich*), and here even the most good-natured German is seized by an unmistakable lust for mastery and a longing for power over other peoples. He forgets how detrimental to the welfare of the German peoples the Roman state-idea had already shown itself to be."[85]

What is, according to Wagner, the true nature of the "German spirit (*deutscher Geist*)"? Hermann Cohen, we recall, wrote in 1916 that the "German spirit is the spirit of classical humanism and true universalism." This was an idea that Wagner shared, and in his case the lesson had probably been impressed on him as a boy by his learned uncle, the classical humanist Adolph Wagner. Wagner himself claims that through study of the classical world of Greek literature the German spirit was able to "remodel the purely human itself . . . in its original freedom" not simply by copying the Greek model but by

84. *Ibid.*, 37–38.
85. *Ibid.*, 38–41, *passim.*

"molding the necessary new form through application of the classical view of the world." To recognize the difference, he says, we need only compare Goethe's *Iphigenia* with that of Euripides. The German concept of classicism, Wagner asserts, is no older than Winckelmann and Lessing.[86]

We recall from the previous chapter Wagner's claim (in "What Is German?") that the "Christian religion pertains to no one national tribe of people," and that "Christian teaching addresses itself to purely-human nature." Only insofar, he adds, as a people "truly comprehends that the content [of the Christian teaching] is common to all human beings (*Menschen*) can that people (*Volk*) truly call itself Christian." What had enabled the German spirit to grasp the essence of Greek art and mold it into a new form was the complete lack of concern with aesthetics shown by the political state; this had as yet found no way to use art for its purposes. Not so with religion. "With religion," writes Wagner in "What Is German?," "matters were otherwise: religion became an affair of interest to the state, and this interest received its stamp and direction, not from the German spirit, but from the un-German, Roman spirit." Tied in with state interests as it was, the Christian religion could not be molded into a new form by the German spirit. Matters were made worse by the development of contending sects, Protestant and Catholic. We are not told by Wagner precisely what form Christianity might have been given by the German spirit, but we may conclude that what he himself looked forward to was a nontrans-cendental Christian humanism, based on the law of love and without any ties to the state.[87]

While Wagner was the first to see, in the person of Lassalle, the coming of the "German-Jewish human being of the future," the idea that a truly symbiotic relationship could exist between the German spirit and the Jewish spirit was as totally foreign to him as the idea of Christian-Judaic symbiosis was to Kierkegaard. To Wagner—as to Marx and to Hess (in his pre-Zionist phase)—the Jewish spirit was the spirit of commercialization. Like Kierkegaard, Wagner was well aware

---

86. *Ibid.*, 40–41.

87. *Ibid.*, 40–42, *passim*. The creed of the American Unitarian Association, "In the love of truth, and in the spirit of Jesus, we unite for the worship of God and the service of man" (adopted in 1865), would probably have found favor with Wagner. *S.v* "Unitarianism," in *The New Columbia Encyclopedia* (1975).

that so-called Christians largely ignored Christ's message of a kingdom
not of this world, and that Christians wanted to be Jews. But to urge
the German spirit in this direction was to misunderstand its true nature. "The German princes supplied the misunderstanding," Wagner
writes in "What Is German?," and "the Jews exploited it." He continues, "In order to open up and make visible to the spirit of alien
speculation a field in which profit could be reaped, it was, after the
rebirth of German poetry and music, only necessary to turn these arts
into hobbies for princes, following the example set by Frederick the
Great, to ignore them, or to assess them in the light of French stereo-
types and judge them wrongly and unjustly."[88]

Instead of a mutually helpful symbiotic relationship, Wagner sees
the German spirit being transformed and distorted by the daimonic,
worldly, and more powerful Jewish spirit.

> It is as if the Jew wondered why so much genius and spirit led here to
> nothing but poverty and failure. He could not understand that where the
> Frenchman worked for *la gloire*, the Italian for *denaro*, the German did
> this *pour le roi de Prusse* [*i.e.*, for little or nothing]. The Jew corrected this
> bungling on part of the German by taking into his own hands the work of
> the German spirit. And so today we see a repulsive, distorted picture of the
> German spirit held before the German people (*Volk*) as its supposed mirror
> image. It is to be feared that in time the people will really come to believe
> that the image of the mirror is that of itself. Then one of the finest features
> of the human race (*menschlichen Geschlechtes*) would perhaps be forever
> destroyed.[89]

For, says Wagner, the belief at the heart of "Bach's spirit, the German
spirit" is that what is "*beautiful and noble did not come to the world
for its advantage, indeed not even for the sake of fame and recognition;* all that is done in the sense of this doctrine is 'deutsch'; because
of it the German is great, *and only what is done in this sense can contribute to the greatness of Germany*" (emphasis in the original).[90]

The postscript of "What Is German?" written in 1878 after the fall of
the Second French Empire and the rise of the Second German Reich—
"un-German," according to Wagner—is the work of a disillusioned

88. Wagner, *Gesammelte Schriften und Dichtungen*, X, 41–43, *passim*.
89. *Ibid.*, 44–45.
90. *Ibid.*, 48.

man. He admits that he had once fallen victim to deception: "What German could have lived through 1870 without being astounded at the forces that were so suddenly revealed here, and at the courage and decision with which the man [Bismarck] who obviously knew something that none of us knew brought into action? Much that was offensive could be overlooked." But that time is past. Wagner now notes, ironically, that the new currency of the Reich is so "originally German" that it is without any value of its own; its value depends on the rate of exchange with the French franc and the English shilling. "Tricky for the ordinary merchant, but very much to the advantage of the banker," adds Wagner. And, now that free trade has been voted in, "the worker goes hungry and industry languishes, but 'business' (*Geschäft*) flourishes." He has been told by a newspaper editor not to suppose that he has a lease on the German spirit. Wagner writes that he has "surrendered the lease" and no longer considers himself qualified to answer the question "What is German?"[91]

Wagner's above-cited sentence "Much that was offensive [about the Franco-Prussian War] could be overlooked" calls for explanation. It is of course true that to many of Wagner's contemporaries, both inside and outside Germany, the war had been provoked by France rather than by Prussia. And by no means dead in their memories in 1870 was a time—hardly more remote from them than the Nazi takeover of Germany is from us today—when Napoleon I had held all Europe in his hand, including the thrones of Spain, Italy, and Sweden. The Second Empire, founded only thirty-seven years after the final defeat of Napoleon I and led by his nephew Louis Bonaparte, immediately became involved in wars against Russia and Austria. French troops, sent by Napoleon III, were the sole support of the short-lived empire of Mexico; the United States helped force their withdrawal in 1867, and Maximilian was left to his fate. Thus the defeat of imperial France by the tiny kingdom of Prussia came as a surprise but hardly as a cause for regret to much of Europe. Looking back on the Second Empire in September, 1870, Gustave Flaubert wrote to a friend: "Everything was false . . . false army, false politics, false literature, false credit, even false *courtisanes*." Two months later, Thomas Carlyle reminded the readers of the *Times* that for three centuries the French, under Francois I, Riche-

91. *Ibid.*, 53.

lieu, Louix XIV, and Napoleon I, had been the European aggressors *par excellence;* "lamentations over fallen and afflicted France," he advised the editors, were "idle, dangerous and misguided."[92]

It was perhaps in the light of history that Wagner was able to rejoice in the victory of Prussia and persuade himself that the penetration of France by Bismarck's armed might was in some arcane sense the equivalent of the penetration of the false French spirit of mode—false mode— by the true German spirit embodied in the music of Beethoven. This notion, one rather difficult to swallow today, is developed at length in his "Beethoven," an essay celebrating the centennial of the composer's birth in 1770. "*Music* breaks through the chaos of modern civilization" (Wagner's emphasis), we are told in this essay. In "What is German?" Wagner expresses doubt that salvation is to be found in a Christianity willing to live in symbiosis with political states; in "Beethoven" he finds salvation in the form of the universal muse of music.[93]

Wagner's period of self-deception as to the nature of the new German spirit was short-lived. The Germany of his dreams—the old Germany of poets and thinkers (*Dichter und Denker*) celebrated for a brief period throughout Europe—was becoming a nightmare. Music had been Wagner's last hope, and he saw that it too had failed. In an open letter to Friedrich Schön in Worms (where the Siegfried of legend lies buried) Wagner wrote on June 16, 1882:

> I have often explained how I held music to be the saving good genius of the German people (*den rettenden guten Genius des deutschen Volkes*), and it was possible for me to show this from the revival of the German spirit from Bach to Beethoven. . . . German music was a holy emanation of the human spirit, and its priests were daimonic, suffering, divine natures (*dämonische leidende göttliche Naturen*). But just as the gospel faded away after the cross of the savior was hawked on all street-corners as an article for barter, so also the genius of German music fell silent ever since it became distorted

92. Flaubert's words cited from T. J. Clark, *The Painting of Modern Life: Paris in the Art of Manet and His Followers* (New York, 1985), 111. Carlyle's letter of November 11, 1870, to the *Times* is reprinted in his *Critical and Miscellaneous Essays* (5 vols.; New York, 1899), V, 49–59, under the title "Latter Stage of the French-German War 1870–71." Only ninety years earlier Edward Gibbon could still term Alsace and Lorraine "recent acquisitions" of the powerful French monarchy (Gibbon, *The Decline and Fall of the Roman Empire,* ed. J. B. Bury [4th ed.; 7 vols.; London, 1906], I, 19).

93. Wagner, "Beethoven," in *Gesammelte Schriften und Dichtungen,* IX, 61–126; *cf.* p. 120.

by trade on the markets of all the world, and its progress celebrated with professional gutter-humor.[94]

Reality was the Second Reich. The seeming economic miracle of the *Gründerjahre*, the years 1871–1873, had produced a bustling business class of the new rich. In 1877, after concertizing in London, Wagner had described that great grimy town, in terms drawn from the *Ring*, as "Alberich's dream . . . Nibelheim, world-dominion, everywhere the press of steam and fog."[95] The same words could be used of the new Germany, where the whip of Alberich was wielded by the so-called Iron Chancellor, Bismarck. The spirit of Prussian militarism, always abhorrent to Wagner, had spread to encompass all Germany. Wagner felt himself to be a stranger in the land. He and Cosima seriously considered emigrating to the United States. In London, Cosima noted in her diaries: "Rehearsal, very moving. After this obliged to discuss our position with R. America? Then never again a return to Germany!" Two days later she writes: "Thoughts of America—never again back to Germany." And on July 27, 1880: "Next summer he [Richard] wants to go to Grafenberg, and then to America, perhaps to stay there, if only to put Fidi [Helferich Siegfried] out of reach of the 'horrible soldier business.'"[96] (Conscription, first successfully introduced by Napoleon I, had by that time spread over Europe.)

Although Wagner had disqualified himself as spokesman for the new German spirit, he continued to speak his own mind. In "Shall We Hope?," an essay published in 1879, Wagner again sounds the chief theme of "What Is German?." "Here it seems to us as if the unity and European place of power that the Germans (*die Deutschen*) lost in the wars of the Reformation had to be sacrificed in order to maintain in-

94. Wagner, "Offenes Schreiben an Herrn Friedrich Schön in Worms," *ibid.,* X, 291–96; *cf.* p. 292. Belief in the saving power of music is implicit in Mazzini's description of music as the "holy" art (see Chapter 3 herein), and George Gissing wrote in 1889: "For, work as you will, there is no chance of a new and better world until the old be utterly destroyed. Destroy, sweep away, prepare the ground, then shall music the holy, music the civiliser, breathe, and over the renewed earth, and with Orphean magic raise in perfected beauty the towers of the City of Man" (Gissing, *The Nether World* [3 vols.; London, 1889], I, 264–65). George Bernard Shaw wrote in 1907 "Bach, Handel, Haydn, Mozart, Beethoven, and Wagner" had made Germany for him "the Holy Land of the capitalist age" (*cf.* Rather, *The Dream of Self-Destruction*, 159).
95. *Cf.* Rather, *The Dream of Self-Destruction*, 86.
96. Cosima Wagner, *Diaries,* I, 963, 965; II, 519.

stead the peculiarity of natural disposition through which they are fitted not indeed to be rulers, but to be ennoblers of the world. What we *must* not be, we also *cannot* be. We could, with the help of all the Teutonic stocks (*germanischen Stämme*) related to us, penetrate the entire world with our peculiar cultural creations without ever becoming world-rulers."[97]

But this was at best the expression of a forlorn hope. The penetration dreamed of by the rulers of Germany was military, not cultural. The new Germany chose to learn from Napoleon I rather than from Wagner. France, after the downfall of Napoleon III, had been humiliated before the entire world: she had been forced to surrender Alsace-Lorraine (taken from the Hapsburgs by Louis XIV in 1697), and to pay an enormous cash indemnity, negotiated jointly by the Rothschilds in Paris and the Bleichröders in Berlin. This "frivolously provoked and frightful war," Wagner wrote in 1880, had ended in a peace treaty leading inevitably to "renewed preparations for war." Wagner continues:

> Recognition of the need and possibility of the real regeneration of humanity caught in the toils of a war civilization could instead have prompted a treaty by means of which the path to world peace might well have been paved: fortresses would have been demolished, not conquered; pledges of peace security, not of war security, would have been taken. But instead historical rights alone were weighed and brutally applied against historical claims; all was based on the right of conquest. It seems that, with the best of intentions, the leaders of nations can see no farther. They all have fantasies of world peace. Napoleon III also had peace in mind—provided that the peace would work to the benefit of his dynasty and France. For these men of power can conceive of peace in no other form than under the widely respected shelter of countless cannons.[98]

Bismarck, too, assures us that he is a lover of peace, Wagner adds, and we would be happy to believe him; but this love has the inconvenient feature of forcing us to preserve peace by waging war. The truth is, says Wagner, that when we look closely at Bismarck "we see Robespierre before us, presiding over the Committee of Public Safety . . . restlessly seeking for the increase of his power." In our time, adds Wagner, "all leaders of states strive after Robespierre's prize."[99] This

---

97. Wagner, "Wollen wir hoffen?," in *Gesammelte Schriften und Dichtungen*, X, 130.
98. Wagner, "Was nützt diese Erkenntis," *ibid.*, 255.
99. *Ibid.*, 254–55, *passim.*

prize is mere power for the sake of more power. We ourselves may fairly read here "the Nibelung's ring" for "Robespierre's prize," and we recall that the power of the Nibelung's ring was won at the cost of forswearing love. "Why," cries Wagner in this same essay, "other than for want of love, is our whole civilization headed for destruction?" ("Woran geht unsere ganze Civilisation zu Grunde als an dem Mangel der Liebe?").[100] Although Wagner's message remains the same as it was in 1848 (in *Jesus of Nazareth*), the hope and belief in the future of humanity with which he expressed it in 1853 (to Franz Liszt) has vanished.[101]

America still remained a last hope. "America, you are better off than our ancient continent . . . useless memories and fruitless strife . . . do not disturb you from within"—thus Goethe in 1831.[102] Wagner could share the hope that old mistakes would not be repeated in the new world, in the American republic at least. As late as 1880 he was still grasping at financial straws in the hope of leaving Germany for the United States.[103] Goethe's words (in the light of the frightful war between the northern and southern states) had proved to be somewhat overoptimistic. But the stain of slavery had been wiped away, however crudely and stupidly, and the restored Union was still unburdened by the huge standing armies that were beginning to press harder and harder on the continent. Nor had the United States yet entered the contest for world power. It was content to fence itself off with the Monroe Doctrine.

In 1876 Wagner was commissioned to compose a festival march for

100. *Ibid.*, 259.

101. *Cf.* the message of the angel in Leo Tolstoy's *What Men Live By:* "I have learned that every man lives not by the care for himself, but for love" (in Tolstoy, *Complete Works*, XII, 359). Tolstoy's story is headed by seven epigraphs on the nature of Christian love, all taken from 1 John 3–4.

102.   Amerika, du hast es besser
          Als unser Kontinent, das alte,
          Hast keine verfallene Schlösser
          Und keine Basalte.
          Dich stört nicht im Innern
          Zu lebendiger Zeit
          Unnützes Erinnern
          Und vergeblicher Streit.

From the *Zahme Xenien*, cited in Richard Dobel, *Lexikon der Goethe-Zitate* (Zurich, 1968), *s.v.* "Amerika."

103. Westernhagen, *Wagner: A Biography*, II, 551–52.

the American centennial celebration. Not long after this he was invited, as he writes, "to personally address the readers of a well-known
New York review on the subject of my artistic opinions and methods."
This Wagner did in the lengthy essay, "The Work and Mission of My
Life," published in two installments in the August and September
issues of the *North American Review*. At the close of the essay, Wagner
recalled the earlier invitation to compose a festival march for the
American centennial with the following words: "It was with special
pleasure that I undertook the task—giving the work the motto (from
Goethe's 'Faust') that seemed best to point to my ideal for the American Union: 'He only has true liberty—true life— / To whom they are
the prize of daily strife.'"[104] Wagner's essay was written in German and
translated into English by an unknown hand. The original essay is no
longer available. Only a few phrases in German remain, either en-
closed in parentheses or left untranslated and embedded in the text
like so many fossils.[105]

"Here, in my own country," Wagner writes in the opening paragraph of "The Work and Mission of My Life," "I have long thought it
best to refrain from all publication of my ideas, experiences, and plans
to any general audience." In 1871 he had brought out a nine-volume
edition of his writings (including the early stories and essays, and the
libretti of his music dramas), but according to Wagner, "the continual
influence of elements fundamentally hostile to me . . . proved powerful
enough to prevent the German public almost entirely from reading my
collected writings." After the success of *The Ring of the Nibelung* at
Bayreuth in 1876, continues Wagner, a company of friends formed a
society, the Bayreuther Patronatsverein, with its private journal the
Bayreuther Blätter. This now seemed to him the proper organ for all
further communication. It had required an invitation from America to
induce him to address the general public on his artistic aims. He adds,

104. Wagner, "The Work and Mission of My Life," *North American Review,*
CXXIX (August, 1879), 107–124 and (September, 1879), 238–58. *Cf.* pp. 107 and
257. The lines are from Faust's monologue at the close of *Faust II:* "Nur der verdient
sich Freiheit wie das Leben / Der täglich sie erobern muss" (11575–76). On the dubious
character of the last acts of Faust, however, see Rather, "Some Reflections on the Philemon and Baucis Episode in Goethe's *Faust*," *Diogenes* (Spring, 1959), 60–73.

105. The only German version available, *Richard Wagners Lebensbericht* (Leipzig,
1884), a brochure of 102 pages, describes itself as a "back-translation" (*Rücküber-
tragung*) of the article in the *North American Review*.

"The 'old' world, and especially that part of it included in our new Germany, will hear no more from me directly on this subject."[106] We saw that Wagner had disqualified himself in 1878 (in the postscript to "What Is German?") as spokesman for the German spirit in the realm of politics; here he disqualifies himself in the realm of art as well.

Wagner reminds his American readers that Beethoven, Weber, and Goethe were still alive in 1813, the year of his own birth, to see the "world-conquering French Caesar" go down to defeat at Leipzig. In those days the German spirit seemed ready to reveal itself in the form of great art as well as ready to supply the energy needed for the "work of founding an independent political civilization." The young men of Germany, inspired by the spirit of Goethe and Schiller, were "laboring everywhere to purify the morals of the people—to ennoble alike their inner and outer life." The student associations had put aside their "old coarseness and brutality" and now spoke vigorously in favor of the "new-born national life." But then their strivings were balked by the ruling class.

> The rescued princes, amid their own diplomatic peace-making, saw all this, and were alarmed at this new strength. They had thought of nothing but the restoration of the Bourbon system and of the spirit of despotism on the thrones of Europe, with which the light hearted Congress of Vienna, after all the long terrors of the war, had thought it could easiest settle all the troubles of the day—at the same time securing for the ruling powers the return of all those pomps and pleasures which the end of the last century seemed to have buried forever. . . . The "Deutscher Jüngling" [German youth] was looked on as a Jacobin; and the *fear* of a national spirit thus misconceived and misinterpreted was the only thing which the rulers of the time seemed to have learned from these hopeful beginnings of a national revival. The wretched, stupefying period of Reaction began. . . . At a time when Beethoven was composing his last and greatest works, when Weber's "Freischütz," "Euryanthe," and "Oberon" were coming into being, when Goethe was finishing his "Faust" . . . we are confronted with this picture of complete oppression of everything German, of the entire destruction of every living nucleus for the development of a domestic or political national life.[107]

Wagner reminds his American audience that it was during this period of reaction and repression—in the German kingdoms and duchies, in France, Russia, and Europe generally—that he passed his boy-

---

106. Wagner, "The Work and Mission of My Life," 107–108.
107. *Ibid.*, 112, 114–15.

hood. When "the city that still ruled the world" (*i.e.*, the Paris of
Charles X, last of the old Bourbons) was shaken by the July Revolution of 1830, he was a youth of seventeen. In what had been Poland,
the Poles rose up against their Russian overlords. "Polish emigrants,
haughty, handsome men, who fascinated me and filled me with the
deepest sympathy for the sad fate of their country, came to Leipsic
[*sic*], and I became acquainted with numbers of them," says Wagner;
and we recall Count Tyskiewicz, the bizarre episode involving the
death of his first wife, and its place in Wagner's scrapped early opera
Die Hochzeit.[108]

As for his inner artistic development at this time, Wagner says that

> a taste for poetry . . . struggled with a taste for music. . . . It was only the
> knowledge of Beethoven's symphonies, gained when I was a boy of fifteen,
> that first decided me finally and passionately in favor of music. . . . Beetho-
> ven's symphonies, to which, though entirely without any special study, I
> devoted myself with passionate enthusiasm, finally gave music in my eyes a
> fairly supernatural power (*eine ganze dämonische Macht*), which, it seemed
> to me, I could not measure by any ordinary outward standard. Their har-
> monies and movements appeared to me rather like ghostly, spiritual forces,
> which seemed to address themselves to me individually, and to take on the
> most fantastic shapes. . . . I had suddenly become a musician, though . . .
> my instinct of poetic imitation, which I had even as a child practiced on
> Shakespeare and the antique tragedies, did not quite leave me. It sought
> rather to pay a tribute, however small, in the shape of some *libretti* which
> I composed, to the mighty Daemon of music that had so taken possession
> of me.[109]

It was in 1829 too that Wilhelmine Schröder-Devrient sang the role of
Leonora in Beethoven's *Fidelio* and made a lasting impression on the
youthful Wagner with her "almost daimonic warmth" (*fast dämonische Wärme*), as he tells us in his autobiography.[110] In "The Work and

108. *Ibid.*, 116. See Chapter 1 herein for the story of Count Tyskiewicz and the plot
of Wagner's *Die Hochzeit*.

109. *Ibid.*, 116. The ghost of E. T. A. Hoffmann's fictitious musician Kreisler peeps
through Wagner's lines (*cf.* Chapter 1 herein). In his autobiography too Wagner says
that music was once for him "a wholly daimonic realm, a mystic, sublime portent"
("durchaus nur Dämonium, eine mystische erhabene Ungeheuerlichkeit" [*Mein Leben*,
I, 39]).

110. Wagner, *Mein Leben*, I, 44. See Chapter 1 herein for Wagner's reference to the
Kundry of *Parsifal* as "a wonderful world-daimonic woman" ("ein wunderbar weltdämonisches Weib").

Mission of My Life" he refers again to the impression made on him by that "great dramatic artist," this time in connection with her perform-ance in Vincenzo Bellini's *Romeo* (*i.e.*, *I Capuleti ed i Montecchi*).[111]

Wagner says that his first completed opera, *The Fairies* (*Die Feen*), was written and composed in the high romantic style of Weber and Heinrich Marschner. But now, under the influence of Johann Heinse (1746–1803), whom Wagner calls an "apostle of a kind of unlimited aesthetic sensuousness," and Heinrich Laube (1806–1884)—the au-thor of *Young Europe* (1833–1837) and, Wagner says, "at that time my personal friend"—his artistic strivings took on a new, revolution-ary turn. Heinse's ideas had reappeared, according to Wagner, in the "new school of 'young German' literature, which attacked with fiery vehemence the life of *old* Germany, now exhausted and moribund under the weight of political oppression."[112] Wagner still had no style or content peculiarly his own, but the daimonic muse nonetheless drove him on.

> I passed into the period in which it may be said that I sowed my musical "wild oats"—a phase which I cannot call a change in my character or even taste, but rather an awakening to the importance of what was living and vigorous. The result of this condition was the writing and composition of a second opera—this time entirely in the French and even in the Italian style—the "Love-Veto" [*Das Liebesverbot*]—a wild, revolutionary, reck-lessly sensuous transformation of Shakespeare's serious "Measure for Mea-sure." Music had now become a living thing to me, instead of a mys-tery. . . . What I had still to attain was the true *ideal form* in which this new life, so indispensable to the perfection of my art, must be embodied.[113]

Fifteen years after Wagner's death, incidentally, George Bernard Shaw picked up and neatly varied a phrase used by Wagner in the above citation. In 1898, in the preface to the first edition of *The Per-fect Wagnerite: A Commentary on the Ring of the Nibelungs* (an im-perfect title), Shaw asserts that he regards himself as peculiarly quali-fied to interpret the *Ring* for the British public, "having learnt more about music than about anything else in my youth, and sown my po-litical wild oats subsequently in the revolutionary school." Previous commentaries on Wagner's *Ring* in English have come, Shaw says,

111. Wagner, "The Work and Mission of My Life," 117–18.
112. *Ibid.*, 117.
113. *Ibid.*, 118.

from the pens of "musicians who are no revolutionists and revolutionists who are no musicians."[114]

Music was perhaps no longer a "mighty Daemon," a "daimonic power" (*dämonische Macht*) or even a "mystery" to Wagner, but it remained, as we shall see in the following chapter, an expression of the female principle (as it is also in Tolstoy's *The Kreutzer Sonata*). The "ideal form" that Wagner attempted to embody in the music drama represents the ideal union, on the public stage, of the female principle of *tone* and the male principle of the *word* to give birth to "the purely human" (*das Reinmenschliche*). This stage performance was not intended to divert a bored public but to elevate and exalt an actively involved audience of men and women in the manner of the classical Greek drama as Wagner saw it.[115] Wagner writes:

> Goethe and Schiller had also striven to develop the spirit of the people by means of the stage; but they were compelled to work far in advance of the theatre's capabilities, as it existed in their time; and it would have been the part of the stage to follow after them—just as the German princes had had to hurriedly follow after the political spirit that had run before them. . . . But when at length German *music* succeeded in inspiring the stage to a complete revival by breathing into it the breath of a new life, this was the decisive moment when an intelligent support of native art, by a power as truly national, should have given the surest confirmation of the victory of German culture over a foreign civilization.[116]

Wagner had in mind here the epochal new music of Beethoven, in particular the *Ninth Symphony* and the words of Schiller's *Ode to Joy* that "break through" into the flow of its fourth movement.[117] He had in mind too the operas of Carl Maria von Weber. But the victorious German culture did not materialize. It was a dream. Wagner con-

114. On Shaw's various interpretations of Wagner's *Ring,* beginning with *Widowers' Houses* (1892) and continuing through the successive prefaces and editions of *The Perfect Wagnerite* (1898–1923) and *Major Barbara* (1905–46), see Rather, *The Dream of Self-Destruction,* 149–67.

115. The impresario in the prelude to Goethe's *Faust* remarks that women theatergoers dress up in their finery and play their roles free of charge. As for the men in the audience, according to Goethe's cynical impresario, some are looking forward to a night of card-playing, others to "a wild night on a whore's bosom" ("eine wilde Nacht an einer Dirne Busen"). See *Faust,* 119–20, 125–26.

116. Wagner, "The Work and Mission of My Life," 113–14.

117. *Cf.* Rather, "The Meaning of Beethoven," in *The Dream of Self-Destruction,* 139–48.

tinues, in "The Work and Mission of My Life": "That this *did* not happen and *could* not happen, showed on the other hand that the regenerated German spirit, in a restored German state, had suffered a most disastrous defeat, from which it has never been able to recover."[118] We note that Wagner, writing in 1879, does not claim a victory, in his own name, for the regenerated German spirit. He knows well enough that his spiritual Bayreuth is a tiny enclave in Bismarck's earthly Second Reich. He knows, and has repeatedly stated, that his ideals are not those of the new, imperial Germany.

When Wagner's revolutionary sympathies as a youth of seventeen were first enlisted—by reports of the French revolt against Bourbon rule in 1830, and by direct acquaintance with members of the Polish resistance against Russian rule—they were purely political. In the widespread European revolts of 1848–1849 Wagner's sympathies were still with the revolution, but they had taken on an added character. "In my belief," he tells his American audience in 1879, "it was only by a complete change in all those political and social relations, of which the degeneration of art was a fitting manifestation, that an artistic revival and especially a revival of the drama was to be brought about." Hence, says Wagner, the "general revolutionary spirit which was growing stronger and stronger all around me . . . now [in 1848–1849] enlisted my zealous sympathy."[119]

Wagner was, in 1849, still interested in social and political betterment for its own sake. As a practicing artist with grand plans in mind for the music drama, he was now interested as well in the betterment of art through social and political renewal. Wagner's ecstatic prose-poem "The Revolution," published in Dresden on April 8, 1849, is art in the service of social revolution, but Wagner tacitly expects the social revolution to be of service to art; the relationship is a dialectical one. ("The Revolution," which castigates a social system that "makes millions the slaves of a few, and makes these few the slaves of their own power, their own riches," foreshadows *The Ring of the Nibelung:* Alberich and his toiling millions are alike slaves of the ring.)[120]

The reader will recall that in 1848—the year of the *Communist Manifesto*—Wagner wrote his sketch of and commentary on *Jesus of*

118. Wagner, "The Work and Mission of My Life," 114.
119. *Ibid.,* 241.
120. Wagner, "The Revolution," in *Richard Wagner's Prose Works,* VIII, 232–38. *Cf.* also Rather, *The Dream of Self-Destruction,* 47–48.

Nazareth; later on he showed it to Bakunin, who was less than impressed. We now find Wagner, in 1879, telling his American audience how he came to lose faith in the power of political and social revolution, unaccompanied by a fundamental change from within, to accomplish anything of lasting value. Wagner's posthumously published *Jesus of Nazareth* shows through in "The Work and Mission of My Life" as Wagner continues to tell of his involvement with the revolution of 1849.

> But, after a brief consideration of its methods, a feeling of doubt began to trouble me, as to whether the *purely human* [emphasis added] element that was at the foundation of the revolution would not be lost sight of amid the prevailing disputes of parties as to the value of different forms of government—the difference between which was, after all, only a matter of preference. It seemed to me that from this basis of general human interests a new civilization might spring which would make men truly free, and which might reach its noblest height in that pure and humanizing art which would be its natural outgrowth. The only element in history which had always attracted and inspired me had been this effort of the [human] race to mutiny against the tyranny of a traditional and legalized formalism; and I could see no triumph of this impulse of the natural man in the mere victory of one party over another. When I saw that this idea of mine, as to what should be the essential motive of a revolution, was utterly misunderstood by the politicians . . . I once more turned my back on the realities of things, and sought my ideal world again.[121]

"While in Germany the unsuccessful revolution yielded to a new reaction," Wagner continues, "I found at last, in the perfect freedom of my exile's home in Switzerland, full and undisturbed opportunity for self-communion and for the uninterrupted contemplation of my ideals. . . . In my first published work 'Kunst und Revolution' (Art and Revolution), I pointed out the connection I had recognized between the state of art and the social and political condition of the modern world."[122] This essay, the first of Wagner's works in the field of the sociology of art, was written in Paris during a two-week period in 1849. It was rejected by the editor of a French political journal but paid for and published in 1849 by Otto Wigand in Leipzig, the same publisher who would reject Hess's *Rome and Jerusalem* thirteen years later.[123]

121. Wagner, "The Work and Mission of My Life," 241–42.
122. *Ibid.,* 243.
123. Wagner, *Die Kunst und die Revolution* (Leipzig, 1849). Wigand also published Wagner's *Das Kunstwerk der Zukunft* (1850). According to Newman, Wagner "sent his

Wagner summarizes the work, for the benefit of his American readers, as follows.

The life of the Greeks served me as the most enduring and brilliant example of such a connection. It was with the union of all the different methods of artistic expression in the noble, finished art-work of its tragic drama, that this people had celebrated, in reverent concord, the divine rites of its strong and noble Hellenic nature. I followed the decline of art that accompanied the decline of Greek influence: I showed how, degenerating under Roman civilization and rejected by the spirit of Christianity, it could no longer, after its revival at the time of the Renaissance, be said to be the free and natural expression of the national life of any one great people—how it was forced to sacrifice its noblest value and its true popular spirit first to the service of the caprices and the wealth of princes and aristocrats, and then to the influence of trade and the hypocrisies of modern society. It is true that, with the downfall of the old inhuman institution of slavery and the spread of the Christian idea of the equality of men, true art found a nobler and broader domain spread before it, in which it might for the first time have attained its highest success as an embodiment of the ideas of the free man in his true and untrammeled relations to his kind. But such a civilization, founded upon liberty, has never come fully into being. The modern man is neither a free nor a consistent being. A thousand different interests divide his shifting life and fill him with perpetual unrest; and it is only in their common slavery to the power of social shams and social necessities that men are really equal. Only some great revolution of humanity at large could make the true liberty of the individual possible; and only a revolutionary movement in such a sense, with such a motive, could be of any saving worth to a true art.[124]

To this Wagner adds, "But that such an art should be the highest ideal expression of a universal and really human civilization, was only conceivable to me, again, in the form of that greatest artistic creation which portrays human life by means of the aid of all the lesser arts united—a work like the Greek tragedy."[125] This is the formula for the Wagnerian music drama in general, but it applies in particular to that

---

essay [*Art and Revolution*], through Liszt, to Wigand, the radical publisher, who accepted it and paid him five Louisdor for it" (Newman, *The Life of Richard Wagner*, II, 121–22). Silberner calls Wigand "one of the most radical publishers in Leipzig," as well as "the leading member of the Institute for the Advancement of Israelite Literature" (Hess, *Moses Hess Briefwechsel*, 66 n.1, 377 n. 3). See Chapter 5 herein for Wigand's rejection of Moses Hess.

124. Wagner, "The Work and Mission of My Life" 243–44.
125. *Ibid.*, 244.

masterpiece on which Wagner labored for more than a quarter of a
century and brought to fruition in 1876—his tetralogy (in reality a
trilogy with a prelude) *The Ring of the Nibelung*.

Wagner's assertion that the art produced by a given society is manifestation of the social and political structure of that society—the society producing both the artist and the conditions governing the work
produced by the artist—will seem to today's reader a version of the
Marxian view of art as superstructure. It is in fact likely that Marx
himself would have approved Wagner's view of the matter, no doubt
after reminding him that economic relationships were the foundation
of political and social relationships. But Marx, like Tolstoy, was aware
of Wagner only as a musician and dramatist. And Wagner himself
seems to have ignored the writings of Marx.[126]

What went wrong with the German spirit in the mother country of
the Germans during the nineteenth century? Wagner has told his
American audience that the best of the German tribes had left central

126. Wagner can hardly have remained unacquainted throughout his life with
Marx's existence and activities, but I have found no reference to Marx (or Engels) made
or reported to have been made by Wagner. As for Marx on Wagner, the index of S. S.
Prawer's *Karl Marx and World Literature* lists six references in the text to a Richard
Wagner. Four of these, however, have to do with the Wagner of Goethe's *Faust* (whom
Goethe neglected to provide with a first name). The fifth is to "that shoemaker-poet
Hans Sachs whom Marx was never to see through Wagner's admiring eyes." In support
of this claim Prawer cites Marx as follows: "Herr Daumer is a continuation of Hans
Sachs, but dry and devoid of all humour" (Prawer, *Karl Marx and World Literature*,
172). Marx's comment is hardly to the disadvantage of the humorous Hans Sachs of
Wagner's *Die Meistersinger*, and Prawer supports his claim with no additional citations.
In the last of the indexed references, Prawer writes: "Marx charges the text of Wagner's
The Ring of the Nibelungs [sic] with grossly titillating misuse of Germanic legend."
Rather confusingly, Prawer then cites from an unidentified work in the Marx-Engels
corpus a passage containing: a direct quotation, unidentified as such, from *Die Walküre*
("whoever heard of a brother embracing a sister as his bride"); a reference to Wagner's
"lewd gods," who "spice their amours with a dash of incest"—the first part presumably
from Marx, the second from Engels; and a quotation ("In primaeval times the sister *was*
the wife, *and that was moral*") from a letter written by Marx in the spring of 1882
(*ibid.*, 364). The passage cited by Prawer may be found in Frederick Engels, *The Origin
of the Family, Private Property and the State, in the Light of the Researches of Lewis H.
Morgan* (New York, 1972), 102 (note to the 1884 edition). Marx's letter of 1882 has
not been preserved; *cf.* Marx and Engels, *Selected Works*, III, 216–17. The mistransla-
tion of "Der Ring des Nibelungen" should not be attributed to Engels, who refers simply
to "Wagner's *Nibelung* text" in the note to the 1884 edition of his account of Lewis H.
Morgan's researches.

Europe long ago and had dispersed themselves to the west—to England as the Angles and Saxons, to France as the Franks, to Spain as the Visigoths, to northern Italy as the Lombards. (This *Völkerwanderung,* or diaspora, was an exodus caused by the inroads of Huns and Slavs from the east.) Remaining at home, says Wagner, were the Germans of Germany (*die Deutschen*), worst exemplified by the "peculiar type of the German 'Philistine.'" This kind of man "lets himself be hampered and hemmed in on every side," and he "lives out his tale of little woes, in pettiness and wretchedness, amid continual bickerings with neighbors like himself."[127]

But what of the revival of the German spirit heralded by the music of Beethoven and Weber, the words of Goethe and Schiller, and "the noble aspirations of Young Germany"?[128] Somewhere there was a worm in the bud. Wagner writes:

> Whoever has given any attention to my own career, and has gathered from my occasional writings some idea of my character and its development, will easily understand that I was precisely the one, among my German countrymen, who must have felt most vehemently the longing for such a new birth of German civilization—somewhere and at some time. The longer I lived, the more I saw the fading away of that vivid memory of our true German culture, which, at the beginning of this century, it seemed that the mighty strength of our great artists was about to awaken and lead to great results. Wider and wider spread before my eyes the heterogeneous web of a civilization entirely foreign to the German race—a web that glittered with two changing colors, the sallow hue of the Restoration, in the old French sense of an oligarchy of petty rulers, and the red hue of Revolution, in the new (and equally French) sense of "Liberty." The interweaving and arrangement of these two textures seemed to me to be undertaken by a third foreign constituent of our national life—that Jewish element whose influence was continually on the increase. How different had been the future of German culture as Young Germany might have imagined it at the period in which I was born![129]

"From Beethoven's symphonies to Meyerbeer's opera—what a fearful stride is this!"[130] Thus Wagner, on the musician whose work and person he had come to despise. "The German mind," Wagner says,

127. Wagner, "The Work and Mission of My Life," 110.
128. *Ibid.,* 115.
129. *Ibid.,* 111–12.
130. *Ibid.,* 119.

"losing more and more of itself . . . let Weber die in a foreign land among strangers; it laid away in the dusty corners of its libraries Goethe's now completed 'Faust' as a dry unintelligible jumble of mysteries . . . and now it deserted Beethoven, whom it pronounced a mere madman, for Meyerbeer . . . and reveled amid the 'revolutionary' music of 'The Huguenots' in dreams of a coming day of freedom."[131] But the reader will recall that "the German mind" was not alone in hailing Meyerbeer as a paraclete: in 1833 Giuseppe Mazzini had called Meyerbeer—along with Gioacchino Rossini, the musician whom Schopenhauer preferred to Wagner—a harbinger of "social music, the music of the future."[132]

As far as Wagner was concerned the art of Meyerbeer was all "coarseness and triviality." But there was, he tells his American audience, another direction for music to take in Germany. "A finer taste and a real artistic talent revived among us and did *its* best, also, to settle our account with the great past," Wagner says. He adds:

> Here, too, a member of that ubiquitous, talented race took the lead. Mendelssohn undertook with his delicate hand—his exquisite special talent for a kind of musical landscape-painting—to lead the educated classes of Germany as far away from the dreaded and misunderstood extravagances of a Beethoven, and from the sublime prospect opened to national art by his later works, as from those rude theatrical orgies which his more refined tastes so detested in the historical opera of his fellow-Hebrew. He was the savior of music in the *salon*—and with him the concert-room, and now and then even the church, did duty as a *salon* also. Amid all the tempests of revolution he gave to his art a delicate, smooth, quiet, cool and agreeably tranquil form that excited nobody, and had no aim but to please the modern cultivated taste, and to give it occasionally, amid the shifting and turmoil of the times, the consolation of a little pleasing and elegant entertainment. A new idea in art was developed—the embodiment in it of a graceful, good-society element quite foreign to the nation's character and social life.[133]

131. *Ibid.*, 120. *Cf.* F. G. Edwards, *Musical Haunts in London* (London, 1895), 52–54. According to Edwards, Weber died of long-standing "consumption" on June 4, 1826, in a house at 103 Great Portland Street. A plaque was affixed to the house in 1894. ("Better late than never," comments Edwards.) Weber finished his overture to *Oberon* at Great Portland Street on April 9, 1826, only three days before conducting the premiere at Covent Garden. His body was buried in the vaults of Moorfield's Catholic Chapel. Eighteen years later the remains were sent to Dresden, largely "upon the initiative of Wagner," according to Edwards. For Wagner's account of the reception of Weber's remains at Dresden, see Wagner, *My Life*, trans. Gray, 296–99.
132. See Chapter 3 herein.
133. Wagner, "The Work and Mission of My Life," 120–21.

Mendelssohn, the "savior of music in the *salon*," detested the operas of Meyerbeer but dreaded the unrestrained expressive power of Beethoven's music. He wanted, we may say, to tame the daimonic spirit of German music. (Had Wagner known of Mazzini's claim, he might have added at this point that Meyerbeer had given us only a debased form of "social music" and that Mendelssohn, although a true enough musical savior, had saved nothing more than "society music.") Mendelssohn's salon music, Wagner continues, was soon complemented by the tasteful genre music of Robert Schumann. The Germans pronounced themselves satisfied. Wagner adds:

> The educated German—who no longer believed in a great living national art, but in his vague longing for political freedom was very fond of using empty phrases about the now forgotten "German element"—saw in these works the noble achievements of a truly reawakened "German art-spirit"; and, contrasting them with the prevailing crude realism and trivial sensuousness of the "international" art which he saw presented to the public, he felt himself bound to admire them enthusiastically when he heard them performed in the more exclusive concert-room. Thus the German intellect degenerated into a condition of complete unproductiveness in art, severing the living and active bonds that bound it to a great national past, and undertaking to create, unaided, an art intended only for "amateurs" and "connoisseurs."[134]

Wagner's answer to the questions of what went wrong with the German spirit in the sphere of music and the arts generally (whether or not we are inclined to give it credence) is clear enough: the burgeoning German spirit had been checked in its development and distorted by the French spirit and the Jewish spirit. The German spirit was weak, almost newly born, at the beginning of the nineteenth century. Royal and imperial France was—despite the vicissitudes of the Bourbons and Bonapartes—an old, well-established, and long-since unified culture, whereas Germany had been split apart by the Reformation and pounded into fragments during the Thirty Years' War. The Jews, although a scattered people without a state of their own, had been unified for millennia by the spirit of Judaism.

The power of the Jewish spirit over the German spirit is Wagner's constant refrain. The relationship, as he sees it, is neither symbiotic nor parasitic. Or if it is parasitic, the German, not the Jewish, spirit has become the parasite. "We are blockheads and have taken everything over from the Jews," Wagner complains to Cosima on October

134. *Ibid.*, 121.

24, 1882.[135] On November 22, 1878, Cosima notes in her diary: "R.
said yesterday, 'If ever I were to write again about the Jews, I should
say I have nothing against them, it is just that they descended on us
Germans too soon, we were not yet steady enough to absorb them.'"[136]
And on January 13, 1879: "Friend [Hermann] Levi stays behind after
our other friends have gone, and when he tells us that his father is a
rabbi our conversation comes back to the Israelites—the feeling they
intervened too early in our cultural circumstances, that the generally
human (*allgemeine Menschliche*), which should have developed from
the German character (*aus dem deutschen Wesen*), in order to have
then benefited the Jewish character as well, was held up in its development by their premature intervention in our affairs, before we as yet
knew who we were. . . . Alone together again, R. and I speak of the
remarkable attraction of individual Jews to him; he says we are getting
a synagogue at Wahnfried!"[137] (This entry in Cosima's diary reports a

135. Cosima Wagner, *Diaries*, II, 937. In the same entry Wagner justifies some un-
specified activities of the Hungarian Jews: "During our walk R.[ichard] told· me the
Hungarian minister has declared that the Jews' struggle is that of the have-nots against
the haves, and thus there is everything to be said for it. 'And that struggle is of course the
most justified of all,' says R." For Wagner's remark in 1881 that governments maintain
their armed forces for "the protection of the haves against the have-nots," see Rather,
The Dream of Self-Destruction, 175.

136. Cosima Wagner, *Diaries*, II, 207. According to Westernhagen, Wagner's remark (that his only objection to the Jews was that they had come to Germany before the
Germans had found their own roots) was reprinted in 1937 in the *Bayreuther Blätter*,
i.e., during the high tide of National Socialism in Germany (Westernhagen, *Wagner: A
Biography*, II, 571).

137. Cosima Wagner, *Die Tagebücher*, II, 290 (the translation of this passage in
Cosima Wagner's Diaries, II, 254, is somewhat faulty). Wagner was depicted as a long-
nosed "Rabbi of Bayreuth" in the anti-Jewish Viennese press of the 1870s and 1880s.
According to one reporter, "Richard Wagner has arranged for the benefit of Jews expelled from Russia [after the assassination of Alexander II in 1881] a special performance of *The Ring of the Nibelung*, in which only kosher Valkyries appear, and the magic
fire flickers under the supervision of the Bayreuth higher rabbinate" (*Cf.* Eduard Fuchs
and Richard Kreowski, *Richard Wagner in der Karikatur* [Berlin, 1907], 138). And in
Vienna's chief newspaper, the *Neue Freie Presse*, a journalist wrote in 1876: "The
Wagner-Semite (*Wagnersemite*) . . . has discovered in the cheerfully aggressive character
of the maestro : . . . distinct traces of an earlier tribal relationship. They say that Wagner
himself . . . looks with displeasure when his name is abbreviated to 'R.' Wagner, because
it could be read as 'Rabbi' Wagner" (cited from Tappert, *Richard Wagner im Spiegel der
Kritik*, 82). According to Fuchs and Kreowski (writing in 1907), "Where once no effort
was spared in accusing Wagner of antisemitic tendencies, he was now [during the 1870s
and 1880s] berated as a servant of the Jews (*Judenknecht*)" (Fuchs and Kreowski,
Richard Wagner in der Karikatur, 138).

puzzling remark made by Levi before his departure; it is discussed in the notes.[138]) Subsequently Levi wrote a letter to his father, the chief rabbi at Giessen, seeking to justify Wagner's fight against "what he calls 'Judaism' (*Judentum*) in music and literature" and predicting that posterity will some day recognize that Wagner was "as great a human being (*Mensch*) as an artist."[139]

138. Cosima Wagner, *Die Tagebücher*, II, 290. The puzzling remark follows immediately after the discussion between Levi and the Wagners on the Jewish problem in Germany. It reads: "The kapellmeister [*i.e.*, Levi] reports on a great movement against Jews in all fields; in Munich it is desired that they be removed from the town council—he hopes that in twenty years they would be extirpated root and branch and the public of the *Ring* given over to another folk, we 'know it otherwise'!" ("—er hofft, in 20 Jahren würden sie mit Stiel und Stumpf ausgerottet und das Publikum des "Ringes" ein anderes Volk abgeben, wir 'wissen es anders'!"). See *Die Tagebücher*, II, 290, for the original, and *Cosima Wagner's Diaries*, II, 254, for a faulty translation. The verb *ausrotten* means, literally, to "root out," hence "extirpate," "exterminate," or "eliminate." If Richard Wagner himself had made this remark it would probably be cited as further and conclusive evidence that he favored the "final solution," *i.e.*, the wholesale slaughter of the Jews. Levi, however, made the remark, and he, the son of a rabbi, was and remained a Jew. Levi was no doubt calling—making use of an unhappy metaphor while doing so—for a new kind of audience for the *Ring*. The "we" closing Cosima's sentence is indeterminate, but it probably refers to the understanding of the *Ring* shared by Levi and the Wagners, rather than to a belief on part of the Wagners that the public attending the *Ring* would continue to be heavily Jewish. Fifty-seven years after Levi made this remark, and three years after the Nazis came to power, appeared a documented account of the mistreatment of Jews in Germany entitled *Der gelbe Fleck. Die Ausrottung von 500,000 deutschen Juden. Mit einem Vorwort von Lion Feuchtwanger* (Paris, 1936). An English translation, entitled *The Yellow Spot: The Outlawing of Half a Million Human Beings: A Collection of Facts and Documents Relating to Three Years' Persecution of German Jews, Derived Chiefly from National Socialist Sources, very carefully assembled by a Group of Investigators. With an Introduction by the Bishop of Durham*, was reviewed in T. S. Eliot's *The Criterion* (July, 1936), 759–60. Here *Ausrottung* is translated as "Outlawing." In the German original Lion Feuchtwanger speaks of the "systematic destruction" (*systematische Vernichtung*) of half a million highly civilized Europeans (p. 5). Feuchtwanger, of course, was referring to the systematic rooting out and destruction of the German-Jewish community, not to the destruction of its individual members. The reviewer of the English translation (possibly T. S. Eliot himself) objected, however, to what he saw as a disparity between the book's title and its contents.

139. Levi's letter to his father, dated April 13, 1882, is translated in the English version of Westernhagen's biography (*Wagner: A Biography*, 571–627). The German version of the letter is given by Gregor-Dellin in an appendix to his edition of Wagner's autobiography. (This appendix is not included in Andrew Gray's translation of Gregor-Dellin's edition.) Levi's letter to his father, as cited by Gregor-Dellin, reads (my translation): "But some day posterity will recognize that W. was as great a human being (*Mensch*) as an artist, which those close to him already know. Even his fight against what he calls 'Judaism' (*Judentum*) in music and in modern literature arises from the

In "The Work and Mission of My Life" Wagner has nothing to say
of the prominence of Jews in music and the arts generally. His concern
is with the warped development of the German spirit. In "Judaism in
Music" he does question this relatively sudden rise to prominence and
his answer is Marxian in character: he seeks for an underlying economic cause and finds it in the growing commercialization of art. (We
recall that in the short story "An End in Paris," written after his first
exposure to the full force of that commercialization, Wagner's dying
musician "R." anathematizes those who have "dared to practice usury
with high chaste art." [140]) We have seen that Disraeli, before Wagner,
asked the same question and answered it by pointing to the inherently
superior character of the Hebrew race. Theodor Lessing, who asked
the same question (with specific reference to Germany) seventy years
after Wagner, left it unanswered. [141] As far as America was concerned,
the question of Jewish predominance in the arts had no relevance in
1879: the population of the United States at that time was approximately 50,000,000, and of this population 230,000 were Jews, that is,
less than half of 1 percent; moreover, nearly 80 percent of these Jews
had been added to the total since 1850. [142]

Repeatedly Wagner insists in "The Work and Mission of My Life"
as elsewhere in his writings that the Germans of Germany proper are
not fitted for *Weltmacht*, world power. It is of interest to recall here

---

noblest motives, and his behavior toward me, toward Joseph Rubinstein, and his earlier
intimate connection with [Carl] Tausig [1841–71], whom he loved tenderly, shows that
he harbors no petty prejudices (*kleinliches Risches*) like those, say, of a rural Junker
(*Landjunker*) or a Protestant bigot (*protestantischer Mucker*)" (Wagner, *Mein Leben*,
II, 788). Edouard Sans has *homme, judaïsme, mesquinerie, hobereau*, and *cagot protestant*, respectively, for the German words given in parentheses above (*Richard Wagner et
la pensée schopenhauerienne*, 248). Joseph Rubinstein committed suicide in Lucerne on
September 22, 1884, nineteen months after Wagner's death. His body was brought back
to Bayreuth and buried there in the Jewish cemetery. For Wagner's letter of January 22,
1882, to Joseph's father, asking him to support his son's "truly religious belief" in the
value of art, and warning him of "certain morbid dispositions" in Joseph that "might
lead to the most regrettable excess" if he were forced to continue his career as a concert
pianist, see Westernhagen, *Wagner: A Biography*, 595–96. Wagner's letter, a model of
sympathetic understanding and psychological insight, is worth reading in full. See also
the senior Rubinstein's reply, after his son's suicide (*ibid.*, 597).

140. *Cf.* Chapter 2 herein.
141. *Cf.* note 30, this chapter.
142. Ruppin, *The Jews in the Modern World*, 53.

that in 1837 Moses Hess, then in his pre-Marxist, pre-Zionist phase, told the Jews the same thing: their destiny was to conquer the world by virtue of their spirit, not by the force of their arms. The Napoleons and Caesars of the world, the so-called world conquerors, are "hateful, petty, brutal, insatiable—because they have nothing at all within and therefore must forever be gobbling up what is without," Wagner had written to Mathilde Wesendonck in 1859.[143] In the penultimate paragraph of "The Work and Mission of My Life" he sums up his message to the citizens of the United States of America.

> It is said that your famous General Grant once prophesied that all the world would some day speak one language. It would only seem possible, at first thought, to conceive of such a language as a kind of universal jargon made up of all manner of heterogeneous ingredients, and equivalent to the destruction of all strong idiomatic expression, and so of all that art which lives only in speech. But those who stood by, at the laying of the cornerstone of my theatre, and heard the singing of "Seid umschlungen, Millionen," in the closing chorus of Beethoven's symphony, could make a similar yet widely different prophecy. They could see that Grant's words might be fulfilled in another fashion than that which the distinguished American had in mind. Such a fulfillment, in fact, we see already: *German music* already unites the nations of the world—even to those beyond the sea—by an ideal bond. Our great masters, by those noble works which have won the admiration of all lands, have made it certain that this alone can ever be the true, natural, living world-language. And let us, who look back to them with heartfelt reverence, see to it that we reach that ideal toward which I have striven unceasingly throughout my life. Let us see to it that the original, pure, vigorous style of this great German music—and of that visible form, the universal drama, in which its spirit is best revealed—shall be preserved to it; so that the influence of the German mind, upon a world which will always need that influence, shall not be perverted and false and therefore worthless, but true, noble, and vigorous, and therefore in the highest degree salutary, beneficent, and broadening in its effects.[144]

The words of Schiller, "Be embraced, ye millions," introduced by Beethoven into his last symphony, tell us, says Wagner, of an ideal embrace, mediated not by the force of arms but by the virtue of the spirit of music.

---

143. *Cf.* Chapter 5 herein on Hess's *Die heilige Geschichte der Menschheit.* Wagner's letter to Mathilde Wesendonck is cited from Rather, *The Dream of Self-Destruction,* 71.
144. Wagner, "The Work and Mission of My Life," 257–58.

The true German Reich is a kingdom not of this world. It is not an earthly Zion. If the Germans are deceived or deceive themselves into believing that they are destined for world power, disaster will surely follow. Siegfried will be slain; Wotan and Valhalla will go up in flames. The ring bearing the curse of Alberich must find its way back to the depths of the Rhine. The message of Wagner's *Ring* was echoed in 1895 by the great French Wagnerian Romain Rolland when he wrote to Wagner's old friend Malwida von Meysenbug complaining bitterly of the honoring of Bismarck in that year, on the occasion of his eightieth birthday. This man, "who founded an empire on millions of cadavers," wrote Rolland, had been given a sword by William II, and the German Kaiser had then told the audience that a sword would be used, if necessary, to preserve the unity of the fatherland. Rolland added: "Don't be vexed with me. It is not a matter of races [*i.e.*, of the French race versus the German race]. It is a matter of souls. To me the soul of the Kaiser has become hateful." And making obeisance to Wagner, he tells Frau von Meysenbug that retribution is on its way: "The Kaiser wears the ring of Siegfried on his finger. He will not escape the curse."[145]

Earlier in this chapter we saw Wagner taking note in 1880 that men of power—such as Bismarck then was, and the two Napoleons had been—could "conceive of peace in no other form than under the widely respected shelter of countless cannons." In consequence, Wagner wrote in the same year, the peoples of Europe, "armed to the teeth for mutual destruction (*Ausrottung*)," were ready "to fall upon and tear each other apart at the first sign from their warlords." But even without this sign, he continued, the intervention of the "blind will," or the occurrence of some "incalculable oversight," might unexpectedly blow away the fruits of peace and cause everything to "fly into the air."

145. Romain Rolland, *Cahiers I. Choix de lettres à Malwida Meysenbug* (Paris, 1948), 133–34. Two decades later Joseph Conrad had an Orwellian vision of war as peace, moustachioed in the style made popular by William II: "Indeed, war has made peace altogether on its own, it has modelled it on its own image: a martial, overbearing, war-lord sort of peace, with a mailed fist and turned-up moustaches, ringing with the din of grand manoeuvres, eloquent with allusions to glorious feats of arms; it has made peace so magnificent as to be almost as expensive to keep up as itself. It has sent out apostles of its own, who at one time went about (mostly in newspapers) preaching the gospel of the mystic sanctity of its sacrifices, and the regenerating power of spilt blood, to the poor in mind—whose name is legion" (Conrad, *Notes on Life and Letters,* 109–10).

A general famine would then add to the toll of deaths.[146] Wagner's fears, discounted by the practical wisdom of the men of power, proved to be well-founded. The long-deferred catastrophe came almost by accident in August, 1914, after a series of unforeseen events beginning with the assassination by Serbian and Croatian nationalists of the Archduke Franz Ferdinand of Austria-Hungary on June 28, 1914. The countless cannons on land and sea—already "Roaring their readiness to avenge," as Thomas Hardy wrote five months before the Great War—proved to be, in the long run, a too fragile shelter for the peace of the world.[147]

146. Wagner, *Gesammelte Schriften und Dichtungen*, X, 252–53; *cf.* also Rather, *The Dream of Self-Destruction*, 178.

147. "From 1871 to 1914 the deterrents were effective," comments a recent historian, "[b]ut if the First World War teaches no other lesson, it can perhaps be said to have illustrated that deterrents cannot be depended upon to deter forever" (Harry Hearder, in the "Editor's forward" to James Joll, *The Origins of the First World War* [London, 1984], ix).

CHAPTER SEVEN

THE INSURRECTION OF WOMAN

To promote a woman to beare rule, superioritie, dominion or empire above any realm, nation, or citie, is repugnant to nature, contumelie to God, a thing most contrarious to his reveled will and approved ordinance, and finallie it is the subversion of all good order, of all equitie and justice . . . The spaniardes are Iewes and they bragge that Marie of England is of the root of Iesse.[1]

John Knox

During the years of Wagner's artistic productivity three separately constituted groups of human beings were seen to be in need of emancipation: women, the proletariat, and the Jews. The distinguishing features of the three groups were, respectively, sex, class (Karl Marx), and race (Moses Hess). Jews and women were alike in that they were to be found at all levels of society and often occupied, openly or in secret, positions of great power. A male Jew could free himself from some of the social disabilities weighing on him by converting to Christianity, if only nominally, although he would then be read out of the Jewish community. A woman could emancipate herself in part by divorcing or simply leaving her husband, but at the cost of losing her social status. If talented, she could then move freely in the Bohemian world of the intelligentsia, adopt a male name, write books, and seek to advance feminism, as did the Baroness Dudevant (George Sand) and the Countess Marie d'Agoult (Daniel Stern) in France.

1. In 1558, when the founder of Scottish Presbyterianism wrote this polemic, Catherine de Medici was Queen of France, Mary Tudor (daughter of Catherine of Aragon and Henry VIII) was Queen of England, and Marie de Lorraine (the mother of Mary, Queen of Scots) was Queen of Scotland. All were Roman Catholics. Elizabeth Tudor succeeded her sister in 1558 and no second blast of Knox's trumpet was heard thereafter.

Associated with the movement to emancipate the female sex was a movement to emancipate the sexual body; in early nineteenth-century France and Germany this was known as the "rehabilitation of the flesh." Also associated were experiments, carried out by small groups of initiates in Europe and the United States, with different forms of sexual bonding between men and women. Some of these experiments took place within a religious context, and in such contexts women were often restored to religious roles from which they had, since the downfall of the Marcionite and Gnostic churches, been rigorously excluded. Expressed in mythic terms, a movement was under way to achieve a better balance between the male and female principles resident in the two sexes—the cloven halves of Plato's primal androgyne. The topic of the present chapter is this many-faceted movement and Wagner's involvement in it.

THE WAGNER QUESTION, THE WOMAN QUESTION, AND THE EBELIAN FEMALE CHURCH

"Wagner is plainly mad." These were the words of Hector Berlioz in 1860 when Wagner was frantically readying *Tannhäuser* for what would prove to be its fiasco at the Paris Opera. The words were mere rhetoric, as was the subsequent reference to Wagner's "exterminating" by the French press.[2] Twelve years later a close study of Wagner's music dramas and theoretical writings led a practicing psychiatrist in Munich to charge that Wagner was literally mad, and that his madness had its base in a warped sense of sexuality. The psychiatrist was Dr. Theodor Puschmann, and his charges were made public in 1872 in a widely read brochure of sixty-seven pages (entitled *Richard Wagner. Eine psychiatrische Studie*) that quickly went into three printings.[3] Puschmann's psychiatric study of Wagner does not preserve "that objectivity of judgment which must be the prime requirement of a scientific work," as its author claims it does, but it makes interesting reading.[4] Cosima Wagner and her husband seem to have taken Puschmann

2. See Chapter 3 herein.
3. Theodor Puschmann, *Richard Wagner. Eine psychiatrische Studie* (Berlin, 1873). Puschmann later achieved eminence as a medical historian. According to Erna Lesky, "Puschmann's statement that the master was not a genius but a lunatic" contributed to his retirement from psychiatry (Lesky, *The Vienna Medical School of the 19th Century*, trans. L. Williams and I. S. Levij, M. D. [Baltimore, 1976], 571).
4. Puschmann, *Richard Wagner. Eine psychiatrische Studie*, 9.

less than seriously, and even managed to extract some humor from the situation.[5]

Puschmann finds that Wagner's Paris short stories read well enough, and he grants that the texts of *Rienzi, The Flying Dutchman, Tannhäuser,* and *Lohengrin* are written with a certain "poetic verve."[6] But he has reservations with respect to the sexual freedom championed in *Das Liebesverbot,* and he has harsh words for the sexual immorality of the later works. Puschmann writes: "Wagner has always accorded sexual arousal a great place in his psychic life, as is especially evident from his own autobiographic jottings. His first great work, 'Das Liebesverbot,' celebrates the 'victory of free and open sensuality,' even though here he remains within the still acceptable bounds of decorum. But so much the more obvious is the erotic element in his most recent works; in 'Tristan and Isolde' he glorifies 'adultery,' in the 'Valkyrie' even 'incest' (*Blutschande*)."[7]

Puschmann was particularly offended by the "frivolity and obscenity" of the expressions to be found in Wagner's writings. From *Siegfried* he cites the young Siegfried's query to Mime: "You made me then without a mother?" And from *Die Walküre* he cites Sieglinde's reference to Siegmund as her "hotly beloved brother." He was most offended by a passage from Wagner's essay *Opera and Drama:* " 'To become a human being,' he [Wagner] writes, 'Beethoven had to become a whole, that is a unified, human being subject to the sexual conditions of maleness and femaleness'—'Beethoven,' he continues, 'found it necessary to contribute to the newly-revived organism, now capable of giving birth, a fructifying seed; and this he took from the generative force of the poet.' "[8]

5. At Karlsruhe on November 24, 1872, Cosima noted in her diaries: "Prof. Nietzsche tells me that in Munich a Dr. Puschmann, lecturer at the university there, has just published a paper in which he proves psychiatrically that R. is mad. That such things are possible and are tolerated!" On April 5, 1873, there is the following entry: "After lunch, when I look long at R., he says, 'I suppose you are making Puschmann studies of me.' I reply that I have no need to do that, since I am completely convinced that both of us are mad." On August 19, 1873, Wagner remarks: "Now, when my name is well-enough known, nobody reads my things, they only read Dr. Puschmann about me, and it has become a pastime to provoke me" (Cosima Wagner, *Diaries,* I, 561, 619, 664–65).

6. Puschmann, *Richard Wagner. Eine psychiatrische Studie,* 45–46.

7. *Ibid.,* 59–60.

8. *Ibid.,* 60. Puschmann's volume and page references to the 1871 edition of Wagner's collected works, from which he is citing, have been omitted here.

Puschmann eventually reaches his diagnostic conclusions. Wagner is a very sick man indeed: he suffers from "erotomania," "physical and psychical impotence," "megalomania," "moral insanity," and "persecution mania."[9] In his private life Wagner "shamelessly treads down the holiest sentiments of human morality, love and friendship." Although Wagner considers himself to be "the greatest man, the genius of the century," his music dramas since *Lohengrin*—which Puschmann, with a flash of wit, calls Wagner's "swan-song"—have been as unsuccessful as they are tasteless or immoral. *Die Meistersinger*—later to become the favorite of Sigmund Freud—has no appeal for the educated public, says Puschmann; it deals with the "mud and filth of everyday life."[10] Nine pages of Puschmann's brochure are devoted to Wagner's "Judaism in Music" and his attitude toward newspapers and journals critical of his works. "It seems," Puschmann writes, "that his consuming envy of the fame achieved by his musical rivals who by chance adhere to the faith of Israel has implanted in him the fixed idea that he is being persecuted by the Jews. Justifying this suspicion are the hard, loveless and often incorrect judgements that he passes on Halévy, Berlioz, Mendelssohn and Meyerbeer."[11]

In the passage from Wagner's *Opera and Drama* that so offended Puschmann's moral sensibilities, the "poet" in question is Schiller, and the "fructifying seed" the words from Schiller's *Ode to Joy* that Beethoven introduced into the *Ninth Symphony*. Tone and word fuse into a whole organism, Wagner goes on to say, with the utterance of Schiller's "Be embraced, O ye millions!"[12] Wagner's metaphor is rooted in the deepest soil of both Indo-European and Semitic lan-

9. *Ibid.*, 26, 31, 51, 59. Respectively, "unnatürliche Steigerung des Geschlechtstriebes," "physische und psychische Impotenz," "Grössenwahn," "moralischer Irrsinn," and "Verfolgungswahn."

10. *Ibid.*, 21, 31. Freud was sixteen years old at the time of Puschmann's writing. On Freud's attitude toward music and his admiration for *Die Meistersinger*, see Paul Roazen, *Freud and his Followers* (New York, 1976), 32–33.

11. Puschmann, *Richard Wagner. Eine psychiatrische Studie*, 39. Puschmann's belief that Berlioz was Jewish, or of Jewish origin, finds no support in Martin Greenberg, comp., *The Jewish Lists: Physicists, Generals, Actors and Writers, and Hundreds of Other Lists of Accomplished Jews* (New York, 1979). The same may be said of Disraeli's belief that Mozart and Rossini were of Jewish origin, and Leon Stein's similar belief with respect to Richard and Cosima Wagner, none of whom appear on Greenberg's lists, which are more than comprehensive (*cf.* the criteria for inclusion given on p. vii).

12. Wagner, *Gesammelte Schriften und Dichtungen*, III, 312–16.

guages. The "seminal word," "creative word" or "logos spermatikos" is the central feature of an ancient but still-malleable creation myth.[13] In the Christian tradition, the savior is the "Word made flesh" (John 1:14). Equally ancient is the other metaphor in the passage from *Opera and Drama* in question. Wagner tells us that in order for Beethoven to become a "whole human being" it was necessary for him to take on both male and female characteristics, and we recall Plato's myth of the primal androgyne. Nineteen years after writing *Opera and Drama* Wagner developed the same idea along slightly different lines. In "Beethoven" (1870), Wagner tells us that the "blind seer Tiresias"— the epicene prophet celebrated by poets from Ovid to Eliot—has his counterpart in the deaf musician Beethoven: what Tiresias "sees" is no more than the visible world of appearances, but what Beethoven "hears" (with his inner ear) and expresses in his music is the voice of reality.[14]

Opera and Drama is a theoretical treatise of some three hundred pages. Wagner sent the manuscript, bound in red, to his musician friend Theodor Uhlig as a Christmas present in 1851, immediately after the publication of the book. In an accompanying private dedication Wagner told Uhlig to take cheer from the binding. "I have endeavoured to reverse Goethe's saying: 'Grey, my friend, is every theory,' so that I may call to you with a good conscience: 'Red, o friend, is this my theory!'" Ellis, who tracked down this private dedication, takes note of Wagner's "semi-political allusion to the revolutionary tendency of the art-theories" embodied in his book.[15]

Shortly after the passage in *Opera and Drama* that offended Puschmann, Wagner tries to define the nature, or essence (*Wesen*), of music. He writes: "*Music is a woman.* The nature of woman is *love;* but this love is *receptive,* and totally *yielding* in its responsiveness. Woman receives her full individuality only at the moment of yielding. She is the maiden of the waves rushing soullessly through the billows of her element until she, through love of a man, first receives a soul" (emphasis

13. *Cf.* Rather, "Alchemistry, the Kabbala, the Analogy of the 'Creative Word,' and the Origins of Molecular Biology."

14. *Cf.* Rather, *The Dream of Self-Destruction*, 139–40. On T. S. Eliot's debt to Wagner in *The Waste Land*, see Chapter 1, note 27, herein.

15. Wagner, *Richard Wagner's Prose Works*, II, x–xi. On Baudelaire's acquaintance with an English translation of *Opera and Drama* published in 1855–56, see chapter 3, note 29, herein.

added).[16] We catch a glimpse here of Hans Christian Andersen's tale of the little mermaid's painful search for a soul, and perhaps also of Wagner's own rather cold-blooded Rhine maidens. But it is more important to note that here Wagner sees music, the female principle, in a subordinate role with respect to the male principle of the word: the "fructifying seed" is more important than the soil to which it is added. As Wagner's ideas developed he gave greater weight to the female principle, and in "Beethoven" (1870) he does an about face and gives tone priority before word in the *Ninth Symphony*.[17]

Woman is most perfect, Wagner continues in *Opera and Drama*, when she remains within the "sphere of the involuntary." Music has achieved perfection of this kind in the work of one musician alone. Wagner writes: "Behold Mozart! Was he by any chance a lesser musician because he was only a musician, heart and soul, because he neither would nor could be anything other than a musician? Look at *Don Giovanni*! Where else has music ever achieved, in abundantly overflowing fullness, such endlessly rich individuality and definitive characterization than here, where the musician was an unconditionally loving woman, in keeping with the essence of his art?"[18] Wagner's "sphere of the involuntary" is the sphere of the mythic creative unconscious, familiar to him from the workings of his own muse as well as from the writings of G. H. Schubert and E. T. A. Hoffmann. Later he would discover it in the writings of Schopenhauer, under a changed name.[19]

So much for "true" music. Wagner then points to the role played by "false" music in Italian opera, French opera, and German opera, respectively that of the "prostitute," the "coquette," and the "prude." Of these three false muses he prefers the first, if he is forced to make a choice. Worst of all is the German prude, for she tries to make a virtue of her own inability to love, and looks at her sisters with Pharisee-like scorn. Moreover she is a hypocrite. "Love never stirs in her bigoted heart, true, but [there is] common, sensual lust in her carefully hidden flesh. We know the conventicles of the pious and the respectable towns where the flower of Muckerism bloomed! We have seen the prude

16. Wagner, *Gesammelte Schriften und Dichtungen*, III, 316.
17. *Cf.* Rather, "The Meaning of Beethoven," in *The Dream of Self-Destruction*, 139–48.
18. Wagner, *Gesammelte Schriften und Dichtungen*, III, 316–17, 320.
19. *Cf.* Rather, "Music, Dreams, and the Unconscious," in *The Dream of Self-Destruction*, 110–38.

descend to every vice practiced by her French and Italian sisters, stained moreover by hypocrisy and, unfortunately, without a trace of originality!"[20]

This obscure (to today's reader) reference to "Muckerism" (*Muckerei*) on the part of Wagner brings us to the subject of a worldwide sexual revolution, now almost forgotten, that took place in Europe and America in the mid-nineteenth century. It seems likely that Wagner's conception of Muckerism took form in the respectable Prussian town of Königsberg, where he arrived in the summer of 1836 in hot pursuit of Minna. Two leaders of the Ebelian Church at Königsberg—whose adherents were called "Muckers" by their enemies—were then standing trial in the Prussian courts. They had been charged with engaging in sexually immoral practices, under the cover of religion, and participating in a secret society (illegal, as such, in Prussia). In Wagner's autobiographical account of his misadventures with the flighty Minna at Königsberg nothing is said of the trial of the Muckers, but it can hardly have escaped his attention.[21]

The Königsberg Muckers receive the lion's share of space in William Hepworth Dixon's *Spiritual Wives,* a book that ran into four editions in England in 1868 and almost immediately appeared in German and Russian translations.[22] Its author states that the "doctrine of the Spiritual wife" is represented in England by the so-called saints of Paxton (Dixon refers to them as "our English Muckers") under the guidance of the Reverend Henry James Prince. This doctrine, Dixon tells us, is found chiefly if not wholly among "men of Teutonic race" (*i.e.,* the English, the Germans, the Scandinavians). In the United States it has flowered out "at Salt Lake City into Polygamy; among New England spiritual circles into Affinities; at Mount Lebanon into Celibate Love;

20. Wagner, *Gesammelte Schriften und Dichtungen,* III, 318–19.

21. Minna and Wagner were married in the church at Tragheim near Königsberg on November 24, 1836. In May of the following year Minna ran off with a wealthy merchant, who soon deserted her. Wagner says in his autobiography that Minna wrote to him later, confessing that she had been unfaithful and asking his forgiveness. He replied, he says, that the chief guilt was his own, and that the affair would never be mentioned again between them (*Mein Leben,* I, 156). Wagner's letter has not been preserved, nor has Minna's, but he refers to it in some detail in another letter written to her twenty-two years later. For the text of this letter, see Newman, *The Life of Richard Wagner,* I, 230–34.

22. William Hepworth Dixon, *Spiritual Wives* (4th ed.; 2 vols.; London, 1868). A German translation of 1868 and a Russian translation of 1869 are listed in the British Museum Catalogue.

at Wallingford and Oneida Creek into Complex Marriage, and in a hundred American cities into some more or less open form of Free Love." These alternative societies believe that they have created "a new earth and a new heaven." To some of them "property was nothing, marriage was nothing," for all of them a new light had been shed on "the higher relation of woman to man in the new kingdom of heaven." Dixon found it striking that three of these singular societies, namely "the congregation of Pietists, vulgarly called the Muckers, at Königsberg, the brotherhood of Princeites at Spaxton, and the Bible Communists at Oneida Creek," had so much in common, and yet had arisen "without concert, in distant parts of the world, under separate church rules, and in widely different social circumstances." All three, he noted, were led by clergymen, took origin in a place of learning and theological study, and affected the form of family life.[23]

For the modern reader, Dixon's book sheds a great light over a side of nineteenth-century life that was increasingly repressed and forgotten as the century grew older and, on the surface at least, more respectable. But for our purposes here—which are to illuminate certain generally overlooked aspects of Wagner's theories of art and society—we need only consider what Dixon had to say of the Muckers of Königsberg, this being the sole instance of the movements studied by Dixon to which Wagner was at all exposed.

Beginning on a note of high comedy, Dixon tells of his initiation in 1867 into the society of "wet Muckers" at Königsberg by a learned lawyer. He is asked, "Have you come to a full consciousness, my much beloved, of the universal prevalence and acceptance of the principle of water?" On replying in the affirmative, Dixon is told: "Now these two principles—the first principle being that of Light, the second principle being that of Water—are the alpha and the omega, the beginning and the end, the sun and the moon, the positive and the negative, the right line and the curve, the conscious and the unconscious, the active and the passive, the male and the female. Their union is creation; their divorce is chaos." Dixon is then given the "seraphic kiss" and told to

---

23. *Ibid.*, I, 79, 85, 87, 227. With reference to the "lawless unions, which are known in America as a state of Free Love," Dixon says that in France and England the parties to such unions know that they must live thereafter under a social ban, but in the United States this is not so. "The great disparity [in number] in the sexes, which in that country makes the female master of every situation, has deprived society of the conservative force engendered by fear and shame. No woman in that country needs to care whether she offends or not" (*ibid.*, II, 226–27).

drink a glass of Roman punch. "Wet Muckerism," the lawyer says, is a society to which many free and learned men subscribe; it represents the "counter-comedy; the movement against the movement; the only answer which in these days science can make to superstition." A wet Mucker is like, "as your people in London say, a Wet Quaker," that is, a "Pasquin" or "Punch."[24] Dixon's interest lay in the field of social behavior rather than secret doctrine, and the lawyer's account of the latter is about all we are given.

The founder of Königsberg Muckerism was Johann Heinrich Schönherr, the son of a noncommissioned officer in the infantry of Frederick the Great. The author of the brief note on Muckerism in the eleventh edition of the *Encyclopaedia Britannica* asserts that the ultimate knowledge Schönherr claimed to have discovered was "so closely analogous to Gnosticism that it might have been taken for a deliberate revival had not Schönherr's lack of education precluded any such idea."[25]

According to Dixon, Schönherr sat in on some of the classes at the University of Königsberg. Despairing of the theologians, he turned to the professors of philosophy with his questions on the immortality of the soul and the eternal destiny of things. Dissatisfied with their dusty answers to his heated questions, Schönherr wandered off. By the side of a stream, in the midst of growing plants, the mystery of the two archprinciples of being was suddenly revealed to him from on high. "Ah, he cried in ecstasy, by the warmth! 'Sun, fire, light,—all of which come from a single principle,—Light—solidify the moist.' Now he felt that he had got the results of nature in his grasp. Light is the male, the vivifier; Water the female, the nurse. Eureka! These two arch-beings— the supreme male and the supreme female—bound in eternal and necessary wedlock, explain everything; for in this great wedlock of principles lies the only chance of the seed of things being brought to life." And then, Dixon says, "Armed with this great discovery, which he thought would replace the crude jargon taught in the schools under the names of science and divinity, the Pauper Paraclete walked to Göttingen, to Jena, to Leipsic, to Königsberg."[26]

24. *Ibid.*, I, 55–61.
25. *S.v.*, "Muckers," *Encyclopaedia Britannica* (11th ed.).
26. Dixon, *Spiritual Wives*, I, iii–v. Dixon finds it fitting that Schönherr's doctrines received a welcome in Königsberg: six centuries earlier the Teutonic Knights had been accompanied in their crusade against the pagans of Old Prussia by the "followers of the Free Spirit," a kind of "secret society" whose doctrines bore a certain resemblance to those of Schönherr.

In Königsberg, Schönherr met and converted to his views Johann Wilhelm Ebel, since 1816 archdeacon of the Lutheran church there.[27] Ebel continued to profess orthodox doctrines in public, but in private he built up a group of devoted followers, drawn chiefly from the Königsberg aristocracy. After Schönherr's death, Ebel was joined by another Lutheran pastor, Heinrich Diestel, described by Dixon as a fiery, headstrong young man. Among the Ebelians it became the woman's role to hear the confessions of sinners, to inflict penance, and to grant absolution. Diestel would seem to have been a constant source of trouble until the young Countess von Derschau "brought him to his knees and a better mind," as Dixon writes. The countess was only one of the strong-willed female Ebelians. The women, in fact, ruled the roost. According to Dixon: "In Ebel's system women were to be nearly all in all. The chief laid himself out to act on them, and through them on the world. They stood nearest to him in rank; they shared his most secret thoughts; they were his friends, his counsellors, his agents. In a word, the Ebelians were a Female Church."[28] Meanwhile the official church "seemed to have no other end in view than to keep women in their place, and find a little amusement for official men."[29]

Dixon does not explain why the worldwide movement exemplified by the Ebelians of Königsberg and their "Female Church" should have been confined, as he says it was, to peoples of Teutonic, that is, Nordic, descent. As we shall see, a movement not wholly different in character, that of the Saint-Simonians, in whose "church" the female principle was co-regent with the male, had been under way in France for some time. But if we agree that the movements described by Dixon in *Spiritual Wives* drew strength from the desire of women to cast off the

27. Dixon states that Ebel's father and grandfather were clergymen, and that the grandfather had been suspended from his office after having made public "certain mystical ideas . . . on the coming of the Paraclete in the flesh" (*ibid.*, I, 101).
28. *Ibid.*, 136–37. Diestel is said to have drawn a conclusion that Ebel found disturbing, namely that "regenerate man and woman, by virtue of his and her regeneration, have opened out to them a wider field and a higher range of love." Not only is God love, but the perfected human being too is love (*ibid.*, I, 159). *S.v.* "Perfection (Christian)," in Hastings' *Encyclopaedia of Religion and Ethics,* especially the last section on the so-called "unethical perfection" of the Albigenses, Brethren of the Free Spirit, Anabaptists, and the Bible Communists and Free Lovers in the United States. *S.v.* "perfected human," in Rather, *The Dream of Self-Destruction,* for Wagner's "perfected" male-female human being and its counterpart, the tonal-musical drama.
29. Dixon, *Spiritual Wives,* I, 51. In Prussia, says Dixon, the church has always been "a branch of the high police."

shackles of a male-dominated church and society, there is some reason
to expect that such movements would flourish more readily in northern Europe. South of the Alps, for well over two thousand years, male-
domination had been an established fact of public life. Scholars have
repeatedly called attention to the startling difference between the position of women in the Homeric writings—where they appear as counsellors, directors, and protectors of men, even as queen-goddesses with
entirely subordinate male consorts—and their position in classical
Greece, a position that has been likened to that of women in China
until recently, and described as "the most degraded and abject to be
found in any civilized country of the Western world."[30] The official
position of women in the Roman world, where father right was the
supreme law, was no better. In the Roman Catholic church, which
took its cue here as elsewhere from the hierarchical structure of the
Roman empire, male domination was divinely represented by the male
God of the Jews. And in the society that the Catholic church helped
shape, the position of women has been welcomed as part of the natural
order of things by one-half of the population and accepted, until recently, with Griselda-like resignation by the other.

   North of the Alps women lost status more slowly. The high regard
in which women were held among the northern tribes, Celts as well as
Teutons, drew the attention and comment of Caesar, Florus, Tacitus,
and other Roman writers. Tacitus, in particular, observed that to the
German tribesmen there was something sacred and foreseeing in a
woman. The counsel of women was sought and followed in peace and
war. "During the reign of the divine Vespasian," Tacitus writes, "we
saw that Veleda was given by many people the status of a *numen*"—
and he goes on to contrast the servile adulation given by the Romans
to deified mortals, for example, Poppaea, wife of Nero, with the true
veneration given by the Germans to the prophetess Veleda.[31] In ma-
triarchal societies property rights descend on the distaff side; as late as
the time of Friedrich Barbarossa the offspring of a freewoman and a

   30. Robert Briffault, *The Mothers: A Study of the Origins of Sentiments and Institutions* (3 vols.; 1927; rpr. New York, 1969), I, 410.
   31. Tacitus, *On Germany,* chap. 8. *Cf.* Tacitus, *C. Cornelii Taciti opera omnia ex
editione Oberliniana,* ed. A. J. Valpy (London, 1821), I, 3263–67 (with extensive
notes). For a good discussion of similar passages in other Roman writers, see Tacitus,
The Works of Cornelius Tacitus, with an Essay on His Life and Genius, ed. Arthur
Murray (Philadelphia, 1840), 537–38 n. 4–6.

slave was free, according to Jakob Grimm, whereas the offspring of a freeman and a slave was legally a slave.[32] The old ways died more slowly north of the Alps.

Ebel was an admirer of Johann Heinrich Jung (known as Jung-Stilling), a mystic who had died in 1817 leaving behind him the prophecy that in 1836 the first great battles of the millennium would be fought. Ebel apparently expected something of the sort to happen. But, as Dixon observes, the devil "seemed ill-disposed to wait . . . [and] opened his campaign a year before the prophetical time." In 1835 a quarrel arose between Count von Finkenstein, an estranged member of the Ebelian group, and his sister, the Countess von Kainitz. In a letter, the count had objected to certain "practices which no honest man or woman could endure" that he claimed were taking place among members of the inner circle. Ebel had powerful enemies, and as a result the matter was brought before the Prussian king's judges. Chief witness for the prosecution of Ebel and Diestel was a physician, Professor Ludwig Wilhelm Sachs, a former member of the group. Sachs was a man, says Dixon, "whose tongue was feared and his talent prized." A Jew, hence unable to occupy a chair at the university, Sachs had offered up himself, his wife, and his infant son to Archdeacon Ebel for baptism.[33] The court relied entirely on Sachs's deposition, and such was the power of Ebel's foes that even after Sachs had thoroughly discredited himself in open court his evidence was admitted.[34] A verdict was returned against Ebel and Diestel; they were removed from the pulpit and sentenced to imprisonment. The sentence was then appealed. Meanwhile, in 1840, Frederick William III was succeeded by Frederick William IV, who, says Dixon, was "known to have lived a Pietist and is said to have died a Mucker." A change of men took place

32. Briffault, *The Mothers,* I, 414–15.

33. Dixon, *Spiritual Wives,* I, 187, 198–99. According to Dixon, Sachs was "a being all brain and nerve, cold in nature, quick in perception, acrid, humorous and splenetic," who "mocked at religion and held women in contempt" (pp. 163, 214).

34. The counsel for the defense produced two documents, addressed to the Countess von Kainitz and signed by Professor Sachs; in them Sachs confessed that he had committed, in Dixon's words, "many and grievous offences against God and man, some of which were absolutely revolting." Sachs granted the validity of the documents, but stated that he had written them at the insistence of the young countess while he was under her spiritual guidance, and that none of the admissions in them were true. His lengthy deposition is given by Dixon in full in the original German (*Spiritual Wives,* II, 294–344).

in high offices, and the sentence was reversed. The archdeacon and Countess Ida, his "most immediate Spiritual wife," retired to Stuttgart, where they are said to have made a convert of Pauline, queen of Würt-temberg. Mucker societies sprang up in Halle, Hannover, Heidelberg, Berlin, Dresden, Barmen, and Elberfeld.[35] It is worth noting that the Moravian Brethren were among Ebel's friends in Königsberg, and that when Ebel's church was closed they lent him their chapel for his services.[36]

Such were the Muckers of the Ebelian Church. To Wagner, as we see from his reference to them in *Opera and Drama* in 1851, they were a sect of sexual hypocrites—male and female Tartuffes. One can imagine his disgust eighteen years later when he himself was accused of wanting to found a Muckerish sect. Complaining of his treatment by the press, Wagner wrote in an open letter to Marie Muchanoff (née Countess Nesselrode) on New Year's day in 1869:

> You can get a very good idea of this and of the way the last-named [gentlemen of the press] use, with respect to me, a provoking tone in order further to hinder any participation in my undertakings, if you will take the trouble to read through the feuilleton of the current New-Year's number of the *Süd-deutsche Presse,* which has just been sent to me from Munich. In it Mr. Julius Fröbel quite calmly denounces me to the Bavarian authorities as the founder of a sect aiming to abolish religion and the state, and to substitute for all this an Opera-house from whence to reign, a sect that in addition offers the prospect of satisfying "Muckerish lusts" . . . We learn here how the idea of love, as the foundation of society, takes form in the head of a Julius Fröbel.[37]

35. *Ibid.,* I, 222–25.

36. *Ibid.,* 219. The Moravian Brethren are known for their cultivation of music and song for religious purposes. So also the followers of Conrad Johann Beissel, whose settlement in Ephrata, Pennsylvania, was matched by Nikolaus Zinzendorf's Moravians in Bethlehem (*cf.* Paul Henry Lang, *Music in Western Civilization* [New York, 1941], 470, 688). Beissel's harmonic system and his idiosyncratic separation of the notes of mu-sical scales into "master" and "servant" tones are discussed at length in the eighth chap-ter of Thomas Mann's *Doktor Faustus.*

37. Wagner, *Richard Wagners gesammelte Schriften,* XIII, 44; Wagner, *Prose Works,* III, 115. In 1870, in his essay "Über das Dirigiren" ("On Conducting"), Wagner wrote: "Some time ago a newspaper editor in South Germany objected to the 'Muckerish' tendencies in my theory of art. The man obviously knew not whereof he spoke; he was simply making use of an opprobrious term. From what in my experience is the nature of Muckerism, the peculiar aim of this revolting sect is, rather, the urgent pursuit of the stimulating and seductive in order to exercise the power of resistance. . . . But the actual scandal of the affair came from the disclosure of the secret of the higher adepts of this

THE INSURRECTION OF WOMAN

Fröbel's charge was repeated with approval three years later by Puschmann in *Richard Wagner: A Psychiatric Study.*[38] Wagner thus became the first of the two great nineteenth-century artists who were declared insane and accused of founding sexually, politically, and religiously subversive sects. The other was of course Leo Tolstoy. In his case the diagnosis of insanity was made by a differently and perhaps less qualified shepherd of souls (a Russian Orthodox priest, Father Ivan), but the condemnation of "Tolstoyism" as a subversive sect came from the Pan-Russian Missionary Congress.[39]

Fröbel's accusation contains a grain of truth, insofar as Wagner dreamed of a brave new world of the future presided over by the muse of music, under the aegis of New Testament love rather than of Old Testament Law, and insofar as he looked forward to the demise of the political state and of its prop, the established Judeo-Christian church. We recall here the words, Wagnerian in spirit, of George Gissing in 1889: "Destroy, sweep away, prepare the ground, then shall music the holy, music the civiliser breathe over the renewed earth, and with Orphean magic raise in perfected beauty the towers of the City of Man."[40]

DAS LIEBESVERBOT, THE YOUNG GERMANY MOVEMENT, AND SAINT-SIMONISM

Das Liebesverbot was Wagner's operatic assault on sexual prudery and hypocrisy in Germany. It was the second of his completed operas but the first to reach the stage.[41] Mounted by the Bethmann theater group, of which Wagner was the new and untried musical director, *Das Liebesverbot* was given its premiere performance in Magdeburg at the Stadttheather on March 29, 1836. This proved to be its only performance during Wagner's lifetime. The full score was first published in 1923, and a few performances then followed in Germany. Some comments on the music of *Das Liebesverbot*—including those

---

sect, among whom the purported aim was inverted, so that resistance to stimulation merely increased the pleasure finally achieved" (Wagner, *Gesammelte Schriften und Dichtungen,* VIII, 321–22). This is a clear reference on Wagner's part to the Königsberg affair.

38. Puschmann, *Richard Wagner. Eine psychiatrische Studie,* 26.

39. Rather, "Tolstoy and Wagner: The Shared Vision," 12.

40. See Chapter 6, note 94, herein.

41. Wagner's earlier completed opera, *Die Feen,* was first performed, five years after the composer's death in Venice, under the baton of Hermann Levi in Munich (Cosima Wagner, *Die Tagebücher,* note to the entry of January 31, 1879, p. 1176).

232   READING WAGNER

of Cosima and Richard Wagner on January 31, 1879—will be found in the notes.[42]

The premiere performance of *Das Liebesverbot* was preceded by Wagner's brief encounter with German prudery in its official form. He tells us in his autobiography that the Magdeburg police found the title of his opera offensive and, partly in view of the near approach of Easter, refused to allow it on the boards. Only after Wagner convinced the authorities that *Das Liebesverbot* was based on "a very serious piece by Shakespeare" and agreed to change its title to *Die Novize von Palermo* (*The Novice of Palermo*) was the performance allowed to take place. Wagner conducted the orchestra, but he says nothing in his autobiography about the music, its performance by the orchestra, or its reception by the audience on the opening night. As for the libretto, he remarks that its "quite unclear presentation" by the performers left the public so completely in the dark that its questionable features went unnoticed.[43]

42. Cosima Wagner's entry reads in part: "Herr R.[ubenstein] played us the Overture to *Das Liebesverbot,* in which the banning theme seems to me very good—soulless, legal, harsh, dramatic; when I say I like the Overture to *Die Feen* better, R.[ichard] observes that the other (*L.-Verb.*) shows more talent. He searches out a few passages but apart from the *'Salve Regina'* (*Tannhäuser*) he finds it all 'horrible' 'execrable,' 'disgusting.'—It is well orchestrated, he says—'that I could do in my mother's womb'—but the Overture is all thunder and lightning" (*Diaries,* II, 263). The annotators point out that Wagner made use of the *Dresdner Amen* in the nuns' chorus (the *Salve Regina*) of *Das Liebesverbot* and that he used it again in *Tannhäuser* (*ibid.,* II, 1058). Curt von Westernhagen writes: "The British première at University College, London in 1965 surprised the critics with its melodiousness: its Italianisms look back to Rossini and forward to the young Verdi. . . . The relentless theme of the decree forbidding love has the function of a genuine leitmotiv, while the melody and harmonization of the 'Salve regina coeli' already contains, note for note, the Grace theme from *Tannhäuser*" (Westernhagen, *Wagner: A Biography,* I, 42–43). To Paul Bekker the music of *Das Liebesverbot* foreshadows the melodic and harmonic chromaticism of *Tannhäuser, Tristan,* and the second act of *Parsifal* (Bekker, *Richard Wagner: His Life in His Work,* 81–85).

43. Wagner, *Mein Leben,* I, 127; Wagner, *My Life,* ed. Gray, 118. A short time later, in Leipzig, Wagner tried to substitute *Das Liebesverbot* for *Die Feen* (which had been accepted but then dropped). He writes: "Director Ringelhardt, whom I hoped to win over by flattery to my undertaking by assigning the role of Mariana to his daughter, who was making her debut at the opera, derived a rather nice pretext for rejecting my work from the trend of the story as he understood it. He stated that if the Leipzig town council were to permit the performance, which he, out of respect for this governing body, very much doubted, he, as a conscientious father, would in any case not allow his daughter to take part in it" (*Mein Leben,* I, 127–28).

A second performance of the opera was then scheduled. About fifteen minutes before curtain time the cuckolded husband of the leading lady (Wagner's Isabella) appeared on the scene and proceeded to bloody the noses of his wife and her lover, the second tenor. As Wagner puts it in his autobiography, the husband thus proclaimed a *Liebesverbot* of his own. A general turmoil ensued, and the director was forced to cancel the scheduled performance. According to Wagner, there were only three persons in the stalls, all of whom were Jews.[44]

Wagner's characterization in 1879 of *Das Liebesverbot* as a "wild, recklessly sensuous transformation" of Shakespeare's *Measure for Measure,* written under the influence of Heinrich Laube and the "new school of 'young German' literature," has already been called to the reader's attention.[45] The nature of this transformation will be examined after a brief account of Shakespeare's play and the sources from which it was drawn.

It seems generally accepted by students of the plays that the central theme of *Measure for Measure* was borrowed by Shakespeare from Geraldi Cinthio's *Hecatommithi,* a collection of tales (in the manner of Boccaccio's *Decameron*) published in 1565. Professor Peter Alexander writes, "There [in Cinthio] Shakespeare found a story belonging to the type in which a woman has to ransom a man, usually her husband, by complying with the desires of some judge in whose power the man lies." Cinthio's variation on the theme makes the man and woman brother and sister. The sister yields herself to the judge on a half-promise of marriage, only to find later that the brother has nevertheless been executed. She appeals to the emperor for justice; the emperor complies by ordering the judge to be executed after he has been made to fulfill his promise to the sister. The newly made wife then pleads for

---

44. Punning on the name of his opera, Wagner writes: "Soviel stellte sich heraus, dass das unter dem Liebesverbot Herrn Pollerts [the angry husband] leidende Paar [the guilty lovers] unfähig geworden war heute aufzutreten." As far as Wagner had been able to ascertain, the audience consisted of "only Frau Gottschalk with her husband and, most remarkably, a Polish Jew in full costume" (*Mein Leben,* I, 128). Earlier Wagner mentioned Frau Gottschalk as a "trustworthy Jewess" who had undertaken to consolidate his debts and seek for means of paying them (*ibid.,* I, 108). In later years Wagner exaggerated this part of the story to amuse Cosima. An entry of September 28, 1878, in her diary reads: "Then he [Wagner] laughs at the thought that Polish Jews would soon be enjoying the *Ring* in Leipzig (at the fair!): 'Well, one of them was my entire audience for *Das Liebesverbot*'" (Cosima Wagner, *Diaries,* II, 158).

45. See "The German Question" in Chapter 6 herein.

the life of her husband. Again the emperor complies, and according to Alexander, the two live "happily ever after."[46]

Shakespeare's two contributions to the traditional plot were a bed-trick and a surrogate woman. Mariana, the surrogate woman, is slipped into the bed of the lecherous judge (Angelo) in place of the virtuous sister (Isabella) of the condemned man (Claudio). Angelo, a bigot and a hypocrite, is deputy governor of Vienna during the duke's supposed absence in Poland, and he is busily engaged in a program of moral reform. (The duke believes such reform is needed, but he is unwilling to carry it out himself.) Claudio has been condemned to death for getting his sweetheart with child. Isabella, a novice of the sisterhood of Saint Clare, pleads for her brother's life. Angelo makes the traditional proposal, but Isabella rejects it out of hand. The duke, who has remained in Vienna all the while, disguised as a friar, subsequently appears and, without revealing his true identity, proposes the bed-trick to Isabella. He justifies it on the grounds that Angelo was, and still is, bound by oath to marry Mariana, and that Angelo had cast her adrift only after her dowry and her brother had been lost in a shipwreck. Isabella readily agrees to act as decoy. She returns to Angelo and promises him satisfaction that very night, if only he will spare her brother. As in Cinthio's version, Angelo decides to have it both ways: he orders the prison provost to bring him Claudio's head by five o'clock. But Claudio is saved by the duke, who, still in disguise, by a show of authority convinces the provost of the prison to bring a surrogate head to Angelo.[47] That night, as arranged, Mariana substitutes herself for Isabella in Angelo's bed. On the following day the duke appears in person and explains what has taken place. He forgives Angelo and—a curious touch—tells Angelo to forgive the provost. Angelo is to fulfill his marriage promise to Mariana, and Claudio is to make an honest

46. William Shakespeare, *The Complete Works of Shakespeare,* ed. Prof. Peter Alexander (4 vols.; London, 1958), I, 172–73. Giacomo Puccini's *Tosca,* based on Victorien Sardou's drama of the same name, is a later variation on the theme. In accordance with tradition, the bigoted and lecherous Scarpia, chief of police in Rome, orders the execution of Floria Tosca's lover to take place in reality after he has promised, in return for her sexual favors, to make the execution a sham. *Tosca* introduces a grim new note: immediately after having secured (as she believes) the survival of her lover, Tosca stabs Scarpia to death with his own knife.

47. The exchange of heads was probably borrowed by Shakespeare from George Whetstone's *Promos and Cassandra,* a dramatized version of Cinthio's story published in 1578. Cf. Shakespeare, *Measure for Measure,* in *Complete Works,* I, 172.

woman of his pregnant sweetheart. The closing lines of *Measure for Measure* tell us that the duke has something in mind for the virtuous Isabella, possibly a marriage proposal.

Wagner shifted the scene of the action from Vienna to Palermo. With the single exception of Friedrich, governor of Sicily during the temporary absence of the king, all the dramatis personae of *Das Liebesverbot* are Sicilians. Friedrich is a German, and Wagner says in his autobiography that this name was chosen simply to characterize him as a German ("um ihn als Deutschen zu charakterisieren").[48] Friedrich is referred to throughout the play as a hypocrite (*Heuchler*) and a German fool (*deutscher Narr*).[49] He is engaged in a morals campaign, as was his prototype in *Measure for Measure,* but the king really is absent. Isabella, Claudio, and Mariana play roles similar to the like-named characters in Shakespeare's play. Wagner's Isabella is told by her friend Mariana (after a silence of three years) that she, Mariana, is the lawful wife of Friedrich, who cast her off as soon as he had won the favor of the king. It was for this reason that she hid herself away in a convent.

Their intimate tête-à-tête is interrupted by the unwelcome news that Claudio has been condemned to death for engaging in an illicit love affair. When Isabella pleads with Friedrich to spare her brother's life, he makes the traditional offer. The furious Isabella threatens to expose him to the people as the hypocrite he is, but Friedrich replies calmly that no one believes him, a cold-blooded German, capable of love. In any case he has merely to explain that he was testing her virtue. The nonplussed Isabella is about to admit defeat, when a sudden inspiration occurs to her: the bed-trick! She will send Mariana, disguised, in her place. Mariana plays her part. Friedrich, of course, has

48. Wagner, *Mein Leben,* I, 123. Were there perhaps other reasons for Wagner's selection of the name? Mariana is the husband of "Friedrich" in Wagner's version, but she is the *sister* of "Frederick" in *Measure for Measure* (named on one occasion only, in act 3, sc. 1, line 214).

49. This and all further citations from the text of *Das Liebesverbot* are taken from the libretto (in German, with an English translation by Richard P. Avrenty) accompanying the first full recording of the opera in 1976, under the musical direction of Edward Downes, assisted by the BBC Northern Symphony Orchestra and the BBC Northern Singers (four records, seven sides, privately recorded). Wagner decided against including the text of *Das Liebesverbot* in his collected works (Cosima Wagner, *Diaries,* July 17, 1871). Instead he included a summary account of the plot, much the same as that given in his autobiography (see Wagner, *My Life,* ed. Gray, 113–18).

ordered the execution to be carried out in any case. Isabella intercepts the order and saves her brother's life. She then incites the people to seize their weapons and overthrow the despicable German tyrant ("Greift zu den Waffen! Auf, zur Rache! / Stürzt ihn, den schändlichen Tyrannen!"). Exposed now as hypocrite, lecher, and villainous betrayer, Friedrich asks for no mercy ("So richtet mich nach meinem eigenen Gesetz!"). Wagner's chorus replies that the old law has been annulled (*aufgehoben*), and that they want to be more merciful than he ("Wir wollen gnäd'ger sein als du!"). Friedrich is forgiven and, reunited with Mariana, leads a procession down the corso to greet the returning king. Isabella, meanwhile, has thrown herself into the arms of Lucio, Claudio's friend, who warned her of her brother's approaching execution. The opera ends happily for everyone, unlike *Measure for Measure.*[50]

In strong contrast to Shakespeare's passively virtuous Isabella, Wagner's Isabella is an activist of heroic stature: *she* devises the stratagem to save her brother's life, *she* intercepts Friedrich's treacherous order to proceed with the execution, *she* calls on the people to arm themselves and overthrow the tyrant. One thinks of *Fidelio* and Wilhelmine Schröder-Devrient, and it is conceivable that Wagner had both in mind when he wrote the part.[51] *Das Liebesverbot* is, as Lichtenberger says, "an apology for the favorite theory of Young Germany, the rehabilitation of the flesh . . . [and] the prudish and hypocritical German is abashed at the dénouement and obliged to recognize that German prudery has no place in happy Italy, that land blessed by sun, gaiety and love."[52] More impressive to the reader today, perhaps, will be the

50. For the sake of brevity I have passed over many parts of the action in *Das Liebesverbot*. There, as in *Measure for Measure*, Lucio is the friend of Claudio who warns Isabella of her brother's approaching execution and pleads with her to intercede. Again as in *Measure for Measure*, Lucio falls in love with Isabella. But Shakespeare's Lucio is ordered by the Duke to be flogged and hanged, for he is unlucky enough to have commited *lèse-majesté* in the presence of the Duke, while the latter was still disguised as a friar. "Slandering a prince deserves it," says the Duke in justifying his harsh sentence (act 5, sc. 1, line 522). The quality of the Duke's mercy is indeed strange.

51. Cf. Bekker, *Richard Wagner: His Life in His Work*, 81.

52. Lichtenberger, *Richard Wagner poète et penseur*, 42. Wagner himself wrote that the returning king would surely see, in the goodness of his heart, "how ill-suited the dismal Puritanism of the German [*Puritanismus des Deutschen*] is to fiery Sicily" (Wagner, *Mein Leben*, I, 127).

strongly profeminist touches in Wagner's portrait of Isabella. Among the characters in *Das Liebesverbot* she alone differs significantly from her prototype in *Measure for Measure*.

Lichtenberger's description of the spirit abroad in Germany when Wagner wrote the libretto of *Das Liebesverbot* in 1834 is worth quoting at length.

> We know well enough the immense repercussions in Germany of the July Revolution [1830] and the triumph of liberal ideas in France. A large part of the German youth . . . rose up against the reactionary regime that Metternich's policies had imposed on Germany, against the censorship that mutilated books and muzzled the press, against the prudery of the old German morality that prevented the free blossoming of élite individualities. This is the period when Heine, converted to Saint-Simonian ideas, shared in the war against literary and political romanticism, when [Ludwig] Börne hurled from Paris his virulent diatribes against the pusillanimous and servile spirit of the German people, when [Karl] Gutzkow in his novel *Wally* and Laube in his novel *Young Europe* preached the doctrine of the "emancipation of woman" (*l'émancipation de la femme*) and of the "rehabilitation of the flesh" (*réhabilitation de la chair*).[53]

"Young Germany" was not an organized group. The phrase made its first appearance in print in the dedication of a series of university lectures on aesthetics by Ludolf Wienbarg, published in 1834. Wienbarg called for literature to be brought in touch with the realities of contemporary life and politics. The first part of Heinrich Laube's political and social novel *Young Europe* had already been published in 1834. Karl Gutzkow's *Wally die Zweiflerin*, a tale that involves a "spiritual marriage" and ends with the suicide of the emancipated Wally after her spiritual husband has undermined her religious beliefs, was likewise published in 1834. In 1835 appeared Theodor Mundt's novel *Madonna*, a feministic and sensual work. The authorities in Germany took alarm. On December 10, 1835, the Bundestag issued a directive calling for action to be taken against the literary school known as Young Germany or Young Literature. Gutzkow was charged with blasphemy and with bringing the Christian religion into disrepute. The second charge was upheld and Gutzkow spent a month in prison in 1836. Laube was expelled from Leipzig. Mundt and Wienbarg appar-

53. *Ibid.*, 39–40.

ently suffered only minor inconveniences. Heinrich Heine, the only
one of the five writers denounced by the Bundestag whose reputation
survives today, was safe in Paris.[54]

The founder of Saint-Simonism was Claude-Henri de Rouvroy,
comte de Saint-Simon (1760–1825), a descendant of the famous duc
de Saint-Simon who had memorialized the court of Louis XIV a century earlier. As Eliza M. Butler points out in *The Saint-Simonian Religion in Germany: A Study of the Young Germany Movement* (1926),
it was the much modified Saint-Simonism of Barthélemy Enfantin, developed after the death of the founder, that influenced the writers of
Young Germany. Specifically it was Enfantin's doctrine of the "rehabilitation of the flesh" and his defense of the rights of women that
attracted these young men, urged on as they were, says Butler, by a
"spirit abroad at the time, manifest all over the world." In the writings
of Saint-Simon himself, Butler can find only a "solitary feminist utterance." Enfantin, on the other hand, reached the conclusion, three
years after the master's death (in 1828), that "God was androgynous,
and that his material manifestation was under male and female form.
Since God was both man and woman the equality of the sexes followed
inevitably." In advocating the enfranchisement of women, Butler admits, the Saint-Simonians might well have claimed to be following the
spirit if not the letter of the master's words. In her opinion, however,
Enfantin was equally indebted to Charles Fourier, not only for his ad-
vocacy of feminism, but also for the germs of the doctrine of the
"emancipation of the flesh."[55]

Saint-Simon's last work, *New Christianity* (1825), is a proposal for
far-reaching social, economic, and religious reform. In its first dialogue, the "reformer," who calls for artists, industrialists, and scientists to improve the Christian religion, tells the "conservative" that
while he admits the divine origin of Christianity its teachings are open
to improvement. "Theology needs to be brought up to date at different
periods, just like physics, chemistry, physiology." All that is of divine
origin in Christianity can, according to Saint-Simon, be reduced to a
single principle, namely that human beings should treat one another as

54. *S.v.* "Wienbarg," "Laube," "Gutzkow," "Mundt," "Heine," and "junges
Deutschland," in Henry and Mary Garland, eds., *The Oxford Companion to German
Literature* (Oxford, 1976).
55. E[liza] M. Butler, *The Saint-Simonian Religion in Germany: A Study of the
Young Germany Movement* (Cambridge, 1926), 2, 7, 14, 50.

brothers. Christianity, understood simply as the religion of brotherly love, is destined to become the religion of all peoples. "Asia and Africa will be converted," Saint-Simon says, and the "true doctrine of Christianity, that is to say the most universal doctrine which can be deduced from the fundamental principle of the divine morality will be realized." But Saint-Simon wants in addition to create an *earthly* temple (a crystal palace of the kind that would appear in London's Hyde Park in 1851). He calls on preachers, poets, painters, musicians, sculptors, scientists, and industrialists to join hands in creating this total work of art. Architects are to build the new temple, painters and sculptors to decorate it, poets to provide poems to be recited within, and musicians will set the poems to music capable of "penetrating to the depths of the soul." The goal of the new religion is spelled out: "New Christianity . . . is called on to organize all peoples in a perpetual state of peace, by allying them all against the nation which tries to gain its own advantage at the expense of the good of the whole human race. . . . It is called on to link together the scientists, artists, industrialists, and to make them the managing directors of the human race. . . . It is called upon to put the arts, experimental sciences and industry in the front rank of sacred studies, whereas the Catholics have put them among the profane branches of study."[56]

We seem to be witnessing here the birth of modern technocracy. For unless science and industry provide an economic base for the superstructure of the temple, Saint-Simon's goal is unattainable. Science and industry must become *the* "sacred studies," and we look for our saviors among the ranks of the scientists (actually, engineers) and industrialists.[57] Armand Bazard, another of Saint-Simon's disciples, argued that the doctrine of the fall had been superseded by the doctrine of prog-

56. Henri Comte de Saint-Simon, *Henri Comte de Saint-Simon (1760–1825): Selected Writings*, ed. and trans. F. M. H. Markham (Oxford, 1952), 83, 104–105. Markham comments that at a time when our view of the nineteenth century is "still too much dominated by the whig view of history, a study of Saint-Simon gives a different, if peculiar, perspective of the development of Europe" (p. v.).

57. A chapter in Friedrich A. Hayek's *The Counter-Revolution of Science: Studies on the Abuse of Reason* (Glencoe, Ill., 1952) is entitled "The Religion of the Engineers: Enfantin and the Saint-Simonians," and about a third of the entire work is devoted to the Saint-Simonians and their influence. Hayek devotes little attention to the topic of feminism, arguing that there was "virtually nothing in the teachings of Saint-Simon to justify this new departure," *i.e.*, Enfantin's "new theories about the position of women and the relation between the sexes" (p. 154).

ress, and that the creation of an earthly paradise lay within human power. But, notes Butler, the more logically consistent minds of Bazard and Enfantin recognized, as the master had not, that a religion of this world, despite its espousal of universal brotherly love in the name of Christ, could not properly be called Christianity.[58]

Saint-Simon is said to have approached Madame de Staël with a marriage proposal: she, the most remarkable woman of the age, and he, the most remarkable man, should unite to produce an offspring more remarkable still.[59] While nothing came of this proposal, it does seem that Madame de Staël strongly influenced the development of the brilliant young Saint-Simonian Eugène Rodrigues, who died in 1830 at the age of twenty-three. Rodrigues is said by a late nineteenth-century French historian of Saint-Simonism to have been the guiding spirit in the transformation of the movement from a philosophy into a religion. A scion of a wealthy Jewish family of financiers, Rodrigues drew spiritual nourishment from "the Bible, the Gospel, and the Koran." He translated G. E. Lessing's *Die Erziehung des Menschengeschlechtes*—a philosophy of religious history already commented on at length by Madame de Staël—into French and provided it with a preface in which he argued that the claims of religion were prior to those of philosophy and science. Rodrigues was in sympathy with efforts that had been made to rejuvenate Christianity and reconcile it with Judaism, but he held that Judaism, Christianity, and the religion of Islam were incapable of becoming "the religion of humanity." Saint-Simonism, with its union of the spirit and the flesh, of the kingdom of God and the kingdom of Caesar, alone could serve that purpose.[60]

After the premature death of Eugène Rodrigues, the three most influential Saint-Simonians were Armand Bazard, Barthélemy Enfantin, and Eugène's brother, Olinde, who was the only one of the three to

58. Butler, *The Saint-Simonian Religion in Germany*, 10.

59. Saint-Simon, *Selected Writings*, 15.

60. Georges Weill, *L'École Saint-Simonienne; son histoire, son influence jusqu'à nos jours* (Paris, 1896), 14–17. Among others drawn to Saint-Simonism at this time, Weill mentions George Sand (with reservations on her part), Franz Liszt, Elisa Lemmonier (the founder of professional schools for women), Victor Hugo, Alexander Dumas *fils* (whose dramas deal with women's rights, sexual equality, and, in *La question d'argent*, Saint-Simonian socioeconomics). Weill says that the social role of literature was neglected during the sway of such "theoreticians of art for the sake of art" as Gautier, Baudelaire, and Flaubert, but that now (*i.e.*, in 1896) it is being cultivated anew by the Ibsens and Tolstoys (*ibid.*, 300–303).

have known Saint-Simon personally. Olinde had also recruited his cousins Emile and Isaac Pereire and some Jewish friends into the movement. Enfantin, an attractive man with a commanding personality, soon began to take the lead. The church that Enfantin had in mind differs in one very important respect from the temple of "New Christianity" described by Saint-Simon himself. Enfantin's priesthood, like his God, is androgynous. *"The preacher is man and woman,"* he wrote, emphasizing the words. And this feature, he adds, "suffices to mark off our priesthood from the Catholic priesthood, as also from the Protestant ministry, in which the wife of the minister has no sacerdotal role." Enfantin speaks also of the "man and woman of the future," of the androgynous "church of the future" and "priesthood of the future" (*sacerdoce de l'avenir*). He writes:

> As for politics, the clergy has the mission of uniting and developing human industry and science; to this end it employs all the resources of art to stir up the masses; the artists awake intelligence and action, they charm the spirit and the senses; the religious ceremonies present to the minds or eyes of the faithful the spiritual or material symbols of faith; like the temple of Jerusalem, the new church is fitted out with the magnificent conquests of industry; like the cathedral of the middle ages, it encloses the treasures of science; its vaults echo with words, song and harmony that inspire meditation, contemplation and prayer; and architecture, painting and sculpture animate the stone and give it force, elegance and beauty to elevate the workers.[61]

"God," proclaimed Enfantin in the Paris *Globe* on April 20, 1832, "has given me the mission to call the *proletarian* and the *woman* to a new destiny."[62] The first "mother" (*mère*, uncapitalized) in the new church was Claire Bazard, the wife of Armand Bazard. Claire, however, came to the conclusion that women were not yet up to the task, explaining to Enfantin that "we feel respect and obedience for the master alone, and the master is, for us, the man." (A view not shared, we recall, by the women of Ebel's church in Königsberg.) It was at this point, presumably, that Enfantin saw the need to engage in a search for the "mother" (*MERE*, capitalized), who would, with his seed, bring forth the new savior. Enfantin's ideas on the "rehabilitation of the flesh,"

61. Barthélemy Enfantin, "De l'homme et de la femme," in *Religion Saint Simonienne. Procès en la cour d'assizes de la Seine, les 27 et 28 aout 1832* (Paris, 1832), 88–97. Many supporting documents are included in this verbatim report of the trial of the Saint-Simonians.
62. Butler, *The Saint-Simonian Religion in Germany*, 22.

and all that was implied in the way of marriage, divorce, and the freedom of sexual relations permissible to the women, had by now moved
ahead of those acceptable to Armand Bazard and Olinde Rodrigues.
Rodrigues eventually yielded to the superior force of Enfantin's character, but in November, 1831, Bazard withdrew completely from the
Saint-Simonian movement.[63]

On April 23, 1832, *PERE* Enfantin, with forty "sons," or apostles,
withdrew to his house at 69 Menilmontant in Paris, in order "to prepare himself and them for a new life, by meditation, by the abolition of
domesticity [some of the "sons" were married men], by works of the
proletariat, and to found the cult by adopting a new costume and
creating a new art."[64] The ranks of these men, who were in their twen-
ties and thirties for the most part, included "scientists, lawyers, doc-
tors, engineers, men with an excellent education behind them, and
many with successful careers in the future, long-headed, clear-sighted
Frenchmen."[65] But the stay of *la famille Saint-Simonienne* at 69 Menilmontant was a short one. The French government, ostensibly for reasons of public morality, but in reality because the Saint-Simonians
were suspected of socialist subversion, decided that the time to disperse
the family had come.[66] On July 1, 1832, M. Maigret, superintendent of
police, armed with official documents and supported by the *gen-
darmerie*, appeared before the door of 69 Menilmontant at 3:00 P.M. to
begin the dispersal. Enfantin named as his trial counsels two women,
Aglâe St.-Hilaire and Cecile Fournel. The court expressed great dismay, and the presiding judge explained that under French law "persons of the female sex" could not serve as counsels. Neither could witnesses for the defense be heard; they refused to take the oath without
express permission from Enfantin himself, and the judge ruled that
such permission invalidated the oath. The *PERE* then addressed the
court, to explain his new role in the search for the *MERE:* "I feel that I
am the precursor of this female Messiah: I am to her what St. John was

    63. *Ibid.*, 17–19.
    64. Enfantin, *Religion Saint-Simonienne*, 19. A list of the "apostles" appears on
pp. 27–30; included among them was a painter, Raymond Bonheur[e], the father of the
Rosa Bonheure who was later to become famous for her paintings of animals, and who
was notorious for wearing men's clothing while at work.
    65. Butler, *The Saint-Simonian Religion in Germany*, 23.
    66. Saint-Simon, *Selected Works*, xxxix. The Saint-Simonians were thought to
have been involved in the Lyons revolt of 1831, the first purely proletarian uprising in
France.

to Jesus; here is my whole life, here is the bond uniting all my acts, all of which are linked by logic, for all spring from my faith in woman."[67] Enfantin, it appears, no longer believed that he and the "mother" would, together, bring forth the new Messiah. The *MERE* herself was the longed-for Messiah; Enfantin, presumably, was not worthy to unloose her shoe's latchet.

After a short trial, the judge and jury found Enfantin and four other senior members of the Saint-Simonian family guilty. Enfantin, Michel Chevalier, and Charles Duveyrier were sentenced to a year's imprisonment. Olinde Rodrigues and Emile Barrault were fined fifty francs each. The quest for the female Messiah, also known as the "free woman," continued nonetheless. It took on an even more fantastic character: Emile Barrault was authorized by Enfantin to set sail for Constantinople in search of the Messiah, for some believed that she would reveal herself there and prove to be of Jewish origin.[68] But when Enfantin was released from prison in August, 1833, it was as if he had suddenly been transformed from the romantic Faust of the first part of Goethe's drama to the practical Faust of the second, now interested in the building of dams and currency reform rather than in amorous intrigues with Gretchens. Enfantin announced that the great task of the future was the piercing of the Suez. He founded the society of which Ferdinand de Lesseps reaped the benefits, and he became secretary-general of the Paris-Lyon railway company. Michel Chevalier became professor of political economy at the College de France. The brothers Emile and Isaac Pereires founded the Credit Mobilier, the most important commercial bank in Paris under the Second Empire.[69]

When Enfantin gave his testimony before the cours d'assises in Paris in 1832, he stated that the true redeemer was a woman; he himself was no more than a John the Baptist, come to bear witness for her; and all his acts were the logical consequence of his "faith in woman." Enfantin's deity, it follows, is no longer an androgyne: God, too, is a

67. Butler, *The Saint-Simonian Religion in Germany*, 30; Enfantin, *Religion Saint-Simonienne*, 19, 32–34.

68. Butler, *The Saint-Simonian Religion in Germany*, 33. A Jewish origin was evidently not thought to be a *sine qua non:* the searchers approached the eccentric and wealthy Lady Hester Stanhope, who had settled down with her retinue in a ruined convent in Lebanon and was known herself to have had visions of a female Messiah. Lady Stanhope declined the offer, but gave the searchers money (*ibid.,* 34).

69. Saint-Simon, *Selected Works*, xi; Butler, *The Saint-Simonian Religion in Germany*, 32–35; Enfantin, *Religion Saint-Simonienne*, 25.

woman. But, as we have seen, Enfantin underwent still another conversion during his year in prison. Butler's attitude toward the feminist
aspect of Saint-Simonism is at times ambiguous. In a remarkable passage she writes: "It is impossible to lose an illusion more completely
and more robustly than Enfantin when he lost faith in the 'mère
suprême,' a monster whom he had created and who for a moment
threatened to overwhelm her master. But Enfantin was no Frankenstein, and the 'mère suprême' no revengeful demon to hunt him to his
death; the life he had given her proved an illusion, she had never lived
at all."[70] In his solitude, says Butler, Enfantin had "originated a truly
great idea, an idea which pushed the 'free woman' completely into the
background." In August, 1833, he told his followers: "You have made
known my face of appeal to woman; that is well. . . . Today I feel that I
must first show my POLITICAL face to the East." The new task in
hand is a practical one: "What must strike us *uniquely* today is THE
PIERCING OF THE SUEZ." And after the "piercing" of the Suez is to
come the "piercing" of Panama.[71] Enfantin has perhaps not so much
lost faith in the "supreme mother" as he has changed his mind about
who she really is, and decided to take her by storm.

    We have seen that when Wagner arrived at Königsberg in the sum-
mer of 1836 the trial of Ebel and Diestel, the two leaders of Dixon's
Ebelian Female Church, reached its climax with the accusatory deposition submitted to the court (on July 15, 1836) by Professor Sachs.
As far as can be ascertained, this was Wagner's first encounter with
Muckerism. He understood it only as one more manifestation of
the German vice of sexual hypocrisy that he had castigated in *Das
Liebesverbot*. In his later writings there is no hint of any awareness on
his part that the feminist cast of the Ebelian church bore any rela-

70. Butler, *The Saint-Simonian Religion in Germany*, 34–35. *Cf.* Sandra M.
Gilbert and Susan Gubar, *The Madwoman in the Attic: The Woman Writer and the
Nineteenth-Century Literary Imagination* (New Haven, Conn., 1979): in chap. 8, entitled "Horror's Twin: Mary Shelley's Monstrous Eve," Frankenstein's monster is unmasked as a female in disguise—as Mary Shelley herself, whose book is said to be a
"revelation of filthy femaleness" from which its author needed to distance herself.
    71. Butler, *The Saint-Simonian Religion in Germany*, 34–35. Butler is in general
profeminist. She asks how Ludwig Börne, a so-called champion of liberty, could have
"condemned one-half of mankind to remain in the state of modified bondage which was
the lot of women in 1830." She attributes this to the "deep-seated oriental instincts of
his race" (*ibid.*, 69).

tionship to the "rehabilitation of the flesh" and the emancipation of women that had aroused the enthusiasm of the Young German writers. But when we recall Schönherr's musings (as recounted by Dixon in *Spiritual Wives*) on the "supreme male," the "supreme female," and the pressing need for the "great wedlock of [male and female] principles," we find ourselves reminded not only of the Wagner of *Opera and Drama* but also of Barthélemy Enfantin and the version of Saint-Simonism that he began to promulgate around 1828.

Wagner's connection with Saint-Simonism is, in any other sense than that mentioned above, nonexistent. He arrived in Paris in 1839, six years after Enfantin was released from prison to begin his new way of life. Heinrich Heine, who had come to Paris in 1831 with some enthusiasm for the "new religion," as he called it, was by now a sceptic, and by 1839 he objected to being called a Saint-Simonian.[72] If Wagner heard anything from Heine on the subject of Saint-Simonism it was probably unfavorable, but there is no evidence that they ever discussed the subject. Nor is there any comment on Saint-Simonism anywhere in Wagner's writings or in Cosima's diaries.[73]

72. *Ibid.*, 88–128, *passim.* Theodor Wehl, in 1886, noted the prominence of Jews (or former Jews, such as Börne and Heine) in the Young Germany movement and offered the following in explanation: "Among the French, the English and other peoples nationality is a very real thing, inborn in them. . . . These peoples either rejected Jewry or accepted it. . . . In Germany it was otherwise: there Jewry, fragmented in its own nationality, driven about the world in all anguish . . . found a people no less shattered in its nationality" (Wehl, *Das junge Deutschland. Ein kleiner Beitrag zur Literaturgeschichte unserer Zeit* [Hamburg, 1886], 5). Whatever validity the statement may have (*cf.* Wagner's remarks of 1878 and 1879 along the same line in Chapter 6, notes 136, 137, and corresponding text herein), its explanatory power is slight: Jews were equally prominent among the Saint-Simonians in France.

73. A French Wagnerian, Maxime Leroy, suggested in 1923 that Wagner was a Saint-Simonian without being aware of it: "Wagner, like the Saint-Simonians, believed that art and religion drew from the same source of life; he wrote in *The Art-Work of the Future* that a work of art is the living representation of a religion; he believed in a religion that replaced the state itself, in an artist-prophet and leader of the peoples, in a 'prêtre-poète' as did [Victor] Hugo and [Alfred de] Vigny, and, like [Auguste de] Gasperini, he united and equally glorified Christ, Apollo god of art, and the poor in *Jesus of Nazareth* and *Art and Revolution*" (Leroy, "Les premiers amis français de Wagner," *Wagner et la France: numéro spéciale de la Revue musicale, 1er Octobre, Paris, 1923* [New York, 1977], 39). Gasperini was a physician, poet, musician, and Wagnerian, with Saint-Simonian sympathies, whom Wagner met in Paris in 1860. His name is frequently mentioned in Wagner's autobiography.

WAGNER, PROUDHON, AND GEORGE SAND

The mother of the future Cosima Wagner, the Countess Marie d'
Agoult, became a writer of some importance shortly after her break
with Franz Liszt in 1844 (when Cosima was in her seventh year).[74] In
her massive *Histoire de la révolution de 1848* the countess, writing
under the pen name of Daniel Stern, summed up the revolutionary
aims of Pièrre-Joseph Proudhon (1809–1865) as follows: "He believed that the revolution needed only to effect the destruction of
everything that shackled the free expression of the social instinct. No
more clergy, no more army, no more property, the absence of all government, *an-archy,* a society controlled, that is, by its own inherent
forces, such was the philosophical idea of M. Proudhon."[75]

But there was one set of chains that Proudhon intended to keep intact and in place. The great libertarian was paradoxically a champion
of the patriarchal family, and a foe of the women's liberation movement. Proudhon was in fact the nineteenth century's most virulent
antifeminist; his dislike of the emancipated free woman is exceeded
only by his hatred of homosexuals. Today's anarchists call Proudhon
the father of their movement, yet almost without exception they champion the emancipation of women and oppose the patriarchal family.
The spiritual sons and daughters of Proudhon, when they came together after his death under the leadership of Bakunin, simply ignored
that part of their heritage. The socialists and communists, generally,
were profeminist almost to a man.[76]

The Countess d'Agoult spoke up for women's rights in her history

74. Cosima, the younger of the countess' two illegitimate daughters by Franz Liszt,
was born on December 25, 1837, at Bellagio on the shores of Lake Como. Hence her
name, according to Sacheverell Sitwell (*Liszt,* 45). He does not explain how it was arrived at. (The Latin name of the lake, since the fourth century, *Lacus Comacinus,* was
probably the starting point.) See Chapter 6, note 47, herein for a discussion of the al-
legedly Jewish ancestry of the Countess d'Agoult.

75. Daniel Stern, *Histoire de la révolution de 1848* (2nd ed.; 2 vols.; Paris, 1862),
II, 17. First published 1850–53 in three volumes.

76. Peter Kropotkin (in 1883) first called Proudhon the "father" of the anarchist
movement (Pierre Haubtmann, *La philosophie sociale de P.-J. Proudhon* [Grenoble,
1980], 226 n. 13). The anarchists were libertarian in their socialist views: Writing in
1871, Bakunin contrasted the "communism scientifically developed by the German
school, and accepted in part by the American and English socialists" with the "Proud-
honism, largely developed and pushed to its last consequences . . . accepted by the proletariat of the Latin countries" (Bakunin, *Oeuvres,* IV, 252). On the association between

of the aborted revolution of 1848, and it may be that her portrait of Proudhon was colored by an awareness of his antifeminist stance.[77] Proudhon, she writes, although feared by some as the "very incarnation of socialism," was hardly more than a "bizarre superfetation of the seed of revolution." Gifted with a talent for irony and paradox reminiscent of Montaigne, Rabelais, or even Voltaire, Proudhon had, to the detriment of his prose style, allowed himself to become drunk on a fiery brew of Hegel, Strauss, and Feuerbach. "All this terminology with which M. Proudhon is pleased to obscure his style, foreign in origin and antipathetic to the genius of the French language, the *antinomies*, the *becoming*, the *being in itself and for itself*, has seemed to French readers who are unfamiliar with German metaphysics the sure sign of great inventiveness and profound knowledge." In her opinion Proudhon was a sophist rather than a true philosopher. As for his economics, she says that he took his mathematical formulations from Fourier, and that the Proudhonian aphorism "property is theft" had been put into print as early as 1780 by Brissot de Warville.[78]

Proudhon's book *What Is Property?* was first published in 1840. A German edition of the French original appeared four years later. While it seems unlikely that Wagner's attention would not have been drawn to *What Is Property?* by Bakunin in the course of their conversations in Dresden, the book is first mentioned by Wagner in a letter written from Paris in 1849. A brief passage from another of Wagner's letters, written two years later, reveals a continuing interest in Proudhon: "Everything in our country is riddled with servility: there is nobody in all France who knows that we are nonetheless human beings, except perhaps Proudhon—and even he is none too clear about it!"

feminism and socialism, Marguerite Thibert writes that "Proudhon, the great trouble-maker, came . . . to effect a brutal rupture of the faithful association between feminism and socialism" (Thibert, *Le féminisme dans le socialisme français de 1830 à 1850* [Paris, 1926], 171).

77. The Countess d'Agoult's treatment of Saint-Simonism with respect to the "rehabilitation of the flesh" is sympathetic in tone, and she looks forward to a time when "equality and fraternity will not be taught to the exclusion of one sex in its entirety" (Comtesse d'Agoult, *Histoire*, I, 33–36; II, 33–34, 38).

78. *Ibid.*, I, 47–48. Bakunin, in 1871, referred to Proudhon's stand against the reconstitution of Poland as an independent state as "the crime of a sophist," whose argument forced him to "portray the police, soldiers and functionaries of the Czar as socialist emancipators" (Bakunin, *Oeuvres*, IV, 464–65).

Three decades later an entry of September 8, 1876, in Cosima's diary tells us that Proudhon and Bakunin are still alive in Wagner's mind. "He [Wagner] tells us Bakunin's views on Russia—that the only way would be to introduce socialism there without the Proudhon theories, since a community already existed among the people there; when Malwida [von Meysenbug] says that many things have altered since the abolition of serfdom, that individualism has become widespread, R. says, 'Yes, civilization always moves in that direction, makes property its goal.'" And returning in a gondola to the Palazzo Vendramin eight days before his death, Wagner, noting that Cosima's gaze is fixed on the shuttered, almost empty palaces of Venice, calls out, "That is property! The root of all evil."[79]

In *Know Thyself* (1881), Wagner asserts that the chief purpose of the modern state is to stand watch over the rights of property. The elaborate and constantly growing apparatus of police and armies existed for the protection of the "haves" (*Besitzenden*) from the "have-nots" (*Nichtbesitzenden*). But the system appeared to be breaking down. "It seems," he writes, "that the state's utilization of the concept of property, in itself apparently so simple, has driven a stake into the body of mankind, on which it cannot but waste away in painful, agonizing disease."[80] Which is to say, in the language of the *Ring:* A state-enforced corpus of laws—Wotan's spear, with its engraved runes of compact—governing the distribution, accumulation, inheritance, and movement in general of property, including money as property, has brought on us an unforeseen, fatal consequence, a disease that is slowly killing our society. This sounds almost like an echo of Lewis H. Morgan's claim of 1877 that a society in which property is the end and aim of all striving "contains the elements of self-destruction."[81] But it is in fact an echo of *What Is Property?*. When Proudhon calls property "theft," his intent is simply to shock the reader into acceptance of his real thesis, which is that the property owner's "right to increase" (*droit de l'aubaine*)—the right, enforced by the state, to demand rents, dividends, interest, or whatever other form the unearned

79. Westernhagen, *Wagner: A Biography*, I, 143, 163; Cosima Wagner, *Diaries*, II, 145, 1004.

80. Wagner, *Gesammelte Schriften und Dichtungen*, X, 267.

81. Lewis Henry Morgan, *Ancient Society; or, Research in the Lines of Human Progress from Savagery, Through Barbarism to Civilization* (1877; rpr. Palo Alto, 1975), 552.

income may take—amounts to the very real theft of another's labor. A parasitic nonproducer is drawing the lifeblood from a producer. In an economic system so based Proudhon finds that a mathematical impossibility is involved. Something, in effect, is being demanded for nothing, and if matters continue to proceed in this fashion, society will inevitably "devour itself." Property is not only theft, it is homicide and suicide.[82]

During the first few years after his flight from Dresden, Wagner put music aside and busied himself solely with writing. *Opera and Drama*, the long and interesting *Communication to my Friends*, and *The Young Siegfried* were completed by 1851. By 1853 the entire *Ring* poem, in a private edition for his friends, was in print. Since this was the time of Wagner's first contact with the ideas of Proudhon, we are perhaps justified in relating the following passage from Proudhon's *What Is Property?* to Wagner's *Ring of the Nibelung*.

> *Property is the right to increase:* this axiom will be for us like the name of the beast of the apocalypse, a name that includes the whole mystery of the beast. We know that whoever penetrated the mystery of this name would obtain understanding of the whole prophecy, and would overthrow the beast. Well, then! It will be by means of a profound interpretation of our axiom that we shall kill the sphinx of property . . . we are going to follow the coils of the old serpent, we shall number the homicidal twistings of this hideous taenia whose head, with its thousand suckers, always lies hidden from the sword of even its most high-spirited enemies. . . . For something other than courage is required to overthrow the monster: it was written that the monster would not die until a proletarian, armed with a magic rod, had taken its measure.[83]

82. Pierre-Joseph Proudhon, *Oeuvres complètes de P.-J. Proudhon,* eds. C. Bouglé and H. Moysset (19 vols.; Paris, 1923–59), V, 245, 262, 267–68; Proudhon, *What Is Property: An Inquiry into the Principle of Right and of Government,* trans. Benjamin R. Tucker (New York, n.d.), 155–56. That by "property is theft" Proudhon means "unearned income is theft," is emphasized by Michel Augé-Laribe in his annotations to the French edition. The simple statement is a commonplace. Augé-Laribe points out that Proudhon had no doubt run across it in the writings of the church fathers, while working as a printer in Besançon, *e.g.,* Saint Basil's "the rich man is a robber," or Saint Jerome's "riches are always the result of theft" (Proudhon, *Oeuvres complètes,* V, 131–32 n. 10). Proudhon was not so much passing a moral judgment as he was putting his finger on what seemed to him a fundamental contradiction in the workings of the economic system.

83. Proudhon, *Oeuvres complètes,* V, 246. Tucker translates "avant qu'un prolétaire, armé d'une baguette magique, l'eût mesuré" as "until a proletaire, armed with a

The proletarian is, of course, Proudhon himself.[84] In Wagner's *Ring* the young outcast Siegfried, wielding the charmed sword Nothung, takes the measure of Fafner, the giant dragon whose coils overlie the stolen gold of the Rhine. A sphinx is confronted and overthrown.[85]

Unlike Wagner, Proudhon has no place in his scheme of things to come for an Antigone or a Brünnhilde—no place for a woman-Titan or Promethean Eve of any kind, rebellious against male authority.[86] Where Wagner, in 1849, summoned up "Holy Antigone" as the goddess of revolution, Proudhon has inscribed on his standard the words spoken to Antigone by Creon: "While I live, no woman shall rule me."[87] For Proudhon, a woman's place is the home. If she will put aside the false dream of equality and admit her physical, intellectual, and moral inferiority to man, Proudhon will allow her to be the angel of the house. He will even worship her, saying, "Queen of grace, mount the altar."[88] But if she rebels, he will, like Creon, cast her out. Closely linked with Proudhon's detestation of the emancipated woman

---

magic wand, had fought with it." But I have adopted his translation, "right to increase," of Proudhon's "droit de l'aubaine."

84. Unlike most of the Saint-Simonists and Fourierists, Proudhon was of proletarian origin. He says of himself: "Born and raised in the bosom of the working class, still belonging to it at heart and by sentiment, and above all by the community of suffering and vows . . . my greatest joy . . . will be to work untiringly . . . for the moral and intellectual amelioration of those whom I am pleased to regard as my brothers and companions" (Proudhon, *Oeuvres complètes*, V, 15–16).

85. *Cf.* Carlyle's claim, made in 1843, that the paradox of poverty in the face of plenty is the riddle of the sphinx, unsolved by the money-based society of his time (cited in Rather, *The Dream of Self-Destruction*, 7). In an address, "The Workers and the Sphinx," delivered in 1867, Bakunin gives his "answer to the enigma, which the Capitalist Sphinx forces us to-day to solve, threatening to devour us if we do not solve it" (*Bakunin's Writings*, ed. Guy A. Aldred [1947; rpr. New York, 1972], 18).

86. On Charlotte Brontë's vision of the "Promethean Eve" and "woman-Titan" in her novel of the Luddite riots, *Shirley* (1849), see pt. 4 of Gilbert and Gubar's *The Madwoman in the Attic*.

87. Antigone has just told Creon that she speaks for mutual love (συνέχθειν). See Sophocles, *The Antigone of Sophocles*, ed. Milton W. Humphreys (New York, 1891), 22 (ll. 23, 25). I have given Creon's response as it appears in Virginia Woolf's profeminist antiwar tract *Three Guineas* (New York, 1938), 259. Woolf's reading of Sophocles' *Antigone* recalls that of Wagner. To her it is a "profound analysis . . . of the effect of power and wealth on the soul." She points out with approval "Antigone's distinction between laws and the Law" and argues that Antigone's words on mutual love in human relationships are "worth all the sermons of the archbishops" (*ibid.*, 124).

88. Proudhon, *Oeuvres complètes*, XII, 502.

is a fear and distrust of the flesh recalling that of the fathers of the church.[89] With the single exception of Leo Tolstoy, Proudhon differs in this respect from almost all other anarchist thinkers who preceded or followed him, as well as from the Saint-Simonians, the Ebelians, and the Young Germans who took the slogan of the "rehabilitation of the flesh" back to their native land.[90]

Proudhon won his reputation as a misogynist and antifeminist in 1846 with his *Economic Contradictions,* confirmed it in 1858 with *On Justice in the Revolution and in the Church,* and sealed it with *Pornocracy, or, Women in Modern Times,* which did not appear in print until after his premature death in 1865. At the end, he felt that the battle had gone badly. "They [women] no longer suffice for their task [at home], and they talk to us of becoming judges, physicians, apothecaries, chiefs of police and wives of chiefs of police; what do I know?—gendarmes, too, and dragoons!" he cried.[91] Proudhon's admirers today can only regret such utterances. Daniel Guérin has recently assembled the passages on the subject of women and sexuality scattered throughout Proudhon's notebooks and published writings. Proudhon's war, says Guérin, was one that "spared neither woman,

89. Jules L. Puech, who notes that Proudhon met with the writings of the church fathers in the course of his work as a printer and proofreader, says that "psychoanalysis would no doubt reveal in him [Proudhon] the repressions that often inspired the violent imprecations found in the holy discourses of the preachers of religion" (Proudhon, *Oeuvres complètes,* XV, 304). In the section on love and marriage in *On Justice in the Revolution and in the Church,* Proudhon cites Chrysostom ("Woman, that sovereign pest!"), Jean de Damas ("Woman is . . . a frightful taenia, with its seat in the heart of man"), Chrysologue ("She . . . is the gate of hell"), Anthony ("Her voice is the hiss of the serpent"), Bonaventura ("lance of the demon"), Eusebius of Caesarea ("arrow of the devil"), and Jerome ("She is the gate of the demon, the path to iniquity, the sting of the scorpion, in sum a dangerous species"). It would be a mistake to suppose that Proudhon was always in complete agreement with the fathers of the church. Nor is he without psychological insight, for he adds, "Our effeminate writers affect great anger on reading these imprecations; it would be simpler to recognize here a desperate homage paid to the power of woman" (*Oeuvres complètes,* XII, 94–95).

90. Together with the destruction of the authoritarian state, the anarchists urged what Proudhon wanted to prevent, namely the destruction of the state-sponsored patriarchal family. In 1871 Bakunin made this clear to his followers in Italy: "Just as we are convinced that by abolishing religious, civil and juridical marriage we restore life, reality and morality to natural marriage, so too we are convinced that individuals, associations, communes, provinces and regions will become much more closely allied when they will no longer be forced to live together by the accursed power of the state" (Bakunin, *Oeuvres,* VI, 384–85).

91. Proudhon, *Oeuvres complètes,* XV, 423.

against whom he nourished a pathologic and phallocratic hatred unworthy of a libertarian, nor the various forms of sexual activity, which
he confounded and, with one and the same disapproval, stigmatized."[92]
Homosexuality is unconditionally condemned. Proudhon actually calls
for the killing of pederasts taken *in flagrante* to be made legally permissible. At another point, he denounces the Fourierists as pederasts.
He proposes eugenic measures, presumably to be carried out under the
new order. "It is necessary to exterminate (*exterminer*) all bad natures
and to renew the sex by eliminating vicious persons, just as the English
remake a race of oxen, sheep, or pigs."[93] A "distaste for the flesh" will
be inculcated, and a "perpetual war" will be waged against "erotic ap-
petites." After carrying out a literary psychoanalysis of the father of
modern anarchism, Guérin finds, of course, that Proudhon's distaste
for sex indicates that he was sexually repressed, and his hatred of homosexuals that he was a repressed homosexual. The "great libertarian," Guérin concludes, was partly responsible for the "sexual repression that today dishonors the so-called 'socialist' countries."[94]

Although Proudhon at times seems bent on forcing on woman a
choice between the roles of housewife (*ménagère*) or whore (*cour-
tisane*), he does admit that she has a small role to play as a teacher of
morality. In *On Justice in the Revolution and in the Church*, Proudhon says that this role gives legitimacy to the woman writer, "since it is
by means of the word, of poetry, and of art, that morality is taught and
propagated." But the woman writer needs the kind of male guidance
that has so far not been forthcoming from the effeminate men who are
attracted to her. In this milieu, says Proudhon, the woman writer "will
at first seem to be a heroine, for as the man becomes effeminate she
becomes his equal." Then, "little by little, as her imagination falls prey
to eroticism, she will sink into a kind of literary nymphomania, and,
while she dreams of emancipation, of equality of the sexes, of perfect
love, she will come to lose herself in the mysteries of Cotytto." Proudhon then has a few harsh words for Charlotte Corday and Madame de
Staël.[95]

92. Daniel Guérin, *Proudhon oui et non* (Paris, 1978), 197.
93. *Ibid.*, 229–30.
94. *Ibid.*
95. Proudhon, *Oeuvres complètes*, XII, 234–41. He says, among other things,
that Charlotte Corday "trafficked with her maidenhead," and that if Napoleon had not
disdained the charms of Madame de Staël, she would not have opposed his policies.

Proudhon next turns to George Sand. A casual acquaintance in the past with Sand's writings has, Proudhon says, given him a "lively sense of repulsion for the author." Assured by mutual friends that he was being unjust to "Madame Sand," continues Proudhon, he read *Indiana, Valentine, Lelia, Mauprat, Jacques, Rose et Blanche, Le compagnon du tour de France, Spiridon, Leone et Leoni, Le secrétaire intime, Teverino,* and the *Histoire de ma vie.* At the Odéon he saw *Francois le Champi, Claudie,* and *Maître Favella.*[96] The effect was not the one looked for by the mutual friends. Instead, says Proudhon, "I did not have curses enough . . . against this woman, whom I called a hypocrite, a villain, a plague of the Republic, a daughter of the Marquis de Sade, deserving to rot in St. Lazare for the rest of her days, whom I saw admired and applauded, God save us, by the puritans of the Republic." In the privacy of his notebooks, Proudhon is unable to contain himself: "this woman writes like she pisses (*écrit comme elle pisse*) . . . O scandal! Does she not dress up as a man, smoke cigarettes, run about Europe with her lovers? . . . I will see justice done on this old whore (*cette vieille catin*)." By 1858, however, Proudhon has changed his mind. He admits that he was wrong in so condemning Sand. She is in fact a "lover of honesty as well as of beauty," and a woman of "talent and character." He now knows what is at the bottom of all her protests. "Madame Sand, in the modesty of her heart, has searched for a man; she has found none. . . . If, at the beginning, she had met . . . the strong, grave man of whom her imagination had need, George Sand, the rebellious bacchante . . . would have become the reformer of love, the apostle of marriage." After this diagnosis of the root cause of all female discontent—reminiscent of Mephi-

---

96. Proudhon, *Oeuvres complètes,* XII, 246. Absent from the list are *Consuelo* and its sequel, *La comtesse de Rudolstadt,* historical novels in which Sand brings the fifteenth-century revolt of the Hussites against Catholicism into relation with the subversive activities of Masonic secret societies in the mid-eighteenth century, and gives full rein to the expresssion of her own libertarian, egalitarian, and fraternal ideals. Absent also are *Jean Zyska* (or *Ziska*) and *Procope le Grande,* two studies of the Hussite wars in Bohemia. Of the four novels categorized as "socialist" by Albert Le Roy (*George Sand et ses amis* [Paris, 1903], 433), only *Le compagnon du tour de France* is on Proudhon's list. That fascinating account of class relationships in France in the 1800s, and of the rival secret societies or "companionships" of journeymen masons and carpenters at the time, should have drawn praise from Proudhon, but perhaps it was not doctrinaire enough for his taste.

stopheles' diagnosis in Goethe's *Faust*—Proudhon is at peace with himself.[97]

In George Sand's first novel, *Indiana* (written in her twenty-seventh year), there is a passage that marks her out as an Antigone, a Promethean Eve, or a Lilith. Here Sand—if it be allowed that the heroine of *Indiana* is her spokeswoman—rejects the supremacy of the male principle in its highest manifestation. Proudhon, with great perspicuity, fixes on this passage and cites it at length in his essay *On Justice in the Revolution and in the Church*. In the following, the words in brackets were omitted by Proudhon, but the emphasis is his own. The passage in question occurs in a letter written by Sand's heroine to her former lover.

> [As for me, I have more faith than you;] I do not serve the same God [but I serve him better and more purely]. Yours is the *God of men*, the king, the founder and the prop of your race; mine is the God of the universe, the creator, the support and the hope of *all created beings*. Yours made everything for you alone; mine made all species, *the one for the other*. You believe yourselves to be masters of the world; I believe that you are only its *tyrants*. [You think that God protects you and authorizes you to usurp the empire of the earth; as for me, I think that he suffers you for a little season, and that the day will come when his breath will scatter you like grains of sand. No, Raymon, you do not know God . . . you believe in nothing. Your education and the need you have of an indisputable power to oppose the brute force of the people have made you adopt without examination the beliefs of your fathers, but the feeling of the existence of God has never touched you to the heart; perhaps you have never prayed to him. As for me, I have but one belief, no doubt the only one that you do not have: I believe in him; but] the religion that you have *invented*, I reject: all your morality, all your principles, are the interests of your society erected by you into laws that you claim to have emanated from God himself [just as your priests

97. Proudhon, *Oeuvres complètes*, XII, 246; Guérin, *Proudhon oui et non*, 220. Proudhon here answers in advance the question posed by Sandra Gilbert and Susan Gubar in 1979: "If the pen is a metaphysical penis, with what organ can females generate literary texts?" (Gilbert and Gubar, *The Madwoman in the Attic*, 7). Changing the metaphorical waters, possibly in deliberate contrast to Proudhon, one of George Sand's admirers writes that the "soul of this admirable woman spills out freely in her books . . . *Commes ces eaux si pures et si belles / Qui coulent sans effort des sources naturelles*" ("Like the waters so pure and so fine / That flow without effort from natural springs"). See Anatole France, "George Sand et l'idéalisme dans l'art," in *La vie litteraire* (4 vols.; Paris, 1888–92), I, 341.

have instituted the rites of their cult to establish their power and wealth over the nations].[98]

The stance taken by Sand in this passage places her in the tradition of the Marcionites and gnostic sectarians in the earliest days of Christianity and their followers down to the nineteenth century. Proudhon chose to see in this passage only the first sign of the "black background of *androphobia [androphobie]* that forms the sky of Madame Sand's romances," and he emphasized its words accordingly.[99]

Juliette Lamber and Jenny d'Héricourt, two young defenders of women's rights, were the target of Proudhon's last trumpet blast against the monstrous regiment of women, a work entitled *Pornocracy, or Women in Modern Times.*[100] Both young women had previously attacked his antifeminist views in print: Jenny d'Héricourt in an article in a Saint-Simonian journal, and Juliette Lamber in a book first published in 1858, entitled *Anti-Proudhonian Ideas on Love, Woman and Marriage.*[101] Juliette Lamber's mother had been the governess of Liszt's illegitimate daughters in the household of the Countess d'Agoult, but the association of Juliette herself with the countess appears to have followed only on the publication of her Bradamantian attack on the great antifeminist.[102] Proudhon's *Pornocracy, or Women in Modern Times*

98. Proudhon, *Oeuvres complètes*, XII, 248–49; George Sand, *Indiana* (2nd ed.; Paris, 1922), 232–33. Sand states in the preface to the edition of 1842 that the cause she defends in *Indiana* is not only "that of half of the human race, it is that of the human race in its entirety, for the unhappiness of woman involves the unhappiness of the man, just as that of the slave involves that of the master" (*ibid.*, 14–15).

99. Proudhon, *Oeuvres complètes*, XII, 249.

100. Proudhon, "La pornocratie ou les femmes dans les temps modernes," in *Oeuvres complètes*, XV, 325–412. The essay is addressed to J*** L*** and Jenny d'H***.

101. The augmented second edition of Lamber's book is entitled *Idées anti-Proudhoniennes sur l'amour, la femme et le mariage, séconde édition augmentée d'un examen critique du livre La Guerre et la Paix* (Paris, 1861). Lamber's views seem quite temperate today: "Since a woman is a human being, [she should have] the right to make use of her physical, intellectual and moral faculties, to obey the laws of her own being, to work out her own fate. Since she represents half the social entity, she has functions that are properly her own in society as in the family" (p. 153).

102. Lamber's admiring contemporaries called her a "true Clorinda, a Bradamante" (Jules L. Puech, Introduction to *La pornocratie ou les femmes dans les temps modernes,* by Pierre-Joseph Proudhon, in *Oeuvres complètes des P.-J. Proudhon,* XV, 315). She was born in 1836, one year before Cosima Wagner, and acquiring along the way the name "Madame Adam," she survived until 1936. According to Marie Monod, the

resembles in tone if not in content the diatribe of John Knox, three hundred years earlier, against the female rulers of England, Scotland, and France.[103] For Proudhon, too, the regiment of women is a monstrous thing, an offense against God and man.

> Pornocracy fits in very nicely with despotism, even with militarism: in Heliogabalus the Roman Empire furnishes us with an example. Pornocracy goes equally well with theocracy. The Gnostics tried this in the first and second centuries of our era, the mystics at the height of the seventeenth century also tended in this direction. In our day we have seen pornocracy ally itself with the bankocracy! Malthus and Enfantin are the twin representatives of modern decadence. But the hour has passed: the world, which looks with indifference at the decline of papal theocracy, turns its back on Malthusian pornocracy.[104]

Proudhon's claim that the Gnostics had mixed a dose of pornocracy in with their theological doctrines can be understood in connection with Sand's rejection of the male God in *Indiana:* a refusal to admit the supremacy of the male principle inevitably leads, he believes, to feminine rule, and this in turn to pornocracy. Gnosticism is (for Proudhon) a feminist heresy. In the notes appended to *Pornocracy,* he goes even further in his general condemnation of the female principle. "I have found in the sects of our era—the Icarians [Etienne Cabet's nonviolent, socialist Utopians], humanitarians, Saint-Simonists, phalansterians—and in artistic and literary Bohemianism of all varieties the same tendencies, the same spirit, the same depravity, as in the Gnostics."[105] The obvious meaning of the phrase "Malthusian pornocracy," namely that of a luxury-loving, effeminate world in which men and women selfishly disobey the Old Testament injunction to increase and multiply, may not have been what Proudhon intended. He could have had in mind the economic doctrines of Malthus, in particular Malthus' theory of rent, rather than his call for the exercise of

---

Countess d'Agoult invited Juliette Lamber to visit her salon after reading the *Idées anti-Proudhoniennes* (Monod, *Daniel Stern, comtesse d'Agoult, de la Restauration à la III*e *Republique, 239).*

103. Knox, like Proudhon, invokes the church fathers as witnesses for the inferiority of women and their unfitness to rule, citing Augustine, Tertullian, Ambrose, Origen, Chrysostom, and Basil, in addition to passages from both the Old Testament and the New Testament.

104. Proudhon, *Oeuvres complètes,* XV, 372.

105. *Ibid.,* 419.

marital restraint in order to check population overgrowth. "Bank-ocracy" (*bancocratie*)—one of Proudhon's neologisms—is the unrestricted right to increase (*droit de l'aubaine*), the rule of unearned increment. Proudhon sees the capitulation of Enfantin and certain of the Saint-Simonians to international high finance as all of a piece with their initial capitulation to the female principle; pornocracy had found its natural ally, bankocracy. The old serpent (or tapeworm), the parasitic "sphinx of property" overthrown by Proudhon in his younger days, turns out to be a woman, perhaps even a Jewish financier.[106]

At this point the blind spot in Proudhon's field of vision is strikingly evident. He cannot see what the later anarchists and libertarian socialists recognized at once, namely that antiauthoritarianism is incompatible (in the nineteenth-century context, at least) with antifeminism. The Gnostics, themselves rebels against the Old Testament God, are Proudhon's enemies insofar as they offer support to the revolt of the female principle against the male. And we have seen that Proudhon stigmatized as androphobia the attack launched by George Sand at the beginning of her career against the morality of the tyrant male God of the Old Testament. Yet in 1851, in his *General Idea of the Revolution in the Nineteenth Century,* Proudhon himself joins forces with Satan.

> More than eighteen centuries ago, a man attempted, as we do today, to regenerate humanity. From the sanctity of his life, his prodigious intelligence and his outbursts of indignation, the Spirit of Revolutions, adversary of the Eternal, believed that it recognized a son. The Spirit appeared before his eyes and said to him, while showing him the kingdoms of the world: I shall give you all, if you will recognize me as your author, and worship me.—No, replied the Nazarene: I worship God and shall serve him alone. The inconsistent reformer was crucified. After him came Pharisees, publicans, priests and kings, more oppressive, more rapacious, more infamous than ever; the revolution, twenty times attempted, twenty times abandoned, remained a question. To me then, Lucifer, Satan, whoever you may be, daimon that the faith of my fathers opposed to God and the Church! I shall spread your word, and ask for nothing in return.[107]

106. In the first stage of their development the Saint-Simonians were despised by Proudhon as worshippers of the feminine principle, in the second as Jews and capitalists (according to Markham). No doubt Proudhon linked the Jewish principle with "bankocracy."

107. Proudhon, "L'Idée générale de la Revolution au XIXᵉ siecle," in *Oeuvres complètes,* III, 307.

Like Sand, Proudhon sides with the gnostic heretics and their later followers in the attempt to overthrow God the Father; unlike Sand, Proudhon fails to see that this implies the overthrow of exclusively male-based authority here on earth as well. In the same essay Proudhon states, "He who denies his king denies his God, and vice versa."[108] Twenty years earlier, in the passage from *Indiana* that Proudhon found so objectionable, Sand had already said, in effect, that she who denies her lord and master denies his God, and vice versa. Writing in 1848, Sand stated that the "Gospel Ethic" had "always been true, even before Christianity put it into words." She added that the Old Testament law of retaliation had been legally abolished and, hopefully, would not be reinstated in our time. And in August, 1870, at the time of the Paris Commune, she wrote to a male friend: "As for me, I am still as red a socialist as ever. But . . . [c]onvictions must never be imposed by force. Such behavior is criminal and senseless, for everything born of violence must perish by violence."[109] Proudhon, by contrast, rejects the Christ of the New Testament as well as the Jehovah of the Old Testament; his Lucifer or Satan is as much anti-Christ as anti-Jehovah. Christ's refusal to accept the offer of the prince of this world means, to Proudhon, only that the world will remain in the hands of the Pharisees, publicans, priests, and kings. Further, to him nonviolence is nonsense; as Juliette Lamber was quick to recognize, Proudhon was committed to the belief that right grows out of might, and not vice versa.

Wherever the female principle lifts its head, Proudhon's heel is raised

108. *Ibid.*, 303.
109. George Sand, *George Sand in Her Own Words*, trans. and ed. Joseph Barry (Garden City, N.Y., 1979), 380, 386, 397. In the introduction, Ellen Moers remarks that when Sand died in 1876, Matthew Arnold predicted that her voice would continue to be heard. But instead, says Moers, "by a process of denigration familiar to experts in women's history, the name of George Sand came to mean to most people not an author at all but a target for labels: transvestite, man-eater, lesbian, nymphomaniac" (*ibid.*, xi–xii). Another devoted reader of Sand was Fyodor Dostoevsky. He tells us—using a familiar phrase—that "everything in the being of this poetess . . . all that was 'universally human' in her . . . was promptly reflected in our Russia" (Sand began to appear in Russian translation in the mid-thirties.) Dostoevsky speaks of Sand's "pride of woman's quest," and of his puzzlement by the contradiction between what he read *in* her and what was said and written *about* her. (The same might be said of that other apostle of the "purely human," Richard Wagner.) "She was," Dostoevsky writes, "perhaps, the most Christian among all persons of her age." See Dostoevsky, *The Diary of a Writer*, trans. Boris Brasol (New York, 1954), 341–350, *passim*.

to strike it down. Quite naturally, his hostility spills over from religion and politics into the field of art. The message of his partly posthumous essay "On the Principle of Art and Its Social Destination" is, in effect, that the muses themselves will play the prostitute where the male principle loses control; pornocracy will extend its sway to the arts.[110] In France this is already the case. All is "shamelessness, venality, prostitution . . . we despise poetry, disfigure our prose, and dance the cancan," he writes. "We cannot live in this state of barbarism." True art should raise us above "banality, vulgarity, triviality, indignity"; it should "civilize, urbanize, polish, ennoble us."[111] Proudhon's views in other respects are not too far from those expressed some years earlier by Wagner in "Art and Revolution." Writing in 1939, Jules L. Puech remarked that Proudhon would also have approved of Wagner's later statement in "Religion and Art": "My ideas on religion came to me from my role as a creative artist in relation to the public. . . . And in this way I found it possible to acquire the conviction that true art can flourish only on the terrain of true morality; thus I gave art a mission so elevated that I found it completely identical with true religion."[112] But Proudhon would certainly have disapproved strongly of Siegfried-Brünnhilde, the perfected male-female human being, and of Wagner's theory of the music drama, where (male) word and (female) tone are joined together to form a new whole. Like the Saint-Simonians, Proudhon wanted to grace his future republic of workers with a temple of the arts and sciences, but it was not to be a temple presided over by an—to him monstrous—androgyne.

KILLING THE MONSTER: LÉVI-STRAUSSIAN STRUCTURES IN WAGNER'S *RING*

Under attack from various sides in the second quarter of the nineteenth century, the male principle seemed ill, perhaps moribund. And the Old Testament God, its magnified projection into the skies of a once geocentric as well as anthropocentric universe, was on his deathbed—so at least Heinrich Heine told the Parisian readers of the *Revue*

110. Proudhon, "Du principe de l'art et de sa destination," in *Oeuvres complètes de P.-J. Proudhon*, XV, 37–282. Jules L. Puech states in the introduction that as early as 1843 Proudhon had insisted that in art the "male principle" must be supreme (*ibid.*, 5).
111. *Ibid.*, 258.
112. *Ibid.*, 33. Puech took the Wagner citation from Guy de Pourtalès' *Louis II de Bavière* (Paris, 1928), 210.

des deux mondes in 1834, just three years after George Sand's denunciation of the all-male deity in *Indiana*. "It is the Jehovah of old who
readies himself for death," wrote Heine wittily. "We have known him
since his cradle in Egypt, where he was raised among calves and divine
crocodiles. . . . We have seen him . . . become in Palestine the little god
of a poor shepherd folk. . . . We saw him emigrate to Rome, the capital, where he renounced every kind of national prejudice. . . . But
nothing could save him! Do you not hear the ringing of the bell? To
your knees! They are bringing the sacraments to a dying God." With a
keen sense for mythical interrelationships, Heine tells the French that
the publication, in Germany, of Immanuel Kant's *Critique of Pure
Reason* in 1781 marked the "January 21st of deism."[113] In this way he
relates the publication of the Königsberg philosopher's book to the be-
heading of Louis XVI on January 21, 1793—a date still fresh in the
minds of his readers. Kant cut through the traditional ontological
proofs of God's existence. Heine gives us to understand, therefore, that
the death of the king of France was a logical, if somewhat delayed,
consequence of the death of God under the guillotine of Kantian
reason.

We may say that the death of Louis XVI under the guillotine on
January 21, 1793, was the concrete representation of an event that had
already taken place in France in the abstract realm of thought: the
death of a social fetish that had been handed down from generation to
generation, namely the collective idea of kingship. The fetish and all its
trappings were still intact, but the apotheosizing eye of faith was no
longer there to work a transfiguration. Carlyle understood this in
1837. "Time was when men could (so to speak) of a given man, by
nourishing him and decorating him with fit appliances to the due
pitch, *make* themselves a king, almost as the Bees do; and what was
still more to the purpose, loyally obey him. . . . So it *was* . . . but so it
no longer is . . . much more lies sick than poor Louis: not the French
King only but the French Kingship; this too, after long rough wear and
tear is breaking down." The year is 1774, and the dying Louis XV is
already half-revealed as a sham-king; nineteen years later the revelation will be complete.[114]

    113. Heinrich Heine, "De l'Allemagne depuis Luther," *Revue des deux mondes*, 4.
trimestre (1834), 408.
    114. Thomas Carlyle, *The French Revolution* (3 vols.; Leipzig, 1851), I, 8–10,
passim.

Sustained by the power of belief alone, a king is a mythical monster, poised and ready to plunge into the abyss if the right question is asked. "Dereified"—as the modern sociologist of knowledge might say—the monster then plunges into nothingness. To Carlyle the fictional character of social reality is obvious. "For ours is a most fictile world," he writes, still meditating on the death of kings, "and man is the most fingent, plastic of creatures." The real external world, even, is in a sense fictile. "An unfathomable Somewhat, which is *Not we;* which we can work with and live amidst,—and model, miraculously in our miraculous Being, and name World." He adds a Carlylean touch to the metaphysics of Johann Fichte.

> But if the very Rocks and Rivers (as Metaphysics teaches) are, in strict language, *made* by those outward Senses of ours, how much more by the Inward Sense, are all Phenomena of the spiritual kind: Dignities, Authorities, Holies, Unholies! Which inward sense, moreover, is not permanent like the outward ones, but forever growing and changing. Does not the Black African take of Sticks and Old Clothes (say, exported Monmouth-Street cast-clothes) what will suffice; and of these, cunningly combining them, fabricate himself an Eidolon (Idol, or *Thing Seen*), and name it *Mumbo-Jumbo;* which he can then pray to, with upturned awe-struck eyes, not without hope? The white European mocks; but ought rather to consider; and see whether he, at home, could not do the like, a little more wisely.[115]

Carlyle, who has not only the French Revolution in mind, is there to warn us that the "Destruction of a Sham Kingship" is always "a frightful process," even though it may be necessary on occasion.[116]

The political state, too, is a mythical monster. Recognizing it as such, Wagner read into the myth of Oedipus the story of the downfall of the state. Wagner's sociopolitical interpretation of the Oedipus myth, derived from Sophocles' trilogy (which is itself a version of the original myth), stands on the same level as Freud's psychoanalytical interpretation of the myth fifty years later. To the psychoanalyst, Freud's version of the Oedipus myth has a privileged status; all other versions (and their creators) are to be interpreted in its light. This privileged status remains even when the acquired, hereditarily transmitted content of the Freudian unconscious is replaced, as it is in the

115. *Ibid.,* 9–10.
116. Thomas Carlyle, *Frederick the Great,* in *The Carlyle Anthology,* ed. Edward Barrett (2nd ed.; New York, 1881), 89.

"sociopsychoanalysis" of Gérard Mendel, by a content of the same character transmitted through sociocultural institutions (the ensemble of myths, legends, laws, customs, economic and artistic practices, political forms, and so on).[117] But the Freudian interpretation is perhaps simply another version of the myth. "If—as I believe—Freud's remarks on the Oedipus complex are an integral part of the Oedipus myth," Claude Lévi-Strauss stated in 1958, "we shall therefore not be hesitant in placing Freud, after Sophocles, among the sources of the myth; these versions deserve the same credence as do others that are older and, seemingly, more 'authentic.'"[118]

There are two Wagnerian versions (in the above sense) of the Oedipus myth that Lévi-Strauss overlooked: first, Wagner's reading, in *Opera and Drama,* of Sophocles' version of the myth; and second, Wagner's transformed version of this reading contained in the *Ring* poem, that is, Wagner's Oedipal reading of the Norse myths on which the *Ring* poem is based.[119] This oversight is the more surprising in view of the fact that Lévi-Strauss, by his own admission, derived his technique of structural analysis from a study of Wagner's work. Writing in 1964, Lévi-Strauss speaks of his worship, from childhood on, "at the altars of the 'god Richard Wagner,'" and he informs us that "if Wagner must be recognized as the indisputable father of the structural analysis of myths . . . it is highly revealing that this analysis was first made *in music.*" Lévi-Strauss continues, "When I suggested that the analysis of myths was comparable to the analysis of a great score . . . I was only drawing the logical consequence from the Wagnerian discovery that the structure of myths reveals itself in and through a score."[120]

Lévi-Strauss has in mind the two-dimensional structure of a musical score. Such a score must be read simultaneously along two axes, ver-

117. Cf. Gérard Mendel, *La révolte contre le père. Une introduction à la sociopsychoanalyse* (Paris, 1968). Mendel states that he rejects the biologically unacceptable Freudian hypothesis of the inheritance of acquired characteristics in favor of the "transmission of the acquired unconscious from one generation to another by society, by the sociocultural institutions" (p. 422).

118. Claude Lévi-Strauss, *Anthropologie structurale* (Paris, 1958), 240, 242. See Claude Lévi-Strauss, *Structural Anthropology,* trans. Claire Jacobson and Brooke Grundfest Schoepf (New York, 1963), 217–18. The English translation omits a few words here.

119. I have discussed both versions in *The Dream of Self-Destruction* (pp. 47–62), without reference to Lévi-Straussian structural analysis.

120. Claude Lévi-Strauss, *Le cru et le cuit* (Paris, 1964), 23. Lévi-Strauss is citing here from Mallarmé's poem of homage to Richard Wagner.

tical and horizontal. The vertical (synchronic) axis gives us static harmony, while the horizontal (diachronic) axis gives us the temporal
flow of the harmony (or of tones, if we are reading and listening poly-
phonically). The unit of musical meaning is a melody, theme, or motif.
It is handed back and forth between various orchestral voices; it may
remain intact or it may undergo transposition, inversion, or some
other change; it may be harmonized or heard together with other
themes. To listen to such a score properly requires understanding and
close attention. The intelligent listener picks out the units of musical
meaning and tries to understand how the composer uses them to con-
vey his message.

As for myth, the basic unit of meaning is a brief narrative statement
which expresses a *relation*, for example, "Oedipus kills his father,"
or "Oedipus immolates the Sphinx." It might seem that this unit,
called by Lévi-Strauss a "mytheme," is *the* constitutive unit, and that
mythemes arranged in temporal order give the totality of the narrative. But the specific character of mythic time—synchronic and diachronic—is only taken account of when we come to see that the true
constitutive units of myth are not isolated relations or mythemes, but
"packets of relations," and that it is "in the form of combinations of
such packets that the constitutive units [of a lower order] acquire a
meaning function." Mythemes coming from the same packet may appear at remote diachronic intervals, and it is only when they have been
grouped together that the demands of mythic time are fully satisfied.
This means in practice that we will treat a myth as "an orchestral score
that some perverse amateur has transcribed, staff after staff, in the
form of a continuous melodic series. Our task is to restore it to its
original form."[121]

But why this attention to myth? Lévi-Strauss, following Saussure,
distinguishes "language" (*langue*) from the actual "speaking" (*parole*)
of language.[122] Language belongs to the reversible, diachronic time
axis, speaking to the nonreversible synchronic axis. Myth, a potenti-
ated form of language, extends along both axes. It tells of events that
have taken place "once upon a time," but it simultaneously binds past,
present, and future together into a timeless, mythical unity. History is

121. Lévi-Strauss, *Anthropologie structurale*, 232–35.
122. *Cf.* Ferdinand de Saussure, *Course in General Linguistics,* trans. Wade Baskin,
ed. Charles Bally and Albert Sechehaye, with Albert Reidlinger (London, 1960), 11–15.
Saussure compares language (*langue*) to a symphony, speaking (*parole*) to its actual performance on a given occasion (*ibid.*, 18).

used as myth. To illustrate his point, Lévi-Strauss says that when a historian evokes the French Revolution, he presents it as a sequence of past events whose distant consequences may still be felt via a series of irreversible intermediary events. To a politician, however, the French Revolution is a reality of another order; it is a sequence of past events, but it is also a scheme for interpreting the present social structure in France and a clue to impending changes in that structure. Says Lévi-Strauss: "Nothing is more like mythic thought than political ideology. In our contemporary societies, perhaps, the one has entirely replaced the other." [123]

Recalling the words of Napoleon to Goethe that fate had been replaced by politics, Wagner once stated that in our day one could not "poeticize" (*dichten*) without "politicizing" (*ohne zu politisieren*). Wagner's decision to use myth as the stuff of his poetic dramas stemmed from his belief that artist and public can communicate only if they share a common world view. The Greeks, he believed, had achieved this in the highest degree. "Greek tragedy," Wagner wrote, "is the artistic realization of the content and the spirit of Greek myth." And myth is timeless. "The incomparable thing about myth is that it is true for all time, and that, however great the poetic compression, it is inexhaustible for all time. The task of the poet is only to interpret it." Of the myths artistically realized and interpreted by the Greek poets, Wagner singled out the Oedipus myth for his special attention. He explains why: "Even today we need only interpret the Oedipus myth in keeping with its innermost nature to win a comprehensible picture of the entire history of humanity, from the beginning of society to the necessary downfall of the state. In the myth the necessity of this downfall is sensed in advance; to carry it out is up to actual history." [124] By

123. Lévi-Strauss, *Anthropologie structurale*, 231.
124. Wagner, *Gesammelte Schriften und Dichtungen*, IV, 33, 53, 65. According to Wagner, myths, folktales, and folk music are anonymous productions of the spirit of the folk. Interpretation of myths and folktales is essential: "In *myth* the common, poetic productive force of the folk grasps phenomena only as they appear to the eye, not as they are in themselves. The enormous multiplicity of phenomena makes at first an impression of unrest on the human being, who is unable to grasp their real connection. In order to overcome the unrest a connection among the phenomena that can be seen as the primary cause is sought for. But the real connection can be found only by the understanding, which grasps the actuality of the phenomena. The connection discovered by someone who grasps the phenomena solely in accord with the immediate impression made by them can only be the work of phantasy, and the cause assigned only the product of poetic, imaginative force" (*ibid.*, 31).

"Oedipus myth" Wagner means the myth as we find it set forth in the Sophoclean trilogy. In Wagner's interpretation of the trilogy the downfall of Creon's male-dominated state is precipitated by the unselfish act of a woman, Antigone. Wagner invokes Antigone in terms that recall his invocation of the goddess of revolution in Dresden two years earlier: "Holy Antigone! I summon you! Let your banner wave, that we may, beneath it, both destroy and redeem!"[125] The redeemer, like the goddess, is a woman.

Lévi-Strauss chose the Oedipus myth—in the form, he says, that it has reached us in "late and fragmentary reductions and literary transformations inspired more by esthetic and moral concerns than by religious tradition or ritual usage, insofar as such preoccupations ever existed with respect to it"—to illustrate his analytical procedure. Figure One gives his tentative, synchronic-diachronic score of the subordinate constitutive units (the "mythemes") of the Oedipus myth. To read off the story of the myth the columns are to be disregarded and the lines are to be read from left to right and from top to bottom. To grasp (*comprendre*) the myth in its entirety we again read from left to right, but now the columns are taken as wholes and the diachronic order from top to bottom is ignored. The columns are to be understood as "packets" of mythemes. The first column has to do with what Lévi-Strauss calls "exaggerated" or "overesteemed" blood relationships. The second column is of the same character, with the sign inverted: here the blood relationships are "underesteemed" or "devalued." The third column has to do with the destruction of mythical monsters, and the fourth with the "difficulty of walking upright." Lévi-Strauss sees the fourth column as the third with the sign inverted. The dragon is a chthonian monster that must be killed before men can arise from the earth, that is, from the sowing of the dragon's teeth ("Spartoi" are *men sown*). The sphinx is a chthonian monster that "attempts, by means of enigmas bearing on the nature of man, to take on the lives of its human victims." The common feature of the third column is, according to Lévi-Strauss, a "denial of the autochthonous origin of the human being." The fourth column is linked by a trait characteristic of beings originating directly from the earth: they walk clumsily or not at all (Lévi-Strauss draws on the myths of North American Indians here). An autochthonous origin of human beings is thus affirmed; the common

---

125. *Ibid.*, 63–64. *Cf.* the passage from Wagner's essay *Revolution* (1849) cited in Rather, *The Dream of Self-Destruction*, 48.

FIGURE ONE:

LÉVI-STRAUSS' MYTHEMES OF THE OEDIPUS MYTH

BLOOD RELATIONSHIPS OVERESTEEMED	BLOOD RELATIONSHIPS UNDERESTEEMED	MONSTERS DESTROYED	MEANING OF NAMES
Cadmus seeks his sister Europa, ravished by Zeus.			
		Cadmus kills the dragon.	
	The Spartoi mutually exterminate each other.		
			Labdacus (father of *Laius*) = "lame" (?)
	Oedipus kills his father, Laius.		*Laius* = "awkward" (?)
		Oedipus immolates the Sphinx.	
			Oedipus = "swollen foot" (?)
Oedipus marries Jocasta, his mother.			
	Eteocles kills his brother, Polynices.		
Antigone buries Polynices, violating the prohibition.			

SOURCE: Claude Lévi-Strauss, *Anthropologie structurale* (Paris, 1958), 236.

feature of the fourth column is that of the third with the sign inverted. When we interpret the Oedipus myth *à l'américaine*, we find that it expresses the difficulty faced by a culture which believes that human beings are autochthonous in coming to terms with "the fact that each one of us is really born from the union of a man and a woman." The Oedipus myth does not solve the problem; it merely juxtaposes it to the related problem: born from different or born from the same? "By this means a correlation is given: the over-evaluation of blood relationships is to their under-evaluation as the attempt to escape from autochthony is to the impossibility to do so."[126]

That Lévi-Strauss constructed his paradigm with mythemes from the very myth that Wagner regarded as most fraught with meaning for our own time seems to be no more than an accident, since he makes no reference whatsoever to Wagner's analysis of the Oedipus myth. As for Freud's interpretation, or version, of the Oedipus myth, Lévi-Strauss finds that it is compatible with his own. The Freudian problem is no longer that of autochthonous versus bisexual reproduction, but it is still the problem of "understanding how *one* can be born of *two*," that of how it is "that we do not have a sole progenitor, but mother and also a father."[127] The Freudian view centers on the killing of the father by the son, and the sexual union of the son with the mother. The two mythemes are supposed to be united as a single wish in the unconscious mind of the son from infancy on. This view, in turn, is related to Wagner's interpretation of the myth as the story of the necessary downfall of the state, in consequence of a series of actions culminating in a "purely human" act of compassion—compassion, that is, based solely on love for another human being *as* a human being—on the part of a woman. Creon, whom Wagner compares at this point to Louis XIV and his empty boast "I am the state," personifies the male-dominated political state. Antigone, the woman in revolt, is the goddess of revolution incarnate. Creon, the brother of Jocasta, is the uncle of Eteocles and Polynices, the sons of Oedipus the king, over whose dead bodies he climbs to the throne. The downfall of this particular "vice of kings" is brought about by a niece rather than, as in the case of *Hamlet*, by a nephew.[128]

126. Lévi-Strauss, *Anthropologie structurale*, 236–39.

127. *Ibid.*, 240.

128. This is more or less passed over by Ernest Jones in *Hamlet and Oedipus* (1949). Jones supposed that he was engaged in the psychoanalysis of "Hamlet" (or of Shakespeare, or both). What he did in fact was to show very convincingly that the story of Hamlet and the story of Oedipus have mythic elements in common. In short, Jones did not lay bare the unconscious motives governing the behavior of "Hamlet"—there is, after all, only a paper Hamlet available for analysis. Instead, Jones recognized structural resemblances between Shakespeare's version of the Hamlet myth and Freud's version of the Oedipus myth. In precisely the same way, *i.e.*, by the literary analysis of texts, the French scholar Ernest Dugit had recognized sixty years earlier that "the story of Orestes is in reality that of Hamlet under another name and in another land." It is ironic that Dugit's words are cited by Jones himself. See Jones, *Hamlet and Oedipus* (Garden City, N.Y., 1954), 110.

The sociopsychoanalytical approach of Gérard Mendel to the Oedipus myth yields somewhat "Wagnerian" findings. In both interpretations revolt against the *father* is identified with revolt against the *state;*
in both an underlying conflict between male and female principles is
discerned. Mendel proposes the following working hypothesis: The
imagined murder of the father (Freud's primal crime) allowed the image of the father to be "interiorized" by Paleolithic man. Liberated
thereby from an immediate relation to "maternal imagos," man was
able, from the Neolithic period on, to "exploit and transform Mother
Nature." Mendel's second hypothesis is that no sooner had the new,
rational, scientific attitude toward nature developed than the transformation and exploitation of nature was associated in the collective mind
with "aggression against maternal imagos."[129] (The pre- and post-
prison "versions" of Barthélemy Enfantin come irresistibly to mind.)
    One additional feature of Lévi-Strauss's understanding of mythic
structure requires our attention here. It bears equally on the structure
of myth and the structure of musical scores. Why is there so much du-
plication, triplication, or quadruplication of the same sequence of
events in myth and in oral literature generally? On his hypothesis,
Lévi-Strauss believes, the answer is obvious: "Repetition has its own
function, which is to render the structure of the myth apparent." The
diachronic-synchronic organization of its mythemes into a table of
rows and columns (Figure 1) gives one layer, so to speak, of the myth.
Others lie behind it or below it. "Every myth therefore possesses a layered structure which shows through to the surface, as it were, in and
by the process of repetition."[130] Obviously, this consideration applies
equally to the successive pages of a musical score. Repetition, of course,
does not mean here repetition unchanged. Themes and mythemes may
be transposed, inverted, given to new voices, supplied with new color-
ing, and otherwise altered, often almost beyond recognition.
    Music, according to both Wagner and Schopenhauer, is the voice of
the unconscious. So also, in its own way, is myth. Both are related to
dreams, where all transformations are possible. Schopenhauer distinguished sharply between the original, "theorematic" dream and the
dream that we remember and retell while awake. The meaning embodied in the "theorematic" dream is not presented plainly in the re-

129. Mendel, *La révolte contre le père,* 172–74.
130. Lévi-Strauss, *Anthropologie structurale,* 254.

membered dream because of the distortion introduced into it by a
"most peculiar, daimonic slyness of wit, otherwise quite foreign to the
dreamer."[131] Much ingenuity may be required for the revelation of
underlying resemblances between different mythemes and their combinations and in the dreamworld of myths. The repetitive, layered
structure of a single myth is characteristic as well of the whole corpus
of myths in a given culture. A full structural analysis of a single myth
may call for study of this whole corpus, together with the myths of
apparented cultures. The same may be said, of course, for the structural analysis of music, literature, painting, and the arts and sciences
generally.

Wagner offers us two versions of the Oedipus myth—the interpretation given in *Opera and Drama,* and the transformation of it present
as one of the two central elements in his poem *The Ring of the Nibelung.* The additional element is Wagner's account of the vicissitudes of
a power-conferring ring, forged by the dwarfs Alberich and Mime
from the stolen gold of the Rhine maidens, and of the fates that over-
take its successive holders. For purposes of comparison, a highly tentative synchronic-diachronic score of Wagner's interpretation of the
Oedipus trilogy, constructed roughly along the lines marked out by
Lévi-Strauss, is given in Figure Two. A similar arrangement of the
mythemes in *The Ring of the Nibelung* is given in Figure Three, the
ring element being brought into play only where it is indispensable. (A
brief account of another Lévi-Straussian analysis of Wagner's *Ring,*
made in 1973 by Jean Mayer, will be found in the notes. Unlike mine,
this analysis is concerned only with the battle for possession of the
Nibelung's ring.[132])

131. Schopenhauer, *Sämtliche Werke,* IV, 308 ("die ganz eigentümliche dem Träu-
menden sonst völlig fremde dämonische Schalkhaftigkeit des Witzes"). See also Rather,
"Music, Dreams, and the Unconscious," in *The Dream of Self-Destruction,* 110–48.

132. Jean Mayer, "Les conflits de races dans 'l'Anneau du Nibelung' de R. Wagner,"
Romantisme, VI (1973), 99–110. In this, the only other Lévi-Straussian analysis of the
Ring of which I am aware, Mayer claims to have revealed the "structure of the work as
Wagner conceived it: that of a conflict of races." Mayer's cyclical diagram shows the
unidirectional course of the ring and the bidirectional stresses among the four conflicting "races." In this elemental conflict, according to Mayer, the Rhine maidens (water)
and the giants (earth) are passive; the gods (air) and the Nibelungs (fire) are active. But
only Siegfried can act freely: "The spirit alone, escaping from matter, is capable of ani-
mating a free conscience and marking off in the universe the race of human beings." The
music of the close of the *Ring* thus celebrates the "end of universal servitude" (*ibid.,*

FIGURE TWO:

WAGNER'S VERSION OF SOPHOCLES' OEDIPUS TRILOGY

BLOOD RELATIONSHIPS OVERESTEEMED	BLOOD RELATIONSHIPS UNDERESTEEMED	MONSTERS DESTROYED
Laius, king of Thebes, unites with Jocasta to father Oedipus.		
	In order to preserve his own life, and that of the state, Laius exposes Oedipus to death.	
	Oedipus survives, reaches maturity and kills Laius, not knowing him as his father.	
		Oedipus immolates the Sphinx.
Oedipus, as king of Thebes, unites with his mother to produce Antigone, Polynices, and Eteocles.		
	Oedipus is exposed. He blinds himself and abandons the kingship. Jocasta hangs herself.	
	The twin kings of Thebes, Polynices and Eteocles, quarrel over the kingship and kill each other.	
	Creon, brother of Jocasta, becomes king. Orders that Polynices be left unburied.	
Antigone buries her brother's body, defying her uncle's command.	Creon orders that Antigone be buried alive.	
	Haemon, son of Creon and lover of Antigone, attempts to kill his father. He fails, and then kills himself.	Creon's rule comes to an end. The state is overthrown by Antigone's act of compassion.

Since the myth of Cadmus and the sowing of the dragon's teeth was not introduced by Sophocles into his Oedipus trilogy, the dragon does not appear as one of the monsters destroyed in Wagner's version of Sophocles' trilogy (Figure Two). Instead, we have the destruction of an equally mythical monster, the state, or Creon's kingship thereof. And the overthrow of the state is accomplished by a woman, or, let us say, by the female principle acting under the compulsion of the unselfish, "purely human" principle of compassion. Wagner calls Antigone's act one of "self-destruction through sympathy" (*Selbstvernichtung aus Sympathie*).[133] The arrow in Figure Two indicates that Antigone's burial of her brother's body in defiance of her uncle's command belongs in both column one and column two. Wagner assimilates Creon's exposure of the unburied body of his nephew Polynices to animals of prey to Laius' exposure of his son Oedipus to almost certain death on the mountainside. In both instances, Wagner sees the ruler intent on preserving his own position in order to preserve the stability of the state. The state (not only the revolution, as we are told) devours its own children—for "reasons of state." Once this Moloch point has been reached, the state, for the safety of us all, must be overthrown.

Figure Three makes plain Wagner's abundant use of repetition in the *Ring* poem. Wotan, who calls himself on occasion a light-elf (*Lichtalbe*), unites with a mortal woman to father the twins Siegmund and Sieglinde, hoping that Siegmund will be able to rescue him from his untenable position. Wotan's double and antagonist, the dark-elf (*Schwarzalbe*) Alberich, unites with a mortal woman to father Hagen, with whose aid he hopes to win back the ring (in Wagner's first version Alberich takes the woman, Queen Grimhilde, by force; in the second, he buys her favors with gold). Wotan's plans for Siegmund are upset by Fricka, and he comes to pin his hopes on Siegfried. Siegfried kills Fafner and takes the ring; he, in turn, is killed by Hagen for the sake of the ring. The incest motif of the Oedipus trilogy is doubly redoubled in the *Ring*, and it reaches a crescendo when Siegfried passes through the

---

109, 110). Mayer's diagram is clearly based on the diagram used by Lévi-Strauss to elucidate the structure of Winnebago marital relationships, in which three small circles, representing water, earth, and sky, lie on the periphery of a great circle; the small circles are connected by lines indicative of possible marriage relationships (Lévi-Strauss, *Anthropologie structurale*, 172).

133. *Cf.* Rather, *The Dream of Self-Destruction*, 63.

FIGURE THREE:

LÉVI-STRAUSSIAN ANALYSIS OF *THE RING OF THE NIBELUNG*

BLOOD RELATIONSHIPS OVERESTEEMED	BLOOD RELATIONSHIPS UNDERESTEEMED	MONSTERS DESTROYED	MEANING OF NAMES
	The giant Fafner kills his brother Fasolt, in a quarrel over possession of the ring.		
Wotan, the all-father, unites with the earth-goddess, Erda, to father Brünnhilde.			*Wotan* = "tyrant," "the furious one," "the bad Lord"
Wotan unites with a mortal woman to father the twins Siegmund and Sieglinde.			
Alberich unites with a mortal woman, the queen of the Gibichungs, to father Hagen.			
Siegmund and Sieglinde unite to bring forth Siegfried.	Fricka, wife of Wotan and guardian of matrimonial law and order, persuades Wotan to sacrifice Siegmund.		*Siegfried* = "the achiever of peace"
Mime claims to be both father and mother of Siegfried.	Brünnhilde disobeys Wotan's command. She tries to save Siegmund and rescues Sieglinde and Siegfried.		*Brünnhilde* = "the shield-maiden"
	Wotan immolates his daughter Brünnhilde in the magic fire.		
		Siegfried kills the dragon Fafner.	
Siegfried unites with Brünnhilde, the half-sister of his parents (whom he first takes for his mother).		Siegfried kills his false foster father, Mime, and renders his grandfather, Wotan, impotent.	*Mime* = "mimicker"
		Brünnhilde returns the ring to the Rhine. Valhalla burns, and the kingdom of the gods comes to an end.	

magic fire to find Brünnhilde (the half sister of his incestuous parents) and, after first taking her to be a man, asks her whether she is his mother! This query was perhaps inserted by Wagner as an indirect reference to the Oedipus trilogy, for it seems out of place otherwise. In the interests of their budding love affair, Brünnhilde quickly disabuses Siegfried of this notion. The female and male principles must enter into conjunction if the perfected human being of the future, in this instance Brünnhilde-Siegfried, is to find its way into the world.

Other resemblances also are apparent. As Laius sacrificed his son Oedipus for reasons of state, so Wotan sacrifices his son Siegmund, once the goddess Fricka has made it plain that the sanctity of *all* compacts is at issue. As Creon ordered Antigone to be buried alive, so Wotan immolates Brünnhilde in the magic fire; in both instances the express command of a male ruler has been disobeyed by a female (out of compassion, according to Wagner) related to him. The riddling question put to Oedipus by the sphinx corresponds to Mime's quizzing of Wotan (in the first act of *Siegfried*) on the subject of race. Siegfried kills his false father, Mime, and renders another father figure impotent (when he breaks the lance of Wotan, who has tried to block Siegfried's path to Brünnhilde's sanctuary). Antigone's purely human act of compassion in burying the body of her brother by sprinkling dust over his corpse is matched by Brünnhilde's freely willed return of the Nibelung's ring to the waters of the Rhine. Creon's downfall, or rather that of his state, follows the one act, the general downfall of Wotan and the old gods the other. The difference is that Wotan recognizes the inevitability of his downfall and helps bring it about.

Figure Three by itself is merely a tentative, obviously incomplete structural analysis of Wagner's *Ring* poem. But when it is taken with Figure Two, the close structural relationships between Wagner's two versions (in the sense of Lévi-Strauss) of the Oedipus myth becomes evident. Figures Two and Three, in turn, have been composed in such a way as to bring out the resemblances of Wagner's two versions of the myth to the structural analysis of the myth given us by Lévi-Strauss (whose analysis, like that of Freud, is simply another version of the myth) in Figure One. It will be seen, however, that the meanings of the names given in the fourth column of Figure Three are not linked by a common idea, as they are in Figure One. The question of the origin of the human being, or, more concretely, the question of the origin of the questioner—the Oedipal question *par excellence*, according to

Lévi-Strauss—is not without relevance to the *Ring:* Mime replies to Siegfried's inquiry along this line that he himself is "father and mother in one."

The liberation of woman as redeemer is evident in Figures Two and Three. Nietzsche's remarks on this topic (written after his break with Wagner) are worth recalling here. He will tell us, Nietzsche says, the real meaning of Wagner's *Ring.* It is as follows: Siegfried, a "typical revolutionary," an "ideologist of revolution," sees the source of the world's ills in the outworn compacts of an effete society, its customs, laws, morals, and institutions generally. Siegfried therefore declares war on such compacts.

> He begins it very early, very early: his birth is already a declaration of war on morality—he is brought into the world by adultery and incest. . . . *Not the saga, but Wagner is the discoverer of this radical twist; on this point he corrected the saga.* . . . Siegfried continues as he has begun: he follows only the first impulse, he throws overboard everything traditional, everything revered, all *fear.* Whatever displeases him he strikes down. He presses an irreverent attack on the old gods. But his chief task is *to emancipate woman*—"to redeem Brünnhilde" . . . Siegfried *and* Brünnhilde; the sacrament of free love; the beginning of the golden age; the Götterdämmerung of the old morality.

Wagner, having learned from Schopenhauer that he himself was a crass optimist, then "translated the Ring into Schopenhauerese." The new scenario, Nietzsche continues, calls for Brünnhilde to have read Schopenhauer's *The World as Will and Representation.* Instead of closing the *Ring* with a hymn to "free love" and a "socialist Utopia," Brünnhilde beckons as an "Indian Circe," and Wagner—not Brünnhilde—is redeemed.[134]

134. Friedrich Nietzsche, "Der Fall Wagner," in *Werke,* ed. Karl Schlechta (3 vols.; Munich, 1954–56), II, 910–11.

CHAPTER EIGHT

HARMONIES AND DISSONANCES

SECRET SOCIETIES, HITLERISM, AND WAGNER'S *PARSIFAL*

Julius Fröbel's charge, made in Bavaria in 1869, that Wagner was or wanted to be the leader of a cult founded on Muckerish sexual principles and dedicated to the overthrow of church and state is not as freakish as it may seem to today's reader. We recall that a few decades earlier the Prussian authorities had accused the leaders of the Ebelian church in Königsberg of conducting a secret society. We recall also Disraeli's claim, made in 1852 in his biography of Lord George Bentinck, that "[d]estruction of the Semitic principle, extirpation of the Jewish religion, whether in the Mosaic or Christian form, the natural equality of man and the abrogation of property are proclaimed by the secret societies, and men of the Jewish race are found at the head of everyone of them."[1] Secret societies did in fact play an important role in Europe and what has recently been termed the "mythology of the secret societies" played perhaps an even greater role.[2]

Exactly one hundred years after Disraeli made the above charge the last of Wagner's music dramas was denounced in Germany as the prototype of future Nazi secret societies. "The glorified blood brotherhood of *Parsifal*," Theodor Adorno wrote in 1952, "is the model for the secret societies and Führer-orders with which the circle at Wahnfried [Wagner's home in Bayreuth] has so much in common; a clique held together by murky eros and despotic fear, terroristically stirred up against all who do not belong to it."[3] We shall see that a similar

---

1. See "Marx, Hess, and Disraeli" in Chapter 5 herein. For a more detailed account of the matter see L. J. Rather, "Disraeli, Freud, and Jewish Conspiracy Theories," *Journal of the History of Ideas*, XLVII (January–March, 1986), 111–31.
2. J. M. Roberts, *The Mythology of the Secret Societies* (London, 1972).
3. Theodor Adorno, *Versuch über Wagner* (Berlin, 1952), 178. *Cf.* the charge, made twenty years earlier by the Viennese cultural historian Egon Friedell, that Freud

interpretation of *Parsifal* had already been made two years earlier in
the United States by Leon Stein, and that Stein's apparently new interpretation of the music drama can be traced back a quarter of a century
earlier to Adolf Hitler, in his role as Wagnerian *Opernführer.*

What is the essential feature of a secret society? According to Pierre
Barrucand, writing in 1968, it is the bond formed by a complex system
of thoughts and attitudes and perhaps strengthened by some shared set
of ceremonies and ritual observances. Barrucand distinguishes between secret societies (*sociétés secrètes*) and clandestine societies (*sociétés clandestines*). The former conceal their secrets but make no attempt to conceal their existence. Clandestine societies, on the other
hand, are criminal, revolutionary, or terroristic in character and hence
find some degree of concealment necessary.[4] The classificatory value of
clandestinity, a relative term, is open to some doubt. It plays no role in
C. W. Heckethorn's nineteenth-century classification of secret societies: religious, military, judicial, scientific, civil, political, and anti-
social. "The [Spanish] Inquisition," Heckethorn writes, "though a
state tribunal, had its secret agents and secret procedures, and may
therefore justly be included in the category of the Secret Societies."[5]
Cooperation between criminal secret societies and state-sponsored secret societies has a history of its own.[6]

In his account of the "mythology" of secret societies, J. M. Roberts
argues that the scale and violence of the changes taking place in Europe during the French Revolution and the Napoleonic Wars were un-

---

was the founder of a "sect . . . with rites, ceremonies, and cathartic conjurations, oracles
and divinations, secret doctrine and its popular version . . . and daughter-sects that con-
demn each other in turn" (Friedell, *Kulturgeschichte der Neuzeit* [3 vols.; Munich,
1927–32], III, 583). For an account of the founding by Freud of his self-styled secret
society of seven guardians of the psychoanalytic tradition, see the chapter "Seven Rings"
in Hanns Sachs, *Freud, Master and Friend* (Cambridge, Mass., 1944).

4. Pierre Barrucand, *Les sociétés secrètes. Entretiens avec Robert Amadou* (Paris,
1968), 14–18, *passim.*

5. Charles William Heckethorn, *The Secret Societies of All Ages and Countries
Embracing the Mysteries of Ancient India, China, Japan, Egypt, Mexico, Peru, Greece
and Scandinavia, the Cabbalists, Early Christians, Heretics, Assassins, Thugs, Templars,
the Vehm and Inquisition, Mystics, Rosicrucians, Illuminati, Freemasons, Skopzi, Camorristi, Carbonari, Nihilists and other Sects* (2 vols.; 1875; rpr. New Hyde Park, N.Y.,
1965), I, xxiv–xxv, 3.

6. The Garduna, a secret society of professional murderers, kidnappers, perjurers,
and forgers, is said by Heckethorn to have worked with the Spanish court and Inquisition (*ibid.*, I, 257–63).

precedented. Two world orders seemed to be in confrontation; the conventional and familiar categories of historical explanation—dynastic rivalries, the personal ambitions of rulers and their advisors, quarrels over succession, and so on—seemed insufficient to account for the course of events. Divine retribution, millenarian expectations, and various "plot theories" of history were then called on. "In the best versions of the great drama of subversion," Roberts observes, "virtually the whole of human history would be exploited for evidence of a conspiracy sometimes seen as almost coeval with man himself." Of these plot theories the most influential was that propounded by the Abbé Augustin de Barruel, a Jesuit priest of noble family, toward the end of the eighteenth century. Barruel traced the revolution in France back to what he saw as its source in the Manichean heresy, by way of the Knights Templars, the peasant revolts in Bohemia and Transylvania, and the subversive activities of continental Freemasonry and the Bavarian Illuminati. His book, called by Roberts "the bible of the secret society mythology," was translated into English, German, Italian, Spanish, Portuguese, and Dutch. It attracted the serious attention of readers as diverse as Edmund Burke and Percy Bysshe Shelley.[7]

The Abbé Barruel's message reached the United States in 1802 in a work by Seth Payson. According to Payson a threefold conspiracy had been brought to light: an "Anti-Christian Conspiracy," an "Anti-Monarchial Conspiracy," and an "Anti-Social Conspiracy." Voltaire, Frederick the Great, Beaumarchais (author of the subversive *Le mariage de Figaro* on which Mozart based his opera), and Diderot were parties to the first of these conspiracies; the French Jacobins, the Illuminati, the "occult Lodges of Free Masons," and assorted "sophisters of Anarchy," were involved in the third. Payson claims that the anti-Christian conspirators conceived the idea of "rebuilding the temple at Jerusalem, with a view to defeating the predictions of Christ." They asked Frederick the Great and the empress of Russia to exert pressure on the "Turkish powers, to whose jurisdiction Jerusalem pertained . . . but the fear of losing many wealthy Jews, whom they [Frederick and the empress] found profitable subjects, and who, in that case, would have repaired to the new temple, prevented the attempt."[8]

7. Roberts, *The Mythology of the Secret Societies*, 146–50, 193–98, *passim*.

8. Seth Payson, *Proofs of the Real Existence and Dangerous Tendency of Illuminism. Containing an Abstract of the Most Interesting Parts of What Dr. Robison and the Abbé Barruel Have Published on this Subject, with Collateral Proofs and Gen-*

Some of the so-called antisocial secret societies shared the humanistic ideals that Wagner in 1853 so forcefully expressed in his letter to Franz Liszt.[9] Of interest in this connection is a documentary history of such societies edited by J. D. F. Neigebauer and published in Leipzig during Wagner's time there as a university student.[10] Using familiar phrases, the editor states that the influence of secret societies on the "education of humankind" (*Erziehung des Menschengeschlechtes*) is beneficial where they are motivated by a "purely human striving" (*reinmenschliches Streben*). The age-old quest for human justice began, he says, with the moralists of ancient Egypt. By way of the ancient Indian gymnosophists, Moses, Pythagoras, and the Essenes, the quest culminated in the ethical teachings of Jesus. Christianity, however, underwent transformation into a militant state religion that rejected Christ's "command of love." Those who, like the Knights Templars, secretly followed the teachings of the Christian Gnostics were put down without mercy. "The ruling powers," says the editor, "wanted no secret societies to be in a position to enlighten humanity; humanity was to obey blindly all that came from Rome; in the thirteenth century, therefore, the first tribunal of the Inquisition was set up in Toulouse to combat the Albigenses, and in the fourteenth century the respected leaders of the Knights Templars ended at the stake."[11]

Neigebauer's picture offers us a simple dichotomy between black and white, between the forces of reaction and the forces of progress. Rudolf Hug, another contributor to the volume, tries to give a more balanced view. As he sees it, the age-old conflict is one between the forces of change—beneficial in intent—and the forces of conservatism. "The one party," he writes, "desires to further the [moral] development of humankind; the other party finds itself thereby startled out of its rest; it believes that it must protect itself from troublesome encroachments by taking retrogressive measures, which are in conflict with the times; the first party, likewise, feels itself to have been injured, and it also goes too far, with the result that the good is left behind."[12]

George Sand's *The Journeyman-Joiner* (1840) contains a brief his-

---

eral *Observations* (Charlestowne, 1802), 27–28, 53–54. This book is not mentioned by Roberts.

    9. See "Wagner's Christianity" in Chapter 5 herein.

    10. J. D. F. Neigebauer, *Geschichte der geheimen Verbindungen der neusten Zeit* (2 vols.; 1831–44; rpr. Leipzig, 1972).

    11. *Ibid.*, Bk. I, i–viii, 10–15, *passim*.

    12. *Ibid.*, Bk. VI, 89.

tory of secret societies. "The secret society," Sand writes, "precisely because it is secret and proscribed, must inevitably fall away from the truth. . . . [I]t replies to intolerance with intolerance, to the blind fanaticism which rejects its ideas with a fanaticism equally blind." So it is that the Knights Templars took on a "double character . . . attributed to the spirit of evil or the genius of good, in accordance with the aspect which writers have chosen to consider."[13] But there is no doubt where Sand's sympathies lie. In *Jean Zyska* (1843), a history of the extreme wing of the Hussite revolt against the Catholic church in fifteenth-century Bohemia, Sand addresses her female readers as follows: "The official religion, the established church, has always followed the same system. The secret church, which still seeks to give itself form, this ideal society of equality, which begins with the teachings of Jesus, traverses centuries of Catholicism under the name of heresy, and with us got as far as the French Revolution, only to reform and take stock of itself in Chartist clubs and communist exaltation, this religion is always the same . . . essentially Christian in principle, evangelical in its successive revelations, revolutionary in its claims and strivings."[14]

Before turning to Wagner's knights of the holy grail in *Parsifal,* a word must be said of Nesta Webster, the most widely read conspiracy theorist of our century. In her first book on the subject, *The French Revolution* (1919), Webster (relying heavily on the Abbé Barruel) attempted to uncover the hidden roles played by the Orleanists, the Bavarian Illuminati, and Frederick of Prussia. In *World Revolution* (1921) she found support for her contention that the Illuminati were the most important secret driving force behind the French Revolution in Sand's novel *La comtesse de Rudolstadt,* calling Sand herself a "revolutionary and Freemason."[15] Drawing inspiration from Disraeli's writings on secret societies, Webster asserted that the Jews had been "behind the Masonic insurrection of 1848 in Germany, which started with the cry of Jewish emancipation and proclaimed as its ultimate purpose the supremacy of Prussia."[16] A symbiotic relationship between Germans and Jews had been in existence—according to Webster—from the eigh-

13. George Sand, *Le compagnon du tour de France* (Paris, 1861), 6–7; Sand, *The Journeyman-Joiner; or, The Companion of the Tour of France,* trans. Francis G. Shaw (New York, 1976), 1–2.

14. George Sand, *Jean Zyska* (Paris, 1867), 24.

15. Nesta Webster, *World Revolution: The Plot Against Civilization* (London, 1921), 81–82.

16. *Ibid.,* 165.

teenth century down to her own time. "To the Ashkenazim," she writes in *Secret Societies and Subversive Movements* (1924), "Germany, even more than Palestine, has appeared to be the Land of Promise." And on their part, the Germans—the Prussians, in particular— found the Jews useful. "From Frederick the Great, who employed the Jew Ephraim to coin false money [in France], to William II, who kept in touch with [Walther] Rathenau by means of a private telephone, the rulers of Germany have always allowed [the Jews] to cooperate in their schemes of world-domination. As the allies of Bismarck, who used them freely to fill his war-chests, the Jews directed the power of the secret societies in the interests of Germany; in 1871 the Jew Bloechreider [*sic*] acted as advisor to the new German Empire as to the best method for wresting indemnities from France."[17]

Like Disraeli, Nesta Webster was a defender of the Old Testament God. In her historical construction the attack launched by the Marcionites and the early Christian Gnostics against that deity represented the first in a series of steps "toward the *deification of humanity* [Webster's emphasis] which forms the supreme doctrine of the secret societies and of the visionary socialists of our day." The Carpocratian Gnostics of second century Alexandria had in fact "arrived at much the same conclusions as modern communists," most notably by "instituting the community of women and indulging in every kind of vice." The chain of heresy reached down into modern times; among its links were the Albigensian Cathars of the French Midi, the Knights

17. Nesta Webster, *Secret Societies and Subversive Movements* (2nd ed.; London, 1924), 365. The following words from Walther Rathenau's address to the youth of Germany in July, 1918, could well have come from Wagner: "Germany does have a mission on earth. It is not the mission of militarism, it is also not the mission of mechanization and technology, although these useful things are not despised, and least of all is it the mission of world-domination. It is the mission that ever was and ever will be: the mission of the pure, incorruptible, unerring and inexorable spirit" (Rathenau, *An Deutschlands Jugend* [Berlin, 1925], 123). Other words too, spoken on this occasion by the strongly anti-Zionist Rathenau, are worth recalling: "I am a German of Jewish stock [*Stammes*]. My people [*Volk*] is the German people, my homeland is the German land, my belief the German belief, which stands above religious denominations" (*ibid.*, 9). "There was once a people that called itself chosen. It was not a bad people, and it gave the world the revelation, many prophets, and a magnificent book. But because of its wicked pride in its chosenness it has been scattered to the four winds, and for two thousand years its children have done penance in blood and tears . . . God forbid that our German people commit this error. We are no chosen people nor do we want to be one" (*ibid.*, 108).

Templars of Germany, the eighteenth-century Bavarian Illuminati, the philosophers of the French Enlightenment, and the Freemasons.[18]

Pan-Germanism and its Jewish allies were replaced after World War I by "the world force we know as Bolshevism" as the chief foe of Western civilization in general and the British Empire in particular, according to Webster, but she recognized that Pan-Germanism was still alive and flourishing in the potentially dangerous movement led by Adolf Hitler. And a new force hostile to the interests of Great Britain had appeared on the scene, that of political Zionism. Webster argued that only a strong British-Moslem friendship could assure the safety of the British Empire, and that to pursue any other course was suicidal. And yet (she wrote in 1930) "to further the schemes of Pan-Judaism—aiming at economic predominance in Palestine over the Near East from Cairo to Baghdad—Great Britain deliberately set out to alienate a friendly and at the same time a warlike race, at the risk of antagonising the whole Moslem world and imperilling the very existence of the Empire."[19]

Nesta Webster's plot-theory is George Sand's with the sign inverted: Sand's heroes are, for the most part, Webster's villains. Both theories are Barruelian in character and inspiration. So also the historical construction put forward by Eric Voegelin in the 1950s and 1960s, in which "progressivism, positivism, Marxism, psychoanalysis, communism, fascism, and national socialism" are grouped together as "gnostic movements," whether of the left or right. Voegelin himself derived his views from the writings of Ferdinand Christian Baur (1835), Jacques Matter (1835), and Johann August Neander (1818), all of whom, he says, saw that the gnostic movement had acquired great social significance in the period of the French Enlightenment.[20]

Although the movement led by Adolf Hitler found a modest place in Webster's plot-theory as early as 1930, it was only after World War II that Hitlerism began to take on some of the mystical trappings once associated with French Jacobinism and, a century later, with Russian Bolshevism. In a work on Hitlerism in relation to Catharism published in France in 1971, for example, we are told of a search by Nazi mysta-

18. Webster, *Secret Societies and Subversive Movements,* 27–32, *passim.*

19. Nesta Webster, *Surrender of an Empire* (3rd ed.; London, 1931), v, 198, 369.

20. *Cf.* Eric Voegelin, *Science, Politics, and Gnosis: Two Essays* (Chicago, 1968), 3–4, 83. On Freudian psychoanalysis perceived as part of the "plot" against Western civilization, *cf.* Rather, "Disraeli, Freud, and Jewish Conspiracy Theories."

gogues for a mysterious Aryan Holy Grail said to be hidden in the
ruins of the Catharist stronghold on Montségur in southern France;
the translator of this work assures us that the "Nazi blasphemy" had
its roots "in the Middle Ages, when the neo-Gnostic heresies, particularly Catharism, forcefully challenged the Church's spiritual authority
everywhere in Europe."[21] Hitler's interpretation of Wagner's *Parsifal*
plays a central role in this work.

As he had done earlier in the case of the *Ring,* Wagner drew freely
on the various sources available to him in writing *Parsifal.* He added
essential ingredients of his own making, above all the enigmatic Kundry, with her Jekyll-Hyde character. The killing of the swan by Parsifal
and Gurnemanz's "zoophilomanic" reaction to the deed are also Wagner's contributions; they are of course intended to make the point that
human compassion must be broadened to include the realm of animal
life. A curious addition, little commented on, is Gurnemanz's remark
to Parsifal when they make their first visit to the powerless grail-king
Amfortas: "You see, my son, that here time becomes space" ("Du
siehst, mein Sohn / zum Raum wird hier die Zeit").[22] Simrock's edition
of Wolfram von Eschenbach's poems *Parzifal* and *Titurel* was, as we
have seen, in Wagner's Dresden collection of books. In von Eschenbach's version of the story, the Holy Grail is a sacred stone, possibly in
the shape of a chalice, entrusted by the powers of heaven to the care of
the grail-knights. Wagner seems to have borrowed from Chrétien de
Troyes' *Perceval,* another twelfth-century version of the story, in which
the grail is a mysterious vessel whose significance Perceval at first fails
to grasp. In adopting the spelling "Parsifal" Wagner went along with
Joseph von Görres' probably incorrect etymological derivation of the

---

21. Jean-Michel Angebert, *Hitler et la tradition Cathare* (Paris, 1971); *cf.* Angebert, *The Occult and the Third Reich: The Mystical Origins of Nazism and the Search
for the Holy Grail,* trans. Lewis A. M. Sumberg (New York, 1974), x–xiii.

22. The criminologist Cesare Lombroso calls Wagner a "downright zoophilomaniac" (*förmlicher Zoophilomane*) in his "Neue Studien über die Genialität," 141–45.
Wagner's reference to the conversion of time into space presumably calls attention to the
"timeless"—eternal, in the *nunc stans* sense of medieval philosophers also taken over by
Schopenhauer—character of the quest for the grail. The notion of time as a fourth di-
mension of space is foreshadowed in Rudolf Lotze's *Mikrokosmos* (1859–64) and was
set forth explicitly by Heinrich Czolbe in 1875. By 1905, when H. G. Wells's *The Time
Machine* was published, the relativity of time and space had become a commonplace
topic. *Cf.* Georg Müller, "Versuch einer Zeittheorie," *Archiv für systematische Philosophie,* XVII (1911), 107.

name from "Parseh-Fal," or "Parsi-fal," meaning "the pure fool" (*der reine Thor*)—a derivation, however, not false to the spirit of the legend.[23]

A useful article on the subject of the Holy Grail appeared in 1913 in Hastings' *Encyclopaedia of Religion and Ethics*. The authors were J. M. E. Ross and Margaret Ross, and the chief English authorities cited are Jessie L. Weston, Arthur E. Waite, and Alfred Nutt. The Rosses isolated five themes in the legend: "The Great Fool Tale," "The Vengeance Quest," "The Unspelling Quest," "The Fisher-King," and "The Lance, the Sword, and the Dish." The Holy Grail proves to be an elusive thing—now the vessel in which Joseph of Arimathea received the blood of Christ from the wound in his side made by the spear of the Roman soldier Longinus (who won his name as late as the First Crusade, when the spear was supposedly found at Antioch), now a chalice or cup used at the Last Supper, now a platter to contain the host, now a stone (as in Wolfram von Eschenbach's *Parzival*), possibly used for the same purpose, now a wonder-working, food-producing talisman. The undying wound of Amfortas is either in the side or (in the Celtic version) in the foot. One derivation of *grail* traces the word back to the Latin *crater* (cup), through *cratalis* and *gradalis,* another to the word *gré* (because of the grace its sight affords the viewer); the later, obviously false derivation from *sang real* (blood royal) has also had its currency. The Rosses note that the grail legend has pre-Christian roots in the West and affinities with the Tammuz or Adonis cult in the East. There is "almost always . . . a question to be asked by the hero; he fails to ask it and draws upon himself the curses of the people of the wasted land; or he asks it partially, and the blight is but partially lifted; by and by he comes to the Grail castle, and asks it fully and successfully." But the writers' quest for the elusive grail and the precise nature of the question are as baffling and endless as the grail-knight's quest itself. The Rosses see the grail as a symbol of the struggle to reach spiritual perfection. They close with these words: "It is noteworthy that Robert de Barron, before the tradition had time to be deeply ecclesiasticized, and Richard Wagner, who had no special ecclesiastical interest to serve, should alike be able to see the spiritual significance of the Grail idea."[24]

23. Gustav Kobbé, *Wagner's Life and Works* (2nd ed.; New York, 1896), 179.
24. *S.v.* "Grail," in Hastings' *Encyclopaedia of Religion and Ethics*.

The "Hitlerian" interpretation of Wagner's *Parsifal* propounded after World War II by Leon Stein and Theodor Adorno and incorporated into their anti-Wagner polemics calls for special consideration. The young Hitler, like many others at the time, was carried away by Wagner's music into a land of fantasy. But it was Wagner's *Rienzi,* rather than *Parsifal,* which first exerted this hypnotic effect on Hitler. Adolf Hitler's boyhood friend August Kubizek made public in 1953 an account of Hitler's life as a frustrated, would-be artist in Linz and Vienna from 1904 to 1908.[25] The two boys met for the first time in the standing-room section of the opera house at Linz; Kubizek was sixteen years old and Hitler fifteen. Over the years they listened together to *Rienzi, The Flying Dutchman, Tannhäuser, Lohengrin, Die Meistersinger,* the *Ring,* and *Parsifal.* Hitler disliked the works of Italian, French, and Russian composers; he vehemently rejected Wagner's (and Kubizek's) belief that music must utter its saving message to all peoples and all nations. As far as can be ascertained from Kubizek's account, Hitler showed little interest in *Parsifal.* After their first hearing of *Rienzi,* however, the two boys climbed the Freinberg in Linz and stood together under the stars. Totally swept away, Hitler seized Kubizek's hands and burst forth in an uncheckable torrent of words. Kubizek says that Hitler was in "a state of ecstasy, a state of complete rapture." What Hitler told Kubizek, in short, was that he too, like Rienzi, intended to become a tribune of the people—the German people—and lead them out of servitude into freedom.[26] Ironically enough, as we have seen, only ten years earlier, Wagner's *Tannhäuser* had inspired the first efforts of Theodor Herzl, Hess's successor in the founding of Zionism, to lead the Jewish people out of the European house of bondage.[27]

25. August Kubizek, *Adolf Hitler, mein Jugendfreund* (Vienna, 1953); Kubizek, *The Young Hitler I Knew,* trans. E. V. Anderson (Cambridge, Mass., 1955). The English translation, unfortunately, omits the Austrian publisher's foreword, with its comments on the character of books published on the subject of Hitler in Germany after the "Götterdämmerung"; it also omits Kubizek's own introductory remarks, in which he expresses his lasting debt to Hitler—"because he [Hitler] succeeded in persuading my father that I, in view of my special musical gifts, belonged in the conservatory and not in the workshop" (*Adolf Hitler, mein Jugendfreund,* 10)—and the closing pages of Kubizek's epilogue, as well as many long passages here and there in the original.

26. Kubizek, *Adolf Hitler, mein Jugendfreund,* 20, 133–34, 236–37; Kubizek, *The Young Hitler I Knew,* 7, 90–101, 190–191 (the translation omits much of the material cited here).

27. Theodor Herzl's *Der Judenstaat* (*The Jewish State*) was first published in 1896. Commenting on its genesis two years later, Herzl wrote: "Heine says that he heard the

German chauvinists were already engaged in exploiting Wagner for their own purposes when the young Hitler first heard *Rienzi*. But when Hitler set forth his racist interpretation of *Parsifal* in the late 1930s, he seems to have been well aware of its idiosyncratic character. According to Hermann Rauschning, a close associate of the führer, Hitler's words were: "The problem is: How can racial degeneration be halted? Must it be as Count Gobineau said? We have drawn the political consequences—no equality, no democracy! . . . Should we form a chosen band [made up] only of those who really know? An order, the Brotherhood of Knights of the Holy Grail, around the holy grail of the pure blood?" Hitler paused for a moment to collect his thoughts. He then continued:

> You must also understand *Parsifal* in quite a different way than it is so commonly interpreted, for example by the blockhead Wolzogen . . . not the Christian-Schopenhauerian religion of compassion is glorified, but the pure noble blood that the Brotherhood of the Knowers has gathered itself together to guard and glorify. There the king suffers from the incurable disease of corrupted blood. There the unknowing, but pure human being is tempted to yield to the lust and intoxication of a corrupted civilization, or to join up with the chosen band of knights who guard the secret of life, pure blood. All of us suffer from the disease of mixed, corrupted blood. How can we achieve purification and atonement? Observe that [in Wagner's *Parsifal*] the compassion through which one becomes a knower (*Mitleid, durch das man wissend wird*) is directed only toward those who are inwardly corrupt and divided. And that this compassion knows of only one treatment, to allow the sick to die. The eternal life provided by the grail is valid only for the truly pure and noble![28]

In a later conversation Hitler told Rauschning that in our time the concept of the nation had become empty of meaning. It must now yield place to the concept of race, a concept not bounded by national geographic borders. (We recall that the race concept championed by Moses Hess as the real motive force of history was likewise unbounded.) When

---

rustle of an eagle's wings over his head as he wrote down certain verses. I too believed that I heard something like a rustle over my head when I wrote this book. . . . My only recreation in the evening consisted in listening to Wagner's music, especially *Tannhäuser*, an opera which I heard as often as it was performed. Only on evenings when no opera was given did I feel doubts as to the correctness of my thoughts" (Herzl, *Theodor Herzls zionistische Schriften*, 17–18).

28. Hermann Rauschning, *Gespräche mit Hitler* (New York, 1940), 216–17.

Rauschning tentatively objected that it might be difficult to apply the race concept to Germany, Hitler remarked: "I understand, of course, as well as all these know-it-all intellectuals, that in the scientific sense there is no such thing as race. But as a farmer and breeder you cannot get along without the concept of race in ordering the products of your breeding. And I as a politician need a concept that makes it possible to dissolve the order hitherto resting on historical circumstances, and to compel and give intellectual underpinning to a new, anti-historical order. . . . No God of the Jews will protect these democracies from this revolution, which will be the exact antithesis of the French Revolution."[29] The watchword of the Enlightenment—liberty, equality, and fraternity—will give way to that of the fascist counterrevolution—authority, inequality, and (racial or ethnic) particularism. Hitler rejects the "God of the Jews" not because that God is an exclusively masculine authority figure (as did Sand and other feminists), not because that God plays racial favorites and is without compassion (as Wagner did), but because he worships a rival twin, the "God of the Germans." Rauschning saw this plainly enough. "One God excluded the other. Behind Hitler's antisemitism a battle of the Gods becomes clearly visible."[30]

Hitler's exegesis of *Parsifal* is implicit in Leon Stein's *The Racial Thinking of Richard Wagner*. Stein pointed out, correctly, that as early as 1848 Wagner had equated Siegfried with Christ and called the Holy Grail of the Christian legend the spiritual equivalent of the treasure of the Nibelungs in the old German saga. " 'Parsifal' then becomes, in truth, the fifth opera of the 'Ring':—'the spiritual ascension of the Hoard into the Grail' [he is citing from Wagner's essay of 1848 on the Nibelung myth] is analogous in its fusion of Teutonic myth and Christian legend to the Wotan-God, Siegfried-Christ amalgam, and a fourth element is added in identifying the Master of all spiritual Knighthoods, Titurel, and his successor, Amfortas, with the medieval Kaiser-concept."[31]

29. Rauschning, *Gespräche mit Hitler*, 218–19. Hitler was incorrect, since botanists, entomologists, and zoologists (as well as most anthropologists) do have a scientific concept of race (subspecies), with which it would be inconvenient to dispense. *Cf.* Baker, *Race*, 65, *passim*. Perhaps Hitler meant only that there was no "German race"; he could hardly have been unaware that Germany was a racial melting pot, as Chamberlain had long since pointed out. *Cf.* Rather, *The Dream of Self-Destruction*, 30–31.

30. Rauschning, *Gespräche mit Hitler*, 221–22.

31. Stein, *The Racial Thinking of Richard Wagner*, 101–102.

Unlike Hitler, Stein did not call for a new interpretation of Wagner's *Parsifal*. For Stein there had been only one proper interpretation all along. Stein's thesis is that Wagner's anti-Judaism misled him into the "dissociation of Jesus from his Judaic sources," and that Wagner's anti-Catholicism led him to mount an "unceasing and unrelenting campaign against what he considered the spiritual inroads of that belief." (According to Stein, Wagner's anti-Catholicism was nearly "as virulent as his anti-Semitism.") Stein asserts that the "two streams of hatred"—against Judaism and Catholicism—ran a parallel course and occasionally merged. Hence Wagner could, on occasion, speak of the "Semitic-Latin Church" (Stein seems unaware that this conjunction was hardly new. Disraeli had long since called Christianity the representative of the "Semitic principle"). Stein claims that since Wagner was unable to pluck Christianity from the hearts of the German people he was forced "to fuse its identities with the Gods of Teutonic legend, to recast the creed, not as a universal religion, but as a belief to be understood only 'Germanly,' just as the legends of 'Parsifal' and 'Tristan,' though not originally German, only became significant and immortal when interpreted 'Germanly.' This ethnocentric desire for racial and cultural exclusiveness, predicated on an immutable, even necessary disjunction of 'races' was destined to be carried to the ultimate conclusions: God was to become a Deutscher Gott and Christianity was converted into a 'Deutsche Religion.'"[32]

Stein inverts Wagner's values with breathtaking audacity. For in "Heroism and Christianity" (1881) we find Wagner pointing out that the sole defect of the most ancient religion of the Aryan race, the religion of the Hindus, is its racial exclusiveness. "Its only flaw was that it was a race-religion" ("Sie hatte den einzigen Fehler, dass sie eine Racen-Religion war"). And without the cue from Hitler it may be doubted that Stein would have read into Wagner's last music drama a celebration of an "ethnocentric desire for racial and cultural exclusive-

32. *Ibid.*, 99, 102–103. According to Stein, Wagner's *Parsifal* is anti-Jewish, anti-Catholic, and anti-Christian. "Far from being a consistent Christian expression," he writes, "it [*Parsifal*] is actually rooted in Paganism, and is in truth *the fifth opera of the Ring*" (*ibid.*, 94–95). Where Nietzsche saw Wagner at the foot of the cross, Stein sees him prostrate before a German oak. There were indeed Germans who read paganism into the *Ring*. Writing in 1899, Chamberlain remarked that "in recent years . . . newly arisen 'Wotan worshippers' have offered up sacrifices on the mountaintops of certain German districts at the time of the solstice." He dismissed them as of no importance (Chamberlain, *Grundlagen des neunzehnten Jahrhunderts*, I, 196).

ness"—a commonly enough celebrated desire in our own day, but one
that goes entirely against the grain of the ideas cherished by Wagner.
Two decades later Robert Gutman (who follows Stein in most respects) accomplished a similar distortion of Wagner's views by means
of selective quotation. Gutman asserts that in "Heroism and Christianity" "Wagner celebrated the Aryans as the globe's noblest race, their
rule and exploitation (*'Beherrschung und Ausbeutung'*) being justified
by ethnologic superiority and this is natural law." What Wagner actually wrote was that "the noblest race *founded a completely immoral
world order* [my emphasis, words omitted by Gutman] in the course of
its rule and exploitation of the lower races, which was fully justified in
a natural sense." Wagner then went on to argue that only on the basis
of the universal moral concord taught by "genuine" (*wahrhaftige*)
Christianity—understood *not* as Judeo-Christianity but as the Christian religion of compassion—could universal harmony be achieved.
(Seventeen years earlier, we recall, Wagner had stated that the "Christian religion belongs to no national tribe.") Wagner's "completely immoral world order" is our present-day "Wotan" world order of force
and fraud.[33] The *Ring,* as Wagner informed Liszt in 1853, depicts "the
beginning and the end (*Untergang*) of the world"—of Wotan's world,
that is to say. The pathway to the new world order is depicted in *Parsifal,* as Eric Eugène pointed out in France in 1973. "After catastrophe
has fallen on the will to power of a world founded on injustice, *Parsifal* comes to show humanity the path of reconciliation with itself and
with its social and natural environment."[34] And here the word *natural*
in Eugène's statement should be given due weight: the path leads to
ecological as well as to sociological reconciliation.

33. Wagner, *Gesammelte Schriften und Dichtungen,* X, 281, 284; Robert W. Gutman, *Richard Wagner: The Man, His Mind, and His Music* (London, 1968), 423. Perhaps to strike a Kiplingesque note, Gutman has "noblest race" and "lower breeds"
where Wagner has "noblest race" and "lower races." Several instances of what Lucy
Beckett generously calls Gutman's "blindness to ordinary considerations of logic" appear in her *Richard Wagner, Parsifal* (Cambridge, 1981), 121–23. Apropos of Wagner's
description of Hinduism as a "race-religion," it is of interest that Toynbee characterizes
Hinduism, Zoroastrianism, and Judaism alike as "Janus-faced," the one face turned
outward to all humanity, the other "turned inwards towards the nation among whom
this potentially universal religion originated" (Toynbee, *A Study of History,* XII, 85–88,
294).
34. Wagner, *Briefe in Originalausgaben,* X, 209; Eric Eugène, *Les idées politiques
de Richard Wagner et leur influence sur l'idéologie allemande 1870–1945* (Paris, 1978),
131.

Theodor Adorno's assertion that a "glorified blood-brotherhood" depicted in Wagner's *Parsifal* became the model for the secret societies and führer-orders of Hitler's Germany is wonderfully obtuse. He could have found a more appropriate model in Exodus, where the worshippers of Yahweh are instructed to daub the side posts of their houses with the blood of a lamb, in order that they may be passed over when their national deity comes at midnight to smite "all the firstborn in the land of Egypt, from the firstborn of the Pharaoh . . . unto the firstborn of the captive that was in the dungeon" (Exodus 12 : 23–29). The Paschal celebration in Wagner's *Parsifal* commemorates an act of self-sacrifice, not an act of wholesale infanticide. Neither Wagner's Jesus of Nazareth nor his Parsifal is modeled after the volcanic and often ferocious Yahweh of the Old Testament.[35]

CATHARISM, WAGNERISM, AND NAZISM: A MYTH OF THE TWENTIETH CENTURY

Catholic and Protestant theologians are rarely in agreement as to the precise nature of the Catharist (Albigensian) heresy. A Benedictine abbot offers a Catholic view.

> The Albigenses have received much sympathy, as being a kind of pre-Reformation Protestant; but it is now recognized that their tenets were an extreme form of Manichaeism. They believed in the existence of two gods, a good (whose son was Christ) and an evil (whose son was Satan); matter is the creation of the evil principle, and therefore essentially evil; and the greatest of all sins is sexual intercourse, even in marriage; sinful also is the possession of material goods, and the eating of flesh meat, and many other things. So great was the abhorrence of matter that some even thought it an act of religion to commit suicide by voluntary starvation, or to starve children to death. . . . Such tenets were destructive not only of Catholicism but of Christianity of any kind, and of civil society itself. . . . In 1208, after the

35. Christianity, says Toynbee, relates to Canaanite agricultural religion rather than to the pastoral religion of Israel. He adds: "It was a Canaanite vegetation-god who sacrificed himself for his people in order that they might draw life from eating his flesh and drinking his blood. The Ugaritic Baal and the Byblian Adonis, not the Israelite Yahweh, were the historic models for the Galilean Jesus Christ" (Toynbee, *A Study of History*, XII, 419–20 n. 5). A little over eighty years ago the eminent biblical scholar and historian of the Near East Eduard Meyer characterized the mass slaughter of the firstborn of the Egyptians as the act of a "bloodthirsty deity," a "demon of the night," in his monograph *Die Israeliten und ihre Nachbarstämme. Alttestamentliche Untersuchungen* (1906; rpr. Darmstadt, 1967), 38.

murder of a papal legate, Innocent III called on the Christian princes to suppress the Albigensian heresy by force of arms, and for seven years the south of France was devastated by one of the most bloodthirsty wars in history, the Albigenses being slaughtered by the thousands and their property confiscated wholesale.[36]

But why, asks a Protestant theologian, should it have been necessary for the Catholic church to mount a bloody seven-year war to destroy a people already so intent on destroying itself? And how had property—"confiscated wholesale"—come into the hands of a people who believed that the possession of material goods was sinful? It seemed obvious that the Catholic apologist had ascribed to the Albigenses as a whole a "degree of asceticism which could hardly have been attempted by more than a very few exceptional members of the inner circle of the body (*Cathari* or *perfecti*)." Nor was the time frame accurate. Albigenses were being put to death as early as 1022; some two hundred were burned at the stake in one day at Montségur in 1245, and the Inquisition continued to persecute the remnants of the sect throughout the thirteenth century. With respect to the dualism alleged to be taught by the Cathars, the Protestant theologian remarks:

> Here again it would seem that the case is not quite fairly presented. The most outstanding point of the teaching of the Albigenses, as against their Catholic opponents, appears to have been the rejection by the former of the doctrine of eternal punishment. The Albigenses believed in the ultimate extinction (at all events as far as the human race is concerned) of evil. The Catholics appear to preach that the great mass of humanity which does not "submit itself to the authority of the Roman Pontiff" will throughout all eternity form part of the kingdom of Satan and remain permanently separated from God. While therefore it seems untrue to say that either the Catholics or the Albigenses acknowledged the existence of two opposing deities, the accusation is more comprehensible if brought against the former than against the latter.[37]

36. Cited from Frank Dodd, *Introduction to the Study of Christianity* (London, 1938), 298.

37. *Ibid.*, 298–99. Dodd argues that the Catholic critic's assessment of the Albigenses is "very much like what a hostile and not wholly informed critic might be expected to say about the regular Catholic clergy. The great religious orders . . . prohibit their individual members from owning personal property, in which indeed they follow the example of the early Christian Church. They also prohibit marriage, and this prohibition applies to the Roman Catholic clergy. All of them forbid the use of flesh meat throughout certain seasons of the year, and some indeed (*e.g.*, the Minims) permanently exclude from their diet such articles as meat, eggs, milk, butter and cheese" (*ibid.*, 299).

So much for the religious issues. The series of events with which we are concerned in this section has little to do with the actual history of the Cathars. The phrase "Catharist phenomenon" was employed in 1979 by the French historian Jean-Louis Biget to designate a particular instance of what he terms the "vulgarization of an imagined history" for social, political, religious, artistic, and commercial purposes. The vulgarization of the myth of Catharism culminated in the 1960s. Biget's account of the process as it took place from 1870 on in antiquarian publications, in local and national newspapers and periodicals, in the writings of poets and novelists, and in dictionaries, encyclopedias, and manuals for use in secondary schools is exemplary.[38] The mythographers of Catharism included poets who saw in the Wagner of *Tannhäuser, Lohengrin,* and *Parsifal* the prototype of a modern knight of an artistic grail (a Parsifal who had successfully called Monsalvat into being at Bayreuth), French anticlericals who wanted to break the bond between the Catholic church and the French army (who saw Wagner as one of their own in his opposition to the secular power wielded by the Catholic church since the days of Constantine), and social reformers who looked on the Cathars as their precursors. Later, after Wagner had been darkened in retrospect by the colors of Nazism, a new generation of mythographers was ready with a new myth in which the composer no longer figured as the good Parsifal but as the evil Klingsor.

An understanding of the way in which Wagnerism was incorporated into the mythography of Catharism in France during the last quarter of the nineteenth century affords a plausible explanation of the curious

---

38. Jean-Louis Biget, "Mythographie du catharisme (1870–1960)," in *Cahiers de Fanjeaux. Collection d'histoire religieuse de Languedoc au XIIIᵉ et au début du XIVᵉ siècles. XIV: Historiographie du catharisme* (Toulouse, 1979), 271–342. This fourteenth volume of the *Cahiers de Fanjeaux* is intended to be (writes one of its editors) not a history of Catharism, but a "history of that history," a history, that is, of "publications appearing from the sixteenth to the twentieth century" (*ibid.,* 7). Charles-Olivier Carbonell, one of whose own contributions to the volume deals with the spread of the myth of Catharism to the mass media in France during the 1960s, makes the point that the use of real or imagined history as propaganda is no novelty: "Leaving aside scholarly works, four centuries of the historiography of Catharism show us that Catharism was never anything more than a receptacle for phantasms with which the living believed they could exorcise the dead" (Carbonell, "Vulgarisation et récupération: le catharisme à travers les mass-média," in *Cahiers de Fanjeaux. Collection d'histoire religieuse de Languedoc au XIIIᵉ et au début du XIVᵉ siècles. XIV: Histoire du Catharisme* (Toulouse, 1979), 361–80.

link between French Wagnerites and the defenders of Dreyfus mentioned by Marcel Proust in *Remembrance of Things Past.*[39] And in this
light the continued attachment of Theodor Herzl to Wagner and his
music dramas, even after the Dreyfus affair had converted him from an
assimilationist into a Jewish nationalist, is less puzzling. The Prince de
Guermantes in Proust's novel becomes a Dreyfusard not for ideological reasons but simply because he has examined the evidence and concluded that Dreyfus is innocent. This was true, no doubt, of the many
prominent French non-Jews who came forward to defend Dreyfus,
and who eventually brought about his rehabilitation. In addition to a
love of truth and justice, however, ideological factors were plainly
operative. The Dreyfusards tended to be republican, even socialist, in
their sympathies; they were usually anticlericals, whether as Protestants who had never forgotten the Saint Bartholomew's Day Massacre,
or as Catholics who resented the secular power of the clergy in France.
The French army, which had accused, degraded, and imprisoned Dreyfus, was antirepublican, royalist, and a bastion of conservative Catholicism. Georges Clemenceau, the future wartime premier of France, is
an interesting case in point: republican, socialist, and anticlerical in his
sentiments, he was a typical Dreyfusard (but as ardent a nationalist as
Proust's Prince de Guermantes). In July, 1898, Clemenceau denounced
a eulogy of the French armed forces given by a Dominican priest a few
days earlier, and he recalled, under the rubric "Always the sword and
the aspergillum!" (*i.e.,* always the army in the embrace of the Catholic
clergy), the medieval "pyres of Jews and of Christian heretics." And
in 1899 a journalist in southern France likened the anti-Dreyfusards

39. The passage (not included in the published novel) reads: "Every time you find a
Dreyfusard, scratch a bit. A little deeper you'll find the ghetto, a foreigner, inversion, or
Wagneromania." It is on this basis that a "philosophical anti-Dreyfusard" explains the
pro-Dreyfus sentiments of the Prince de Guermantes, whose anti-Jewish stance otherwise is well-known: first, the Prince's wife is of Bavarian noble blood (the foreigner);
second, she is said to be in love with Charlus (the invert); third, she is known to be a
"passionate Wagnerian" (Wagneromania). In this way, concludes the philosophical anti-
Dreyfusard, "the foreign influence worked its effects on him [the Prince] in an occult
fashion" (Proust, *A la recherche du temps perdu,* II, 1185). Proust may have chosen not
to include this passage in the text of his novel because it fits him more closely than it
does the Prince de Guermantes. The "Marcel" of the novel is Dreyfusard, Wagnerian,
French, and heterosexual. Proust himself was Dreyfusard, Wagnerian, homosexual, and
Jewish (on his mother's side of the family) by descent, although Catholic by religion.

to the "Jesuits who exterminated the Albigensians in the thirteenth century."[40]

"Romanticism," says Biget, "first revived the troubadours, those perfect bards of love." The Albigensians soon found a place among the heroes of freedom. In Germany, for example, Nikolaus Lenau concluded his epic poem *Die Albigenser* (1842) with these lines: "The Hussites follow the Albigensians and bloodily avenge their sufferings; after Huss and Zyska come Luther, Hutten, the Thirty Years War, the rebellion of [the Calvinists of] Cévennes, the Bastille-stormers, and so on." Eighteen years earlier, *The Albigenses,* a Gothic novel by Charles Robert Maturin, had been published in England. Maturin came from a family of clerics, members of the Anglican Church of Ireland, and he was himself curate of St. Peter's in Dublin. His family, which was of French origin, had found refuge in Ireland after the revocation of the Edict of Nantes by Louis XIV in 1685. Maturin stated that his novel was patterned after the romances of Walter Scott, and there are in fact some curious correspondences between Maturin's Albigensian heretics and the Covenanters of Scott's *Old Mortality.*[41]

---

40. Biget, "Mythographie du catharisme," 284–85. The Society of Jesus, however, was not founded until the sixteenth century. According to Biget, the theme of the "sword and the aspergillum" (*sabre et du goupillon*) was first heard at the time of the crusade against the Albigensians (*ibid.,* 284). Dante, in his denunciation of the temporal power wielded by the Roman popes, writes:

> L'un l'altro ha spento, ed è giunta la spada
> Col pastorale, e l'un con l'altro insieme
> Per viva forza mal conviene che vada

("One has extinguished the other, and the sword is joined to the crozier, and the one must perforce go badly with the other")

(*Purgatorio* XVI, 109–111)

For *sabre et goupillon* we have *spada col pastorale.* (Dante, incidentally, is nowhere mentioned in Biget's article).

41. Biget, "Mythographie du catharisme," 284–85. A new (1975) French translation of the poem is listed in his bibliography. The citation is taken from Nicolaus Lenau, *Die Albigenser. Freie Dichtungen* (Stuttgart, 1860), 170 (my translation). Maturin's novel has recently been reprinted (*The Albigenses: A Romance* [4 vols.; New York, 1974]). In his foreword to the novel, James Gray calls Maturin an "Irish parson, haunted by the remembrance of atrocities and persecutions visited upon his French forbears" (*ibid.,* I, viii). Maturin's Albigenses, like Scott's Covenanters, seek refuge in the mountains; their preachers, like those in *Old Mortality,* constantly pour out verbal fire and brimstone. Maturin writes: "It is also a curious, but indisputable matter of fact, that

A synthesis of the various constitutive strata of the Catharist myth was achieved between 1860 and 1870 by Napoléon Peyrat and embodied in his three volume *Histoire des Albigeois*. Protestant, anti-Catholic, romantic, nationalist, revolutionary, regionalist, religious, libertarian, democratic-bourgeois, socialist, and esoteric elements were all combined in this mythic history. Peyrat—a poet, preacher, and visionary rather than a historian—called the Catharist stronghold of Montségur a "Sion of the Essenes," a "Platonic Delphi of the Pyrenees," a "fortress of the Paraclete," a Hussite "Tabor of the Cathars," and a "Golgotha of the Johannite faith." Montségur was also "our aerial tabernacle," and the "throne of Esclarmonde." Esclarmonde, heroic sister of the Count de Foix, played another role than Helen in Peyrat's self-styled iliad of the peoples of the Pyrenees. She was (to those enthusiasts who wanted to raise a monument in her honor shortly before the Great War) a "Joan of Arc of the Midi."[42] Meanwhile, the Catholic party developed what Biget terms an "inverse mythology" (*mythologie inversée*) of Catharism. Catholic churchmen castigated the peoples of the south for their atavistic predisposition to heresy, and in 1892 the Bishop of Albi announced in a pastoral letter to his flock that the Albigensian heresy rested on the "perverse maxim, 'Neither God nor Master.'"[43]

Mysticism and esotericism seem to have developed in the course of the nineteenth century as the reverse aspect of positivism, scientism, and naturalism. The influence of Asiatic religions, in particular of the religions of India, was felt in France after 1840, and between 1890 and 1900 the spiritualist movement was strengthened by the Catharist re-

---

the majority of [the Albigenses] were as tenacious of certain texts and terms of the Old Testament, as their legitimate descendants, the English Puritans . . . like them they assumed Jewish names, fought with Jewish obduracy, and felt with Jewish hostility, even toward those of their community who differed from them in a penumbra of their creed . . . this vituperative and maledictory mode of devotion . . . had become, from their adoption of the Jewish phraseology, too much the habit of the Albigeois" (*ibid.*, I, 137–38, 155). For Wagner's comments on *Old Mortality*, see Chapter 1 herein.

42. Biget, "Mythographie du catharisme," 279–80, 283–84; *cf.* Carlyle's description of the medieval *Nibelungenlied* as a "Northern Iliad," William Morris' and Eirikr Magnusson's characterization of the Volsunga saga as an "Epic of the North" that should be to "our race what the Tale of Troy was to the Greeks," and Houston Stewart Chamberlain's remarks along the same line (Rather, *The Dream of Self-Destruction*, 4, 9, 35).

43. Biget, "Mythographie du catharisme," 285–86.

vival. Among the Provençal poets and men of letters who cultivated the occult aspect of Catharism was the self-styled "Sar" (*i.e.*, king) Joséphin Péladan, who claimed to be a descendant of the Assyrian kings. In 1888 Péladan revived the Order of the Rosy Cross. More important for our purposes was Péladan's grafting of the grail-legend onto Catharism. The abandoned fortress of the Cathars on Montségur was identified with the stronghold of the grail-knights of *Lohengrin* and *Parsifal* on Monsalvat. In 1893 the Gnostic church of France restored to Montségur its status as an episcopal seat, and Jules Doinel, an archivist by profession, was installed as primate of the Albigenses.[44] But the great mass of the French people, in the south as well as in the north, remained untouched by these developments. For the purposes of propaganda, Catharism was still a dead issue. Between 1885 and 1907 a number of attempts, all failures, were made to exploit the Catharist myth for political and economic ends by identifying the small landholders and impoverished winegrowers of the Midi with the Catharist rebels. The bankers in the north of France were likened to Simon de Montfort and the other French barons who had slaughtered the Cathars wholesale in the thirteenth century.[45]

After the Great War a revival of neo-Catharist mysticism and occultism took place in France and Germany. Catharism was variously linked to Celtic druidism, to the hyperborean solar cult of Thule, to Visigothic gnosis, to Hindu religions, and to pre-Roman culture by persons whom Biget describes as "erudite autodidacts, capable of the most extraordinary syntheses and of the most fantastic rapprochements between phenomena of apparently unrelated character." While some of these erudites evoked the spirits of the Tibetan masters or the

44. *Ibid.*, 293–94. As early as 1836 an attempt was made to show that the grail legend was of Provençal origin (Charles-Olivier Carbonell, "D'Augustin Thierry à Napoléon Peyrat: un demi-siècle d'occultation [1820–1870]," in *Cahiers de Fanjeaux. Collection d'histoire religieuse de Languedoc au XIIIᵉ et au début du XIVᵉ siècles. XIV: Histoire du catharisme* [Toulouse, 1979], 153–54.

45. Biget, "Mythographie du catharisme," 301–302. The wine industry of southern France had been hard hit by the depredations of the grape louse, *Phylloxera vastatrix*. This insect pest had reached France from the United States by way of vines sent for grafting. Eventually, the affected vineyards were replanted with louse-resistant American vines. *Cf.* Houston Stewart Chamberlain's argument for Jewish assimilation: "We have, however, reason to hope and believe that the Jews, like the Americans, have brought us not only a new pest but also a new vine" (Rather, *The Dream of Self-Destruction*, 32).

spirit of the Lady Esclarmonde, others searched in the ruins of Montségur for a Johannite evangel that had not been "falsified by Rome."
Among them was Otto Rahn, an enthusiastic young German Wagnerian. Biget writes, "Shortly after [Rahn's] *The Crusade Against the
Grail* appeared, Hitlerism came into power. This work, with its references to Wagner, its exaltation of paganism and Germanism, offered
itself to the Nazi régime for political exploitation." Rahn did little
more than repeat the mythography of Peyrat and Péladan. In *The
Court of Lucifer* (1937) Rahn's message came through more forcefully: "Hatred for the Catholic Church, [which is] Mediterranean and
'judaized' because it reveres Christ. The true god is Lucifer, the bearer
of light, the god of love, principle of the forces of nature, Nordic sun-
god, 'Apollo' of Thule and the Aryans of India, the quintessential god
of Germanism. It was he whom the Cathars had venerated. The Crusade had attempted to exterminate the worshippers, descendants of
the Visigoths, of the German gods."[46]

A mythical Wagner was in this way incorporated into both German
and French versions of Catharist mythography. The real Wagner was
not only unaware of the events described above (since almost all of
them took place after his death), but also, as far as one can tell, uninterested in the Albigensian heresy. Wagner may perhaps have known
of Lenau's poem *Die Albigenser,* but if so, he failed to discuss it with
Cosima at any time between 1869 and 1883.[47] Sixteen years after
Wagner's death, Houston Stewart Chamberlain displayed an equal
lack of concern with the subject of Catharism in his *Foundations of
the Nineteenth Century*. Mythography, however, makes strange bed-
fellows. "Dante was the supreme pontiff of the Cathar sect," Jean-
Michel Angebert tells us, "and his *Divine Comedy* was written with
the express purpose of exalting his faith in the Cathar religion and
heaping abuse on the Papacy for having unleashed the Albigensian
persecution. . . . Sufficient proof is found in Hitler's bedside book *The*

46. Biget, "Mythographie du catharisme," 308–313. Otto Rahn, *Kreuzzug gegen
den Gral. Die Tragödie des Katharismus* (3rd ed.; Stuttgart, 1974). Although Rahn is
said to have been an agent of the Nazi SS, he wrote in the mid-thirties that it had become
impossible for him to live in Germany. Rahn was found in March, 1939, frozen to death
in the Austrian Alps (Rahn, *Kreuzzug*, 305).

47. Lenau's name does not appear in the index of Cosima Wagner's *Diaries*. It is
absent also from the index of Glasenapp's biography of Wagner, as are references to
Catharism or Albigensianism.

Genesis [*sic*] *of the 19th Century,* whose author, H. S. Chamberlain, exalts the heretic Dante and the movement *'Los von Rom'* (Away from Rome)." And in a certain Nazi fortress, where Heinrich Himmler presided as grand master over an "order claiming to descend from the Templars and the Teutonic Knights," the initiates of the order never tired of hearkening back to the times of medieval esotericism. Wagner, says Angebert, was one of the "two prime initiators of the Third Reich," the other being Nietzsche.[48] Dante, Hitler, Himmler, Chamberlain, Nietzsche, and Wagner are thus thrown together to bubble in the same conspiratorial pot.

Although the names of Eugène Aroux and Gabriele Rossetti are not listed in the index of Angebert's book it is likely that his version of Dante as heretic, Cathar, and foe of Roman Catholicism derives from these two writers. Aroux's book, published in 1854 in Paris, was entitled *Dante, Heretic, Revolutionary and Socialist: Revelations of a Catholic in the Middle Ages.* Arthur Waite, after bringing the reader's attention to the carefree way in which Aroux linked the Manichees, Albigenses, Cathars, Templars, Ghibellines, troubadours, Dante, the Freemasons, anticlericalism, gnosticism, revolution, socialism, and the pursuit of the Holy Grail, remarks that with such canons of evidence the old tales of Captain Macheath and Dick Turpin could be construed as "records of a secret attempt to re-establish the Roman hierarchy in Britain."[49]

Aroux relied heavily on Gabriele Rossetti's Dante studies of a few decades earlier. The father of the four Rossettis (Christina, Dante Gabriel, William, and Maria) was, like the man whose writings he undertook to interpret, a political exile. He arrived in England from Italy, by way of Malta, in 1824, and he found for himself a poorly paid post as a professor of Italian literature at King's College, London. An

48. Angebert, *The Occult and the Third Reich,* 31–32, 116, 119. In the original version (*Hitler et la tradition Cathare*) Chamberlain's book is referred to by its French title, *La genèse du XIXᵉ siècle.*

49. Eugène Aroux, *Dante hérétique, revolutionnaire et socialiste. Révélations d'un catholique sur le moyen age* (Paris, 1854); Arthur Edward Waite, *The Hidden Church of the Holy Grail: Its Legends and Symbolism Considered with the Affinity with Certain Mysteries of Initiation and Other Traces of a Secret Tradition in Christian Times* (London, 1909), 530–37, 708. Waite apparently knew that Wagner was being incorporated into the Catharist myth, for on p. 527 of his book he speaks of the attempt on the part of "a few zealous and undiscriminating minds" to identify "Mont Ségur" with "Mont Salvatch" [*sic*].

English translation of his work on Dante appeared in 1834.[50] Eugène
Aroux took over Rossetti's unorthodox interpretation of the *Divine
Comedy* in its entirety, but what the fiercely anti-Romanist Italian
praised in Dante was sheer heresy to the devout French Catholic.[51]
Rossetti's overall theme is a familiar one. There exists, he claims, a certain body of esoteric teachings, rooted in Manichean dualism, and
"called the Gay Science in the middle ages." These teachings have
flowered in the "secret doctrines" of modern times. "This great system
of secret instruction invites us to cast a rapid glance over the five distinct
epochs of the sect. The first is very ancient; the second was in the middle
ages; the third, in the time of Dante; the fourth in the last century; and
the fifth in our own day."[52] Aroux himself characterizes Dante in terms
that would fit Proudhon or Bakunin.

> We have, finally, been forced to assert that he [Dante] had as his goal the
> destruction of the Catholic Church, the abolition of the noblesse of race,
> the elimination of the inheritance of property (which is based, he says, on
> theft and injustice), a complete reversal of position and lot between those
> who possess and those who groan in poverty. . . . [Dante's] plans for social

50. Gabriele Rossetti, *Disquisitions on the Antipapal Spirit Which Produced the
Reformation; Its Secret Influence on the Literature of Europe in General and of Italy in
Particular,* trans. Caroline Ward (2 vols.; London, 1834).
51. For example, Rossetti (*ibid.,* I, 62–63) points out that the dimensions of the
lowest circle of hell given in Dante's *Inferno* are precisely those of the traditional circum-
ference of Rome. And he says that the words—called "unintelligible" by a host of commentators—with which the seventh canto opens should be printed as *Pap' è Satan, Pap'
è Satan, Aleppe. Aleppe* is the Hebrew word *aleph* (prince), and the meaning of the line,
then, is "The Pope is Satan, prince of this hell." Aroux accepts this interpretation (without crediting Rossetti, however) in his book. Of Rossetti, Aroux writes: "Attributing, no
doubt unjustly, to the clergy the exile that has overtaken him and condemned him to end
his days in a strange land, he nourishes a hatred of Rome equal to that of the old
Ghibelline poet. . . . Rome is, for him, the cause of all Italy's ills: ambition, greed, intolerance and persecution have made Rome the plague of humanity" (Aroux, *Dante hérétique,* 439–40).
52. Rossetti, *Disquisitions on the Antipapal Spirit,* II, 185–86. The book concludes with a letter to Sir Charles Lyell (professor of geology in King's College), to
whom it was dedicated. Rossetti says that he will no doubt be called an "ignorant madman" by foes who have already called him a "new Turpin," a "rabbinical illustrator," a
"cabalistic commentator" and a "harlequin annotator." He reminds Lyell that Chaucer,
too, once "fled from England to escape the wrath of the catholic clergy, and stopped at
Padua"; there he met Petrarch and derived from him the allegorical materials for the tale
of Griselda (*ibid.,* 245–59).

regeneration, like the programs of all reformers, liberators and saviors of society in promising everything, happiness, security, liberty, riches, though they have nothing . . . differ not at all from the false utopias for which our age has shown itself to be so deplorably credulous.

And like the critics of our day who profess to admire Wagner's music but to despise the man and what they suppose he stood for, Aroux praises the *Divine Comedy* as "one of the most sublime products of the human spirit," but calls Dante himself an atheist. He was, says Aroux, "one of those men without faith and without honor who, miserably pursuing their vain egoistical interests, dream of and lay plans for revolution, with the hope of raising the edifice of their fortunes on the bloody ruins."[53]

While Chamberlain frequently refers to Dante in the *Foundations of the Nineteenth Century,* he seems to be unaware of the Manichean heretic and revolutionary socialist Dante depicted some fifty years earlier by Aroux and Rossetti. Nevertheless, Chamberlain sees Dante as a heretic of sorts, if only an unconscious one, and says that if the poet were alive today the Catholic church would brand him an atheist. "It is a poor, short-sided orthodoxy which tries to whitewash Dante today," Chamberlain writes, "instead of openly admitting that he belongs to the most dangerous class of genuine protesters." And he asks, "How could a man of Dante's intellectual acumen regard himself as an orthodox Roman Catholic and yet demand the separation of secular and ecclesiastical power, as well as the subordination of the latter to the former?"[54] Chamberlain contrasts Dante unfavorably with St. Francis of Assisi. "Few things are more instructive than a comparison between these outpourings of a man who had become altogether religious and now gathers his sinking strength to sing exultingly to all nature this rapturous *tat tvam asi* and the orthodox, soulless, cold confession of faith of the learned, experienced politician and theologian Dante in the twenty-fourth canto of his *Paradiso.*" And Chamberlain calls Dante's

53. Aroux, *Dante hérétique*, 450, 454.
54. Chamberlain, *Foundations of the Nineteenth Century*, II, 97–98, 104–107. Some fifty years earlier, Schopenhauer (to whom Gabriele Rossetti was unknown) wrote: "One can hardly avoid thinking that behind it [the *Inferno*], for Dante himself, lurks a secret satire on the fine order of this world; a very peculiar taste would otherwise have to be ascribed to someone who derived pleasure in depicting rousing absurdities and endless scenes of torture" (Schopenhauer, *Sämtliche Werke*, V, 523).

proposal that supreme power be transferred from the hands of a pope to those of an emperor "monstrous." Dante will simply have "replaced one tyrant by another."[55]

Wagner gave no attention to Dante the politician and heretic but, with reservations, he admired Dante the poet. An entry of April 27, 1880, in Cosima's diary reads:

> Much talk about Dante in the past few days, R[ichard] is put off by his receding forehead, and the rigid dogmatism in his poem is disturbing. He says that there are certain things human beings have been able to express only in symbols, and the church has committed the crime of consolidating these and forcing them on us as realities through persecution; it is permissible for art to use these symbols, but in a free spirit and not in the rigid forms imposed by the church; since art is a profound form of play, it frees those symbols of all the accretions the human craving for power has attached to them. But Dante did not follow this method.[56]

Dante could not follow this path—followed by Wagner in *Parsifal*—because the church demanded that he treat the symbolic as the real. If we accept the views of Rossetti and Aroux, of course, the *Divine Comedy* allegorically depicts the Rome of the popes as a kind of inferno; but Wagner, as far as we know, regarded Dante as a faithful son of the Catholic church.

The passage from Cosima's diary is so plainly stated that it hardly requires further comment. Wagner's "free spirit," engaged in a profound form of play with symbols which express the otherwise inexpressible, is that of any great artist at work; opposing it is the spirit of

55. Chamberlain, *Foundations of the Nineteenth Century*, II, 144, 425.

56. Cosima Wagner, *Diaries*, II, 470. Wagner added that the life of St. Francis of Assisi was exploited by the Roman church "at the very time the most genuine Christians, the Waldenses, were being persecuted" (*ibid.*). The relationship between the Albigenses and the Waldenses is disputed, but that both groups were persecuted by the Catholic church can hardly be doubted. (Wordsworth touches on the subject in his *Ecclesiastical Sonnets*, pt. 2, no. 14:

> Then followed the Waldensian bands, whom Hate
> In vain endeavours to exterminate,
> Whom Obloquy pursues with hideous bark
> . . . Nor lacks this sea-girt Isle a timely share
> Of the new Flame, not suffered to expire.

See Wordsworth, *The Poetical Works of William Wordsworth*, ed. Thomas Hutchinson, rev. by Ernest de Selincourt [London, 1960], 339).

dogma, freezing the symbols into a fixed reality, belief in which is enforced by the sword and the stake. And in *Parsifal* and in his words to Cosima, Wagner again rejects the human "craving for power"—the Nietzschean will to power, which is itself merely an inversion of Schopenhauer's denial of the will. Earlier he had allegorically depicted that craving in the misuse of the gold of the Rhine by Wotan and his dark counterpart, Alberich. Here he senses it in the forced manipulation of symbols to gain power over human souls—symbols which, like the Rhinegold itself, should have been left to the care of the Muses. Wagner had written of Dante two years earlier:

> Insofar as his great poem was a product of his time, we find it almost repulsive. But it attracted the attention of his contemporaries precisely because it depicted as realities the ideas of medieval religious spookery (*Glaubensspuk*) current in his time. Freed, as we are now, from the ideas of that age, yet drawn by the incomparable force with which he depicts them for us, we find it necessary to make an almost painful effort to put them aside so that the sublime spirit of the poet, in its ideal purity, may, as judge of the world, act on us in freedom—and that the nature of this action has been rightly understood even by posterity is more than uncertain. Hence for us Dante can take on the look of a gigantic apparition, condemned to fearful solitude by the workings of his time.[57]

Here Wagner seems to see Dante as a Prometheus. But his fiery message was rendered almost unintelligible by the ruling spirit of the age.

We return again to Biget's account of the changing course of Catharist-Albigensian mythography. He points out that during World War II a British writer, Hannah Closs, depicted Catharism as a "quest for knowledge and liberation." A few years later the spirit of the French maquisards of 1944 was evoked jointly with that of the embattled thirteenth-century Cathars against a backdrop of what Biget calls "folkloric esotericism." Of Zoé Oldenbourg's Catharist romance *Les Brûlés* (translated into English in 1961 as *Destiny of Fire*), Biget remarks that it "projects into the past a set of problems peculiar to our age: conquest and occupation, repression and partisan warfare." He considers it significant that the Catharist mythographers made their breakthrough into the mass media in France precisely at a time when the revolt in Algiers had made the French public as a whole acutely aware of that set of problems.[58] (Here the Algerian partisans played

57. Wagner, *Gesammelte Schriften und Dichtungen*, X, 93–94.
58. Biget, "Mythographie du catharisme," 319, 323–24.

the role of Cathars, or maquisards, and the French themselves were
the murderous oppressors, perhaps with the paratrooper commander
Jacques Massu as Simon de Montfort.) The Cathars and their modern
representatives were, in the popular mind at least, still on the side of
the angels.

But an antimyth, in which the Cathars appeared in a politically bad
light, had come into being. No doubt its genesis owed something to
Otto Rahn's activities at Montségur in the thirties. Biget takes note
also of an attempt made by Philéas Lebesque, as early as 1938, to trace
the Nazi mystique of "race," "blood," and "will" to medieval Catharism. Lebesque argued that Hitler had found a revelation and a guide
in "the cycle of Parzival," and that behind Hitler stood a secret order
of Cathars. Although Lebesque's article was picked up and cited four
decades later in a work by Christian Bernadac entitled *Le mystère
Otto Rahn. Du catharisme au nazisme* (1978) it attracted little attention when it first appeared.[59] In contrast, a novel of adventure by Pierre
Benoît, member of the French Academy and a native of Albi, reached a
very large audience. This was *Montsalvat* (1957), a melange of Catharism, Wagnerism, grail-mystique, occultism, and esotericism generally. *Montsalvat* does not offer us the antimyth; Catharism and Wagner are presented in this novel in a favorable light. But, says Biget,
Montsalvat "finally situates Germanism and Hitlerism in the province
of Catharism and the grail; it thus prefigures in magisterial fashion the
annexation of the mythology of medieval Provençal to the imaginary
domain of Nazism at the close of the nineteen-fifties."[60]

In the section of his monograph entitled "Catharism and Nazism =

59. *Ibid.*, 314.
60. *Ibid.*, 322. The action of Benoît's *Montsalvat* takes place in 1944, in France,
Spain, and Palestine. Allusions are made to the writings of Otto Rahn, and one of the
grail-seekers is a member of the German *Wehrmacht*. The chapter headings in Benoît's
novel are drawn from the grail-song in act 3, sc. 3, of Wagner's *Lohengrin*. The grail,
here a crystalline chalice, is eventually recovered by a mysterious young woman who
seems to represent both the spirit of Catharism and the sacred dove of *Lohengrin, Parsifal,* and the gospels. She passes it on to her co-searcher, a professor of medieval studies
at Montpellier and a specialist in Catharism. The closing note of Benoît's *Montsalvat*
echoes that of Wagner's *Götterdämmerung:* As Brünnhilde returned Alberich's ring to
the waters of the Rhine, so the professor, after journeying to Palestine, returns the sacred
chalice to the waters of the Jordan. A dove briefly circles overhead as the grail slowly
sinks beneath the waves (Benoît, *Oeuvres romanesques* [7 vols.; Paris, 1966–1970], V,
1492).

a 'myth of the 20th century'" Biget remarks that *Der Mythus des 20.
Jahrhunderts* (1930), a work by the Nazi ideologist Alfred Rosenberg,
is often cited in support of the antimyth that Catharism equals Nazism.
Biget sums up the relevant aspect of Rosenberg's book as follows.

> There are certain connections between the romantic view of Catharism,
> Peyrat's ideas on the genius of the Provence (*génie d'oc*), the glory of race
> and the grandeur of the struggle for freedom, and the racist ideas of Rosen-
> berg. But these convergences have no connection whatsoever with Nazi
> doctrine: *The Myth of the Twentieth Century*, a bulky and prolix work of
> almost five hundred pages, disposes of Catharism in four or five lines that
> pigeon-hole it along with an assortment of heresies. . . . Catharism means
> almost nothing to him, any more than it meant for other leaders of the
> Third Reich.[61]

Another distinguished historian of Catharism, Jean Duvernoy,
agrees with Biget's rejection of this "myth of the 20th century." Duvernoy points out also that the ideologists of Nazism never attacked the
Old Testament God—unlike the Catharists, who remained true to
their anti-Yahwist gnostic heritage.[62] Nazism was in many ways an
anti-Catharist movement. For one thing, it was male-dominated and
antifeminist: the dearth of prominent females among the Nazis contrasts rather startlingly with their relative abundance among the Communists. And one of the documents included in a recent book on
Hitler and secret societies by René Alleau is the transcript of a Vichy
radio broadcast on May 4, 1943, indiscriminately attacking gnostics,
occultists, Freemasons, Bavarian Illuminati, and Jews.[63] The Old Tes-

61. Biget, "Mythographie du catharisme," 314–15. Alfred Rosenberg, *Der
Mythus des 20. Jahrhunderts* (189–194th ed.; Munich, 1942). Rosenberg states: "The
history of the Albigenses, Waldenses, Cathars, Arnoldists, Stedingers, Huguenots, Re-
formists, and Lutherans, together with the history of the martyrs of free investigation,
and the presentations of the heroes of Nordic philosophy, presents the sublime picture of
a gigantic battle for *character-values*" (p. 88). Two pages later he says that the German
Waldenses received a warm welcome in "Gothic-Albigensian Provence." Rosenberg's
book was only less widely circulated than Hitler's *Mein Kampf*.
62. Jean Duvernoy, *Le catharisme: l'histoire des cathares* (Toulouse, 1979), 345.
Duvernoy briefly discusses the mythography of Catharism in an appendix, "Prolonge-
ments et histoire littéraire," pp. 335–45.
63. René Alleau, *Hitler et les sociétés secrètes* (Paris, 1969). The Nazi-controlled
Vichy broadcast included the following passage: "We say again that other Jewish elements, more or less related to Judaism either in spirit or by way of the Kabbala, have
contributed to the formation of Freemasonry, although it would be premature to claim

tament God of the Jews had long since been received in Germany as a *deutscher Gott,* a German God. Other than to expel the Jews from the partnership, the Nazis did nothing to change this state of affairs. The most assiduous worshipper of the national deity was Hitler himself, proud celebrator of the "triumph of the will" at Nuremberg.

A final step in the exploitation of the Catharist myth was still to come. Some ten million television viewers in France on March 29, 1966, were presented with the story of the Cathars, and the program had as one of its results a vast pilgrimage, by automobile, to Montségur on the following Sunday. The myth had been modestly exploited in the interests of tourism even in the days of Napoléon Peyrat, but now commercial interests were aroused on a larger scale. "In real Cathar country, Montségur is also a fine cheese," an advertisement in the *Dépêche du Midi* of August 7, 1973, informed its readers, and it reminded them of the "terrifying history of Montségur," as told in the romances of the Duke de Levis-Mirepoix, "member of the French Academy." For the discriminating tourist "vin de Cathares" was available with the cheese. The sixth annual Catharist motorcyclist rally took place in 1978 at the foot of Montségur, and young people were urged to ski the slopes of the Monts d'Olmes "in real Cathar country," on the grounds that "les cathares sont sympas." Biget's closing words are much to the point. "The fancied image of Catharism," he writes, "has no relevance whatsoever to the history of the medieval past, but it tells us a great deal about the successive presents on which it is projected."[64]

MUSICO-SOCIOLOGY: WAGNER'S CHRISTIAN HARMONY

The Spinoza of Auerbach's biographical novel *Spinoza. Ein Denkerleben* discovers at the crucial point in his spiritual growth that he is a "son of humanity" and no longer a "son of Israel." Likewise, the Jesus of Wagner's posthumously published sketch *Jesus von Nazareth* re-

---

that Freemasonry was of Jewish origin. Gnostics, alchemists, Protestant deists of the school of John Toland, Bavarian Illuminati, Encyclopedists, in a word, all who were passionately attached to natural religion, took part in its creation. . . . To conclude, we may say that between Jews and Masons there is a close alliance and collusion in anti-Christian activities" (*ibid.,* 301).

64. Carbonell, "Vulgarisation et récupération," 364; Biget, "Mythographie du catharisme," 288, 332.

jects the temptation to become an earthly Messiah of a purely Jewish kingdom of this world, and goes forth to preach a universal kingdom not of this world.[65] It is possible, even likely, that the rejection of Jewish particularism by Wagner's Jesus owed something to Auerbach's Spinoza, for the conversations of Wagner and Auerbach on the Jewish question took place during the years between the publication of the novel in 1837 and the writing of the sketch in 1848–1849.[66]

The mottos "compassion" (*Mitleid*) and "the purely human" (*das Reinmenschliche*)—rather than Constantine's *in hoc signo vinces*— would seem to have accompanied Wagner's mind's-eye view of the universal kingdom of humanity. They would have been equally acceptable in this role to Auerbach (and Tolstoy). We recall that when Wagner, in the 1860s, looked back on his conversations with Auerbach in Dresden in the 1840s he saw the writer as someone who had learned compassion through suffering. And in one of the tales of life in the Black Forest that first brought him to Wagner's attention, Auerbach has a village Jew show active compassion for a cast-off Christian woman. It is no accident that in this tale the phrase "the purely human" makes two appearances. This phrase, widely used at the time, simply means that confessional barriers to the spread of compassion, to the sharing of a common humanity, have been overthrown.[67]

In Wagner's "The Art-Work of the Future" (1849) the following passage occurs.

> The life-need (*Lebensbedürfniss*) of life-needs is, however, the love-need (*Liebesbedürfniss*). As the conditions of natural human life are given in the

65. *Cf.* Chapter 5, note 96, herein.

66. *Cf.*, "Wagner's Christianity" in Chapter 5 herein for an account of these conversations. There are no references to Spinoza in Wagner's autobiography. Cosima's diaries contain a single reference, in an entry dated June 6, 1870: "Yesterday evening he [Wagner] spoke a long time about philosophy and said that from Plato to Kant there had been no real progress; that Spinoza, for instance, who had acknowledged the wickedness of the world, had still taken this world as it appears to us for the reality" (Cosima Wagner, *Diaries*, I, 230).

67. Auerbach, "Schlossbauers Vefele," in *Werke*, I, pt. 2, pp. 53–83. *Cf.* the physician Rudolf Virchow's assertion in 1866: "The care of the ill is in the highest sense a *purely human* task. Among civilized peoples the hospital has long since ceased to be an institution serving confessional purposes. A general hospital does not turn away from its threshold a heathen or believer in another faith. It leaves each of its wards free to pray or not, and if so to whom. It cares for him as a *human being*, were he the most depraved human being or a known criminal" (Virchow's emphasis; Virchow, *Collected Essays on Public Health and Epidemiology*, ed. L. J. Rather [2 vols.; Canton, Mass., 1985], II, 18).

love-bond (*Liebesbund*) of the subordinated forces of nature that longed for sympathy, redemption, and, merging into something higher, precisely the human being (*Mensch*), so also the human being finds sympathy, redemption, and satisfaction likewise only in something higher. And this something higher is humankind, the community of human beings (*die menschliche Gattung, die Gemeinschaft der Menschen*). For there is only one thing higher than the individual human being and this is humanity as a whole.

How can such community be achieved? Wagner answers that it can be achieved only by giving instead of taking. Unselfish love, alone, truly satisfies the love-need. "Human beings can satisfy the love-need only by giving, that is by giving themselves to another human being and, in the highest case, to humanity as a whole. The horrible thing about the absolute egoist (*den absoluten Egoisten*) is that he sees in other human beings merely the natural factors of his existence, and that he consumes them—although at times in a very peculiar, barbarically cultivated way—as fruits and animals of nature, never wanting to *give,* that is, but only to *take.*"[68]

In 1854 Wagner (in the course of explaining the meaning of the *Ring* poem) wrote to his friend August Röckel: "Egoism truly comes to an end only in the merging of an 'I' ('*Ich*') with a 'thou' ('*Du*'), but the 'thou' does not present itself at once when I place myself in conjunction with the whole world: 'I' and 'the world' are nothing more than 'I' alone; the world becomes fully actual for me only when it has become for me a 'thou,' and this it becomes only in the presence of a beloved individual."[69] Which is as much as to say: Only a whole human being (*Mensch*), formed by the conjunction of a man and a woman, is capable of entering into the community of human beings (*die menschliche Gattung, die Gemeinschaft der Menschen*).

Wagner states in *Opera and Drama* that "the purely human" con-

68. Wagner, *Gesammelte Schriften und Dichtungen*, III, 68–69.

69. La Mara, *Richard Wagner an August Röckel* (Leipzig, 1903), 29–30, cited in Rather, *The Dream of Self-Destruction*, 66. Martin Buber's book *I and Thou* (*Ich und Du*) was first published in 1923. Hermann Cohen's use of the "I-thou" concept in 1908 is said to have been "logical" rather than "ontological" (Cohen, *Reason and Hope*, 29). Wagner's use would seem to fall into the same character as Buber's, *i.e.,* the "ontological." Wagner was at this time still devoted to the philosophy of Ludwig Feuerbach, whose writings were haunted from beginning to end by the "I-thou" relationship, according to Marx W. Wartofsky, *Feuerbach* (Cambridge, 1977), 34–35.

stitutes the nature or essence (*Wesen*) of humankind (*der mensch-lichen Gattung*). An isolated individual, that is, cannot be a whole hu-man being, much less part of the human community. (It is worth noting that Wagner uses the term *Gattung* here, with its built-in mean-ing of "consort" or "spouse," rather than a more biological term, such as *Rasse*.) The artistic roots of Wagner's leading idea now appear. He speaks of the necessary conjunction between tone and word, between emotion and understanding, between head and heart. Goethe's "eter-nal feminine," or "eternal womanly" (*das ewige Weibliche*), says Wag-ner, draws the egoistic male principle into a larger union: "Bound only by love into a human being, the male and the female [principles] draw nourishment from the purely human."[70] And in "A Communication to My Friends" he argues that only a combined art form, namely the mu-sic drama, can adequately express a purely human content: "A content solely comprehensible to the understanding is communicable solely in verbal language, but the more [the content] is enlarged to include the emotional factor, the more it needs a [mode of] expression that in the end only tonal language can offer with the corresponding fullness. Thus the content of what the poet-musician has to express is entirely intrinsically specified: it is *the purely human, free of all convention*."[71]

Wagner's "musico-sociological" procedure is best illustrated by the following passage from *Opera and Drama*. Here a discussion of key relationships in music is at once a discussion of social relationships among groups of human beings. The vocabulary calls for careful at-tention.

> The key (*Tonart*) is the most closely bound and interrelated family (*Fami-lie*) of the whole class of tones (*ganzen Tongattung*), but it shows itself as truly related to the whole class of tones only where—due to an inclination on the part of an individual member of the tone-family—it advances to an

70. Wagner, *Gesammelte Schriften und Dichtungen*, IV, 102.

71. *Ibid.*, 318. For Wagner's treatment of Schiller's "mode," or "convention," in his analysis of Beethoven's *Ninth Symphony*, see Rather, *The Dream of Self-Destruc-tion*, 145–46. Wagner's debt to Schiller's conception of "the purely human" in art is discussed by Marie Haefliger Graves in her dissertation, *Schiller and Wagner: A Study of Their Dramatic Theory and Technique* (Ann Arbor, Mich., 1938), 92, *passim*. See also Henri Lichtenberger, "Schiller jugé par Wagner," in *Études sur Schiller. Bibliothèque de philologie et de littérature moderne* (Paris, 1905), 199–212. On Wagner's conception of "the purely human" in relation to the ideas of Ludwig Feuerbach, see chap. 4 of Rudolf Louis' *Die Weltanschauung Richard Wagners* (Leipzig, 1898).

involuntary conjunction with other keys. Here we can very appropriately compare the key to the old patriarchal tribal families (*Stammfamilien*) of human stocks (*menschlichen Geschlechter*): due to an involuntary error the members of these families thought of themselves as separate rather than as members of the whole class of human beings (*Besondere, nicht als Glieder der ganzen menschlichen Gattung*). Inflamed by unaccustomed rather than by accustomed appearances, sexual love on the part of the individual alone passed over the barriers of the patriarchal family and formed alliances with other families. Christianity, in a prophetic transport, announced the unity of all human beings (*die Einheit der menschlichen Gattung*). Music, the art that has Christianity to thank for its fullest development, took that gospel within and shaped it in the new language of tones into a rich, ravishing pronouncement to the sensuous feelings. Comparing the primal patriarchal national melodies, those characteristic family heirlooms of separate tribes (*Stämme*), with the melody that has been made possible through the development of Christianity, we find that there, characteristically, the melody almost never moves out of one given key, seemingly having fused with it immovably. The melody possible for us, on the contrary, has acquired the most many-sided and remarkable ability to connect by means of harmonic modulation the initially-struck chief key with the most distant tone-families [*i.e.*, keys], so that in a larger composition (*Tonsatz*) the primal relationship of all keys appears, as it were, in the light of one particular chief key.[72]

By means of a musical metaphor, Wagner is saying here what he has already said in "The Art-Work of the Future" and will say again in his letter to Röckel: When a loving couple recognizes its members to be one and the same, the first step toward the attainment of universal human community has been taken. With "absolute egoism" thus overthrown by the development of an "I-thou" relationship, the way is then opened to the formation of unions of greater and greater scope. The process culminates in the union of all human beings under the sign of "the purely human." Alternatively, we may say that Wagner has used a socially based metaphor to recount the musical steps taken toward the recognition of the primal unity of all keys in the course of the development of Christian harmony.

Early in the present century a well-known musicologist of the time

---

72. *Ibid.*, IV, 148–49. The Siegfried of Wagner's *Ring* breaks the barrier posed by the runically-engraved spear of convention held in his way by the patriarchal god Wotan, passes through the magic chromatic fire of Loge, and, in uniting himself with Brünnhilde, takes the first step toward "the purely human."

remarked that the musical meaning of Wagner's analogy between tribal families and tonal families was clear enough to the student of harmony. If one recognized the second tetrachord of any ordinary major scale to be the first tetrachord of the next key (in the usual order), one saw that the leading note of the first tetrachord was the mediant of the new key. The leading note is, as it were, a "youthful member of the family who is . . . awaiting the opportunity to unite himself with a neighbouring or modulative tetrachord."[73] So much is true, but we should recognize also that Wagner's chief aim was not to teach harmony by analogy but to grasp the social meaning of the historical development of the materials used in musical composition.

In the course of development leading from the ancient Greek modes to modern tonality and equal temperament there was a time, so we are told by another musicologist, when the "relation of different keys to one another was almost beyond human conception."[74] Wagner's aim is to break through the barriers separating one key from another, just as it is his aim to break through the barriers that separate human beings from each other. By following this path he attains his goal, the musico-social realm of the purely human. Musical modulation is thus the equivalent of social assimilation. In Wagner's system tonality remains intact: the keys are shown to be separated by no impassable barriers, but they do not, for this reason, vanish from the earth. The key-defining interval of the perfect fifth is in a sense highly democratic, that is, in the system of keys so defined the tonic of one key may be considered as the dominant of the fifth below it and so on, as we move around the ring of harmonically tempered keys.

The chromatic style in music—culminating in Wagner's *Tristan and Isolde*—has in recent years occasioned some interesting sociological reflections. Charles Rosen points out that all three masters of the classical diatonic style were actively involved in its overthrow. Haydn's self-created artistic personality "prevented, by its assumption of an easy-going generality, the full development of the subversive and revolutionary aspect of his art." The music of Mozart, "shockingly voluptuous" in its expression of suffering and terror, wears a mask of sheer

73. Edwin Evans, Sr., *Wagner's Teachings by Analogy* (London, n.d.), 5–6. Evans (1874–1945) also published new translations of Wagner's "Judaism in Music" and *Opera and Drama*.
74. *S.v.* "Modes, Ecclesiastical" and "Modulation" (by Sir C. Hubert Parry), in *Grove's Dictionary of Music and Musicians*.

physical beauty, but in its own time, says Rosen, it often evoked "uneasiness and even dismay." Mozart's assault on the musical language
that he himself had helped create was mounted with the aid of a chromatic style later exploited by Chopin and by Wagner. "The powerful
chromaticism that [Mozart] could employ with such ease comes near
at moments to destroying the tonal clarity that was essential to the significance of his own forms, and it was this chromaticism that had a
real influence on the Romantic style, on Chopin and Wagner in particular." As for Beethoven, his attack on the established order is "naked."
All great art is subversive, insists Rosen. Great art "attacks established
values, and replaces them with those of its own creation; it substitutes
its own order for that of society."[75]

Only by "recreating in our own minds the conditions under which
[Mozart's music] could still seem dangerous," Rosen tells us, can we
understand the uneasiness and dismay that it occasioned among his
eighteenth-century contemporaries.[76] Robert Craft, however, in calling
attention to the chromaticism, syncopations, dotted rhythms, explo-
sive accents, and "almost Wagnerian" volume of Mozart's *Don Giovanni*, remarks rightly that, while the music may still terrify us, its
"impact on Mozart's audience . . . may scarcely be imagined."[77]

To place ourselves once again within the spirit of past times is not as
impossible as Goethe said it was (*Faust*, 575–79), but the recreated
Zeitgeist is inevitably somewhat bloodless. We need the testimony of
contemporary witnesses. Who would today *feel* the music of *Tannhäuser* as the expression of a "falling back into Spinozism," as an "ab-

75. Charles Rosen, *The Classical Style: Haydn, Mozart, Beethoven* (New York,
1972), 325–26. *Cf.* E. T. A. Hoffmann (writing in 1810 in a study of Beethoven's *Fifth
Symphony*): "In Haydn's composition the expression of a childlike, cheerful disposition
prevails. His symphonies lead us into an endless green meadow, into a lusty, colorful
crowd of happy human beings. . . . A life full of love, of bliss, before sin (*wie vor der
Sünde*), of eternal youth . . . Mozart leads us into the depths of the spirit world. Fear
encircles us, but without agony, and more as an intimation of the infinite . . . the night of
the spirit world dissolves into a bright purple glimmering . . . Beethoven's instrumental
music, too, opens up for us the realm of the monstrous and the immeasurable." And in
Hoffmann's essay "Old and New Church Music" (1814) we read: "Haydn, Mozart
[and] Beethoven developed a new art, the first germ of which showed itself indeed as
early as the middle of the eighteenth century" (E. T. A. Hoffmann, *Schriften zur Musik;
Nachlese* [Munich, n.d.], 35–36, 230).
76. Rosen, *The Classical Style*, p. 325.
77. Robert Craft, *Current Convictions: Views and Reviews* (New York, 1977), 28.

dication of the self" rooted in "materialism and socialism," as did Amiel in Geneva in 1857?[78] Or that the Page of Mozart's *Figaro* represents the first stage of the "musical-erotic," Papageno in *The Magic Flute* the second stage, and *Don Giovanni,* with its "irresistible and demoniac" seductiveness, the third stage of a dialectical development in which music has the role of a "love-potion," as did Kierkegaard in 1843?[79] Or that music heard in the nineteenth century could strike some of its listeners as a devil's elixir, unethical and conducive to depravity, as it did Auerbach and Tolstoy?[80]

Chromatic is said to be derived from χρωματίκος, the name of one of the ancient tetrachords, the notes of which were formerly supposed to be similar to the chromatic scale of modern times.[81] It is difficult to say whether the visual or aural sense of the term came first, or, indeed, whether it makes sense to ask. Lévi-Strauss has pursued "chromaticism" into the jungle-world of myth. He cites the following passage from Jean-Jacques Rousseau's *Dictionnaire de musique* (1767): "Chromaticism comes from the Greek χρῶμα, which means color . . . this particular style adds beauty and variety to the diatonic through its semitones, which produce, in music, the same effect as is produced in painting by the variety of colors." In the corpus of South American myths with which Lévi-Strauss is concerned, it appears that *visual* chromaticism takes the place of *aural* chromaticism in the Western tradition, where, Lévi-Strauss says, "from Plato and Aristotle on," the latter has been "treated . . . with the same mistrust and credited with the same ambiguity." An Arecuna myth about the origin of fish poison,

78. Amiel, *Journal,* 81–82.

79. Søren Kierkegaard, *Either/Or: A Fragment of Life,* trans. David F. and Lillian Marvin Swenson (2 vols.; Princeton, 1949), I, 63–69, *passim. Cf.* E. T. A. Hoffmann's claim of about three decades earlier that the "magic power of music works like the wondrous elixir of the wise, a few drops of which make all drinks splendid and delicious. . . . The lyre of Orpheus opens the gates of Orcus" (Hoffmann, *Schriften zur Musik,* 36). Robert Craft notes that we have become accustomed to associate *Tristan und Isolde* with "unholy eroticism" and to pass over the eroticism of Mozart's operas. With reference to Wagner's *Tristan* and Mozart's *Cosi fan tutte,* Craft writes: "In comparison, the passion and voluptuousness of Wagner's music-drama are purity itself, portraying a love which is true unto death" (Craft, *Current Convictions,* 19). See also Craft's discussion of Kierkegaard's views on Mozart in the same volume.

80. See Chapter 5, note 109 and corresponding text, herein. The reaction of some listeners today to rock music (and the accompanying lyrics) at once comes to mind. Little sensitivity is required here, for the "diabolism" is often overt.

81. *S.v.* "chromatic," in *Grove's Dictionary of Music and Musicians.*

for example, "includes an episode . . . which presents the fragmentation of the rainbow as the cause of the anatomical discontinuity of
living species." Lévi-Strauss continues:

> Behind the juxtaposition of seemingly incongruous themes, we can dimly
> perceive the action of a dialectic . . . of the chromatic and the diatonic. It is
> as if South American thought, being resolutely pessimistic in inspiration
> and diatonic in orientation, invested chromaticism with a primordial malef-
> icence of such a kind that long intervals, which are necessary in culture for
> it to exist and in nature for it to be "thinkable" to men, can only be the
> result of the self-destruction of a primal continuity, whose power is still to
> be felt at those rare points where it has survived its own self-destructiveness:
> either to the advantage of men, in the form of poisons they have learned to
> handle; or to their own disadvantage, in the form of the rainbow over
> which they have no control.

After pointing out that in Guiana the rainbow is called by the name of
the opossum, and that the opossum of myth is a "giver of life and a
giver of death," hence a "chromatic being," Lévi-Strauss abruptly
shifts gears from the world of myth to the world of the music drama.

> I will not go so far as to suggest that Isolde can be reduced to an "opossum
> function." But, since the analysis of South American myths has led us to
> consider fishing or hunting poison as a combinatory variant of the seducer,
> who is a poisoner of the social order, and to see both poison and seducer as
> two modalities between nature and culture of the domain of short [i.e.,
> chromatic] intervals, we may conclude that the love philter and the death
> philter [in Wagner's Tristan] are interchangeable for reasons other than
> those of simple expedience, and we may thus be prompted to reflect anew
> on the fundamental causes of the chromaticism in Tristan.[82]

Lévi-Strauss does not mention the reflections of Wagner himself, in
1850, on the meaning of the dissolution of tonal barriers, nor those of
Oswald Spengler in Munich at the time of the Great War. Wagner, as
we have seen, looked on the positive side: the barriers were not dis-
solved so much as surmounted, in the name of progressively higher
unions. To Spengler, however, the aural chromaticism of Wagner's Tristan marked not only the dissolution of the old musical order but the
end of Western civilization as a whole. Calling Tristan the "giant key-
stone of Western music," Spengler sees the curve of the musical arc de-

82. Lévi-Strauss, *The Raw and the Cooked*, 278–81, *passim*.

clining from then on into old age and death. Here, Spengler tells us in
The Decline of the West, "the last of the Faustian arts died."[83]

Spengler linked Wagner's chromatic style to that of Edouard Manet,
the first of the French impressionists. "Between Wagner and Manet
there is a deep relationship, which is not, indeed, obvious to everyone
but which Baudelaire with his unerring flair for the decadent detected at
once." And Spengler describes Wagner's music in Turneresque terms.

> For the Impressionists, the end and culmination of art was the conjuring up
> of a world in space out of strokes and patches of colour, and this was just
> what Wagner achieved with three bars. A whole world of soul could crowd
> into these three bars. Colours of starry midnight, of sweeping clouds, of
> autumn, of the day dawning in fear and sorrow, sudden glimpses of sun-
> lit distances, world-fear, impending doom, despair and its fierce efforts,
> hopeless hope—all these impressions, which no composer before him had
> thought it possible to catch, he could paint with entire distinctness in the
> few tones of a motive.[84]

Using a metaphor that goes back before Wagner himself to Kant and
Jean Paul, Spengler says that a Wagnerian motive "comes up out of the
dark terrible deeps" [*i.e.,* the depths of the unconscious]. "Whatever
this is," he concludes, "it is neither painting nor music, in any sense of
these words that attaches to previous work in the strict style."[85]

Spengler was conscious only of the dissolution of the old forms, and

83. Oswald Spengler, *The Decline of the West,* trans. C. F. Atkinson (2 vols. in 1;
New York, 1939), I, 291; Spengler, *Der Untergang des Abendlandes* (2 vols.; Munich,
1918), I, 393. *Cf.* Wagner's use of *Untergang* (*i.e.,* a "going-under") at the close of his
essay "Judaism in Music." There too—as in his treatment of tonal relationships in
Opera and Drama—the emphasis is on the unity achieved rather than on the threat
posed by the dissolution of the old barriers. In connection with Spengler's masterpiece,
cf. W. M. Flinders Petrie's almost simultaneous claim that music was the last of the
Western fine arts to reach maturity, and that in our day only science and technology are
open to further development, in his comparative chronological study of civilizations (Petrie, *The Revolutions of Civilisation* [London, 1912], 96–97.) Similarly, Spengler advises young men to "devote themselves to technics instead of lyrics, the sea instead of the
paintbrush, and politics instead of epistemology" (Spengler, *The Decline of the West,*
I, 41).

84. Spengler, *The Decline of the West,* I, 292.

85. *Ibid.,* 292–93. See Chapter 1 herein for Wagner's account of the circumstances
under which the opening motive of the *Ring* came to him at Spezia, as he lay on his bed
in a "somnambulistic" state.

he tends to overlook the carefully structured character of Wagner's music, taken on its own terms.[86] More important to ask at this point are the conclusions drawn by Spengler from his initial thesis that individual, discrete "folk-souls," Apollinian, Magian, Faustian, and the like, are forever separate and mutually unassimilable—quite unlike Wagner's tribal families of tones. These souls spring up from a particular soil, flourish for their thousand-year day, grow old and die, or remain in a petrified state, frozen in a dying posture, over additional thousands of years—as in the case of the civilization of ancient Egypt. The repudiation of the Faustian folk by such men as Wagner and Marx in the name of a higher unity is, says Spengler, an act of self-repudiation committed by a "Faustian nihilist."[87] Spengler admits, however, that the "idea of a socialist Nirvana has its justification insofar as European weariness clothes its flight from the struggle for existence with the slogans of world-peace, humanity and the brotherhood of human beings."[88]

As Spengler sees it, with the eye of the morphologically aware naturalist-historian, the various, plantlike folk-souls that spring from a particular soil of the planet Earth to give rise to organically integrated cultures are forever separate, peculiar, and unassimilable—incapable of dialectical union in a higher synthesis or of joining together in Wagner's universal harmony. Such an outcome constitutes the repudiation of self, and a "lie of life" (*Lebenslüge*), says Spengler, borrowing the latter phrase from Henrik Ibsen. And Spengler concludes, "This lie of life is the foundation of [Wagner's] Bayreuth . . . and a trace of the lie clings to the whole of political, economic, and ethical socialism."[89]

Spengler to the contrary, in our own day this so-called lie of life

86. *Cf.* Curt von Westernhagen, *The Forging of the 'Ring': Richard Wagner's Composition Sketches for Der Ring des Nibelungen*, trans. Arnold and Mary Whittall (Cambridge, 1976), *passim.*

87. Spengler, *The Decline of the West*, I, 357.

88. Spengler, *Der Untergang des Abendlandes*, I, 498; *Decline of the West*, I, 357.

89. *Ibid.*, I, 510–11; Spengler, *The Decline of the West*, I, 363–64. To emphasize the fact that Spengler's "folk" is not a biological category, John R. Baker cites the following passage from *The Decline of the West*: "*Völkerformen* may change their speech, race, name, and country; so long as their soul lasts, they engulf men of any thinkable origin and remodel them. . . . One certainly does not suppose that a *Volk* was ever held together by mere unity of bodily inheritance. . . . It cannot be often enough repeated that his physiological origin exists only for science . . . and that no *Volk* has advanced itself for *this* ideal of 'pure blood'" (Baker, *Race*, 54).

must be recognized as life's deepest truth. A livable world will continue to elude us unless we repudiate, as Wagner—however imperfectly— did, the belief that peoples, races, tribes, classes, and the human sexes themselves are discrete entities, forever set apart from each other and incapable of musically harmonious bonding or fusion at the higher level of pure humanity.[90]

90. "Both Fascism and Communism are theocratic, in the sense that they place temporal and spiritual authority in the same hands. But whereas Communism aspires to be a universal religion like Christianity, and welcomes disciples of all races, the German fascists have reverted to a tribal faith strangely resembling that of the early Semites. Hitler's German God is like Jahve, the volcano-god whom the Hebrews are said to have followed after the death of Moses (*cf.* Freud's *Moses and Monotheism*). The German conquest of Europe is conducted in the same spirit as the Hebrew conquest of Canaan, the Promised Land, this being an earlier synonym of *Lebensraum*" (Malcolm Cowley, "Communism and Christianity," in *The Flower and the Leaf,* ed. Donald W. Faulkner [New York, 1985], 14).

BIBLIOGRAPHY

Not listed here are *Grove's Dictionary of Music and Musicians,* Hastings' *Encyclopaedia of Religion and Ethics,* and other standard works of reference cited in the chapter notes. A few books and articles referred to in passing have also been omitted.

Ackerknecht, Erwin. *Rudolf Virchow: Doctor, Statesman, Anthropologist.* Madison, Wis., 1953.

Adorno, Theodor. *Versuch über Wagner.* Berlin, 1952.

————. *Mes souvenirs.* 3rd ed. Paris, 1880.

Alleau, René. *Hitler et les sociétés secrètes.* Paris, 1969.

Amiel, Henri Frédéric. *Amiel's Journal: Being the Journal Intime of Henri Frederic Amiel.* Translated by Mrs. Humphrey Ward. New York, 1928.

Angebert, Jean-Michel. *Hitler et la tradition Cathare.* Paris, 1971.

————. *The Occult and the Third Reich: The Mystical Origins of Nazism and the Search for the Holy Grail.* Translated by Lewis A. M. Sumberg. New York, 1974.

Aquinas, Thomas. *Divi Thomae Aquinatis summa theologica.* Editio altera. 6 vols. Rome, 1894.

Ariosto, Lodovico. *Orlando Furioso. Translated into English Heroical Verse by Sir John Harington (1591).* Edited by Robert McNulty. Oxford, 1972.

Aroux, Eugène. *Dante Hérétique, revolutionnaire et socialiste. Révélations d'un catholique sur le moyen age.* Paris, 1854.

Auden, W. H. *New Year Letter.* London, 1941.

Auerbach, Berthold. *Werke.* 15 vols. in 4. Leipzig, 1913.

Augier, Emile. *Théâtre complet.* 6 vols. Paris, 1885–86.

Bainton, Roland. *Christian Attitudes Toward War and Peace: A Historical Survey and Re-evaluation.* New York, 1960.

Baker, John. *Race.* Oxford, 1974.

Bakunin, Mikhail. *Bakunin's Writings.* Edited by Guy A. Aldred. 1947; rpr. New York, 1972.

———. *Oeuvres.* 6 vols. Paris, 1907–13.

Balzac, Honoré de. *Oeuvres complètes.* Edited and annotated by Marcel Bouteron and Henri Longnon. 40 vols. Paris, 1912–40.

———. *The Works of Honoré de Balzac.* Translated by J. Walker McSpadden. 36 vols. New York, n.d.

Barrucand, Pierre. *Les sociétés secrètes. Entretiens avec Robert Amadou.* Paris, 1968.

Barton, Bruce. *The Man Nobody Knows.* Indianapolis, 1924.

Baudelaire, Charles. *Baudelaire: Correspondance.* Edited by Claude Pichois and Jean Ziegler. 2 vols. Paris, 1966–73.

———. *Oeuvres complètes.* Edited by Marcel Ruff. Paris, 1968.

———. *Oeuvres complètes de Charles Baudelaire.* Edited by Jacques Crepet. 19 vols. Paris, 1923–53.

Beckett, Lucy. *Richard Wagner, Parsifal.* Cambridge, 1981.

Béguin, Albert. *L'Ame romantique et le rêve: essai sur le romantisme allemand et le poésie française.* Paris, 1946.

Bein, Alex. "The Jewish Parasite: Notes on the Semantics of the Jewish Problem, With Special Reference to Germany." *Leo Baeck Institute Yearbook,* IX (1964), 3-40.

Bekker, Paul. *Richard Wagner: His Life in His Work.* Translated by M. M. Bozman. 1931; rpr. Westport, Conn., 1971.

Benoît, Pierre. *Oeuvres romanesques.* 7 vols. Paris, 1966–70.

Bernard, Claude. *An Introduction to the Study of Experimental Medicine.* Translated by Henry Copley Greene, A.M. New York, 1949.

Biddis, Michael. *Father of Racist Ideology: The Social and Political Thought of Count Gobineau.* New York, 1970.

Biget, Jean-Louis. "Mythographie du catharisme (1870–1960)." In *Cahiers de Fanjeaux. Collection d'histoire religieuse de Languedoc au XIIIᵉ et au début du XIVᵉ siècles. XIV: Historiographie du catharisme.* Toulouse, 1979.

Blake, William. *Blake: Complete Writings with Variant Readings.* Edited by Geoffrey Keynes. London, 1966.

Blau, Joseph L. *Modern Varieties of Judaism.* New York, 1966.

Bourdeau, Jean. *Les maîtres de la pensée contemporaine.* Paris, 1910.

Briffault, Robert. *The Mothers: A Study of the Origins of Sentiments and Institutions.* 3 vols. 1927; rpr. New York, 1969.

Brontë, Charlotte. *Shirley.* Leipzig, 1849.

Brown, Norman O. *Life Against Death: The Psychoanalytic Meaning of History.* New York, 1959.

Bryant, William Cullen. *The Iliad of Homer.* Boston, 1870.

Buber, Martin. "Old Zionism and Modern Israel." *Jewish Newsletter,* XIV (June, 1958).

Burton, Robert. *The Anatomy of Melancholy.* 3 vols. 1931; rpr. London, 1961.

Butler, E[liza] M. *Heinrich Heine: A Biography*. London, 1956.

———. *The Saint-Simonian Religion in Germany: A Study of the Young Germany Movement*. Cambridge, 1926.

Carbonell, Charles-Olivier. "D'Augustin Thierry à Napoléon Peyrat: un demi-siècle d'occultation (1820–1870)." In *Cahiers de Fanjeaux. Collection d'histoire religieuse de Languedoc au XIIIe et au début du XIVe siècles. XIV: Histoire du catharisme*. Toulouse, 1979.

———. "Vulgarisation et récupération: le catharisme à travers les mass-média." In *Cahiers de Fanjeaux. Collection d'histoire religieuse de Languedoc au XIIIe et au début du XIVe siècles. XIV: Histoire du catharisme*. Toulouse, 1979.

Carlebach, Julius. *Karl Marx and the Radical Critique of Judaism*. London, 1978.

Carlyle, Thomas. *The Carlyle Anthology*. Edited by Edward Barrett. 2nd ed. New York, 1881.

———. *Critical and Miscellaneous Essays*. 5 vols. New York, 1899.

———. *The French Revolution*. 3 vols. Leipzig, 1851.

Carroll, Lewis. "Some Popular Fallacies About Vivisection." *Fortnightly Review*. XXIII (June, 1875), 845–54.

Cecil, Lamar. "Jew and Junker in Imperial Berlin." *Leo Baeck Institute Yearbook*, XX (1975), 47–48.

Celsus. *De medicina*. Translated by W. G. Spencer. 3 vols. London, 1948.

Chamberlain, Houston Stewart. *The Foundations of the Nineteenth Century*. Translated by John Lees, with an introduction by Lord Redesdale. New York, 1914.

———. *Die Grundlagen des neunzehnten Jahrhunderts*. 5th ed. 2 vols. Munich, 1904.

Clark, T. J. *The Absolute Bourgeois: Artists and Politics in France*. 1973; rpr. Princeton, 1982.

———. *The Painting of Modern Life: Paris in the Art of Manet and His Followers*. New York, 1985.

Cobbe, Francis Power. "The Scientific Spirit of the Age." *Contemporary Review*. LIV (July, 1888), 126–39.

Cohen, Arthur A. *The Myth of the Judeo-Christian Tradition*. New York, 1957.

Cohen, Hermann. *Deutschtum und Judentum. Mit grundlegenden Betrachtungen über Staat und Internationalismus*. Giessen, 1915.

———. *Reason and Hope: Selections from the Jewish Writings of Hermann Cohen*. Translated by Eva Jospe. New York, 1971.

Cohn, Robert Greer. *Towards the Poems of Mallarmé*. Expanded edition. Berkeley, 1980.

Conrad, Joseph. *Notes on Life and Letters*. Garden City, N.Y., 1900–1925.

Constant, Benjamin. *Oeuvres*. Paris, 1957.

Cowley, Malcolm. *The Flower and the Leaf.* Edited by Donald W. Faulkner. New York, 1985.

Craft, Robert. *Current Convictions: Views and Reviews.* New York, 1977.

Curtius, Ernst. *Essays in European Literature.* Translated by Michael Kowal. Princeton, 1973.

Cuvier, Georges. *The Animal Kingdom arranged in conformity with its Organization. With Additional Descriptions of all the Species hitherto named, and of many not before noticed.* Translated by Edward Griffith and others. 16 vols. London, 1827–36.

Dante Alighieri. *La Divina Commedia.* Edited by Cesare Garboli. Turin, 1954.

Deathridge, John, and Carl Dahlhaus. *The New Grove Wagner.* New York, 1984.

Disraeli, Benjamin. *Coningsby; or, The New Generation.* Leipzig, 1844.

———. *Lord George Bentinck: A Political Biography.* 4th ed., rev. London, 1852.

———. *Sybil; or, The Two Nations.* Leipzig, 1845.

———. *Tancred; or, The New Crusade.* 2 vols. Leipzig, 1847.

D' Israeli, Isaac. *Amenities of Literature, Consisting of Sketches and Characters of English Literature.* London, 1884.

Dixon, William Hepworth. *Spiritual Wives.* 4th ed. 2 vols. London, 1868.

Dobel, Richard. *Lexikon der Goethe-Zitate.* Zurich, 1968.

Dodd, Frank. *Introduction to the Study of Christianity.* London, 1938.

Dole, Nathan Haskell. *The Life of Count Tolstoi.* New York, 1929.

Dombrowski, Daniel A. "Vegetarianism and the Argument from Marginal Cases in Porphyry." *Journal of the History of Ideas,* XLV (January, 1984), 141–43.

Dostoevsky, Fyodor. *Crime and Punishment.* Translated by Constance Garnett. New York, 1917.

———. *The Diary of a Writer.* Translated by Boris Brasol. New York, 1954.

Dujardin, Edouard. *Les lauriers sont coupées.* Paris, 1888.

———. *Le monologue intérieur, son apparition, ses origines, sa place dans l'oeuvre de James Joyce et dans le roman contemporain.* Paris, 1922.

———. *Les premiers poètes du vers libre.* Paris, 1922.

———. "La Revue wagnérienne." In *Wagner et la France: numéro spéciale de la Revue musicale,* 1er Octobre, Paris, 1923. New York, 1977.

Dumas, Alexandre, *fils. Théâtre complet.* 8 vols. Paris, 1893–1925.

Duvernoy, Jean. *Le catharisme: L'histoire des cathares.* Toulouse, 1979.

Edwards, Amelia Ann. *A Thousand Miles up the Nile.* London, 1877.

Edwards, F. G. *Musical Haunts in London.* London, 1895.

Eliot, George. *Daniel Deronda.* 2 vols. New York, 1876.

———. *The George Eliot Letters.* Edited by Gordon S. Haight. 6 vols. New Haven, Conn., 1954–55.

———. "Liszt, Wagner, and Weimer." *Fraser's Magazine,* LII (1855), 48–62.

Enfantin, Barthélemy. *Religion Saint-Simonienne. Procès en la cour d'assizes de la Seine, les 27 et 28 aout 1832.* Paris, 1832.

Engles, Frederick. *The Origins of the Family, Private Property and the State, in the Light of the Researches of Lewis H. Morgan.* New York, 1972.

Ettmüller, Ludwig. *Die Lieder der Edda von den Nibelungen. Stabreimende Verdeutschung.* Zurich, 1837.

Eugène, Eric. *Les idées politiques de Richard Wagner et leur influence sur l'idéologie allemande 1870–1945.* Paris, 1978.

Evans, Edwin, Sr. *Wagner's Teachings by Analogy.* London, n.d.

Evans, Michael. *Wagner and Aeschylus: The 'Ring' and the 'Oresteia.'* London, 1982.

Fenollosa, Ernest. *The Chinese Character as a Medium for Poetry.* Edited with a foreword by Ezra Pound. New York, 1936.

Feuerbach, Ludwig. *The Essence of Christianity.* Translated from the second German edition by Marian Evans [George Eliot]. New York, 1957.

———. *Sämtliche Werke.* Edited by Wilhelm Bolin and Friedrich Jodl. 13 vols. in 12. Stuttgart, 1959–64.

Fitzgerald, F. Scott. *This Side of Paradise.* New York, 1920.

Flaubert, Gustave. *Bouvard et Pécuchet.* 2 vols. Paris, 1945.

Fontenay, Elisabeth de. *Les figures juives de Marx.* Paris, 1973.

France, Anatole. *La vie littéraire.* 4 vols. Paris, 1888–92.

French, Richard D. *Antivivisection and Medical Science in Victorian Society.* Princeton, 1975.

Freshel, M. R. L., ed. *Selections from Three Essays by Richard Wagner with Comment on a Subject of Such Importance to the Moral Progress of Humanity that it Constitutes an Issue in Ethics and Religion.* Rochester, N.H., 1933.

Freud, Sigmund. "Eine Schwierigkeit in der Psychoanalyse." *Imago,* V (1917), 1–7.

Friedell, Egon. *A Cultural History of the Modern Age.* Translated by C. F. Atkinson. 3 vols. New York, 1931–53.

———. *Kulturgeschichte der Neuzeit.* 3 vols. Munich, 1927–32.

Fuchs, Eduard, and Richard Kreowski. *Richard Wagner in der Karikatur.* Berlin, 1907.

Der gelbe Fleck. Die Ausrottung von 500,000 deutschen Juden. With a foreword by Lion Feuchtwanger. Paris, 1936.

Gilbert, Sandra M., and Susan Gubar. *The Madwoman in the Attic: The Woman Writer and the Nineteenth-Century Literary Imagination.* New Haven, Conn., 1979.

Gilbert, Stuart. *James Joyce's Ulysses: A Study.* New York, 1934.

Gissing, George. *The Crown of Life.* New York, 1899.

———. *A Life's Morning.* London, 1947.

———. *London and the Life of Literature in Late Victorian England: The*

Diary of George Gissing, Novelist. Edited by Pierre Coustillas. Hassocks, Sussex, 1978.

——. *The Nether World.* 3 vols. London, 1889.

——. *Our Friend the Charlatan.* Edited by Pierre Coustillas. Rutherford, N.J., 1976.

——. *The Private Papers of Henry Ryecroft.* New York, 1903.

——. *The Whirlpool.* London, 1915.

Gladstone, William E. "'Robert Elsmere'" and the Battle of Belief." *Nineteenth Century,* XXIII (May, 1888), 766–88.

Glasenapp, Carl Friedrich. *Das Leben Richard Wagners.* 6 vols. Leipzig, 1911.

Gobineau, Joseph Arthur, Comte de. *Essai sur l'inégalité des races humaines.* 4 vols. Paris, 1853–55.

——. *Essay on the Inequality of the Human Races.* Translated by Adrian Collins. New York, 1915.

Golther, Wolfgang. *Richard Wagner als Dichter.* Berlin, 1904.

Goltz, Friedrich L. *Gesammelte Abhandlungen über die Vernichtungen des Grosshirns.* Bonn., 1886.

Gotthelf, Felix. "Schopenhauer und Richard Wagner." In *Viertes Jahrbuch der Schopenhauer-Gesellschaft.* 1915; rpr. Nendeln, Liechtenstein, 1968.

Graves, Charles L. *Mr. Punch's History of Modern England.* 4 vols. London, 1921–22.

Graves, Marie Haefliger. *Schiller and Wagner: A Study of Their Dramatic Theory and Technique.* Ann Arbor, Mich., 1938.

Greenberg, Martin, comp. *The Jewish Lists: Physicists, Generals, Actors and Writers, and Hundreds of Other Lists of Accomplished Jews.* New York, 1979.

Guérin, Daniel. *Proudhon oui et non.* Paris, 1978.

Guichard, Léon. *La musique et les lettres au temps du romantisme.* Paris, 1955.

Gumplowicz, Ludwig. *Ausgewählte Werke.* 4 vols. Aalen, 1973.

Gutman, Robert W. *Richard Wagner: The Man, His Mind, and His Music.* London, 1968.

Harich, Walther. *E. T. A. Hoffmann; Das Leben eines Künstlers.* 2 vols. Berlin, 1920.

Harnack, Adolf von. *Marcion: Das Evangelium vom fremden Gott.* 1929; rpr. Darmstadt, 1960.

Haubtmann, Pierre. *La philosophie sociale de P.-J. Proudhon.* Grenoble, 1980.

Haug, H. *Vergleichende Erdkunde und alttestamentliche geographische Weltgeschichte.* Gotha, 1894.

Hayek, Friedrich. *The Counter-Revolution of Science: Studies on the Abuse of Reason.* Glencoe, Ill., 1952.

Heckethorn, Charles Williams. *The Secret Societies of All Ages and Countries Embracing the Mysteries of Ancient India, China, Japan, Egypt, Mexico, Peru, Greece and Scandinavia, the Cabbalists, Early Christians, Heretics,*

Assassins, Thugs, Templars, the Vehm and Inquisition, Mystics, Rosicrucians, Illuminati, Freemasons, Skopzi, Camorristi, Carbonari, Nihilists and Other Sects. 2 vols. 1875; rpr. New Hyde Park, N.Y., 1965.

Heidegger, Martin. *Einführung in die Metaphysik.* Tübingen, 1953.

————. *Holzwege.* Frankfurt am Main, 1950.

Heine, Heinrich. "De l'Allemagne depuis Luther." *Revue des deux mondes,* 1. trimestre (1834), 473–505; 4. trimestre (1834), 373–408, 633–78.

Herzl, Theodor. *Der Judenstaat. Versuch einer modernen Lösung der Judenfrage.* Leipzig, 1896.

————. *Theodor Herzls zionistische Schriften.* Edited by Dr. Leon Kellner. 2 vols. in 1. Berlin-Charlottenburg, 1905.

Hess, Moses. *Rom und Jerusalem; Die letzte Nationalitätenfrage; Brief von Moses Hess.* Edited by Theodore Zlocisti. Tel Aviv, 1935.

————. *Moses Hess Briefwechsel.* Edited by Edmund Silberner with the assistance of Werner Blumberg. S-Gravenhage, 1959.

————. *Philosophische und Sozialistische Schriften, 1837–1850.* Edited by Auguste Cornu and Wolfgang Monke. Berlin, 1961.

————. *Rome and Jerusalem.* Translated by Rabbi Maurice Bloom. New York, 1959.

Hitler, Adolf. *Mein Kampf.* 2 vols. in 1. Munich, 1939.

Hoffmann, E. T. A. *Poetische Werke.* 12 vols. Berlin, 1957–62.

————. *Poetische Werke.* 6 vols. Berlin, 1958.

————. *Schriften zur Musik. Nachlese.* Munich, n.d.

Hook, Sidney. "Morris Cohen—Fifty Years Later." *American Scholar,* XLV (1976), 426–35.

Hüffer, Franz. "Richard Wagner." *Fortnightly Review,* XVII (March 1, 1872), 265–87.

————. *Richard Wagner and the Music of the Future.* London, 1874.

Hutchings, Monica, and Mavis Caver. *Man's Dominion: Our Violation of the Animal World.* London, 1970.

Huysmans, Joris-Karl. *A rebours.* Paris, 1965.

Huxley, Thomas Henry. *Lay Sermons, Addresses, and Reviews.* New York, 1870.

Jacobson, Anna. *Nachklänge Richard Wagners im Roman.* Heidelberg, 1932.

James, William. "The Moral Equivalent of War." *McClure's Magazine,* XXXV (August, 1910), 463–68.

————. "Remarks at the Peace Banquet." *Atlantic Monthly,* XCIV (December, 1904), 845–47.

Joll, James. *The Origins of the First World War.* London, 1984.

Jones, Ernest. *Hamlet and Oedipus.* Garden City, N.Y., 1954.

Jones, Robert Emmett. *Gérard de Nerval.* New York, 1974.

Kierkegaard, Søren. *Das Buch über Adler.* Translated by Hayo Gerdes. Düsseldorf, 1962.

————. *Either/Or: A Fragment of Life.* Translated by David F. Swenson and Lillian Marvin Swenson. 2 vols. Princeton, 1949.

————. *Søren Kierkegaard's Journals and Papers.* Edited and translated by Howard V. Hong and Edna H. Hong, assisted by Gregor Malantschuk. 4 vols. Bloomington, Ind., 1967–75.

————. *Søren Kierkegaard. The Last Years: Journals 1853–1855.* Edited and translated by Ronald Gregor Smith. New York, 1965.

————. *Die Tagebücher.* Translated by Hayo Gerdes. 5 vols. Düsseldorf/Köln, 1962–74.

Knox, John. *The First Blast of the Trumpet Against the Monstrous Regiment of Women.* Edited by Edward Arber. London, 1895.

Knust, Herbert. *Wagner, The King, and "The Waste Land."* University Park, Pa., 1967.

Kobbé, Gustav. *Wagner's Life and Works.* 2nd ed. New York, 1896.

Kraeling, Emil G. *The Old Testament Since the Reformation.* 1955; rpr. New York, 1969.

Kubizek, August. *Adolf Hitler, mein Jugendfreund.* Vienna, 1953.

————. *The Young Hitler I Knew.* Translated by E. V. Anderson. Cambridge, Mass., 1955.

Kulka, Otto Dov. "Richard Wagner und die Anfänge des modernen Anti-semitismus." *Bulletin des Leo Baeck Instituts,* IV (April, 1961), 281–300.

Lamber, Juliette. *Idées anti-Proudhoniennes sur l'amour, la femme et le mariage, seconde édition augmentée d'un examen critique du livre La Guerre et la Paix.* Paris, 1861.

Lang, Paul Henry. *Music in Western Civilization.* New York, 1941.

Langan, Thomas. *The Meaning of Heidegger: A Crucial Study of an Existentialist Phenomenology.* New York, 1959.

Lanier, Sidney. *The Science of English Verse and Essays on Music.* Edited by Paull Franklyn Baum. Baltimore, 1945.

Laqueur, Walter. *The Israel-Arab Reader: A Documentary History of the Middle East Conflict.* New York, 1969.

Lassalle, Ferdinand. *Ferdinand Lassalle; Der Mensch und Politiker in Selbstzeugnissen.* Edited by Konrad Haenisch. Leipzig, 1925.

Lenau, Nicolaus. *Die Albigenser. Freie Dichtungen.* Stuttgart, 1860.

Lenin, Vladimir Il'ich. *Lenin on the Jewish Question.* Edited by Hyman Lumer. New York, 1974.

Leon, Abram. *The Jewish Question: A Marxist Interpretation.* New York. 1970.

Le Roy, Albert. *George Sand et ses amis.* Paris, 1903.

Leroy, Maxime. "Les premiers amis français de Wagner." In *Wagner et la France: numéro spéciale de la Revue musicale, 1er Octobre, Paris, 1923.* New York, 1977.

Lesky, Erna. *The Vienna Medical School of the 19th Century.* Translated by L. Williams and I. S. Levij, M.D. Baltimore, 1976.

Lessing, Theodor. *Europa und Asien, oder, Der Mensch und das Wandellose; Sechs Bücher wider Geschichte und Zeit.* Hannover, 1923.

Levin, Harry. *James Joyce: A Critical Essay.* New York, 1941.

Lévi-Strauss, Claude. *Anthropologie structurale.* Paris, 1958.

———. *Le cru et le crit.* Paris, 1964.

———. *The Raw and the Cooked: Introduction to a Science of Mythology: I.* Translated from the French by John and Doreen Weightman. New York, 1975.

———. *Structural Anthropology.* Translated by Claire Jacobson and Brooke Grundfest Schoepf. New York, 1963.

Lichtenberger, Henri. *Etudes sur Schiller. Bibliothèque de philologie et de littérature moderne.* Paris, 1905.

———. *Richard Wagner poète et penseur.* 5th ed., rev. Paris, 1911.

Lilienthal, Alfred M. *The Zionist Connection: What Price Peace?* New York, 1978.

Lombroso, Cesare. "Neue Studien über die Genialität." *Schmidts Jahrbücher der in- und ausländischen gesammten Medicin,* CCXCIII (1907), 117–48.

Louis, Rudolf. *Die Weltanschauung Richard Wagners.* Leipzig, 1898.

Lovejoy, Arthur O. *The Great Chain of Being.* Cambridge, Mass., 1936.

Lowrie, Walter. *Kierkegaard.* London, 1938.

Lukács, Georg. *The Destruction of Reason.* Translated by Peter Palmer. Atlantic Highlands, N.J., 1981.

McHarg, Ian L. *Man: Planetary Disease.* The 1971 B. Y. Morrison Memorial Lecture. Presented in cooperation with the North American Wildlife and Natural Resources Conference, Portland, Oregon. Washington, D.C., n.d.

Magee, Bryan. *Aspects of Wagner.* London, 1968.

Mallarmé, Stéphane. "Hommage." *Revue wagnérienne,* January 8, 1886, p. 335.

———. "Richard Wagner, rêverie d'un poète français." *Revue wagnérienne,* August 8, 1885, pp. 195–200.

Mann, Golo. *Deutsche Geschichte des neunzehnten und zwanzigsten Jahrhunderts.* Frankfurt am Main, 1958.

Mann, Heinrich. *Little Superman.* New York, 1945.

———. *Der Untertan.* Leipzig, 1918.

Mann, Thomas. *Doktor Faustus. Das Leben des deutschen Tonsetzers Adrian Leverkühn erzählt von einem Freunde.* Frankfurt am Main, 1951.

———. *Doctor Faustus. The Life of the German Composer Adrian Leverkühn as Told by a Friend.* Translated by H. T. Lowe-Porter. New York, 1948.

Martin, Jay, ed. *A Critical Collection of Essays on "The Waste Land."* Engle-
  wood Cliffs, N.J., 1968.
Martin, Stoddard. *Wagner to "The Waste Land": A Study of the Relationship
  of Wagner to English Literature.* London, 1982.
Marx, Karl. *Capital.* Edited by Frederick Engels. 3 vols. New York, 1967.
―――. *A World Without Jews.* Translated by Dagobert D. Runes. 4th ed.
  New York, 1959.
―――. "Zur Judenfrage." In *Deutsch-Französiche Jahrbücher.* 1844; rpr.
  Darmstadt, 1967.
Marx, Karl, and Frederick Engels. *Collected Works.* New York, 1975−
―――. *Selected Works.* 3 vols. Moscow, 1969.
Marx, Karl, and Friedrich Engels. *Werke.* 38 vols. Berlin, 1959−71.
Mayer, Jean. "Les conflits de races dans 'l'Anneau du Nibelung' de R. Wag-
  ner." *Romantisme,* VI (1973), 99−110.
Mazzini, Giuseppe. *Filosofia della Musica.* Edited by Adriano Lualdi. Milan,
  1943.
―――. *Life and Writings of Joseph Mazzini.* 6 vols. London, 1890−91.
Mendel, Gérard. *La révolte contre le père. Une introduction à la sociopsy-
  choanalyse.* Paris, 1968.
Meyer, Eduard. *Die Israeliten und ihre Nachbarstämme. Alttestamentliche
  Untersuchungen.* 1906; rpr. Darmstadt, 1967.
Mitchell, Jerome. *The Walter Scott Operas.* University, Ala., 1977.
Mochulsky, Konstantin. *Dostoevsky: His Life and Work.* Translated by
  Michael A. Minihan. Princeton, 1967.
Monod, Marie Octave. *Daniel Stern, comtesse d'Agoult, de la restauration a
  la IIIe république.* Paris, 1927.
Morgan, Lewis Henry. *Ancient Society; or, Research in the Lines of Human
  Progress from Savagery, Through Barbarism to Civilization.* 1877; rpr.
  Palo Alto, Calif., 1975.
Morris, G. L. K. "Marie, Marie, Hold on Tight." *Partisan Review,* XXI
  (March-April, 1954), 231−33.
Müller, Georg. "Versuch einer Zeittheorie." *Archiv für systematische Philoso-
  phie,* XVII (1911), 107−10.
Neigebaur, J. D. F. *Geschichte der geheimen Verbindungen der neusten Zeit.*
  2 vols. 1831−44; rpr. Leipzig, 1972.
Nerval, Gérard de. *Oeuvres.* Edited by Henri Lemaitre. 2 vols. Paris, 1966.
Newman, Ernest. *The Life of Richard Wagner.* 4 vols. New York, 1933−47.
―――. *Wagner as Man and Artist.* Garden City, N.Y., 1937.
Nietzsche, Friedrich. *Gedichte und Sprüche.* Leipzig, 1916.
―――. *Werke. Kritische Gesamtausgabe.* Edited by Giorgio Colli and Maz-
  zino Montinari. 8 pts. Berlin, 1967−77.
Niven, Charles D. *History of the Humane Movement.* New York, 1967.

Passage, Charles E. *Dostoevski the Adapter: A Study in Dostoevski's Use of the Tales of Hoffmann.* Chapel Hill, N.C., 1954.

Payson, Seth. *Proofs of the Real Existence and Dangerous Tendency of Illuminism. Containing an Abstract of the Most Interesting Parts of What Dr. Robison and the Abbé Barruel Have Published on this Subject, with Collateral Proofs and General Observations.* Charlestowne, 1802.

Peacock, Thomas Love. *Works.* 10 vols. London, 1924–34.

Petrie, William Matthew Flinders. *The Revolutions of Civilisation.* London, 1912.

Piroué, Georges. *Proust et la musique du devenir.* Paris, 1960.

Pound, Ezra. *Literary Essays of Ezra Pound.* Edited by T. S. Eliot. New York, 1968.

———. "Vorticism." *Fortnightly Review,* CII (September 1, 1914), 461–71.

Prawer, S. S. *Karl Marx and World Literature.* Oxford, 1978.

Proudhon, Pierre-Joseph. *Lettres de Pierre-Joseph Proudhon.* Edited by Daniel Halévy and Louis Gouilloux. Paris, 1929.

———. *Oeuvres complètes de P.-J. Proudhon.* Edited by C. Bouglé and H. Moysset. 19 vols. Paris, 1923–59.

———. *What Is Property: An Inquiry into the Principles of Right and Government.* Translated by Benjamin R. Tucker. New York, n.d.

Proust, Marcel. *A la recherche du temps perdu.* 3 vols. Paris, 1969.

Puech, Jules L. Introduction to *La pornocratie ou les femmes dans les temps modernes,* by Pierre-Joseph Proudhon. In *Oeuvres complètes de P.-J. Proudhon,* edited by C. Bouglé and H. Moysset. 19 vols. Paris, 1923–59.

Puschmann, Theodor. *Richard Wagner. Eine psychiatrische Studie.* Berlin, 1873.

Rahn, Otto. *Kreuzzug gegen den Gral. Die Tragödie des Katharismus.* 3rd ed. Stuttgart, 1974.

Rathenau, Walther. *An Deutschlands Jugend.* Berlin, 1925.

Rather, L. J. "Alchemistry, the Kabbala, the Analogy of the 'Creative Word' and the Origins of Molecular Biology." *Episteme,* VI (1972), 83–103.

———. *The Dream of Self-Destruction: Wagner's 'Ring' and the Modern World.* Baton Rouge, 1979.

———. *The Genesis of Cancer: A Study in the History of Ideas.* Baltimore, 1978.

———. "The Masked Man[n]: Felix Krull is Siegfried." *Opera Quarterly,* II (1984), 67–75.

———. "Old and New Views of the Emotions and Bodily Changes: Wright and Harvey versus Descartes, James and Cannon." *Clio Medica,* I (1965), 1–25.

———. "On the Source and Development of Metaphorical Language in the History of Western Medicine." In *A Celebration of Medical History: The*

Fiftieth Anniversary of the Johns Hopkins Institute of the History of Medicine and the Welch Medical Library. Baltimore, 1982.

————. "On the Use of Military Metaphor in Western Medicine: The *bellum contra morbum* of Thomas Campanella." *Clio Medica,* VII (1972), 201–208.

————. "Some Reflections on the Philemon and Baucis Episode in Goethe's *Faust.*" *Diogenes* (Spring, 1959), 60–73.

————. "Tolstoy and Wagner: The Shared Vision." *Opera Quarterly,* I (1983), 12–24.

Rauschning, Hermann. *Gespräche mit Hitler.* New York, 1940.

Roazen, Paul. *Freud and His Followers.* New York, 1976.

Roberts, J. M. *The Mythology of the Secret Societies.* London, 1972.

Rod, Edouard. "Wagner et l'esthétique allemande." *La revue contemporaine, littéraire, politique, et philosophique,* July 24, 1885; rpr. Geneva, 1971, pp. 305–15.

Rolland, Romain. *Cahiers I. Choix de lettres à Malwida Meysenbug.* Paris, 1948.

————. *Cahiers VI. Printemps Romain. Choix de lettres de Romain Rolland à sa mère.* Paris, 1954.

Röpke, Wilhelm. *The German Question.* Translated by E. W. Dickes. London, 1946.

Rosen, Charles. *The Classical Style: Haydn, Mozart, Beethoven.* New York, 1972.

Rosenberg, Alfred. *Der Mythus des 20. Jahrhunderts.* 189th-194th ed. Munich, 1942.

Rossetti, Gabriele. *Disquisitions on the Antipapal Spirit Which Produced the Reformation; Its Secret Influence on the Literature of Europe in General and of Italy in Particular.* Translated by Caroline Ward. 2 vols. London, 1834.

Rousseau, Jean-Jacques. *Collection complète des Oeuvres.* 17 vols. Geneva, 1782–89.

Ruppin, Arthur. *The Jews in the Modern World.* London, 1934.

Sachs, Hanns. *Freud, Master and Friend.* Cambridge, Mass., 1944.

Saint-Simon, Henri, Comte de. *Henri Comte de Saint-Simon (1760–1825): Selected Writings.* Edited and translated by F. M. H. Markham. Oxford, 1952.

Sand, George. *Le compagnon du tour de France.* Paris, 1861.

————. *La comtesse de Rudolstadt.* Paris, 1921.

————. *Consuelo.* 3 vols. Paris, [1856].

————. *Indiana.* 2nd ed. Paris, 1922.

————. *Jean Zyska.* Paris, 1867.

————. *The Journeyman Joiner; or, The Companion of the Tour of France.* Translated by Francis G. Shaw. New York, 1976.

————. *Mouny-Robin.* Paris, 1869.

————. *George Sand in Her Own Words.* Translated and edited by Joseph Barry. Garden City, N.Y., 1979.

Sans, Edouard. *Richard Wagner et la pensée schopenhauerienne.* Paris, 1969.

Saussure, Ferdinand de. *Course in General Linguistics.* Translated by Wade Baskin. Edited by Charles Bally and Albert Sechehaye, with Albert Reidlinger. London, 1960.

Shahak, Israel. "The Divide Between Israel's Two Nations." *Middle East International,* August 10, 1984, p. 13.

Schopenhauer, Arthur. "On Religion." In *Parerga and Paralipomena: Short Philosophical Essays,* translated by E. F. J. Payne. 2 vols. Oxford, 1974.

————. *Sämtliche Werke.* Edited by Wolfgang Freiherr von Lohneysen. 5 vols. Stuttgart, 1960–65.

————. *Schopenhauers Gespräche und Selbstgespräche nach der Handschrift ἐις ἑαυτον.* Edited by Edward Griesbach. Berlin, 1898.

————. *The World as Will and Representation.* Translated by E. F. J. Payne. 2 vols. 1958; republished with minor corrections, New York, 1969.

Schubert, Gotthilf Heinrich von. *Die Symbolik des Traumes.* 1814; rpr. Heidelberg, 1968.

Schuler, John. *The Language of Richard Wagner's Ring des Nibelungen.* Lancaster, Pa., 1908.

Scott, Walter, Sir. *Count Robert of Paris.* 2 vols. New York, 1880.

————. *The Life of Napoleon Buonaparte.* 9 vols. Edinburgh, 1835.

————. *Old Mortality.* Leipzig, 1846.

Servières, Georges. "Les visées de Wagner sur Paris." In *Wagner et la France: numéro spéciale de la Revue musicale, 1ᵉʳ Octobre, 1923.* New York, 1977.

Shakespeare, William. *The Complete Works of Shakespeare.* Edited by Professor Peter Alexander. 4 vols. London, 1958.

Shaw, George Bernard. *Man and Superman.* New York, 1939.

Shelley, Percy Bysshe. *Shelley's Prose, or the Trumpet of a Prophecy.* Edited by David Lee Clark. Albuquerque, 1954.

Sitwell, Sacheverell. *Liszt.* London, 1955.

Smith, Morton. *Hope and History, An Exploration.* New York, 1980.

————. *Tannaitic Parallels to the Gospels.* Philadelphia, 1951.

Sophocles. *The Antigone of Sophocles.* Edited by Milton W. Humphreys. New York, 1891.

Spengler, Oswald. *The Decline of the West.* Translated by C. F. Atkinson. 2 vols. in 1. New York, 1939.

————. *Der Untergang des Abendlandes.* 2 vols. Munich, 1918.

Spielrein, Sabina. "Die Destruktion als Ursache des Werdens." *Jahrbuch für psychoanalytische und psychopathologische Forschungen,* IV (1912), 464–503.

Spinoza, Baruch. *Benedicti de Spinoza opera omnia quotquot reperta sunt.* Edited by J. von Vloten and J. P. N. Land. 4 vols in 2. The Hague, 1914.

————. *The Chief Works of Benedict de Spinoza*. Translated from the Latin by R. H. M. Elwes. London, 1891.

Stark, Werner. *The Sociology of Knowledge: An Essay in the Aid of a Deeper Understanding of the History of Ideas*. London, 1958.

Steele, Joshua. *An Essay Towards Establishing the Melody and Measure of Speech*. 1775; rpr. as No. 172 of *English Linguistics 1500–1800*. Edited by R. C. Alston. Menston, Eng., 1969.

Stein, Leon. *The Racial Thinking of Richard Wagner*. New York, 1950.

Steiner, George. *After Babel: Aspects of Language and Translation*. New York, 1975.

Stern, Daniel. *Histoire de la Revolution de 1848*. 2nd ed. 2 vols. Paris, 1862.

Stevenson, Lloyd G. "Science Down the Drain." *Bulletin of the History of Medicine*, XXIX (1955), 1–26.

Suarès, André. "La première lettre de Baudelaire à Wagner." *La Revue musicale*, November 1, 1922, pp. 1–10.

————. "Sur Wagner." In *Wagner et la France: numéro spéciale de la Revue musicale, 1ᵉʳ Octobre, 1923*. New York, 1977.

Symons, Arthur. *The Symbolist Movement in Modern Literature*. Rev. ed. New York, 1919.

Tacitus. *C. Cornelii Taciti opera omnia ex editione Oberliniana*. Edited by A. J. P. Valpy. London, 1821.

————. *The Works of Cornelius Tacitus, with an Essay on His Life and Genius*. Edited and annotated by Arthur Murray. Philadelphia, 1840.

Tappert, Wilhelm. *Richard Wagner im Spiegel der Kritik*. Leipzig, 1903.

Thackeray, William Makepeace. *Stray Papers*. Edited by Lewis Melville. London, 1901.

————. *Works*. 22 vols. Boston, 1899.

Thibert, Marguerite. *Le féminisme dans le socialisme français de 1830 à 1850*. Paris, 1926.

Tolstoy, Alexandra. *Tolstoy: A Life of My Father*. Translated by Elizabeth Reynolds Hapgood. New York, 1953.

Tolstoy, Leo. *The Complete Works of Count Tolstoy*. Translated by Leo Wiener. 24 vols. Boston, 1904.

————. *Journal intime*. Translated from the Russian by Natacha Rostova and Mgte. Jean-Debrit. Paris, 1917.

————. *My Religion, by Count L. N. Tolstoi*. Translated from the French by Huntington Smith. New York, 1885.

————. *Recollections and Essays*. Translated by Aylmer Maude. 1937; rpr. London, 1961.

————. *Tolstoy's Letters*. Selected, edited, and translated by R. F. Christian. 2 vols. London, 1978.

————. *What Is Art? and Essays on Art*. Translated by Aylmer Maude. 1930; rpr. London, 1938.

————. *What Then Must We Do?* Translated by Aylmer Maude. 1935; rpr. London, 1960.

Toynbee, Arnold. *A Study of History.* 12 vols. New York, 1939–64.

Tucker, Robert C. *Philosophy and Myth in Karl Marx.* Cambridge, 1967.

Twain, Mark. "Concerning the Jews." *Harper's New Monthly Magazine,* XCIX (September, 1899), 527–35.

Virchow, Rudolf. *Collected Essays on Public Health and Epidemiology.* Edited by L. J. Rather. 2 vols. Canton, Mass., 1985.

Voegelin, Eric. *Science, Politics, and Gnosis: Two Essays.* Chicago, 1968.

Vordtriede, Werner. "Richard Wagners 'Tod in Venedig.'" *Euphorion,* LII (1958), 378–96.

Wagner, Cosima. *Die Tagebücher.* Edited by Martin Gregor-Dellin and Dietrich Mack. 2 vols. Munich, 1976–77.

————. *Cosima Wagner's Diaries.* Edited by Martin Gregor-Dellin and Dietrich Mack. Translated by Geoffrey Skelton. 2 vols. New York, 1978–80.

Wagner, Richard. *Die Kunst und die Revolution.* Leipzig, 1849.

————. *Das Kunstwerk der Zukunft.* Leipzig, 1849.

————. *Gesammelte Schriften und Dichtungen.* 10 vols.; 1887–88, 2nd ed.; rpr. Hildesheim, 1976.

————. *Jesus von Nazareth. Ein dichterischer Entwurf aus dem Jahre 1848.* Leipzig, 1887.

————. *Mein Leben.* 2 vols. Edited by Wilhelm Altmann. Leipzig, 1923.

————. *Mein Leben.* Edited by Martin Gregor-Dellin. 2 vols. Munich, 1969.

————. *My Life.* Translated (from Martin Gregor-Dellin's edition) by Andrew Gray. Edited by Mary Whittall. Cambridge, 1983.

————. *Richard Wagners Briefe in Originalausgaben.* Edited by Erich Kloss. 17 vols. in 9. Leipzig, 1910–13.

————. *Richard Wagners gesammelte Schriften.* Edited by Julius Kapp. 14 vols. in 5. Leipzig, 1914.

————. *Richard Wagner's Letters to August Roeckel.* Translated by Eleanor C. Sellars. Bristol, 1897.

————. *Richard Wagner an Mathilde Wesendonck.* Berlin, 1904.

————. *Richard Wagner's Prose Works.* Translated by William Ashton Ellis. 8 vols.; 1895–99, 2nd ed.; rpr. St. Clair Shores, Mich., 1972.

————. *Richard Wagner: Stories and Essays.* Edited by Charles Osborne. London, 1973.

————. *Sämtliche Briefe.* Edited by Gertrud Strobel and Werner Wolf. Leipzig, 1967– .

————. *Selections from Three Essays by Richard Wagner with Comment on a Subject of Such Importance to the Moral Progress of Humanity that it Constitutes an Issue in Ethics and Religion.* Edited by M. R. L. Freshel. Rochester, N.H., 1933.

———. "The Work and Mission of My Life." *North American Review,* CXXIV (August, 1879), 107–24 and (September, 1879), 238–58.

Waite, Arthur Edward. *The Hidden Church of the Holy Grail: Its Legends and Symbolism Considered in the Affinity with Certain Mysteries of Initiation and Other Traces of a Secret Tradition in Christian Times.* London, 1909.

Wartofsky, Marx W. *Feuerbach.* Cambridge, 1977.

Webster, Nesta. *Secret Societies and Subversive Movements.* 2nd ed. London, 1924.

———. *Surrender of an Empire.* 3rd ed. London, 1931.

———. *World Revolution: The Plot Against Civilization.* London, 1921.

Wehl, Theodor. *Das junge Deutschland. Ein kleiner Beitrag zur Literaturgeschichte unserer Zeit.* Hamburg, 1886.

Weill, Georges. *L'Ecole Saint-Simonienne; son histoire, son influence jusqu'à nos jours.* Paris, 1896.

Weiner, Marc A. "Richard Wagner's Use of E. T. A. Hoffmann's 'The Mines of Falun.'" *19th Century Music,* V (1982), 210–14.

Weininger, Otto. *Ueber die letzten Dinge.* Posthumously published, with a biographical preface by Dr. Moriz Rappaport. 6th ed. Vienna, 1920.

Weltsch, Robert. "Introduction." *Leo Baeck Institute Yearbook,* IX (1964), xv.

Westernhagen, Curt von. *The Forging of the 'Ring': Richard Wagner's Composition Sketches for Der Ring des Nibelungen.* Translated by Arnold and Mary Whittall. London, 1976.

———. *Richard Wagners Dresdener Bibliothek.* Wiesbaden, 1966.

———. *Wagner: A Biography.* Translated by Mary Whittall. 2 vols. London, 1978.

Weston, Jessie L. *From Ritual to Romance.* Cambridge, 1920.

———. *The Legends of the Wagner Drama: Studies in Mythology and Romance.* 1903; rpr. Boston, 1977.

White, Lynn, Jr. "The Historical Roots of Our Ecological Crisis." *Science,* CLV (1967), 1203–1207.

Wilson, Pearl Cleveland. *Wagner's Dramas and Greek Tragedy.* New York, 1919.

Wolfson, Harry Austryn. *The Philosophy of Spinoza.* 1934; rpr. New York, 1958.

Wolzogen, Hans von. *E. T. A. Hoffmann und Richard Wagner; Harmonien und Parallelen.* Berlin, 1906.

Woolf, Virginia. *Three Guineas.* New York, 1938.

Woolley, Grange. *Richard Wagner et le symbolisme français: Les rapports principaux entre le wagnérisme et l'évolution de l'idée symboliste.* Paris, 1931.

Wordsworth, William. *The Poetical Works of William Wordsworth*. Edited by
Thomas Hutchinson. Revised by Ernest de Selincourt. London, 1960.
Wysewa, Teodor de. "Le pessimisme de Richard Wagner." *Revue wagnér-
ienne,* July 8, 1885, pp. 167–70.
———. "La religion de Richard Wagner et la religion du comte Leon de
Tolstoi." *Revue wagnérienne,* October 8, 1885, pp. 237–55.

INDEX